VIKING AGE YORKSHIRE

MATTHEW TOWNEND

BLACKTHORN PRESS

Blackthorn Press, Blackthorn House
Middleton Rd, Pickering YO18 8AL
United Kingdom

www.blackthornpress.com

ISBN 978 1 906259 39 6

© Matthew Townend 2014

Printed and bound by CPI Group (UK) Ltd, Croydon, CR0 4YY

For Natasha, Robin, and Kit

CONTENTS

ACKNOWLEDGEMENTS

I am very grateful to the many friends and colleagues who have given me help and guidance in various ways. My especial thanks are due to Steve Ashby and Tom Pickles, who generously read through the book in draft form, and suggested many improvements. I am also grateful to Alan Avery of the Blackthorn Press, for inviting me to write this book in the first place, and for his patience and support while I have been writing it. Finally, and above all, I wish to thank my family: my wife, Natasha Glaisyer, and our two sons, Robin and Kit, to whom this book is dedicated with gratitude and love.

CONVENTIONS AND ABBREVIATIONS

A number of conventions employed in this book should be noted:

(1)   Places within the county of Yorkshire are normally identified by their pre-1974 riding, as follows:

ER = East Riding
NR = North Riding
WR = West Riding

(2)   Personal names are cited in a variety of forms. There is no simple, consistent means of modernizing or regularizing Anglo-Saxon and Norse personal names, and on the whole I have used the forms which are most frequent in modern scholarship; occasionally, in the treatment of Norse names in particular, I have decided simply to use an un-modernized Old Norse form.

(3)   In quoting from primary sources, I have normally used published translations where they are available, though occasionally I have preferred to use my own, or to adapt published versions slightly. I have, however, silently changed the forms of personal names (and, occasionally, place-names) used in the translations I quote from, in order to bring them in line with my usage elsewhere in the book.

(4)   The referencing system used is normally author-date (with full publication details provided in the Bibliography), but for a small number of works that are cited with high frequency I have employed abbreviations as follows:

ASC = Whitelock 1961
EHD = Whitelock 1955
PNERY = Smith 1937
PNNRY = Smith 1928
PNWRY = Smith 1961-63

LIST OF MAPS AND ILLUSTRATIONS

INTRODUCTION

APPROACHING THE HISTORY
OF VIKING AGE YORKSHIRE

The Middleton Cross

The first illustration, at the centre of this book, shows a famous piece of stone sculpture from Viking Age Yorkshire [Figure 1a]. At the time of writing, the Middleton Cross, as it is commonly known, is displayed in the north aisle of St Andrew's Church, Middleton, near Pickering [NR]. The main panel of this tenth-century sculpture shows a warrior, viewed front on and surrounded by his weapons. To the viewer's left (the warrior's right) is a tall spear, while to the viewer's right (the warrior's left) can be seen, from top to bottom, a round shield, a sword, and a large axe – a distinctive Scandinavian weapon – on which his hand seems to rest. Across his waist, attached to his belt, is a short sword or knife, and on his head there sits a plain conical helmet – no theatrical (and apocryphal) Viking horns are to be found here, and indeed the headwear might possibly be not even a helmet but rather a hat or cap. The warrior's legs seem a little bent, and his feet point to the left (the viewer's right). This main panel forms part of the cross-shaft, and above the panel the sculpture is topped by a ringed cross-head decorated with interlace – a distinctive form from the north of England in the Viking Age.

This compelling piece of sculpture, which apparently brings us eye-to-eye with a Viking Age warrior, has been much reproduced in books and articles on the Vikings. But it fully came to light only in 1948, when it was removed from the church tower at Middleton in the course of repairs.[1] In 1956 Alan Binns argued that the sculpture depicts a Viking warrior lying in his grave, surrounded by his armoury of weapons, and this interpretation was generally accepted; the presence of such a quantity of grave-goods, moreover, surely indicated that this warrior was pagan.[2] But in 1973 James Lang drew attention to the two beads or pellets above

1

the figure's shoulders, and also to the strips between his legs.[3] This is not a dead warrior in his grave, Lang suggested, but rather a living one seated on his ceremonial throne or 'gift-stool', with the pellets above marking the top of the seat's pillars, and the strips below marking its legs. Lang's interpretation continued to accentuate a martial identity for the figure depicted, but matched it with an equal emphasis on his jurisdiction and largesse. So in this view we are coming face-to-face not so much with a ferocious pagan warrior, as with a tenth-century member of the local landed gentry.

Moreover, if the weapons are no longer to be seen as grave-goods, then the grounds for seeing this as a pagan figure disappear. The panel is, after all, surmounted by a cross-head, and the monument as a whole – presumably a funerary monument for the figure represented on it – was found built into Middleton church, and no doubt derived from either the church itself or its churchyard. Victoria Thompson has therefore supplemented Lang's interpretation by suggesting that the surrounding weapons can be viewed not only as literal, physical ones, but perhaps also as spiritual ones – in other words, as the 'weapons of faith' of which St Paul writes in Ephesians Chapter 6.[4] Such a view takes us even further from the supposed pagan warrior in his grave, and offers instead an interpretation which foregrounds Christian piety and scriptural iconography.

The warrior panel on the Middleton Cross raises even more questions when viewed in the context of other sculptural scenes from the same site – indeed, from the very same stone, for the reverse of the cross-shaft shows a serpent or dragon-like creature crammed into the panel [Figure 1b]. A front leg can be seen across the top of the panel, with a paw or claw top left; a rear leg can be seen a quarter of the way up on the right-hand side. Two prominent eyes punctuate the animal's head, below which are a pair of odd-looking jaws (indeed, viewed upside down, the jaws are unavoidably reminiscent of a rabbit's ears). Twining across and even through the animal are various bands of interlace, forming something of a compressed mesh at the bottom of the panel. The serpent is unquestionably Scandinavian in its aesthetic, but although it has affinities with the so-called Jellinge style, art historians have found it difficult to fit it into the canonical art movements of the period. The reason for this is its poor quality in terms of design and workmanship – 'almost inconceivably incompetent', according to one standard work on Viking art – which raises questions about the access enjoyed (or not enjoyed) in Middleton to top-quality sculptors.[5] Furthermore, it has been suggested that the Middleton serpent represents an inadequate attempt at copying art styles that are seen more successfully on sculptures found in York – which makes the Middleton example look like a somewhat clumsy rural attempt to emulate urban sophistication.[6] So our Middleton warrior-sculpture, celebrated though it is, may be the product of a cultural periphery rather than centre, even though its frequent reproduction nowadays may give the impression that it is an object that comes from the heart of

2

Viking England. And what does the serpent signify? Is it some sort of Christian image, perhaps the dragon-devil of Revelation 20, seeking unsuccessfully to attack the soul of the departed?[7] Or is it simply a form of Scandinavian space-filler, chosen for decorative rather than symbolic reasons?

The so-called Middleton Cross is not, in fact, the only Viking Age cross from Middleton. Parts of no fewer than seven other stones have been found at the site. Three of these boast similar-looking (though less elaborate) warrior-figures, who are adorned with similar conical helmets or hats on their heads and/or similar knives or short swords at their waists. One of them is also, rather more clearly, seated on a chair, and sports a forked beard, in the Scandinavian style. Art historians date all four of these warrior stones to the tenth century, together with the four other stones from Middleton (all of which show Scandinavian interlace); indeed, all the warrior stones may possibly be the work of the same sculptor.[8] If one is familiar with the Middleton Cross only from its reproduction in books on the Viking Age, it can be something of a surprise to learn that, even at this one site, it is far from unique. And if one assumes that such sculptures were funerary monuments (as is generally thought), then an obvious question is what the relationship may have been between the men who are commemorated by, and on, the monuments. Who were they, and were they related to each other? Do we have here four generations of Viking warriors, each succeeding the other as lord of Middleton? Or – if some or all of the crosses are by the same hand – were at least some of the dead men contemporary with each other? Middleton is a planned village, its streets (re-)laid out in a grid pattern at some point in the early Middle Ages, and this implies a central, controlling lord; but whether the re-planning of Middleton pre- or post-dates the sculptures (or indeed is contemporary with them) is hard to know, and thus it remains uncertain whether we are seeing successive generations of lords or a contemporaneous plurality.

We can be sure, though, that the portraits that are being offered are not naturalistic ones, drawn from life, but rather are formal, and formulaic. And a further question that might arise is whether or not the men commemorated here were genuinely warriors, veterans of Viking Age campaigns. Are these formulaic monuments analogous to the standardized war graves of later conflicts? Possibly, but it must be equally possible that although the family – or families – who patronized the church at Middleton chose to depict their dead in conventional martial poses, they did in fact derive their wealth and prosperity from the land, or even from trade – in other words, they were a country elite who continued to hark back to a warrior identity that now lay firmly in the past, not unlike eighteenth-century aristocrats who wished to be painted in classical costume.

To de-militarize the Scandinavian lords commemorated on the Middleton sculptures may seem like an interpretation too far; and it is indeed possible that the men commemorated were warriors who had seen battle. There is no danger of

3

modern scholarship white-washing the traditional image of the Vikings as violent warriors, bringing trauma and grief to much of western Europe. The Vikings were violent: warfare and violence played a central part in the world-view of at least some of them, and it is effectively certain that the domain of Middleton passed into Scandinavian hands as the result of war.[9] But not all imagery depicting Viking Age Scandinavians as ferocious warriors should be taken at face value, and that includes images produced or patronized by the Scandinavians themselves; in many respects the popular stereotype of the Vikings as great warriors is one that was initially propagated by Viking Age Scandinavians themselves – with, so far, over a millennium of success.

It is worth returning, therefore, to the undeniable fact that the Middleton Cross is a Christian monument, and most likely a grave marker. Whatever else they were, the wealthy elite who put up the cross and its associated sculptures were patrons of the church at Middleton. We will see in due course that there is ample evidence for the Vikings having disrupted and even destroyed ecclesiastical structures during their raids, wars, and conquests; and the Vikings who did so were pagans. But within a few decades at most, such heathen conquerors had been transformed into at least outwardly pious Christians, supporting, rebuilding, and sometimes even founding local churches, and choosing to bury their dead within their graveyards. The tower of St Andrew's Church, Middleton, and parts of the nave, are pre-Norman – possibly pre-Viking, but more likely tenth- or eleventh-century.[10] The fact that some of the Scandinavian crosses were, in the twentieth century, re-discovered built into the fabric of the tower, having been re-used as building material, would suggest that some period of time elapsed between the carving of the monuments and the building of the tower, though it is possible that the crosses were used for later repair rather than original construction. Either way, the combination of church and monuments indicates a pious local elite in the Anglo-Scandinavian period.

There are further issues, too. The place-name Middleton is an Old English one (that is, in the language of the Anglo-Saxons), not an Old Norse one (the language of the Vikings).[11] The linguistic contact between the speakers of these two different languages demands attention, and suggests a number of questions; it will be discussed further in Chapters 4 and 5 of this book. But for the present we can note the important points that pieces of Scandinavian sculpture are not necessarily to be found in places with Scandinavian names, and that the Old English nature of the place-name indicates that Middleton was originally an English settlement that later passed into the possession, or at least under the influence, of a Scandinavian elite (or, strictly speaking, an elite with marked Scandinavian tastes, though this may be an excessively fine distinction).[12] A decorated piece of eighth- or ninth-century stonework, now built into the tower, also implies (unless it was imported from elsewhere) that Middleton was a pre-

Viking site.[13] So the quest for Yorkshire's Viking history inescapably means an investigation into the interaction of English and Scandinavian elements; it is rare that the Scandinavian component can be considered in isolation.

Moreover, the place-name Middleton – in the form *Mid(d)eltun* – is first recorded only in 1086, in the pages of Domesday Book.[14] In other words, the Yorkshire site that has produced one of the most famous pieces of Viking Age sculpture from anywhere in England is not in fact mentioned in any historical source from the Viking Age itself. This, we will see, is overwhelmingly the norm: although there are a good number of contemporary written sources for the history of Viking Age Yorkshire, very few texts refer to individual villages or settlements, and for much of the time our primary sources must be physical or archaeological. As soon as we dip below the level of grand narrative, written history may not be able to help us very much, at least before the later tenth century.

This book has begun with a discussion of the Middleton Cross not only to present immediately, from the very start, the more complex and nuanced, and less exclusively blood-spattered, picture of Viking Age England that our sources enable us to construct; but also to make a number of obvious but nonetheless important points about the nature of historical inquiry for this period. The first is that much of our evidence for the history of Viking Age Yorkshire is likely to be open to varying interpretations, and to have received a diversity of explanations. Historical evidence does not simply speak for itself, with an unmistakable, unambiguous voice. Rather, it speaks only when it is spoken to: different questions will receive different answers, and the questions we ask are certainly likely to vary from scholar to scholar, and from decade to decade. The second point to make is that our evidence for the history of Viking Age Yorkshire is not a fixed and finalized body of material. Rather, it is changing all the time, most obviously in the form of archaeological discoveries; and the new finds are likely to give rise to new questions, and hence to new interpretations. And a third point is that the history of Viking Age Yorkshire requires an interdisciplinary approach, involving a wide variety of both written and unwritten sources.

The Middleton sculptures, then, enable us to perceive a tenth-century elite who were settled in England but preferred Scandinavian ornament for their aesthetic, who were Christian patrons of their local church but who chose to commemorate their dead in Viking postures, and who engaged creatively with English culture but still held on to their Scandinavian heritage. In response to scholarly inquiry, the Middleton sculptures tell an eloquent story, easily grasped at least in its outlines: of Scandinavians who came to Yorkshire in the Viking Age, first as warriors and then as settlers, and who left an indelible mark on the county's history and culture.

Sources for Viking Age Yorkshire

What, then, are the main sources with which we shall be concerned in this book? We shall begin with a consideration of the written evidence.

Our primary sources are to be found in three main languages: Old English (the language of the Anglo-Saxons), Old Norse (the language of the Vikings), and Latin (the language of the church); and occasionally we shall engage with texts in other languages as well, such as Old Irish and Anglo-Norman or French. Most of our written sources are the product of the Anglo-Saxon side of things, and by far the most important single source in this category is the *Anglo-Saxon Chronicle* [Figure 2].

The unitary title of the *Anglo-Saxon Chronicle* conceals what is, textually, an extremely complicated work, surviving in a number of different versions whose inter-relationships are both complex and perplexing.[15] These different versions share many of the same entries (or parts of entries), but also differ significantly from one another in terms of the information they include and the things they are interested in. Six main manuscripts survive, austerely labelled A to F in modern scholarship, and all have been re-edited in recent decades to high scholarly standards.[16] Five of these, A to E, are written in Old English, while F is a bilingual version in Old English and Latin. The earliest extant version is A, sometimes also called the 'Parker Chronicle', after the archbishop of Canterbury, Matthew Parker, into whose possession it passed in the sixteenth century. The *Anglo-Saxon Chronicle* as a text was first compiled in the early 890s, put together out of diverse historical traditions and earlier Latin records, almost certainly at the court of King Alfred 'the Great', though how far the *Chronicle* remained an official, royal production in later decades is a matter for debate.[17] Manuscript A, probably written in Winchester, is not the original version of the *Chronicle*, but in terms of distance of copying it is relatively close to that supposed original. This A-text was updated at various stages in the tenth and early eleventh centuries, but it is much less full for these later decades than for its earlier, Alfredian core.

Manuscripts B and C are related, and are distinguished by their inclusion for the early tenth century of the so-called 'Mercian Register', an originally separate set of annals with a focus on Mercian politics and persons.[18] C continues much later than B (which ends in 977) and has traditionally been attributed to the monastery of Abingdon, though a persuasive case has recently been made for an association with, or particular interest in, the earls of Mercia.[19] The C-text shares with D and E a detailed and eloquent account of the reign of King Æthelred 'the Unready' (978-1016).

With manuscripts D and E we come to those versions of the *Chronicle* which are usually labelled as its 'Northern Recension'. The two manuscripts derive, at some remove, from a shared ancestor in which an Alfredian exemplar was filled out, for the pre-Viking period, with a great deal of northern material derived from a variety of sources, including Bede's *Ecclesiastical History of the English People* (*Historia Ecclesiastica Gentis Anglorum*). This Northern Recension was most plausibly put together for one of the West Saxon-appointed archbishops of York, probably in the second half of the tenth century, but other provenances are possible.[20] Up until the year 1031 the texts of D and E are quite similar, but by no means identical; after 1031 they diverge substantially.

The D-text we will come back to in a moment. E is known alternatively as the 'Peterborough Chronicle', as it was unquestionably written there in the twelfth century: for the annals from 1031 to 1121, E is a copy of a version of the *Chronicle* that was kept at Canterbury, but from 1122 to 1154 it is an original composition, especially interested in events that impacted on the monastery of Peterborough itself. It is thus the version of the *Chronicle* that kept going the longest, well into the post-Conquest period. The bilingual F is based predominantly on E.

The D version of the *Chronicle* will be quoted frequently in this book. For a long time it was attributed to Worcester, and occasionally York, as its text shows a strong interest in the church and clerics of both places. But in the 1990s two scholars, Patrick Wormald and G.P. Cubbin, argued forcefully that D's defining affiliations were not with a place, but rather with a person: namely Ealdred, bishop of Worcester from 1046 to 1062, and archbishop of York from 1060 to 1069.[21] Moreover, it is quite possible that the ancestor of D came to Ealdred via his most important predecessor as archbishop of York, Wulfstan II (1002-23).[22] Late Anglo-Saxon bishops and archbishops were not always to be found in their diocese: instead, they were itinerant to a substantial degree and spent a considerable amount of time at the royal court (itself itinerant). The advocacy of Ealdred as perhaps the key element in the genesis of D (though other origins have also been suggested) indicates that it may be misleading to think in terms of locating a manuscript to a particular place, rather than to a particular person or circle.

Although the format of the *Anglo-Saxon Chronicle* is that of year-by-year annals, it is important to realize that the entries were not usually written contemporarily, a year at a time, like diary entries. Rather, it is clear that, for much of the time, the *Chronicle* was written in retrospective blocks (though these must, one assumes, often have drawn on annalistic memoranda of some sort). So, for example, the famous Æthelredian *Chronicle*, which supplies the most withering of critiques of the policies of Æthelred the Unready, was not actually written during Æthelred's reign itself, but rather shortly after the end of that reign: it is thus a retrospective document, written with some degree of hindsight, and the same is likely to be true of much of the *Chronicle*.[23] In this respect as well as others, the *Anglo-Saxon Chronicle* differs considerably from the main Irish source with which we will be concerned, the *Annals of Ulster*, which gives invaluable information, on a year-by-year basis, about the history of Scandinavian kings and warlords in Ireland, and political relationships between Dublin and York.[24]

A number of Latin texts derive from, or are indebted to, the vernacular *Anglo-Saxon Chronicle*. A *Life of King Alfred* (*Vita Ælfredi Regis*) was written in the 890s by Asser, one of the king's clerics who was originally from Wales but later became bishop of Sherborne; and the *Anglo-Saxon Chronicle* was Asser's single most important source.[25] Similarly, a historical *Chronicle* (*Chronicon*) was put together by Æthelweard, descendant of Alfred's older brother Æthelred I of Wessex, and ealdorman of 'the western provinces' (Somerset, Dorset, and Devon); this was probably composed in the 980s, but possibly in the 990s.[26] Æthelweard edited and supplemented the *Anglo-Saxon Chronicle* with other information which reflected his particular views and interests – which included the history and culture of the Scandinavians in England, and the Viking wars of the late ninth and early tenth century.[27] The *Annals of St Neots* is an early twelfth-century compilation that draws heavily on the *Anglo-Saxon Chronicle*, among other sources.[28] And also in the early twelfth century a number of Anglo-Norman historians, writing in Latin, relied heavily on the *Chronicle* in their attempts to make sense of the pre-Conquest past, the most important of whom, for our purposes, were John of Worcester and William of Malmesbury.[29] The *Chronicle* was also used as the main source for an important work in French, Geffrei Gaimar's verse *History of the English* (*Estoire des Engleis*), composed in Lincolnshire in the 1130s.[30]

More locally significant for the history of Yorkshire is the complex and important *History of the Kings* (*Historia Regum*) which survives as an early twelfth-century Northumbrian text associated with Symeon of Durham.[31] A related text is Symeon's *Tract on the Origins and Progress of this the Church of Durham* (*Libellus de Exordio atque Procursu istius hoc est Dunhelmensis Ecclesie*), earlier known by the simpler title of the *History of the Church of Durham* (*Historia Dunelmensis Ecclesie*): for the Viking period this mostly draws on earlier, known sources, but it does include some additions and expansions which are not found in those earlier sources.[32] For the eighth century, the *History of the Kings*, which has a composite and highly complex origin, preserves a very important set of Latin annals which were kept in York, and which acted as one of the sources for the Northern Recension of the *Anglo-Saxon Chronicle*. For the Viking period, the *History of the Kings* does not offer such a full account, but it still contains a good deal of information about the Viking Age north which is not duplicated elsewhere, since one of its component parts was a collection of northern annals running from 888 to 957.[33] This collection of northern annals may itself be of composite origin, and it has been suggested that two separate sets of annals have been combined (one running to 933, one from 934 onwards).[34] It is unclear whether all the annals were composed in the same place, and their origin has been variously ascribed to York, to somewhere else in Yorkshire (perhaps Ripon [WR]), and (perhaps most plausibly) to Chester-le-Street. But their value is indisputable: Peter Hunter Blair claimed that they supply 'an account of the wars between the Vikings and the English which is altogether more trustworthy and more accurate chronologically' than that in the *Anglo-Saxon Chronicle*, and that 'every detail in it suggests that, as it now survives, it is a genuine record of the tenth century, untouched except for minor slips on the part of copyists'.[35] Perhaps even more intriguing, though more edited in transmission, is the material preserved in the *Flowers of Histories* (*Flores Historiarum*) of Roger of Wendover, an early thirteenth-century monk of St Albans. For his knowledge of early northern history, Roger used a text of the *History of the Kings*, but he also seems to have had access to some further tenth-century annals, apparently from York: these annals are not preserved anywhere else, and they show a special interest in the history of York and its Viking kings; it is, for example, Roger who preserves the fullest account in English sources of the expulsion and death of Eric Bloodaxe, the last Scandinavian ruler in York.[36] That one or more chronicles may have been kept at York in the tenth century (presumably in Latin) is, of course, a tantalizing prospect, and it has even been suggested that echoes of these York annals can be heard in some Old Norse kings' sagas.[37] The use of Latin for the annals preserved in both the *History of the Kings* and Roger of Wendover suggests that the tradition of history-writing in Northumbria in the tenth century was different from that in Wessex and Mercia, where the *Anglo-Saxon Chronicle* had instituted a switch to the vernacular.[38]

Another unusually precious and important text is the *History of St Cuthbert* (*Historia de Sancto Cuthberto*), as it is one of the few works known to have been composed in the north of England during the late Anglo-Saxon period and which survives in its entirety.[39] Written in quite simple Latin, it provides an account of the life of St Cuthbert, the great Northumbrian saint, and (more importantly) of the history and land-holdings of the clerical community that were the guardians of his cult – first on Lindisfarne and then, following their Viking Age wanderings, at Chester-le-Street (where they may have compiled the tenth-century annals preserved in the *History of the Kings*), and finally at Durham. The *History of St Cuthbert*'s narrative is episodic and far from fluent, and its sources were evidently miscellaneous, including Bede, charters, estate memoranda, and (most enticingly) oral traditions: indeed, the text gives us an unusual opportunity to access oral stories that seem to have been circulating in late Anglo-Saxon Northumbria – about Cuthbert, and about the Vikings – as part of the institutional memory of Cuthbert's community. The *History of St Cuthbert* is the only Anglo-Saxon text, for example, that uses the term *Scaldingi* to refer to the Scandinavian conquerors of Northumbria – an apparent echo of the Danish dynasty called the *Skjöldungar*.[40] But the exact date of the *History* is very hard to establish, as there are conflicting indicators: some features of the text point to a mid tenth-century origin for the work, some to an early eleventh-century origin, some to a mid eleventh-century one.[41] It may well be that the text went through successive stages of composition and revision, imperfectly reconciled, all of which have left their mark on the work.

Histories and chronicles are not the only narrative texts of value for this study, though they form our main textual sources for the second half of the ninth century and the first half of the tenth. For the subsequent period – the later tenth century and the eleventh, after the Viking kingdom of York had been subsumed into the English state under a southern king – a wider range of narrative sources becomes available, especially in terms of hagiography and biography. For this later period there also exists, for the first time, some wealth of more administrative and documentary sources, such as laws, political tracts, and above all charters (recently re-edited by David Woodman).[42] The apex of such administrative sources is of course Domesday Book, compiled in 1086.[43] The precise purpose of Domesday Book remains a ground of inquiry and dispute – is it primarily a record of ownership or a resource for taxation? – but as a source it has received a very great deal of skilful study and elucidation.[44] A particular point of emphasis in recent scholarship is that, in order to know how to use it for historical study, we need to understand the processes by which Domesday Book was compiled and its data assembled. This is especially pertinent for Yorkshire, which formed part of 'Circuit 6' for the Domesday commissioners (together with Lincolnshire, Nottinghamshire, Derbyshire, Rutland, and Huntingdonshire). David Roffe has demonstrated that, not only was Yorkshire the first county in Circuit 6 to be surveyed, but Circuit 6 was also the first set of returns to be edited down and entered into Domesday Book itself.[45] The consequence of this is that the survey for Yorkshire is provisional and disorganized in its scope and presentation: 'uncertainty persisted throughout the drafting of the text', and the survey cannot be taken as a reliable (let alone systematic and exhaustive) guide to conditions on the ground.[46] In other words, apparent peculiarities in the Yorkshire Domesday may be due as much to the process of the text's composition as to the structure of local society.

For the vast majority of settlements in Yorkshire (and, therefore, for most Norse place-names of significance), Domesday Book is the point at which they first enter the historical record. It has been calculated that, in Domesday Book, some 49% of place-names (which is to say, of settlement or vill names) in the East Riding are either Old Norse in origin or Scandinavianized in form, and 46% in the North Riding; even in the less Scandinavianized West Riding, the figure is 31%.[47] This is therefore a convenient place to notice the central importance of place-names (and, to a lesser degree, personal names) for the study of Viking Age Yorkshire; the history of the region would be unwriteable without them. In the study of the Scandinavian place-names of Yorkshire we are indebted to two scholars in particular, A.H. Smith and Gillian Fellows-Jensen. Smith produced the county surveys for the three ridings for the English Place-Name Society: the North Riding in 1928, the East Riding (including the City of York) in 1937, and the West Riding

10

in 1961-63.[48] These are the fundamental resource for the investigation of Yorkshire's place-names, but they were produced on widely different scales: the North Riding and East Riding surveys are single volumes, and thus are largely confined to major names (with the important addition of Smith's study of York street names in the East Riding volume), whereas the West Riding survey extends to no fewer than seven volumes (plus a one-volume index covering the whole of Yorkshire) and gives a wealth of detail for minor names, especially field-names.[49] Fellows-Jensen produced her monograph *Scandinavian Settlement Names in Yorkshire* in 1972, the first of three volumes examining Scandinavian place-names across England; she also published the fundamental study of Scandinavian personal names in the county.[50] As with Smith's county surveys, the (deliberate) restrictions of Fellows-Jensen's volume should be noted: her study is confined to names for settlements recorded in Domesday Book or earlier, and thus she does not include names which are minor, topographical, or first recorded after 1086. The works of Smith and Fellows-Jensen are indispensable, and will supply the place-name evidence to be discussed in this book; but it is worth observing that the minor names of the North and East Ridings remain less well studied (or even collected) than those of the West Riding. It is also worth noting that – as in all disciplines – place-name scholars are by no means unanimous on all points of interpretation, from the meanings of individual names to the significance of larger patterns, and for some place-names the standard reference works present differing etymologies. But the general level of agreement is high: the principles governing the composition and meaning of place-names have been well studied and are well understood, and place-name studies are not a free-for-all.[51]

This completes our review of the main Anglo-Saxon (and early Norman) texts, written in either Old English or Latin, which will be drawn on in this book. The situation on the Old Norse side of the picture is rather different. During the Viking Age itself, the Old Norse language was – except for a very few, brief inscriptions – never written down in the Roman alphabet, and it was certainly never written down in manuscripts. In other words, although the Old Norse language was used for many purposes and in many spheres in Viking Age England, it was primarily an oral language, existing in the medium of speech and sound, and not in writing. We should not, however, equate the oral with the ephemeral. On the contrary, anthropological and historical study has shown that in oral cultures the spoken word can be both powerful and enduring, and that memories in oral cultures can be astonishingly capacious.[52]

One of the most enduring forms of memorization in Viking Age culture was poetic.[53] So-called skaldic poetry – the term simply comes from the Old Norse word for 'poet' – was a form of occasional and situation-specific poetry that reached its fullest expression at the courts of Viking Age rulers and other patrons. Skaldic encomia were composed to celebrate and perpetuate the fame of their

11

subjects, either within life or after death, and skaldic diction and metre could be exceptionally ornate – both for aesthetic and mnemonic purposes. As we will see, the activities of Viking Age kings in northern England were sometimes commemorated in verse, and such poetry is now an invaluable contemporary source, both for the events that happened and, equally, for the attitudes and ideas of the patrons and poets responsible for such verse.

How, though, has oral poetry from the Viking Age survived to us? The answer is that such skaldic praise-poems were not composed to be recited only once; rather, they were memorized and passed on across decades and even centuries, their accurate transmission largely guaranteed by their elaborate poetic form (which meant that misremembering would usually lead to an unmetrical poem). Literacy in the Roman alphabet came to Scandinavia in the eleventh century, with the increasing Christianization of the region, and our earliest Old Norse prose writings, preserved in manuscripts, date from the twelfth century. In the late twelfth and thirteenth centuries there was an explosion of Old Norse historical writing, in Norway and especially Iceland, telling the stories of Viking Age kings. Such 'kings' sagas' (*konungasögur*) used and quoted earlier skaldic verse as one of their most important sources, and, together with a number of poetic treatises from the same time (most famously, Snorri Sturluson's *Edda*), they preserve for posterity a huge body of Viking Age verse. Such kings' sagas (such as Snorri's *Heimskringla*) also contain many details, and tell many stories, that are not corroborated by earlier poetry, as do certain 'legendary sagas' (*fornaldarsögur*) and 'sagas of Icelanders' (*Íslendingasögur*); such information is not to be neglected, but it is of secondary status as historical evidence, and must be weighed carefully. But when such material is all gathered together, one can see that the Norse sagas have quite a lot to say about events in Viking Age Northumbria.[54]

There is, of course, one important exception to the statement made above that the Old Norse language was an exclusively oral one in the Viking Age. We possess many hundreds of runic inscriptions from Viking Age Scandinavia, in which Old Norse is written in runic script rather than the Roman alphabet; such inscriptions are mostly carved on stone, occasionally wood or bone or some other substance.[55] But the corpus of Old Norse runic inscriptions from Viking Age England is very small – fewer than 20 at the present count – and currently only one of these (brief, and largely incomprehensible) is from Yorkshire.[56] Norse runic inscriptions from England are far outnumbered by inscriptions in English and Latin, in the Roman alphabet.[57]

Such inscriptions take us from the textual to the material and artefactual, and bring us to the question of unwritten, archaeological evidence. This is, of course, vast, but it is also – like the textual evidence – patchy in its distribution. Both forms of evidence, textual and archaeological, are partial – semi-chance survivals of what may once have existed, and in need of careful handling to gauge

12

whether they are representative or exceptional. As we will see, some aspects of Viking Age England can be, and have been, very greatly illuminated by archaeological evidence; others, hardly at all. It is also the case that, for the early medieval period at least, one crucial difference between archaeological and textual evidence is that the latter is effectively closed, while the former is still growing.[58] Of course, it is possible that, for example, a late copy of a hitherto unknown charter may come to light, but it is highly unlikely that there will be many, or even any, major new discoveries in terms of Anglo-Saxon written sources; and the test for textual scholars is how to squeeze the most information out of their exiguous, and often laconic, sources. For archaeology, though, the possibility of new discoveries is ever-present; the quantity of metal-detected finds in the last twenty years, for instance, has been truly revelatory. This is both a blessing and a challenge. It is a blessing in that new finds are always likely to cast new light on old questions (and to give rise to new questions). But it is also a challenge, in that any generalization or conclusion runs the risk of being premature, and hypotheses founded on archaeological evidence may possess a greater degree of provisionality than those founded on textual sources: distribution maps can go out of date very quickly.

Rather than being reviewed here, one at a time, different forms of archaeological evidence — some excavated, some metal-detected — will be introduced at various points in this book as they become most relevant, above all in Chapters 4 to 6. But two particular forms of material evidence should be noted as being of especial importance, and in both cases the evidence-type straddles the disciplines of archaeology and history (including art history and linguistic history).

The first of these is coinage. Coins are one of the most important forms of evidence we possess for the political history of the Viking kingdom centred on York, and many distinguished numismatists have given their attention to the Viking coinage of Northumbria; Michael Dolley and Mark Blackburn should be mentioned in particular. Coins have often been recovered singly, through metal-detecting, but sometimes also in great abundance, in the form of hoards, many of which contain metalwork and bullion as well as coins; and James Graham-Campbell and Gareth Williams have been the leading scholars to work on these northern hoards.

The meaning and motivation of hoards remains imperfectly understood, though their discovery has the power to thrill and tantalize with a glimpse of an individual life or moment.[59] Who deposited the hoard? Why? What happened to prevent them from recovering it? Every hoard, arguably, is a sign of at least two moments of crisis or trauma: the one that led to its burial, and the one that caused it not to be recovered. Some hoards may also be ritual deposits; this is certainly the case in mainland Scandinavia.[60] The presence of datable coins in many hoards means that we are often able to pin-point their time of deposition fairly narrowly, and sometimes the probable date of a hoard correlates persuasively with known

13

political or military events, and thus enables us to reconstruct a plausible (though not, of course, certain) context for its deposition.

In many ways the narrative that is able to be constructed through numismatic study is superior to that which can be assembled from textual sources: as we will see in Chapters 2 and 3, it is coinage that best enables us to plot the reigns of the different Scandinavian rulers of York, to appreciate the character and reach of their bureaucratic machinery, and to access the ideologies of power they wished to project.[61] Of course, the numismatic evidence has its patchiness and imbalances too: the discovery of coin hoards has a random element to it (though the deposition of hoards may not have been random), and for some kings we have vastly more coins, and thus more evidence, than for others.[62]

The second form of material evidence that is especially important for this book is stone sculpture, as we have already seen with the introductory example of the Middleton Cross. As we will see in Chapters 5 and 6 in particular, several hundred pieces of Viking Age sculpture are preserved in Yorkshire, at over a hundred separate sites, nearly all ecclesiastical. What is particularly valuable about this sculptural evidence, in addition to its quantity and variety, is its distribution: on account of its weight and non-portability, most of the sculptures that survive, it is assumed, do so in the locations where they were originally erected a thousand years ago, and thus for many places and regions within the county the sculpture is our best evidence for local culture and activity in the Viking Age. Much of this evidence was recovered in the later nineteenth century and the earlier twentieth (like the Middleton Cross): although a few items are preserved *in situ*, most of the sculptures were uncovered through church repair and restoration, often having been re-used as building material in the post-Viking period. The sculptural evidence has also been superbly well served by scholarship: the pioneering figure in the study of Yorkshire sculpture was the artist and author W.G. Collingwood (1854-1932), who published a series of seminal surveys before and during the First World War.[63] More recently, the whole county has been covered in three volumes, two by James Lang and one by Elizabeth Coatsworth, as part of the on-going 'Corpus of Anglo-Saxon Stone Sculpture'; neighbouring areas (County Durham and Northumberland, Cumbria, and Lancashire and Cheshire) have also, very helpfully, been surveyed in the same project.[64]

This completes our introductory review of the main types of evidence to be discussed in this book, out of which a narrative history of Viking Age Yorkshire can be constructed. But before such a history, and such a narrative, can at last begin, we need finally to ask what exactly we mean by the designation 'Viking Age Yorkshire'.

Defining the Region

Is it an anachronism to talk of 'Yorkshire' during this period, and – whether it is or not – is it a useful term, and a useful unit, for writing Viking Age history? The first point to note is that, whatever answer one gives to these questions, there are at least a number of distinguished precedents, of scholars taking a county-based approach to the pre-Norman past: the most important of these are probably John Blair's ground-breaking volume on Oxfordshire, and Peter Sawyer's history of Lincolnshire.[65] Yorkshire itself has not previously received such a study, but there have been important histories of the larger unit of the Anglo-Saxon kingdom of Northumbria, most recently by Nicholas Higham and David Rollason; and such a regional approach is well established in early medieval history.[66] In many respects, the closest fore-runner to the present volume, in its attempt to combine political history, settlement history, and cultural history, is Alan Binns' 1963 pamphlet, *The Viking Century in East Yorkshire*, a compact work of continuing value.[67]

The geographical scope of the present study, then, is unashamedly the modern county of Yorkshire, even though, of course, at many points it will be necessary to look beyond the county in order to understand what was going on within it. But the following paragraphs will seek to demonstrate that, although the name 'Yorkshire' is a slight anachronism when it comes to Viking Age history, the area or political unit that it designates is not.

Let us begin with the suffix 'shire'. This comes from the Old English word *scīr*, which meant a portion of territory. Simon Keynes defines the Anglo-Saxon shire as 'a district, in most cases conceived as a part of a larger whole, which served as a unit or organising principle of local government for military, legislative, financial, and other administrative purposes'.[68] So, for example, each shire lay under the authority of an ealdorman or earl, and each had its own shire-court and its own shire-reeve or king's representative (whence the modern word 'sheriff'). The shires south of the Thames are probably of pre-Viking Age origin, but those between the Thames and the Humber are tenth- or eleventh-century in origin, being administrative structures created by the expansionist West Saxon kings and their successors.[69] Yorkshire is the only shire north of the Humber to have taken shape before the Norman Conquest, and thus the only shire north of the Humber to feature in Domesday Book (1086), the survey of which is structured according to a shire-by-shire format; it is also, of course, by far the largest county in England. Most of the shires north of the Thames were named after a central important place (Bedfordshire after Bedford, and so on), and Yorkshire clearly follows this principle. But while most of the midland shires were created 'without any respect for the underlying 'tribal' complexion of the region, and with the appearance, therefore, of a system imposed from above', Yorkshire is likely to represent a

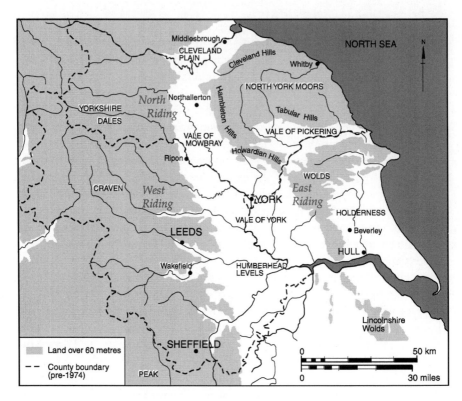

Map 1 The county of Yorkshire

different case (as, too, do the East Anglian shires of Norfolk and Suffolk).[70] The creation of the county of Yorkshire will be returned to below.

Meanwhile, in terms of territorial extent we should note that the Anglo-Saxon kingdom of Northumbria comprised two originally separate kingdoms: Bernicia to the north, and Deira to the south. The modern scholarly names *Bernicia* and *Deira* are Latinized forms of originally Old English names, but those Old English names themselves were certainly in existence by the seventh century at the latest.[71] The boundary between these two kingdoms seems to have lain along the River Tees, but by the mid seventh century the two kingdoms had been politically unified, into a single Anglo-Saxon kingdom north of the Humber.[72] To the south, the boundary of the kingdom of Deira, and later of Northumbria, ran westwards along the Humber estuary, and then either along the River Don or a little further south: a poem in the *Anglo-Saxon Chronicle* for 942 names Whitwell and Dore, near Sheffield [WR], as marking the frontier between Mercia and Northumbria, which is also more or less the boundary between Yorkshire and Derbyshire in Domesday Book, while the *Chronicle* entry for 919 also indicates

16

that (at least at that period) Manchester was regarded as lying within Northumbria.[73]

As we shall see in later chapters, the Scandinavian conquest of Northumbria, and subsequent Scandinavian settlement, primarily affected the area covered by the old kingdom of Deira, so much so that Bernicia resumed something of its former independent existence (with the community of St Cuthbert developing their own power base in the buffer zone between the rivers Tyne and Tees).[74] Place-name evidence indicates that major Scandinavian settlement extended a few miles north of the Tees, but no further.[75] Kenneth Cameron thus suggested that the county of Yorkshire 'represents the district controlled by the Danish army with its headquarters at York'.[76] The idea of an army 'headquarters', with its implications of a modern garrison town, may be a little misleading, but the recognition that the county of Yorkshire correlates roughly with the extent of the Viking polity centred on York is likely to be correct. It is surely not a coincidence, moreover, that under Viking assault the Anglo-Saxon kingdom of Northumbria fissured along the fault-line between its own constituent kingdoms of Deira and Bernicia. So the county of Yorkshire is likely to correlate, broadly speaking, both with the Viking kingdom of York and with the old kingdom of Deira.

This is at least the case east of the Pennines; the situation west of the Pennines is more problematic. In Domesday Book, parts of what are now Lancashire and Cumbria are included under the returns for Yorkshire, but this is because these lands lay within the diocese of the archbishop of York, and the north-western shires had not yet come into existence; it does not mean that they were constitutionally part of Yorkshire. (More difficult to interpret, in terms of its Domesday treatment, is the status of Craven: this is also counted with Yorkshire in the Domesday survey, as one might expect, but it is not included as part of the West Riding, as it later became.[77]) As for pre-Viking Age Northumbria, there is no doubt that in certain periods its rule extended westwards, into what are now Lancashire, Cumbria, and Dumfries and Galloway.[78] But we do not know precisely the extent of the old kingdoms of Deira and Bernicia, especially in the west, and they may have fluctuated over time: as David Rollason has suggested, in mapping early medieval kingdoms it may be more fruitful to think in terms of heartlands and border zones, rather than strictly delimited political boundaries of a modern sort.[79] The situation in the Viking Age itself is even more murky, and whether the Viking kings of York exerted authority west of the Pennines is unclear. Some lines of argument might suggest that they did: as we will see in Chapter 3 in particular, in the first half of the tenth century the history of the kingdom centred on York was intimately tied up with that centred on Dublin, and travel and communication between the two Viking cities must have been frequent; in which case, control of the main overland route between the two will have been important.[80] Furthermore, Gareth Williams has pointed out that Viking Age hoards tend to be of a similar composition on both sides of the Pennines, and thus, he has suggested, they do not readily support a distinction between a 'Kingdom of York' and a looser 'North-West'.[81] On the other hand, single finds of coins do support such a distinction, at least in economic terms: very few single finds of Scandinavian York coins have been discovered west of the Pennines (the vast majority, in fact, have been found in the vicinity of York itself and in the East Riding), and single finds may give us a better indication of monetary networks, and of the circulation of coinage, than hoards do – which may reveal rather the transportation (and concealment) of wealth along routes of travel.[82] It is also the case, of course, that other kingdoms and polities were exerting an influence over the north-west in the tenth century, not least Strathclyde (which was extended south-eastwards in this period), and in many respects modern Cumbria has a different linguistic and ethnic history to Yorkshire.[83] Lancashire may be different, and may be the most plausible area to attach to the 'Kingdom of York' in terms of cultural connections and, possibly, political authority, especially if we take the southern boundary of pre-Viking Northumbria in the west as having been the Mersey rather than the Ribble.[84] Nonetheless, the subsequent history of the north of England indicates that east and west were not to be welded together into a single unit: to repeat the point made above, our best interpretation is that the modern county of Yorkshire corresponds roughly with the old Anglo-Saxon kingdom of Deira, and it is likely therefore to correspond also to the Viking kingdom centred on York. For all these reasons, this book will assume that the Viking kingdom of York was essentially to be found east of the Pennines – while being alert to possible extensions to the west (and indeed, at certain times certain Viking kings of York also exerted authority south of the Humber too).

We can now return to the county name 'Yorkshire'. This is first recorded in the early 1060s, when a writ of King Edward 'the Confessor', relating to Beverley Minster [ER], begins as follows: 'King Edward sends friendly greetings to earl Tostig and all my thegns in Yorkshire [*Eoferwicscire*]. And I inform you that Archbishop Ealdred has my consent and full permission to draw up a *privilegium* for the lands that belong to St John's minster at Beverley.'[85] Although preserved only in later manuscripts, this writ must date from the first half of the 1060s: Ealdred became archbishop of York in 1060, and Tostig ceased to be earl of Northumbria in 1065. In the *Anglo-Saxon Chronicle* also, the name 'Yorkshire' first appears in entries for the 1060s (though as noted earlier, such entries are not necessarily strictly contemporary). Tostig was removed as earl in 1065, following an uprising against him by the Northumbrian elite (discussed further in Chapter 8 of this book). The rebellion began when, as the D-text records, 'all the thegns in Yorkshire and in Northumberland [*on Eoforwicscire and on Norðhymbralande*] came together and outlawed their earl Tostig'.[86] Other versions of the *Chronicle* have different wording: version C simply says 'all the thegns of Yorkshire [*on*

Eoferwicscire]', while version E does not mention Yorkshire but states instead that it was the 'men of Northumbria [*Norðhymbra*]' who assembled.[87] The significant phrasing here is that of the northerly D-text, in that it draws a meaningful distinction between two different units within the region of Northumbria, namely Yorkshire and Northumberland, which presumably equate roughly with the old kingdoms of Deira and Bernicia. A further phrase in version C's annal for 1066 is worth noting also: after capturing York, King Harald Hardrada of Norway moved east to Stamford Bridge [ER] because he had been promised that hostages would be brought to him there 'out of all the shire [*of ealre þære scire*]'.[88] The appearance of references such as these imply, then, that the formally designated shire of 'Yorkshire' came into existence in roughly the mid eleventh century. This conclusion is also suggested by earlier negative evidence. In tracking the movement of Cnut and his army during the battles of 1016, the *Anglo-Saxon Chronicle* (versions C, D, and E) records that he 'went out through Buckinghamshire into Bedfordshire, from there to Huntingdonshire, and so into Northamptonshire, along the fen to Stamford, and then into Lincolnshire; then from there to Nottinghamshire and so into Northumbria towards York [*swa to Norðhymbron to Eoforwic weard*]'.[89] The chronicler name-checks the counties that Cnut and his army pass through on their journey to York, but ends by specifying 'Northumbria'; this implies that 'Yorkshire' did not yet exist as a designation for the unit of territory within which York was to be found.

The etymology of the city after which the shire took its name is, of course, very well established.[90] Originally a British name *Eburācon* (probably 'place abounding in yew-trees'), this is recorded in Roman sources as *Eburacum* or *Eboracum*. Through folk-etymology, this Romano-British name was Anglicized by the Anglo-Saxons to *Eoforwīc* ('boar settlement'). In the Viking Age this Old English form was in turn Scandinavianized by Old Norse speakers to *Jórvík* (Old Norse **jórr* '(wild) boar' was cognate with Old English *eofor*, but is not recorded outside of names; the more common variant is *jöfurr*, which developed the meaning 'leader, prince'). The first certain occurrence of the name-form *Jórvík* in our textual record comes in skaldic verse of the second half of the tenth century, though it has been suggested that a blundered attempt at the Old Norse form of the name occurs on some York coins of the 920s.[91] It is from the Norse form of the name that the Modern English form *York* descends. However, it is worth noting that, as the *Anglo-Saxon Chronicle* and other works attest, the Old English form also continued to be current through the tenth and eleventh centuries (and beyond), as indeed did the Latin name in written sources, and it is interesting that it is the Old English form that is the base for the shire-name found in eleventh-century records – a further confirmation, perhaps, that the creation of the shire was the work of an English-speaking authority. As we will see in Chapters 4 and 5, the co-existence of English and Norse forms of names for the same place was one of the linguistic facts of life in Viking Age Yorkshire.

But if the name 'Yorkshire' did not come into existence until the eleventh century, then it is worth asking what the territory was called during the period when Viking kings held power in York (866-954). How did the Scandinavian rulers and settlers refer to their own region, and how did their contemporaries elsewhere in England define it? The answer to this question has, in effect, already become clear: the area or political territory was sometimes named by some form of reference to Northumbria, and sometimes by some form of reference to York. In modern scholarship the favoured term is 'the Viking kingdom of York' (or sometimes 'the Viking kingdom in Northumbria'). This is, it is true, a modern designation, and not one that is found in tenth-century records.[92] But it is not for that reason to be distrusted or rejected, for it probably equates pretty well to the terms by which contemporaries referred to the Scandinavian polity north of the Humber. A number of examples will serve to illustrate this point.

To take 'Northumbria' first. 'Northumbria' is not quite an early medieval term, as Anglo-Saxon sources refer to *Norðhymbre* 'the Northumbrians, those living north of the Humber', a people rather than a place. The concept and term are first found for sure (in Latin) in Bede, who writes in his early eighth-century *Ecclesiastical History* of the *gens Nordanhymbrorum* ('the people of the Northumbrians').[93] But after the Viking conquest, and the splitting of the kingdom, the term persisted through the tenth and eleventh centuries, for instance in the *Anglo-Saxon Chronicle*. A scale of meanings seems to develop, so that while it sometimes retains a more collective geographical sense, as of the pre-Viking kingdom (that is, both Deira and Bernicia combined), often it seems to refer only to the area of Scandinavian rule and settlement (that is, only Deira). So, for example, the more collective sense seems to be attested in the entry for 920 in the A-text of the *Anglo-Saxon Chronicle*, which states that those who submitted to King Edward 'the Elder' were 'the king of the Scots and all the people of the Scots, and Rægnald, and the sons of Eadwulf and all who live in Northumbria [*on Norþhymbrum bugeaþ*], both English and Danish, Norsemen and others'.[94] But counter-examples of a more restricted use can readily be found: revealing in their usage are the entries for 926 and 927 in the D-text of the *Chronicle*, which state that, following the death of 'Sihtric, king of the Northumbrians [*Norðhymbra cyng*]', King Athelstan 'succeeded to the kingdom of the Northumbrians [*Norðhymbra rice*]; and he brought under his rule all the kings who were in this island: first Hywel, king of the West Welsh, and Constantine, king of the Scots, and Owain, king of the people of Gwent, and Ealdred, son of Eadwulf from Bamburgh'.[95] What these entries tell us is, first, that the 'kingdom of the Northumbrians' was a recognized political unit, and, second, that it excluded the territory ruled from Bamburgh, the old kingdom of Bernicia. Similarly, the entry

20

for 954 in the D-text of the *Chronicle* records that 'the Northumbrians [*Norðhymbre*] drove out Eric, and Eadred succeeded to the kingdom of the Northumbrians [*Norðhymbra rice*]'.[96] The 'Northumbrians' here must be Eric's subjects, and this would again seem to exclude the old kingdom of Bernicia, as this was (once more) under the governance of the high-reeves of Bamburgh at this time. This distinction persisted after the region had been incorporated into the kingdom of England, and the Viking kings were no more: in the later tenth and eleventh centuries, the royally-appointed earls of Northumbria normally exercised authority south of the Tees, while the old Bernicia continued as a separate entity, though sometime the earls of Bamburgh held the earldom of Northumbria as well.[97]

What the *Chronicle* entries indicate, then, is that in the first half of the tenth century what modern scholars call 'the Viking kingdom of York' was called, at least sometimes, 'the kingdom of the Northumbrians'. This suggests that, in the tenth century, the term 'Northumbrian(s)' itself experienced certain changes in sense, or the development of new senses. In one of its meanings it became geographically restricted, so that often the term referred only to the old Deira, and not to Deira and Bernicia (though this older, collective sense was still able to be activated). But one of the other meanings of 'Northumbrian(s)' that developed seems to have been 'Scandinavian(s)' – or more precisely, 'Scandinavian(s) ruling or settled north of the Humber'. So, for instance, the *Anglo-Saxon Chronicle* entries for 900 and 910 refer to 'the army in Northumbria [*here on Norðhymbrum*]', but that for 893 (also in a military and political context) simply to 'the Northumbrians [*Norþhymbre*]'.[98] Within the *Chronicle*, these terms seem more or less synonymous, and all refer to the Scandinavian forces and peoples settled north of the Humber. An even clearer indication comes in Æthelweard's Latin *Chronicle*. Æthelweard seems at times to use the term 'Northumbrians' precisely to mean 'Scandinavians settled in Northumbria': in 899, for example, he records 'a disturbance on a very great scale among the English [*Anglos*], that is the bands who were then settled in the territories of the Northumbrians [*Northhymbriorum*]' – a statement which only makes sense if the latter group (the Northumbrians) does not include the former group (the English).[99] It is worth noting, though, that it is only in English sources that the term 'Northumbrian(s)' shows this change in meaning. The Old Norse equivalent *Norðimbrar* 'Northumbrians' – clearly borrowed from English – only appears twice in Viking Age sources (skaldic praise-poems from the late tenth and early eleventh centuries), and on both occasions the *Norðimbrar* are the enemies in battle of the kings concerned (Olaf Tryggvason and Cnut): this does not exclude the possibility that the term is showing a finer shade of meaning, but the likelihood is that it is functioning more or less as a geographically-inflected synonym for 'the English'.[100]

To return to English sources: alongside the persistence and indeed alteration of the term 'Northumbrian(s)', we should also note the practice of referring to Viking rule by reference to York itself. When Viking rulers established themselves north of the Humber, it was usually chronicled in contemporary sources in terms of gaining York, as we shall see in Chapters 2 and 3. This is not surprising: York was of course the one city in Northumbria, the one mint, the one archbishopric, and so on; to gain control of York was clearly, in many ways, to gain control of Northumbria, and of no other polity in the Anglo-Saxon period can one observe a closer identification between city and kingdom than that between York and Northumbria in the Viking Age. So the political and strategic importance of York is self-evident; it is not self-evident, though, that the polity centred on York should sometimes be named after it, but this does seem to have been the case. So, for example, the *History of the Kings* records a military expedition in 941 by 'the men of York [*Eboracenses*]', where context indicates that the forces referred to are the supporters of Northumbria's Scandinavian ruler.[101] Equally intriguing is a usage in the Mercian Register for 918, where 'the people of York [*Eforwicingas*]' are said to have made political overtures to the ruler of Mercia (and it should be noted that the term *Eforwicingas* does indeed mean 'the people of York', and not 'the York Vikings').[102] Whereas the *History of the Kings'* *Eboracenses* are a military group, the Mercian Register's *Eforwicingas* are not necessarily so, and indeed might equate with the 'councillors of the Northumbrians [*Norðhymbra witan*]' found elsewhere in the *Anglo-Saxon Chronicle*.[103]

In Viking Age England, there is an obvious parallel for styling a political unit after its fortified urban centre, and this is the so-called 'Five Boroughs' of the southern Danelaw: Derby, Leicester, Lincoln, Nottingham, and Stamford. That York may sometimes have been thought of in the same way is suggested by a unique and cryptic reference in the *Anglo-Saxon Chronicle* for 1015 to the 'Seven Boroughs'. The identity of the two extra boroughs is debated, but a common assumption is that they are York and Torksey.[104] The difference between York and the Five Boroughs, of course, is that the Scandinavian rulers of York inherited the idea (and the reality) that what they were ruling was a kingdom, and that they themselves were kings and not merely earls.[105] This was probably a significant difference, both practically and ideologically.

So we might conclude that two systems of nomenclature overlapped in tenth-century usage: the political unit ruled over by Scandinavian kings north of the Humber was known both after the fashion of an old Anglo-Saxon kingdom (Northumbria) and also after the fashion of the new Scandinavian polities south of the Humber (York). Such naming practices reflected both continuity and innovation, and that no universal, hard-and-fast name was established may be due to the fact that those who lived through its times had no way of judging whether it would prove ephemeral or long-lived. That they often chose to hold on to a traditional term (Northumbria) is hardly surprising.

We can conclude, therefore that – taking all of the foregoing into consideration – 'Yorkshire' can indeed be regarded as a meaningful unit for the purposes of Viking Age history (as it equates with the 'Viking kingdom of York'), even though the name itself does not come into existence before the mid eleventh century. Two further terms also merit briefer, prefatory discussion before this chapter can close, namely 'the Danelaw' and the very word 'Viking'.

'The Danelaw' is a popular term in modern scholarship, used to designate the great area of eastern and northern England settled and, at least for a period, ruled by Scandinavians from the late ninth century onwards.[106] The term is undoubtedly Old English in origin (*Dena lagu* 'law of the Danes'), but it is never used in ninth- or tenth-century sources. It is, in fact, an early eleventh-century coinage, apparently created by a specific individual, Archbishop Wulfstan II of York, to refer to an area characterized by distinctive (Scandinavian) jurisdictional practices: it is thus a cultural term that has a geographical dimension to it, and all the early attestations of the phrase occur in Wulfstan's writings.[107] It is also, therefore, a term that only came into existence once the areas of Scandinavian settlement had passed into the control of the West Saxon kings of England, and its deployment to refer to those Scandinavian areas in the ninth and tenth centuries is thus anachronistic; but it remains, nonetheless, a useful term, and a useful category, for the purposes of modern study.

As for 'Viking' itself, this is also a modern term, at least in current usage: it is a nineteenth-century re-introduction of an Old Norse word (*víkingr*).[108] The Old Norse word *víkingr* ('raider, warrior'), of uncertain etymology, is recorded in poetry and runic inscriptions from the Viking Age itself, sometimes with a positive sense but more often with a pejorative one ('enemy raider'); and the term never seems to bear the collective ethnic sense 'Scandinavian'.[109] The Vikings, in other words, did not normally call themselves 'the Vikings'. *Víkingr* is, however, quite a common personal name or nickname (it is the first element, for example, of the Yorkshire place-names Wigginton and Wiganthorpe [both NR]).[110] An apparent Old English cognate, *wícing*, also existed with the sense 'raider, pirate': this probably pre-dated the Viking Age, and it was not adopted by the Anglo-Saxons as their default term for the new Scandinavian raiders (whom they more often referred to as *Dene* 'Danes, Scandinavians', or *hæðene* 'heathens').[111]

For modern usage, though, the etymology of 'Viking' is not important, and it is not worth being purist about the current use of the term. For at least a hundred years it has been fully recognized that the Modern English noun 'Viking' (with or without a capital 'V') has both a narrower, more technical meaning (a Scandinavian raider of the ninth and tenth centuries) and a wider, more cultural one (any or every Scandinavian person of the ninth and tenth centuries).[112] The same is true –

indeed, even more so – of the corresponding adjectival or attributive use (as in the very phrase 'the Viking Age'). Over the years, some scholars and writers, either wary of the term 'Viking' or simply seeking variety, have preferred the adjectives 'Danish' or 'Scandinavian', or the hybrid terms 'Anglo-Danish' or 'Anglo-Scandinavian', though 'Danish' now tends to be used in modern scholarship with a precise geographical sense ('from Denmark'), rather than as a generalized term for Scandinavians of whatever origin.[113] The adjective 'Norse' has moved in the opposite direction, more often (as in this book) now bearing the generalized sense of 'Scandinavian', rather than its older sense as a synonym for 'Norwegian'.

Under its title of *Viking Age Yorkshire*, then, this book tracks the 200 year period that takes us from the Viking kingdom of York to the Anglo-Scandinavian Yorkshire of the eleventh century. The history of Yorkshire will be placed within that of Northumbria more fully, but it will also be separated out as far as possible, as the area of Deira had a very different history in the Viking Age from that of Bernicia. The book will foreground the Vikings, and the impact of Scandinavian conquest, settlement, and culture on the region, but the title, it should be noted, is *Viking Age Yorkshire*, and not *The Vikings in Yorkshire*: the continuing importance of the Anglo-Saxon element in the culture and history of the region will not be neglected, nor the centrality of the contact between Scandinavians and English. Seven chapters follow this introduction: the first two will narrate the military and political history of the region in the Viking Age; the next three will explore questions of settlement, contact, and culture; and then the last two will take the story forward beyond the period of Viking rule, as Northumbria became part of a unified kingdom of England. The last chapter will also consider, as an epilogue, the echoes and commemoration of Yorkshire's Viking heritage in the centuries after the Norman Conquest.

THE EARLY VIKING KINGS OF YORK

The Fall of York

We can begin our narrative proper with the entry for the year 867 in the *Anglo-Saxon Chronicle*. Under that year the *Chronicle* records the fall of York to the great Viking army that was then at large in the country:

> In this year the army went from East Anglia to Northumbria, across the Humber estuary to the city of York. And there was great civil strife going on in that people, and they had deposed their king Osberht and taken a king with no hereditary right, Ælle. And not until late in the year did they unite sufficiently to proceed to fight the raiding army; and nevertheless they collected a large army and attacked the enemy in York, and broke into the city; and some of them got inside, and an immense slaughter was made of the Northumbrians, some inside and some outside, and both kings were killed, and the survivors made peace with the enemy.[1]

King Alfred's biographer, Asser, adapting the *Chronicle*'s account shortly after its composition, clarifies (or embellishes) a few of its details, especially with regards to the battle at York:

> Osberht and Ælle combined forces and assembled an army, and went to the city of York. On their arrival, the Vikings immediately took to flight, and endeavoured to defend themselves within the fortifications of the city. When the Christians noticed their flight and panic, they too determined to pursue them within the fortifications of the city and to breach the wall; and this they did. For in those days the city did not yet have firm and secure walls. After the Christians had breached the wall as they had intended, and the majority of them had got into the city along with the Vikings, the Vikings, driven on by grief and necessity, attacked them fiercely, cut them to pieces, put them to flight, and overthrew them inside and outside. Virtually the entire force of Northumbrians was annihilated there, and the two kings were killed; but the remainder, who escaped, made peace with the Vikings.[2]

The word translated as 'Vikings' here is *pagani* 'pagans' in the original Latin, and so Asser makes the battle for York a conflict explicitly between Anglo-Saxon Christians and Scandinavian pagans.[3] But other sources saw Osberht and Ælle's defeat as being directly tied to their actions as enemies of the church: the *History of St Cuthbert* claims that both kings had stolen estates from the community of St Cuthbert, and even that Ælle had been staying at one of these stolen estates (Crayke [NR], ten miles north of York) prior to their unsuccessful attack on the Viking army in York.[4]

It is also worth considering a further version of the fall of York, in Symeon of Durham's *Tract on the Church of Durham*. Although it is a later source, Symeon's *Tract* gives us the fullest account of these events, and seems to be coherent in the narrative that it offers:

> In the year of Our Lord's Incarnation 867 [...] the aforementioned heathen army captured York on 1 November and ranged hither and thither, filling everywhere with blood and lamentation. They destroyed monasteries and churches far and wide with sword and fire, and when they departed they left nothing except roofless walls.[5]

Symeon records that the Viking army did not on this occasion go any further north than the River Tyne, and his narrative continues:

> Driven by necessity, the kings of the Northumbrians (that is, Osberht and Ælle) were reconciled to each other, and the Northumbrian peoples gathered together a not inconsiderable army and strove in every way possible to cripple the enemy's power.
> So, led by two kings and eight counts, they burst into York on 21 March, and fought stubbornly, some on the inside, some on the outside. At first the enemy was terrified by the sudden arrival of the attackers, but then they resisted fiercely, and on both sides there was savage fighting. At length both the aforementioned kings fell with most of their men.[6]

Symeon's account thus makes clear what is ambiguous in the *Anglo-Saxon Chronicle*, namely that there were in fact two battles at York.[7] In this period, the 'chronicle year' began on 24 September, with the so-called Caesarean Indiction, so we would now allocate the first battle, on 1 November, to 866, and it has been suggested that the Vikings may have attacked deliberately on this date – All Saints' Day – as it was a major Christian feast-day, and any assault would have the maximum disruptive effect; attacking on feast-days was a well-established Viking ploy.[8] In this first battle, the Viking army captured York; in the second battle, four and a half months later on 21 March 867, the Anglo-Saxon forces attempted unsuccessfully to regain the city. At York as elsewhere, the Vikings clearly had a talent for exploiting factional strife in the Anglo-Saxon kingdoms.[9] That Symeon had good sources regarding the fall of York is suggested by the fact that, in another of his works, he reveals the unique detail that, upon the capture of the city in 866, the archbishop of York, Wulfhere, withdrew to Addingham in Wharfedale [WR].[10]

The fall of York in 866-67 is well recorded in English sources, and features in Irish and Welsh annals as well. But the significance of the event was also appreciated on the Scandinavian side, and a number of Old Norse texts narrate or allude to it. However, where the *Anglo-Saxon Chronicle* and later versions construct their account in terms of regional history, and the demise of the kingdom of Northumbria, the Scandinavian sources make everything much more personal. The earliest extant Norse source to allude to the fall of York – a poem – dates from the 1020s or 1030s, a full century and a half after the event itself. The text concerned reveals starkly how traditions about the conquest had been re-shaped since the 860s:

And Ivar, who resided at York [*Jórvík*], had Ælle's back cut with an eagle.[11]

The poet here is the important skald Sigvatr Þórðarson, framing and commencing his encomium to King Cnut, the Danish conqueror of England, with a meaningful backward glance to the first Scandinavian conquest of the country. But instead of the teeming crowd-scenes of the *Anglo-Saxon Chronicle*, Asser, and Symeon, Sigvatr reduces the fall of York to an interpersonal conflict between two individuals. On the English side is Ælle (and Osberht is not mentioned at all): instead of being dismissed as 'a king with no hereditary right [*ungecynd cyning*]' (as in the *Anglo-Saxon Chronicle*), Ælle seems in Norse tradition to have become a sort of representation of Anglo-Saxon inheritance and rule, frequently invoked in the context of Scandinavian triumphs in England.[12] On the Scandinavian side is his conqueror, Ivar, known in later Old Norse sagas as *Ívarr inn beinlausi* 'Ivar the Boneless'. Those sagas, especially the *Story of the Sons of Ragnarr* (*Þáttr af Ragnars sonum*), present an elaborate, family-based explanation for Ivar's desire to defeat Ella (as the Norse sources call him) and conquer Northumbria: they tell how Ella captured Ivar's supposed father, the legendary Viking Ragnarr *loðbrók* 'hairy trousers', and villainously put him to death in a snake-pit; whereupon Ivar and his brothers, as self-respecting Viking sons, had no alternative but to take their revenge upon Ella, conquering his kingdom and putting him to death by the shameful method known as the 'blood-eagle', in which a victim's lungs were pulled out and gorily arranged in the shape of an eagle's wings.[13]

The genuineness or otherwise of the blood-eagle has been much debated.[14] It is clear that, with these Old Norse sources, we are observing a process in which historical traditions are re-configured and re-imagined, primarily (one assumes) through a sequence of oral re-tellings. Sigvatr's stanza is our earliest Norse source for these versions, and so it is worth noting that, first, these re-tellings and re-configurations seem to have taken place within the Viking Age itself, rather than in the later, post-Viking period; and second, that these colourful oral stories still retain some substance of historical worth. As we know from the *Anglo-Saxon Chronicle*, the deeply obscure Ælle/Ella was indeed the king of York at the time of the city's fall. With regards to the leader or leaders of the Viking army that vanquished Ælle, later sources record more varied traditions, but ones which can nonetheless be reconciled. Sigvatr Þórðarson, as we have seen, acclaims Ivar as the conqueror of Ælle. The *History of St Cuthbert*, however, attributes that role to a Scandinavian called Ubba (Old Norse *Ubbi*), who is associated in his campaign with another war-leader called Halfdan (Old Norse *Hálfdanr*, *Healfdene* in English sources).[15] It seems likely, however, that in historical reality Ivar, Ubba and Halfdan were brothers, three of the leaders of the Viking Great Army.[16] Ivar, above all, was an exceptionally important figure for the history of Viking Age Britain: probably of Danish origin and known in English sources as *Inwær*, in Irish ones as *Imair*, and in Latin ones (in England at least) as *Hinguar*, he effectively established the dynasty of Scandinavian kings who were to rule in England and Ireland in the ninth and tenth centuries.[17]

The traditions and stories surrounding the fall of York in 866-67 were thus extensive, diverse, and long-lived. And no wonder: the consequence of the event was that for nearly a century, until the expulsion and death of Eric Bloodaxe in 954, York formed the centre of a Scandinavian kingdom in the north of England. The purpose of this and the next chapter, then, is to offer an account of the military and political events of the nine decades between 866 and 954 – a time that more than one scholar has called 'the Viking century' in Yorkshire.[18] But before such a narrative can begin, we should briefly take stock of both Northumbria and Scandinavia at the start of our period.

The Beginnings of the Viking Age

Looking back to the time before the Vikings came, King Alfred, in the preface to his translation of Pope Gregory the Great's *Pastoral Care* (*Cura Pastoralis*), recalled 'how – before everything was ransacked and burned – the churches throughout England stood filled with treasure and books'; and, moreover, how 'there was a great multitude of those serving God'.[19] Of no part of the country was this truer than pre-Viking Age Northumbria. Gregory had sent a mission to convert the Anglo-Saxons in 597, and in the reign of Edwin (616-33), Northumbria had taken a decisive shift to Christianity. Edwin himself was responsible for the construction of the first minster in York, within the grounds of the old Roman fortress.[20] Christian learning and culture flourished in the north-east of England, at least at elite level, and our evidence for this is both archaeological and textual.[21] Above all, Bede's *Ecclesiastical History of the English People*, completed in the early 730s, gives a powerful account of the progress of Christianity within England as a whole, and in Northumbria in particular: Bede's pages contain a host of memorable saints, kings, and miracles, and Bede also articulated a potent and influential vision of the Anglo-Saxons unified as one people, under the authority of one archbishop, and in a New Covenant with God as one of his chosen peoples.[22]

But although Bede may have seen the Anglo-Saxons as forming one Christian people (the *gens Anglorum*, as in the title of his work), they were not unified politically. Instead, at the time when Bede was writing, the various Anglo-Saxon polities had shaped themselves into seven main kingdoms – the so-called Heptarchy – of Northumbria, Mercia, East Anglia, Wessex, Sussex, Kent, and Essex. By the time of the arrival of the Viking Great Army in 865, these seven had been reduced to four, as Sussex, Kent, and Essex had all come under the sway of Wessex.[23] As noted in the previous chapter, Northumbria itself originally comprised two separate kingdoms, Bernicia to the north of the River Tees and Deira to the south. These had become united politically by the mid seventh century, but it is clear – not least from their subsequent histories in the Viking Age – that the territories covered by these two kingdoms were not simply amalgamated, and their differences effaced.

In terms of the old Bernicia, Bede's Jarrow probably represents the high-point of Christian culture and scholarship; in terms of Deira, that accolade surely belongs to York in the second half of the eighth century, the time of Archbishop Ælberht and the great scholar Alcuin (though York was also an important trading centre in the Anglian period). Under Alcuin's leadership, the cathedral school at York became one of the greatest centres of learning anywhere in Europe at the time: it was for that reason that Alcuin was recruited by the Frankish ruler Charlemagne, the most powerful monarch in Europe, to advance his own programme of cultural renovation.[24] At some point in the 780s or early 790s, probably after he had moved to Charlemagne's court, Alcuin used Bede's *Ecclesiastical History* as a source to compose an encomiastic poem about his home city. York is presented as an earthly paradise:

> Through York flows the Ouse, its waters teeming with fish,
> along its banks stretch fields laden with flowers,
> all about the countryside is lovely with hills and woods,
> and this beautiful, healthy place of noble setting
> was destined to attract many settlers by its richness.[25]

There is an unintended irony in the last line. Alcuin was thinking of the Romans and the Anglo-Saxons, but in the century following there were to be other settlers, from the north, who were attracted by York's richness and fertility.

Alcuin's poem also gives us a sense of York's extraordinary literary wealth in the pre-Viking period, providing a catalogue of the library that Ælberht had built up at the Minster school:

> There you will find the legacy of the ancient fathers:
> All the Roman possessed in the Latin world,
> Whatever famous Greece has transmitted to the Latins,
> Draughts of the Hebrew race from Heaven's showers,
> And what Africa has spread abroad in streams of light:
> The perceptions of father Jerome and of Hilary,
> Of bishop Ambrose, Augustine, and
> Of saint Athanasius, the writings of astute Orosius,
> The teachings of Gregory the Great and of pope Leo,
> The glowing words of Basil and Fulgentius,
> Of Cassiodorus and John Chrysostom;
> The teaching of Aldhelm and of Bede the master,
> The writings of Victorinus and Boethius,
> And the ancient historians Pompey and Pliny,
> Of keen-minded Aristotle and of Cicero the great rhetorician [...][26]

So the list goes on, referencing many more classical and Christian writers. This list, perhaps more than any other source, gives us a sense of the cultural heights attained in pre-Viking York, and its poignancy is greatly increased by knowledge of the calamity that was soon to befall the city.[27]

A complementary account of some of the physical treasures of pre-Viking Northumbria can also be found in Alcuin's poem. Alcuin's evocation of some of the artworks with which York Minster was adorned by Archbishop Ælberht is revelatory:

> In the spot where Edwin, the warrior king, was baptized
> the bishop raised a great altar
> and covered it with gold, silver, and jewels,
> dedicating it in the name of St Paul,
> the universal teacher, whom he loved with all his heart.
> High above this altar he hung a chandelier,
> which held three great vessels, each with nine tiers.
> At the altar he erected the noble standard of the cross
> covering it entirely with most precious metals.
> It was all on a grand scale and built on a lovely design,
> weighing many pounds in pure silver.

He erected another altar and covered it too
with pure silver and precious stones,
dedicating it both to the martyrs and to the Cross.
He ordered a large cruet to be made in pure gold
and of great weight, from which the priest
celebrating holy mass could pour wine into the chalice.[28]

Although York Minster was of course exceptional, another poem gives us a sense of the similarly precious treasures with which a lesser church or monastery might be endowed. Æthelwulf's *On Abbots* (*De Abbatibus*) is an early ninth-century Latin poem, influenced by Alcuin's poem on York, which commemorates the leaders and history of an un-named monastery in Northumbria, a dependent cell of Lindisfarne; the most likely – though not certain – identification is that the monastery concerned was that at Crayke, near York (later to be seized by Ælle prior to his defeat and death in the fall of York in 867).[29] Like Alcuin, Æthelwulf celebrates the treasures of his church:

> Many men wished to hang up numerous bowls, which would give soft light in the rectangular church, and others set up ensigns of shining metal [...] Some gave orders for the writing of sacred books [...] and these are covered by plate of bright ductile gold; and similarly men adorned the altars of the blessed church. And somebody dressed the altar of our lady, who is noble by origin, in the flames of gems and in yellow gold.[30]

For Alcuin and Æthelwulf, such treasures were offerings to the glory of God; for Scandinavian raiders, of course, they would be just loot, waiting to be plundered. We now possess very few high-quality artworks from pre-Viking York and its environs, but the famous Anglian 'Coppergate Helmet' is one surviving example of what eighth-century York was capable of: secular rather than ecclesiastical, but nonetheless decorated with a Christian inscription.[31]

Another remarkable object that we possess from pre-Viking York is a fragment of stone sculpture, recovered from the church of St Mary Bishophill Junior, which depicts two men facing one another [Figure 3].[32] These men are not clerics or saints, and, although secular figures are rarely shown on pre-Viking sculpture, there is no reason to doubt that what we have here is a portrait of two prosperous citizens from early to mid ninth-century York. They wear long garments, with belts or girdles. The one on the left has a hood, and also a horn hanging from his belt, while the one on the right has a decorative collar, and a short sword which he is grasping with his left hand. Both seem to have moustaches, and the one on the right sports a very full head of hair. It is not clear what they are standing on. In terms of actions, the two men may be clasping hands, perhaps in greeting or agreement. They themselves, or certainly their children or grandchildren, will have lived to see the fall of the city to the Scandinavians in 866.

It is from Northumbria to Scandinavia that we should now turn. The peninsula of mainland Scandinavia in the late Iron Age (sometimes called the Vendel Period) was a region of petty kingdoms.[33] It was also, of course, pagan. Denmark, as the most southward-facing and 'Europeanized' part of Scandinavia, was a partial exception to both these statements, where state formation had advanced the furthest by the late eighth century, and the force of Christian missionaries (and neighbouring Christian kings) was beginning to be felt. But even Denmark cannot be said to have been securely converted before the mid tenth century, and the regions of Norway and Sweden remained pagan even longer. Nonetheless, the eighth and ninth centuries saw an extraordinary eruption out of Scandinavia, continuing into the tenth and even eleventh centuries, as raiders, traders, and settlers surged out both east and west: the Viking Age.

What were the causes of this Viking expansion? Why did the region of Scandinavia exhibit movements and behaviours in the eighth to tenth centuries of a sort that the rest of northern Europe had experienced some four centuries earlier (for example, in the migration of the Anglo-Saxon peoples to Britain)? The reasons have, of course, been much debated.[34] A traditional explanation for Viking Age expansion was over-population in Scandinavia – in other words, an insufficiency of resources in terms of land, food, or wealth – and this explanation goes back at least to the eleventh century. The German cleric Adam of Bremen, writing his *History of the Archbishops of Hamburg-Bremen* (*Gesta Hammaburgensis Ecclesiae Pontificum*) in the 1070s, claimed of the Norwegians in particular that 'poverty has forced them […] to go all over the world and from piratical raids they bring home in great abundance the riches of the lands'.[35] As an extra twist to the over-population argument, it has been suggested that there may have been a disproportion in the sex ratio in Viking Age Scandinavia, with men significantly outnumbering women – a disproportion exacerbated, or even unwittingly caused, by the apparent infanticide of female babies.[36] There may be considerable truth in the 'insufficiency of resources' argument, but the point is perhaps better made if one thinks in terms of a drag-chain rather than a push-chain: that is, it may be more revealing to ask what attracted Scandinavians to Britain and continental Europe, rather than what propelled them out of their homelands. The answer is that England and Frankia were immensely rich countries, both in terms of moveable wealth – loot – and agricultural resources.[37] As Alfred the Great was to recall, eighth-century England, and the churches of Northumbria in particular, had more than enough treasures to attract the eye (as also did Ireland), and such prosperity may well have acted as a magnet either for those wishing to better their lot through migration, or (at least to begin with) for young men who wished to establish themselves in life through the acquisition of wealth – especially at a time when there seems to have been very little silver or gold circulating in Scandinavia.[38] Substantial amounts of British and Irish metalwork – much of it stripped from ecclesiastical settings – have been found in ninth- and early tenth-century graves in Norway, and especially female graves: this suggests that insular loot had an important role to play in Viking Age gift-exchange and marriage settlements.[39]

Political developments on a larger scale are also likely to have been a factor in the Viking explosion. The eighth to tenth centuries in Scandinavia were a period in which the practices and ideologies of kingship were changing in important ways.[40] Competition for power and resources seems to have led to a volatile and unstable political environment, in which a new form of more predatory kingship came to the fore – an escalation of the Iron Age world of multiple small kings, each supported by their own warband.[41] As the period progressed, power came to reside in fewer and fewer hands, and the reach of a more centralized kingship grew longer and stronger. In Norway, the key figure was Harald Fairhair (Old Norse *Haraldr hárfagri*), to be remembered as the king who, to a large degree, unified the country under one ruler; his key battle, at Hafrsfjorden, was fought in probably the 880s.[42]

Later Icelandic sagas present a romanticized, but not purely fictitious, account of the consequences of Harald's unification. Norwegians who were unable to tolerate the rise of such tyranny, and who had the necessary means at their disposal, vacated the country, and sought new lands in which to live free from royal compulsion. As *Egil's Saga* states:

> King Harald took careful stock of the noblemen and the powerful farmers and all those whom he suspected of possible revolt. He made each do one of two things, either enter his service or leave the country [...] Many men fled away from this oppression out of the country, and many waste lands were then settled, both east in Jamtland and Halsingland, and in the west lands, the Hebrides, the Dublin area, Ireland, Normandy in France, Caithness in Scotland, the Orkneys, Shetland and the Faroes. And at that time Iceland was discovered.[43]

The sagas' claim that Viking Age migrants were a freedom-loving elite, a sort of egalitarian aristocracy, is obviously coloured with a large dash of myth-making; but the fundamental idea, that Viking Age movement was a response to the re-distribution of scant resources in mainland Scandinavia, undoubtedly rings true, and is consonant with other indicators.

Finally, there was a technological element in the onset of the Viking Age. Up until the eighth century, long-distance travel by sea in northern Europe involved hugging the coast, moving along the land in a series of steps, as ship-building, or navigational skills, or nautical ambition, seem not to have been sufficient for cross-ocean voyages. The Viking Age changed all that. Advances in seamanship, and breakthroughs in construction (aided, no doubt, by more centralized powers of coercion and organization), meant that a ship could now be built and crewed which could sail directly, and swiftly, across the North Sea, from Norway to northern Britain; and a shallow keel meant that the same ship could penetrate far inland up-river.[44] As Alcuin was to write, 'such a voyage was not thought possible'.[45] The same shipbuilding skills that could convey a party of raiders to the Northumbrian coast could equally well facilitate long-distance trade, and also transport families of settlers, with their goods and animals, over the Atlantic to Ireland and the Northern and Western Isles of Scotland, to the Faroes and Iceland, and, in time, even to Greenland and North America.

Technological developments, political and economic pressures, and individual ambitions all combined to produce the most appalling of smash-and-grabs. The monastery of Lindisfarne was attacked in 793, apparently without warning, and the *Anglo-Saxon Chronicle*'s record of the event is well-known (in the northern D and E versions; it is not in the Alfredian A-text):

> In this year dire portents appeared over Northumbria and sorely frightened the people. They consisted of immense whirlwinds and flashes of lightning, and fiery dragons were seen flying in the air. A great famine immediately followed those signs, and a little after that in the same year, on 8 June, the ravages of heathen men miserably destroyed God's church on Lindisfarne, with plunder and slaughter.[46]

Fiery dragons do not lie: the ominous signs noted by the *Chronicle* – and also by Alcuin, who recorded bloody rain falling from the roof of York Minster – are a means of predicting, and communicating, the full horror of what was to follow later in the summer.[47] A famous piece of sculpture from Lindisfarne shows a band of warriors brandishing swords and axes in terrifying fashion [Figure 4].[48] This cannot be proven to be a commemorative image of the 793 raid, and it may be a representation of one of the signs of the end of the world; but even so, it seems probable that its unparalleled iconography has been shaped by Lindisfarne's experience as the object of Viking attack: the axes, in particular, are a tell-tale Scandinavian sign.

When he heard the news of the 793 raid, Alcuin sent out a number of heart-felt and traumatized letters, including to the survivors of the Lindisfarne community itself.[49] He wrote to its abbot, Higbald:

> When I was with you your loving friendship gave me great joy. Now I am away your tragic sufferings daily bring me sorrow, since the pagans have desecrated God's sanctuary, shed the blood of saints around the altar, laid waste the house of our hope and trampled the bodies of the saints like dung in the street [...] What assurance can the churches of Britain have, if St Cuthbert and so great a company of saints do not defend their own? Is this the beginning of greater suffering, or the

outcome of the sins of those who live there? It has not happened by chance, but is the sign of some great guilt.[50]

Alcuin had read Bede closely, and he took from the earlier writer the idea that the English people, like the Israelites of the Old Testament, enjoyed a covenantal relationship with God. And so, in the midst of his sense of sheer shock, and his fear for the future ('Is this the beginning of greater suffering?'), Alcuin reached for the idea of the covenant, with its resultant implication that God was chastising those whom he loved, on account of their sin or backsliding, and using the Vikings as his agents for doing so: 'it has not happened by chance'.[51] Alcuin also composed a 240-line poem on the sack of Lindisfarne.[52] There is relatively little in the poem on the raid itself ('how painful to everyone was that day when, alas, / a pagan warband arrived from the ends of the earth'); rather, as he does also in his letter to Higbald, Alcuin situates the event within both general reflections on earthly mutability and a sequence of prior Biblical and Christian examples of reversal and impermanence. But current times do seem more grievous:

> Why should I only deal mournfully with distant times
> And lament the miserable days of the ancients in my poetry,
> When throughout the world the present age endures worse things
> And the earth now grieves in doleful subjection?

This 'doleful subjection' is to pagan forces, and Alcuin again invokes a covenantal interpretation of recent events ('So too omnipotent God tested the saints through savage blows').

It is not quite clear whether Lindisfarne should enjoy the unenviable distinction of being the first place in England to be raided by Viking ships. For one thing, in a letter to the Northumbrian king Æthelred I (the same letter in which he had written that 'such a voyage was not thought possible'), Alcuin reveals that the Northumbrian aristocracy, in the wicked luxuriousness of their lifestyle, seem to have been copying Scandinavian fashions, which would indicate at least some form of prior contact. 'Consider the luxurious dress, hair and behaviour of leaders and people', Alcuin writes to the king. 'See how you have wanted to copy the pagan way of cutting hair and beards. Are not these the people whose terror threatens us, yet you want to copy their hair?'[53] Although some scholars have wished to claim extensive contacts across the North Sea in the eighth century, the evidence for this is very meagre, and our contemporary sources are marked by a sense of shock at the newness and unexpectedness of the Viking attacks.[54]

The *Anglo-Saxon Chronicle* also offers an alternative candidate for the first Viking raid on England, in its entry for the year 789:

> In this year King Brihtric married Offa's daughter Eadburh. And in his days there came for the first time three ships [of Northmen] and then the reeve rode to them and wished to force them to the king's residence [*cyninges tun*], for he did not know what they were; and they slew him. Those were the first ships of Danish men which came to the land of the English.[55]

This is the entry as it stands in version A (and the *cyninges tun*, to which the reeve tried to force the shipmen, is more likely to have been a place of imprisonment than a royal villa).[56] Later or alternative texts expand on a number of points: versions C, D, and E of the *Chronicle* add that the ships came from Hordaland (in western Norway), while Æthelweard records that the name of the unfortunate reeve was Beaduheard, and the *Annals of St Neots* claim that this incident took place at Portland in Dorset.[57] The *Chronicle's* entry is clearly retrospective, recognizing the significance for the future of an event that can hardly have seemed portentous at the time ('Those were the first ships of Danish men which came to the land of the English'). 'Danish' (*Denisc*) is here used, as often in the *Chronicle*, as a catch-all term for Scandinavians, and it does not indicate precise geographical knowledge; 'heathen' (*hæðen*) is the most frequent alternative, as noted in the previous chapter and as seen in the 793 Lindisfarne entry. Since Brihtric reigned from 786 to 802, Beaduheard's death at Portland cannot be dated to an exact year.

Alcuin had been fearful that Bede's Jarrow would suffer the same fate as Cuthbert's Lindisfarne, and he wrote to the community there, appealing again to the idea of a covenant:

> Who is not afraid of the terrible fate that has come upon the church of St Cuthbert? So mend your ways, lest the righteous perish for the sins of the wicked [...] You live near the sea from which this danger first came. In us is fulfilled what once the prophet foretold: 'From the North evil breaks forth, and a terrible glory will come from the Lord' [Jeremiah 1.14, Job 37.22]. See, the pirate raids have penetrated the north of our island.[58]

But to no avail: Jarrow was attacked the following year, in 794, in a raid recorded in versions D and E of the *Anglo-Saxon Chronicle*. But after that, perhaps surprisingly, the *Chronicle* goes quiet for a few decades. This is not likely to be because Viking raids slackened off; indeed, they may have been becoming so frequent as to be no longer quite so newsworthy. But the *Chronicle* itself becomes less expansive in its entries for this period, and some years have no entry at all. That the English were continuing to suffer Viking tribulations at this time is, however, forcefully demonstrated by a sequence of early ninth-century Mercian charters that testify to Scandinavian raids and even camps in Kent, while Roger of Wendover records under the year 800 that, in Northumbria, 'the most impious army of the pagans cruelly despoiled the churches of Hartness and Tynemouth, and returned with its plunder to the ships'.[59] We should therefore be aware that the *Anglo-Saxon Chronicle*'s coverage of Viking raids in the first half of the ninth century is, for whatever reason, patchy and incomplete.[60]

But in 835 the Vikings do re-appear in the *Chronicle*: 'In this year heathen men ravaged Sheppey'.[61] In 836 King Ecgberht of Wessex (Alfred's grandfather) is said to have 'fought against the crews of 35 ships [25 in some versions] at Carhampton, and a great slaughter was made there, and the Danes had possession of the battle-field', while in 838 a 'great naval force [*micel sciphere*]' arrived in Cornwall.[62] In the 840s, the reporting of attacks increases further, all clustered in the south of England, but that this is probably an illusion created by the *Chronicle*'s Wessex-centred perspective is again suggested by an event recorded by Roger of Wendover, under the year 844:

> Æthelred, king of the Northumbrians, was expelled from the kingdom, and Rædwulf succeeded to the kingdom; and when, hastily invested with the crown, he fought a battle with the pagans at Elvet [in Durham], he and ealdorman Alfred fell with a large part of their subjects, and then Æthelred reigned again.[63]

Roger's chronology may be askew here by a decade or more, and numismatic evidence suggests that Rædwulf may have reigned until the late 850s.[64] Either way, it is clear that by the mid ninth century Viking armies were at large in Northumbria, and fighting major battles.

An ominous shift is recorded in the *Anglo-Saxon Chronicle* in 851:

> For the first time, heathen men stayed through the winter on Thanet. And the same year 350 ships came into the mouth of the Thames and stormed Canterbury and London.[65]

King Æthelwulf (Alfred's father) fought an important battle against this army at a place called *Aclea*, and the Chronicler, composing in the early 890s, writes that the king 'inflicted the greatest slaughter on a heathen army that we ever heard of until this present day'. Notwithstanding this success, Viking forces continued to arrive through the 850s and 860s, over-wintering in Sheppey as well as Thanet (with thus an implied target of London and the interior). Eventually, in 865, the *Chronicle* records that a 'great army [*micel here*]' came to England and over-wintered in East Anglia.[66] This 865 'Great Army' was led by Ivar and others of his family. It was intent on conquest and not just plunder, and its scale of ambition has been described as 'breathtaking'.[67] In terms of national history, it must be regarded as one of the most important military forces ever to have entered England. And as we have seen, its first success, the following year, was the capture of York.

The First Viking Kings of York

As we begin to trace the Scandinavian rulers of York, it must be admitted that the history and chronology of northern Britain during the period of Viking kings, 866 to 954, is often confused and difficult to reconstruct. The current scholarly understanding of the period began in the 1970s with the work of Alfred Smyth, who combined English and Irish sources to construct a unified history of the Viking kingdoms centred on York and Dublin.[68] Smyth showed persuasively how the histories of these two Viking cities were inextricably related, at least in political and dynastic terms, with Viking leaders appearing first in one place and then the other, and often succeeding one another across the Pennines. Smyth's work did not escape criticism by any means, especially for his use of late and debatable sources; but his work on Viking Age York and Dublin remains a very significant achievement, and it put the study of the subject on a new footing.[69] More recently, Smyth's framework and chronology have been re-assessed by Clare Downham and Alex Woolf, who have sought to query, confirm, or reject Smyth's interpretations, often on a point-by-point basis; and the account that follows draws very gratefully on the work of these and other scholars.[70]

As we know, our story proper begins in 866. The army that attacked York on 1 November had arrived the previous year:

> A great heathen army came into England and took up winter quarters in East Anglia; and there they were supplied with horses, and the East Angles made peace with them.[71]

Although this statement occurs in the *Anglo-Saxon Chronicle* entry for 866, the *Chronicle*'s year begins on 24 September, and so (as it is recorded taking up winter quarters) the Viking army must have arrived in late 865. Where exactly the Great Army came from is not clearly stated in our sources: mainland Scandinavia would seem a self-evident assumption, but it is also highly likely that at least some of the leadership and army had already been campaigning in Britain (especially Ireland) and Frankia.[72] As Shane McLeod has shown, a trail of pre-865 Carolingian coins found in England indicates that at least some members of the Great Army arrived with Frankish wealth in their pockets; in Yorkshire, examples have been retrieved at Settle [WR], York Minster, and Coney Street, York.[73] As for what the Great Army was doing for the first twelve months after its arrival in late 865, this is also unclear: presumably it was assembling its provisions in East Anglia, before moving north for the assault on York in late 866, and perhaps also waiting for re-inforcements to arrive.[74]

How big was a *micel here*? The size of early medieval armies is a matter of dispute, and in any case it is clear that the Great Army was exceptional and not typical.[75] In the 1960s the historian Peter Sawyer argued that contemporary accounts of the magnitude of Viking armies were greatly exaggerated, and that they were to be numbered only in the mere hundreds, not thousands.[76] These claims were definitively answered by Nicholas Brooks, however, who demonstrated that major Viking armies were likely to comprise several thousand members at least.[77] Brooks' argument was based on a number of grounds: the consistency between insular and continental sources in estimating the size of Viking fleets; the size of the fortifications the major Viking armies occupied and the (better recorded) size of the Anglo-Saxon forces required to withstand them; and (of course) the scale of devastation of the Viking armies and their success in war: in terms of speed and decisiveness, the military conquests of the Great Army were unlike anything seen in Anglo-Saxon England in the previous three centuries. Archaeological investigations at two Viking 'winter-camps' in England have recently strengthened Brooks' case yet further: these were massive sites, clearly occupied by a very large number of people.[78] At least a couple of recent estimates have placed the strength of the Great Army as somewhere in the region of 10,000, though it is possible that this is still an under-estimate.[79] Moreover, although the family of Ivar probably had Danish origins, it should not be assumed that the Great Army was 'mono-ethnic'; on the contrary, Viking armies, especially large ones that remained in the field over a lengthy period, were likely to be composite and cosmopolitan in their make-up.[80] For fifteen years the Great Army's campaigns were the main focus of Viking activity in western Europe, a fact which gives a good indication of the size and importance of the enterprise.[81]

After the fall of York, the *Anglo-Saxon Chronicle* records the army as moving down into Mercia in late 867, to over-winter in Nottingham and, after inconclusive fighting, to make peace with Burgred, king of the Mercians. And then in late 868 the army returned to York, 'and stayed there one year', before moving south again in late 869 through Mercia and into East Anglia, to over-winter in Thetford and defeat and kill King Edmund of the East Angles – rapidly to be commemorated as St Edmund, the first English saint (but not the last) to be martyred at the hands of the Vikings.[82] The Great Army, the *Chronicle* records, 'conquered all the land [*þæt land all geeodon*]' of the East Angles, and it may be significant that this phrase is not used earlier to describe their success in Northumbria, at York.[83] From East Anglia, the Great Army went westwards, in 871, into Wessex, and from this point the *Chronicle*'s narrative becomes a good deal fuller and more emotive – the reason being, of course, that this is the moment at which the Viking army came into contact and conflict with Alfred the Great, the crucial figure behind the *Chronicle*'s compilation.

According to the *Chronicle*, the Great Army over-wintered in London in 871-72, making another peace with the Mercians, and then late in 872 moved northwards again, at least for a time, when it returned briefly to Northumbria – for reasons that will be explained shortly – and then over-wintered in Torksey in Lincolnshire (where the site of its winter-camp has been discovered by metal-detectorists, and many objects recovered).[84] The next year it moved to Repton in Mercia, where Viking fortifications have been excavated.[85] There, they drove out King Burgred and appointed a puppet-king called Ceolwulf in his place (dismissed by the *Chronicle* as 'a foolish king's thegn'), and – we should note the recurrence of the phrase – 'conquered all the land [*þæt land all geeodon*]'.[86] At Repton, in late 874, it seems there was a division in the Great Army: one part, led by the kings Guthrum, Oscetel, and Anwend, went to East Anglia, while another part, led by Halfdan, went north:

> Halfdan went with part of the army into Northumbria and took up winter quarters by the River Tyne. And the army conquered the land [*þæt land geeode*] and often ravaged among the Picts and the Strathclyde Britons.[87]

In the entry for the following year, 876, there occurs a famous sentence that is cryptic and under-stated, but of utmost importance for our present concerns: 'And that year Halfdan shared out the land of the Northumbrians, and they proceeded to plough and to support themselves' [Figure 2].[88]

There is one archaeological site in Yorkshire that offers a more material access to these events of the early to mid 870s. In 2004 the so-called 'Ainsbrook hoard' was reported, found by two metal-detectorists somewhere at a riverine location 'within striking distance of York' ('Ainsbrook' is a code-name, devised so as not to reveal the location of the site to other metal-detectorists; the find-spot is also sometimes referenced as simply 'a riverine site in North Yorkshire').[89] The site was initially reported as a possible Viking boat-burial on account of the presence of a large quantity of iron rivets, though this view was soon abandoned; two bodies were subsequently excavated, which have been given a 'radiocarbon determination' in the tenth century.[90] The 'Ainsbrook hoard', as first reported, included weights and scales, silver ingots, two swords, and a small number of Anglo-Saxon coins, including three of King Burgred of Mercia: these enable it to be dated to sometime after 874.[91] The same site, through metal-detectorist activity, had previously yielded hundreds of small finds, such as weights, brooches, ingots, hack-silver and even hack-gold (that is, chopped up pieces), fragments of weapons, and lots of Northumbrian coins (suggesting activity on the site prior to the Viking arrival). Some high-quality Viking loot was also uncovered, such as a gilded copper-alloy book mount and an ornamental stud, perhaps from an ecclesiastical vessel. Moreover, the site was located within a ditch, and the area enclosed was enormous – some 76 acres. All these features suggest that its closest similarity is with the better-recorded Viking winter-camp at Torksey (from 872-73), though the size of the 'Ainsbrook' site is even greater than that of Torksey.[92]

A speculative interpretation would therefore be as follows. The *Anglo-Saxon Chronicle* conscientiously gives the locations of the Great Army's winter-camps in 871-72 (London), 872-73 (Torksey), 873-74 (Repton), and 874-75 (by the Tyne). But it does not identify a winter-camp for 875-76. This may mean that Halfdan's army was dispersed before the winter (and after 24 September, when the *Chronicle* year begins), in which case the famous settlement of Northumbria should be dated to 875 rather than 876. But if Halfdan's army did stay together through one last winter, just prior to his sharing out of the land, then the 'Ainsbrook' site may be best interpreted as the location of their camp – or at least of one of their camps. The numismatic evidence (Burgred's 874 coins) would fit perfectly with this suggestion. 'Ainsbrook' is thus far and away the most important Viking Age site in Yorkshire currently awaiting publication, and when full details are made available they will no doubt change significantly our understanding of aspects of the 860s and 870s.

At this point we need to pause to take stock of where we have got to, and to ask a number of questions. The first is the nature of the conquest of York in 866. To begin to understand this we need to supplement the *Anglo-Saxon Chronicle*'s account with those of other sources. Symeon of Durham, in his *Tract on the Church of Durham*, records that, after the defeat of Osberht and Ælle at York in 867, 'the Danes set up Ecgberht as a king over the surviving Northumbrians, but he ruled only over those who lived to the north of the river Tyne, and that under the authority of the Danes'; the *History of the Kings* gives a similar account, and adds that Ecgberht ruled for six years.[93] Symeon then records that, a little later, 'the Northumbrians expelled their king Ecgberht and their archbishop Wulfhere from the kingdom, and set up as their king a certain man called Ricsige'.[94] The *History of the Kings* more or less agrees, and states in 873 that 'Ecgberht, king of the Northumbrians dying, had Ricsige as his successor, and he reigned for three years. And Wulfhere was re-instated in his archbishopric', and in 876 that 'King Ricsige of the Northumbrians died, and Ecgberht the second reigned over the Northumbrians beyond the River Tyne'.[95]

This is all a bit puzzling, but collation with the *Anglo-Saxon Chronicle* does enable us to make sense of some parts of the narrative. The otherwise unmotivated visit to Northumbria made by the Great Army in the entry for 873 must have been due to the expulsion of Ecgberht and Wulfhere, the former of whom, we should recall, had been appointed as a puppet-king. But it is not clear whether Ecgberht was re-instated (and then died), or whether the Great Army chose to endorse Ricsige's rule instead; it is also unclear whether there is any connection between the Great Army's 873 visit and the re-instatement of Wulfhere as archbishop.

Let us re-quote the key statements from the *Anglo-Saxon Chronicle* for 875 and 876:

875. Halfdan went with part of the army into Northumbria and took up winter quarters by the River Tyne. And the army conquered the land [*þæt land geeode*].
876. Halfdan shared out the land of the Northumbrians, and they proceeded to plough and to support themselves.[96]

The obvious explanation is that the 866-67 conquest brought the Deiran part of Northumbria (that is, effectively, the area of Yorkshire) under direct Scandinavian control, but that the Bernician part, beyond the Tyne, was governed via a sub-king; and this would explain why Asser describes Halfdan as 'king of one part of the Northumbrians'.[97] This does indeed seem possible, except that the expulsions and re-instatements of 873 involved the archbishop of York as well as King Ecgberht, suggesting a native revolt within Deiran Northumbria as well as Bernician, unless the archbishop was not actually to be found in York; and we are ignorant of who was left in charge of York and Deiran Northumbria after 867, even if Halfdan was regarded as its ultimate ruler. To solve these problems, a couple of scholars have proposed that Archbishop Wulfhere himself may have been the Vikings' ruler in southern Northumbria in this period (though if such was the case, one might perhaps have expected Symeon of Durham, our best-informed source on Archbishop Wulfhere, to have said so, unless he wished deliberately to conceal the fact).[98] As an alternative explanation, Alex Woolf has suggested that it was the whole of Northumbria which lay under the rule of Anglo-Saxon sub-kings between 866 and 876, and that the apparent distinction between Deira and Bernicia in these years was only drawn by Symeon himself in the early twelfth century.[99] This too is possible, and it clears up some of the mystery; but it does not explain why the *Anglo-Saxon Chronicle* should claim that Halfdan 'conquered all the land' of the Northumbrians in 875 (since on Woolf's model it had already been conquered in 866), and nor does it really leave room for both Halfdan and Ecgberht II to be rulers of Northumbria from 876 onwards.

Perhaps we might refine or supplement these interpretations by suggesting that there was, in some way, a two-stage conquest of Northumbria: a first stage in 866-67, in which the Viking army conquered York and somehow became able to dictate the terms of political rule in Northumbria (both Deiran and Bernician), and a second stage in 875-76, in which they dispossessed the ruling elite of land and power, and subjugated Northumbria (especially Deiran Northumbria) directly to themselves. This is perhaps supported by the *Chronicle*'s recurrent statement that the Viking army 'conquered the land': in the original Old English, the phrase literally means that they 'went through' the land – implying an on-the-ground thoroughness to their conquest that had perhaps not occurred up to that point. Furthermore, we might possibly read the *Chronicle*'s references to Northumbria in 875 and 876 as referring solely to Deiran Northumbria: place-name evidence, as noted already, indicates that there was little subsequent Scandinavian settlement north of the Tees valley, and we shall see in Chapter 3 that in the early tenth century the degree of political control exerted by Scandinavian kings over Bernician Northumbria fluctuated considerably, often to the degree of being non-existent. So Halfdan's settlement of 875-76 would look to be the point at which a unified Northumbria broke along the old fault-line between the two kingdoms.

But even if we interpret our sources as indicating a two-step conquest, we must be careful not to downplay the significance of the 866 fall of York. Although the Great Army, in its early years of conquest, preferred the option of setting up Anglo-Saxon subject-kings, and although there is no positive evidence for ruling Scandinavian kings resident in Northumbria before 875-76 (except, perhaps, for the year the Great Army spent at York in 868-69) this does not mean that the events of 866 were unimportant, with business proceeding as usual afterwards, with just a different overlord. Quite the contrary: the Scandinavian conquest of York was a deeply disruptive event, and our best evidence for this is monetary.

The pre-Viking Age kingdom of Northumbria had a thriving but largely self-contained coin economy, especially in the circulation of brass *stycas*.[100] But this economy seems to have come to an abrupt end at the time of the Viking conquest of York; Osberht, one of the two kings defeated and killed by Ivar's forces, is the last Northumbrian ruler to whom *stycas* can be attributed, and although *stycas* have been found at the putative winter-camp of 875-76 (perhaps used in 868-69 also?), it is significant that no coins were minted under the puppet-kings of 867-75.[101] Similarly, no coins dating from after the 860s have been found in Fishergate, the part of York that seems to have been the *wic* or trading emporium of Anglian York: this suggests severe discontinuity in the trade economy of the city (and therefore the region), and the Fishergate site ceased to be used in the 860s.[102] Coins stopped circulating in Northumbria in any significant quantity, and important so-called 'productive sites', such as that at South Newbald [ER], where trade had been conducted and from which many pre-Viking coins have been retrieved, were suddenly abandoned.[103] Over twenty Northumbrian coin hoards have been dated to the mid 860s, including six from York itself.[104] All of this amounts to a clear sign of a society, and a city, in crisis. As one numismatist has written, what this mass of hoard evidence suggests is that 'the issue of coin was interrupted not by some administrative breakdown but by some violent disturbance': the Viking conquest of 866 delivered a profound shock to the kingdom of Northumbria.[105]

A simpler question, in the midst of all this, is what had happened to Ivar – remembered in Scandinavian tradition as the military genius at the head of the Great Army and the man responsible for the capture of York in 866. The answer is that he had turned his attention to Ireland, and as a result he received little attention from English chroniclers compared with Irish ones – though Æthelweard explicitly recognizes him as the leader of the Great Army and twice characterizes him as a *tyrannus* ('tyrant').[106] He died in Ireland in 873, and the *Annals of Ulster* acclaimed him as 'king of the Norsemen of all Ireland and Britain'.[107] Ivar's sons seem to have restricted their attention to Ireland, but his grandsons and great-grandsons, as we will see, played a central role in the politics of tenth-century York. We should also note here the usage in Irish sources of the terms 'White (or Fair) Foreigners' and 'Dark Foreigners' to refer to the Scandinavians. The significance of these terms has been much debated: according to some scholars, the terms indicate a contrast between Norwegians and Danes, but more recently it has been argued that the import is rather of 'old' and 'new', with the 'New (Dark) Foreigners' being the dynasty of Ivar and its supporters, in which case the distinction would be more chronological than ethnic.[108]

The rule in Northumbria of Halfdan, apparently Ivar's brother, was short-lived. Irish annals indicate that, like his brother, his next campaign was in Ireland, where he too was killed, at Strangford Lough in 877.[109] The *History of St Cuthbert* more colourfully claims that 'the wrath of God and of the holy confessor [Cuthbert] fell upon him' when he was in Northumbria, and that as a consequence 'he began to rave and to reek so badly that his whole army drove him from its midst, and he was chased far across the sea and was never seen again'.[110] The third brother, Ubba, seems to have been killed in Devon in 878.[111]

'Halfdan shared out the land of the Northumbrians, and they proceeded to plough and to support themselves'. The nature, extent, and consequences of the Scandinavian settlement, recorded so tersely by the *Anglo-Saxon Chronicle*, will form the subject of Chapter 4; in the present chapter, we are concerned rather with the political and military history of the Vikings in Northumbria. And so we should turn to the next known king of York, Guthred or Guthfrith (Old Norse *Guð(f)røðr*), an obscure figure to whom an extraordinary story is attached. This story is told in the *History of St Cuthbert*, following on immediately from the departure of Halfdan:

> At that time St Cuthbert appeared in the night to the holy abbot of Carlisle named Eadred, firmly commanding him as follows: 'Go', he said, 'over the Tyne to the army of the Danes, and tell them that if they wish to be obedient to me, they should show you a certain young man named Guthred son of Harthacnut, the slave of a certain widow. In the morning you and the whole army should offer the widow the price for him, and at the third hour [take him] in exchange for the price; then at the sixth hour lead him before the whole multitude so that they may elect him king, and at the ninth hour lead him with the whole army upon the hill which is called *Oswigesdune* and there place on his right arm a golden armlet, and thus they shall all constitute him king'.[112]

According to the *History*, Abbot Eadred did exactly as Cuthbert commanded him, and with success: the Viking army responded with obedience rather than violence, and Bishop Eardulf (officially of Lindisfarne, but by now on the move) then appeared, bringing with him the body of St Cuthbert, 'over which the king himself and the whole host swore peace and fidelity as long as they might live, and this oath they faithfully observed'.

This unlikely tale is, however, confirmed to a degree by Æthelweard's *Chronicle*, which records Guthred's death in 895:

> Guthred, king of the Northumbrians, died on the nativity of St Bartholomew, the apostle of Christ [24 August]. And his body is entombed in the city of York in the high church.[113]

Guthred is the first Viking ruler known to receive such Christian obsequies, and his burial in York Minster does seem to indicate a new phase of Christian kingship among the Scandinavians in Northumbria – though Æthelweard does also describe him, cryptically, as a 'hateful king [*rex foetidus*]'. His description of Guthred as 'king of the Northumbrians [*rex Northhymbriorum*]' should also be noted: as remarked in Chapter 1, Æthelweard appears often to use the term 'Northumbrians' in the sense of 'Scandinavian settlers in Northumbria', as opposed to the native English population, and Asser also seems to refer to 'the Northumbrians' in this sense, when he records an alliance that was formed in the 880s between (presumably) Guthred and the sons of Rhodri Mawr, king of Gwynedd.[114]

Of course, the story of Guthred, as told in the *History of St Cuthbert*, raises more questions than it answers.[115] To begin with, why should a slave be distinguished by a patronymic ('Guthred son of Harthacnut')? In the Viking Age, the Scandinavian use of patronymics was not primarily for purposes of identification, but rather 'as a means of boasting of the bearer's family connections'.[116] So the implication may be that Guthred was really a royal and divinely-anointed child concealed in domestic service – a sort of proto-Havelok (to invoke a more famous legend from medieval Lincolnshire) – and this implication is made explicit in a later version of his story, in the *Chronicles of the Church of Durham* (*Cronica Monasterii Dunelmensis*), a text which may date from the late eleventh century but is more likely to be later.[117] Guthred's name is one that is well attested in the ninth century among Scandinavian leaders in Ireland, so it is quite possible – whether or not one places any credence on the story in the *History of St Cuthbert* – that he was part of the dynasty of Ivar; this would certainly help to explain his acceptance at York.[118] On a larger scale, the story of Guthred raises the question as to whether the Scandinavians of Northumbria were already Christian at the time of his accession to the throne, or whether the story is acting as a kind of fable or allegory, precisely to represent their process of conversion. The question of conversion and Christianization will be explored more fully in Chapter 5, but certainly from this point onwards we cannot assume that the Viking kings of York, and their followers, were pagan – though as we shall see, some of them unquestionably continued to be so.

Of the events (and indeed the length) of Guthred's reign we know little, though the little that we do know does not really support the *History*'s claim that the Scandinavians of Northumbria 'faithfully observed' their oath of peace and fidelity for as long as they lived. The *Anglo-Saxon Chronicle* has a long and confusing entry for the year 893, which records a wide-ranging campaign around the south coast of England by the Scandinavian armies of Northumbria and East Anglia, in spite of the fact that previously 'the Northumbrians and East Angles had given King Alfred oaths'.[119] Æthelweard adds that, in a separate incident that year, one 'Sigeferth the pirate [*piraticus*] arrived from the land of the Northumbrians with a large fleet, ravaged twice along the coast on that one expedition, and afterwards sailed back to his own land'; the sequel, the following year, was an apparent peace embassy from Wessex to York led by the ealdorman Æthelnoth, and when this embassy is combined with Guthred's alliance with the sons of Rhodri Mawr, we can gain a sense of the York Viking kingdom putting down roots, and engaging in diplomatic relations and not simply military ones.[120] From entries such as these, the clear picture also emerges that, although previous decades had witnessed settlement by Scandinavians in areas they had conquered, such areas still maintained, or could rapidly raise, substantial armies, perhaps reinforced from overseas. The *Anglo-Saxon Chronicle*, well into the tenth century, continues to use the word *here* ('army') to refer to the Scandinavian communities now to be found in England, as if they are only semi-demobbed; the equivalent Latin usage can be found in the *History of St Cuthbert*'s story of Guthred, where Abbot Eadred is commanded to go to the 'army of the Danes [*exercitus Danorum*]'.[121]

The *History of St Cuthbert* preserves one more story about Guthred, narrated out of chronological sequence at the very end of the text (and thus likely to be of eleventh-century provenance); it is also strangely inconsistent on this very subject of the ability of Northumbria's Scandinavian kings to raise an army with ease.[122] The *History* tells that an army of Scots 'crossed the Tweed with an innumerable multitude and devastated the land of St Cuthbert and despoiled the monastery of Lindisfarne'. In response Guthred, oddly, could only raise 'a very small army' (perhaps the rest of his warriors were away plundering Wessex?). Assailed, like the great King Alfred, by 'many and various cares', Guthred is saved from despair by the appearance of St Cuthbert in his dreams. The saint re-assures him with the promise of a miracle the next day when Guthred confronts the Scottish host: 'at the first clash', he predicts, 'the earth will be opened up and will let them drop alive into Hell'. And so it happens: early the next morning the Scots are punctually 'swallowed alive by the gaping earth'. The coherence and chronology of this story are highly problematic, to say the least, and transparently indebted to a Biblical exemplar (Psalm 106:17); the *History* itself declares the story

46

to be 'a miracle of God and St Cuthbert greatly to be heeded and praised'.[123] Moreover, the very last paragraph of the work, immediately following, celebrates Guthred as the king who laid down the law that any land acquired by St Cuthbert (or rather, by his community) should be the saint's forever and immune from any other claims; 'and if anyone were to attempt in any way to infringe on this, he would be damned with eternal anathema'. Guthred, then, was remembered strongly, well over a century after his death, as a Christian king – indeed, as the ideal type of the Scandinavian convert king – and his commemoration as the guarantor of St Cuthbert's estates is a remarkable accolade.

In order to track the Viking kings of Northumbria in the decade after Guthred's death, we need to turn to the evidence of coins – a form of evidence which is now both very full and very revealing.[124] As we saw earlier, pre-Viking Northumbria had a thriving coinage based on brass *stycas*, which came to a sudden end at the time of the Scandinavian conquest. The minting of coins did not then return to York until some thirty years later; but thereafter, from about 895 right through to 954, the Scandinavian rulers of York oversaw the production and circulation of a substantial coinage in their names.

Thirty years is a long time in monetary terms, and the disjunction between the end of the *stycas* and the beginning of the Scandinavian coinage meant that the Viking kings of York had to start 'from scratch': there was probably no minting expertise to draw on in late ninth-century Northumbria, no surviving moneyers to turn to.[125] In spite of this, the Scandinavian coinage of York bursts upon the scene in the mid 890s with an independence, innovativeness, and sheer vigour that are startling. The first two Scandinavian kings of York for whom we possess coins – and in abundance – are, according to the coin inscriptions, rulers called SIEFREDVS or SIEVERT and CNVT [Figure 5a].[126] (A solitary coin in the name of Guthred has also been found, but this seems to have been struck in the southern Danelaw, which has its own, separate coinage history.[127]) The first name, SIEFREDVS/SIEVERT, equates to the Old Norse name *Sigfrøðr*, and the ruler concerned is presumably to be identified with the *Sigeferð piraticus* who raided southwards from Northumbria in 893; his coins are ascribed to the period c.895-900. Sigeferth seems to have come to Northumbria from Ireland, as the *Annals of Ulster* record that in 893 there was a 'great dissension' among the Scandinavians of Dublin and 'they became dispersed', with one party following an earl called Sigeferth.[128] However, a ruler with the second name, Cnut (Old Norse *Knútr*), whose coins are dated c.900-905, is entirely absent from the *Anglo-Saxon Chronicle*, Æthelweard's *Chronicle*, the *Annals of Ulster*, or any other contemporary work – a fact which offers a sobering reminder of the incompleteness of our textual sources for this period. But Alfred Smyth pointed out that a number of later Icelandic sagas preserve a story of an invasion of Northumbria by a Scandinavian leader called Knútr, who fought two battles, one north of Cleveland and one at Scarborough [NR]; and it may well be that this story represents a distant echo of the rule of the CNVT REX named on York coinage.[129] It is also perhaps worth recalling here that Guthred's father, according to the *History of St Cuthbert*, was called Harthacnut (Old Norse *Hörðaknútr*) – a name sometimes represented only by its second element, Cnut. Since, as we shall see in later chapters, Scandinavian naming patterns often alternated every two generations (so that grandsons were given their names of their grandfathers), it is possible – if the chronology works – that the Scandinavian ruler on these coins was Guthred's son (it is also conceivable, though surely not likely, that he was Guthred's father). That this suggestion has value is supported by the recent discovery (in a hoard found at Silverdale, Lancashire, in 2011) of a unique coin bearing the inscription AIRDE CONVT: this looks, just about, like an acceptable rendering of the name Harthacnut (though the cross-bar on the initial A is missing), and the coin has been given a provisional dating bracket of c.900-910.[130] Perhaps, then, the same ruler issued coins occasionally under the full name of Harthacnut, but more usually under the short form of Cnut.

Independence, innovativeness, and vigour: more should be said about these three qualities of the early York coinage. Its independence can be appreciated from a negative characteristic. Although the Scandinavian rulers of York seem not to have had any local expertise to draw on, they did not therefore turn to the moneyers of the Anglo-Saxon kingdoms of Wessex and Mercia for either their personnel or their practices.[131] It is true that the new coins were silver pennies, as in Southumbrian England, not brass *stycas*, but the weight standard of the new coins was not derived from contemporary Anglo-Saxon usage: rather, it corresponded both to the weight standard of the old Northumbrian *stycas* – suggesting that some coins were still available in York to act as a model in this regard at least – and also to the standard of the recently instituted coins of the southern Danelaw (suggesting, perhaps, co-operation between the new Viking polities in northern and eastern England). Nor did the early issues copy the Anglo-Saxon habit of naming the moneyer on the coins produced under his authority. And when the York coinage did, a little later, start to include the names of moneyers, these were very often continental names – suggesting that the Scandinavian authorities of early tenth-century York turned to Carolingian Frankia for technical support rather than to Anglo-Saxon England; indeed, even the shape of the extant York coin-dies resembles Carolingian ones rather than Anglo-Saxon.[132]

The innovativeness and vigour of the coinage complement its independence. The early coins of York boast many features of decoration that are hard to parallel elsewhere, and collectively demonstrate no fewer than forty different designs.[133] It goes without saying that, in order to produce such a confident and varied suite of designs, and to operate such a well-organized coinage, considerable bureaucratic machinery is required; and this is a point that will be discussed further in Chapter 6, when we consider the city of York itself in the Viking period. Many of these design features are conspicuously Christian in their iconography, and are seemingly inspired by Northumbrian Christian art, rather than by other coins produced elsewhere – apparently confirming that, as the *History of St Cuthbert* suggests, the early Scandinavian rulers of York had converted to Christianity from Guthred onwards. So, for example, the early York coins are decorated with crosses of various shapes and formats; they are inscribed with Latin quotations from the liturgy; and most remarkably of all, one design sets out the four letters of the name 'CNVT' in cruciform shape, so that reading clockwise does not work, and one is required instead to make the sign of the cross with one's eyes – a devotional arrangement that is, in Mark Blackburn's words, 'quite unprecedented on any European coinage' [Figure 5a].[134]

As we shall see increasingly in this narrative, the first half of the tenth century was an extremely unstable time in Northumbria. One reflection of this instability is the number of hoards which have been recovered dating from this period. At the time of writing, nearly twenty hoards have been discovered in northern England that date from the first three decades of the tenth century.[135] The largest is the Cuerdale hoard (c.905-10), and the second largest the Vale of York hoard (though it is, in fact, a distant second: Cuerdale contained over 7,500 coins compared to the Vale of York's 617). These hoards vary in their composition: some are made up only of coins, and some of other forms of silver (such as arm-rings, ingots, and hack-silver), but the majority are mixed, comprising both coins and bullion. A number of the most important hoards were discovered in the nineteenth century (such as the Cuerdale hoard, found in 1840), and their contents have neither been fully preserved nor fully recorded; but several have recently been uncovered through the contemporary activity of metal-detectorists (such as the Vale of York hoard, found in 2007), and these have been much more exhaustively catalogued.

It is precisely because of the immensity of the Cuerdale hoard that we possess the varied coins of Sigeferth and Cnut in such great abundance – even though, textually speaking, they are among the most obscure of the Scandinavian rulers of York. Cuerdale is on the River Ribble, near Preston in Lancashire, and the valleys of the Ribble and Aire are thought to have constituted the main route between Dublin and York.[136] The Scandinavians of Dublin suffered a great defeat in 902, as the *Annals of Ulster* record: 'The heathens were driven from Ireland, i.e. from the fortress of Áth Cliath [...] and they abandoned a good number of their ships, and escaped half dead after they had been wounded and broken'.[137] One consequence of this expulsion seems to have been the shadowy conquest of the Wirral area by a Scandinavian leader named Ingimund.[138] Another is likely to have been the putting together of the treasure deposited at Cuerdale. In addition to its 7,500 coins (over 3,000 of which were from York), the Cuerdale hoard contained

30 kg of silver bullion, in the form of jewellery, ingots, and hack-silver, and the styles and affinities of much of this metalwork reveal that the bullion hoard was assembled in, or exported from, Ireland. But the presence in the hoard of vast numbers of York coins indicates that this bullion from the west was combined with coinage from the east to create an unparalleled store of wealth. One obvious interpretation is that this was, in some way, 'an army pay-chest', compiled for the purposes of campaign in either Ireland or England.[139]

To return to our chronology of kings: in 900 a further ruler had appeared in Northumbria, but this one was not Scandinavian. The *Anglo-Saxon Chronicle* (here quoted from the C-text) gives us the essential account:

> In this year Alfred the son of Æthelwulf died [...] Then the atheling Æthelwold, his father's brother's son, rode and seized the residence at Wimborne and at *Twinham*, against the will of the king [Alfred's son, Edward 'the Elder'] and his councillors. Then the king rode with the army till he encamped at Badbury near Wimborne, and Æthelwold stayed inside the residence with the men who had given allegiance to him; and he had barricaded all the gates against him, and said that he would either live there or die there. Then meanwhile the atheling rode away by night, and went to the Danish army [*here*] in Northumbria, and they accepted him as king [*underfengon hym to cinge*] and gave allegiance to him.[140]

Æthelwold was the son of Æthelred I of Wessex, Alfred's older brother and immediate predecessor as king. This indicates the problem: Alfred and his supporters seem to have wanted to introduce a principle of father-to-son inheritance, whereas previously succession to the throne had not followed such a clear line, and kings were succeeded not just by their sons but by other male relatives who were accorded the throne-worthy title of *æðeling*.[141] The point is made very clearly through the A version of the *Chronicle*, the most 'Alfredian' manuscript: the sentence that records Æthelwold's acclamation as king in Northumbria is conspicuously absent from A's account, as if the very idea of Æthelwold being king at all, anywhere, must not be recognized. And the family of Alfred did triumph in this respect: all the tenth-century kings of Wessex and England traced descent from him. The numismatic evidence, though, confirms what the A-text wishes to deny: a small number of York coins exist which were minted in the name of a ruler ALVVALDVS, a recognizable rendering of the name Æthelwold.[142]

Two years later Æthelwold, backed by the Northumbrian *here*, attacked the south of England. The *Chronicle* records that he 'came hither across the sea [*hider ofer sæ*]' – a surprising phrase to use if Æthelwold was simply sailing down the east coast of England, unless he had made an unrecorded visit to Scandinavia (or conceivably Ireland or Frankia) to gather more troops.[143] Æthelwold persuaded the

Scandinavian *here* in East Anglia to join his campaign, and together they harried across Mercia and into Wessex itself. In return Edward the Elder took his army into Scandinavian territory in the southern Danelaw, and the climactic battle was fought between Æthelwold's forces and Edward's Kentish contingent. Of this battle, Æthelweard's *Chronicle* declares poetically that 'they clashed spears, brandished swords, and in either hand the spear was much shaken'.[144] The site of the battle is given in the Mercian B-text of the *Anglo-Saxon Chronicle* as *æt þam Holme*, and the most plausible identification of this place is Holme in Huntingdonshire.[145] The *Anglo-Saxon Chronicle* also preserves a roll-call of the distinguished Kentish dead, and additionally names several of their opponents:

> On the Danish side King Eohric was killed, and the atheling Æthelwold, whom they had chosen as their king, and Brihtsige, son of the atheling Beornoth, and Ysopa the *hold* and Oscetel the *hold* and also very many with them, whom we cannot name now. And a great slaughter was made on both sides, but more of the Danes were killed, though they remained in possession of the battle-field.[146]

Eohric (perhaps Old Norse *Jórekr*) was probably the Scandinavian king of East Anglia, and *hold* (Old Norse *höldr*) is a Scandinavian term of high rank. As for Brihtsige, son of Beornoth, his identity is unknown, though Dorothy Whitelock's view was that 'the names suggest that these were descendants of ninth-century kings of Mercia'.[147] As the tenth century progressed, the Battle of Holme continued to be remembered as an important event, especially in Kent; over fifty years later, for example, a charter granting land to Christ Church, Canterbury, looked back to the time when 'all the men of Kent were summoned to the battle at the *Holme*' – as well it might, for the donor's father was one of the men of Kent killed there.[148] Although the *Anglo-Saxon Chronicle* judges the Danes to have 'remained in possession of the battle-field', they had lost both their leaders, and Edward seems to have emerged in the stronger position: the consequence was a peace treaty, agreed at Tiddingford in Bedfordshire, between Edward and both 'the East Angles and the Northumbrians'.[149]

This concord did not endure, however, and the *Chronicle* for 910 disapprovingly states that 'the army in Northumbria broke the peace, and scorned every privilege that King Edward and his councillors offered them, and ravaged over Mercia'. This may not have been without provocation, for in the previous year, according to the *Chronicle*, Edward sent an army into 'the territory of the northern army [*norðhere*]' which ravaged and raided for five weeks and 'killed many men of those Danes'.[150] The hostilities of 910 resulted in an even greater battle than that of Holme, fought at Wednesfield, near Tettenhall in Staffordshire.[151] The northern annals preserved in the *History of the Kings* do not state the outcome of the battle, but the southern *Anglo-Saxon Chronicle* claims a decisive victory for the West Saxons:

[Edward] sent his army both from the West Saxons and the Mercians, and they overtook the Danish army when it was on its way home and fought against it and put the army to flight and killed many thousands of its men. And there were killed King Eowils and King Halfdan and Earl Ohter and Earl Skurfa, and Othulf the *hold*, and Benesing the *hold*, and Olaf the Black and Thurferth the *hold*, and Osfrith Hlytta, and Guthfrith the *hold*, and Agmund the *hold* and Guthfrith.[152]

Æthelweard's *Chronicle* adds a third king killed at the battle, named Ivar.[153] These Old Norse names, some garbled in the recording, are the closest we can get to identifying individual members of the Scandinavian ruling elite in early tenth-century Northumbria.[154] Most of them are now irretrievably obscure, though the presence of a nickname or two (such as Olaf 'the Black') suggests that they may have been more than just names to those recording their demise. But we can at least discern something of the hierarchy among the Scandinavian aristocracy in England: kings, earls, and *hold*s. Furthermore, it is possible that the recurrence of the names of previous rulers (Ivar, Halfdan, Guthfrith or Guthred) might indicate some family connection with those earlier kings. Were the defeated Ivar, Halfdan, and Eowils all kings of Northumbria, or were two of them based elsewhere, and if so where? Did the death of all three kings at the Battle of Tettenhall mark a point of crisis for the Vikings of York?

Our poor knowledge of York kings in this period is not aided by the city's coinage, to which we should now return to conclude this chapter. The Christian iconography of Sigeferth and Cnut was continued in the next series of issues, the so-called St Peter coinage [Figure 5b].[155] But these coins do not have the name of the king on them, and state instead SCI PETRI MO ('St Peter's mint' or 'money'). The dedication of York Minster is to St Peter, so the Christian message of these coins seems both local and ecclesiastical or institutional; their model, very clearly, is the series of St Edmund coins produced in the southern Danelaw from the late ninth century onwards – coins which do somewhat different work in expressing the Christian affiliations of the new Scandinavian rulers there, as St Edmund, king of East Anglia, had been martyred by Ivar's Great Army in 869 in the very process of conquest.[156] It may be reasonable, as with the coins of Sigeferth and Cnut, to see clerical input in the design of the St Peter coinage, though how extensive this was can be disputed, as we shall see in the next chapter; one feature of some of the coins is the presence of a pagan Thor's hammer. We do not know which ruler instituted the St Peter coins: it might have been one of the kings killed at the Battle of Tettenhall, or it might have been an unnamed and unrecorded predecessor, ruling after Cnut. Remarkably, though, the St Peter coins were the only coinage-type minted at York between c.905 and 927 – with one spectacular interruption, as we will soon see in the next chapter, as we follow the story of York's Viking kings forward into their last decades.

THE LATER KINGS OF YORK

FROM RÆGNALD TO ERIC BLOODAXE

The Descendants of Ivar

The first ten years of Edward the Elder's reign set the pattern for the next four and a half decades of conflict. Scandinavian kings come and go in Northumbria, wars are waged and battles fought, boundaries are pushed forwards and back. But the years after the Battle of Tettenhall seem to mark the beginning of a new phase in the conflict between Northumbria and Wessex, a phase that can be read in terms of two dynasties squaring up to one another to determine who would control the kingdom of Northumbria. On the Scandinavian side stand the descendants of Ivar 'the Boneless': Irish annals in the early tenth century label a number of Scandinavian leaders as *ua Ímair* 'grandson of Ivar', as if Ivar's dynasty was achieving a greater sense of identity and common purpose at this time. On the English side, opposed, stand the descendants of Alfred 'the Great'. The Anglo-Saxon kings were trying to push their borders northwards and drive out the Scandinavian rulers of York; the Scandinavians were trying to hold on to, or re-conquer, the north, and ideally to extend their borders southwards into the old kingdom of Mercia. Edward the Elder, in the years after Tettenhall, had been consolidating his position through a systematic programme of building *burh*s – fortified towns – along the frontiers of his kingdom, gradually pushing eastwards and northwards: for example, Buckingham in 914, Bedford in 915, Huntingdon in 917, Stamford in 918.[1] The events of these years are traditionally known as the West Saxon re-conquest of the Danelaw, but it is now recognized that the prefix 're-' in 're-conquest' is inappropriate: the southern kings of Wessex were in fact conquering fresh territory for themselves, adding new lands to their domains and in the process creating, for the first time, something like the shape of England that has endured.[2]

Thus it is that Dublin seems to become more important in this period, or at least the political connections between the Scandinavian kingdoms centred on Dublin and York become more prominent, and better able to be construed. Dublin was regained by the Scandinavians in 917, after which the dynasty of Ivar seems to have had a sustained and even programmatic intention to control the two cities together; and the re-established Viking kings of Dublin seem also to have established an alliance with the kings of Alba, in central Scotland.[3] Of course, Scandinavian York and Dublin had been connected to one another ever since the days of Ivar himself, and also through the years following – as indicated, for example, by the dazzling Cuerdale hoard. But they should not be regarded as identical 'twin Viking cities': their development and culture, from religion to architecture, were in some regards very different.[4]

A decisive attempt to re-establish strong Scandinavian rule in Northumbria came hard on the heels of the re-acquisition of Dublin, through the actions of the domineering leader known in modern historiography as, variously, Rægnald or Ragnall (Old Norse *Rögnvaldr*), acclaimed as one of the 'grandsons of Ivar'. The history of York and Northumbria in Rægnald's time is extremely obscure, at least in terms of constructing a consistent narrative, but there are indications enough that it was an extremely important moment, as it ushered in what scholars have tended to call the 'Hiberno-Norse' phase of Northumbria, in contradistinction to an earlier (and later) 'Anglo-Danish' phase – though the rigidity of such categories can be queried.[5]

Our best approach to Rægnald is through a review of what our main sources have to say about him. He makes two appearances in the *Anglo-Saxon Chronicle*, on both occasions in entries wrongly dated to 923. Versions D and E record that 'In this year King Rægnald won York [*gewan Eoforwic*]', while the 'Alfredian' version A (in an entry partly quoted already in Chapter 1) includes him among a group of northern rulers who submitted to Edward the Elder's authority:

> Then [Edward] went from [Nottingham] into the Peak district to Bakewell, and ordered a borough to be built in the neighbourhood and manned. And then the king of the Scots and all the people of the Scots, and Rægnald, and the sons of Eadwulf and all who live in Northumbria, both English and Danish, Norsemen and others [*ægþer ge Englisce ge Denisce ge Norþmen ge oþre*], and also the king of the Strathclyde Welsh and all the Strathclyde Welsh, chose him as father and lord.[6]

The significance, and indeed truthfulness, of this second entry has been debated, but more immediately we should note that both of these events are misdated by the *Chronicle*, by three or four years.[7] Under 919 the *History of the Kings*, more correctly, records that Rægnald 'took York by storm [*irrupit Eboracum*]', while the

Annals of Ulster note Rægnald's death in 921.[8] So Rægnald 'won York' in 919, and submitted to Edward in 920.

The identity of Eadwulf, whose sons are grouped with Rægnald and 'all who live in Northumbria', is important here. The *Annals of Ulster* record the death of Eadwulf himself in 913 and describe him as 'king of the Saxons of the North', while Æthelweard's *Chronicle* denies him royal status but explains that 'he ruled as reeve of the town called Bamburgh'.[9] He thus seems to have been head of the ruling family in possession of what one might think of as 'English' Northumbria, the old Bernicia, north of the Tees. This is confirmed by what our sources have to say about Rægnald's main battle – or battles – at Corbridge.

The *Annals of Ulster* for 918 record that Rægnald fought a battle against the Scots 'on the bank of the Tyne in northern Saxonland'.[10] The *History of St Cuthbert* – the crucial source – includes not one but two short narratives in which Rægnald wins a battle at Corbridge. The first goes as follows:

> King Rægnald came with a great multitude of ships and occupied the territory of Ealdred son of Eadwulf, who was a favourite of King Edward, just as his father Eadwulf had been a favourite of King Alfred. Ealdred, having been driven off, went therefore to Scotland, sought aid from King Constantine, and brought him into battle against King Rægnald at Corbridge.[11]

Because this first narrative dates the battle to the lifetime of Bishop Cuthheard of Chester-le-Street (who died in 915), scholars traditionally believed that Rægnald did indeed fight two battles at Corbridge, in probably 914 and 918.[12] But more recent recognition of the *History*'s peculiar narrative technique, in which chronology is often confused and the same events are frequently narrated more than once, at different points in the text, has led to the simplifying suggestion that the reference to Bishop Cuthheard is a mistake, and there was, in fact, only one battle of Corbridge – in 918, a date that agrees well with the statements of the *Anglo-Saxon Chronicle* and the *History of the Kings* that Rægnald conquered York in 919.[13]

More certain than the chronology of Rægnald's career in Northumbria is his impact. At the time of his arrival in York, roughly forty years had passed since Halfdan had 'shared out the land of the Northumbrians'. The Scandinavian kings of York had converted to Christianity and instituted a fairly stable and successful coinage. But the Norse of Dublin, the new 'Hiberno-Norse' entering Northumbria, had not converted at such an early date, and nor had they adopted the practice of issuing coins.[14] There was thus something of a pagan and primitive tang about them – certainly in the eyes of English observers, and perhaps also among the settled Scandinavians of Northumbria.[15] The *History of St Cuthbert* characterizes Rægnald as 'pagan [*paganus*]' and 'accursed [*maledictus*]', and contains hair-raising stories about the heathen depredations perpetrated by his followers (and the grim, deserved ends they came to); his time was thus remembered as a period of pagan resurgence in Northumbria, and ecclesiastical trouble.[16] Rægnald seems also to have attained a position of lasting fame in Scandinavian legend: he is probably the original for the Rögnvaldr who came to be counted as one of the sons of the legendary Viking Ragnarr *loðbrók*.[17]

York coins bearing the name of a king RAIENALT or RACNOLDT are currently ascribed to the period c.919-21 – a dating, it should be noted, which is established from hoard evidence, and not simply based on the textual sources.[18] It is Rægnald who interrupts the long run of St Peter coinage, and in ostentatious ways. In addition to the re-instatement of the king's name on York coins, the iconography of Rægnald's coins includes the pagan emblem of a Thor's hammer, the martial embellishment of a bow and arrow [Figure 5c], and a portrait of the king himself, with prominent forked beard – the only contemporary representation of a Scandinavian king that we possess from Viking Age York.

Current scholarly understanding, then, based on both textual and numismatic evidence, would ascribe Rægnald a relatively brief reign in York, from probably 919 to 921, whereas earlier commentators, guided by the belief that there were two battles at Corbridge, and working prior to the revised understanding of the coin chronology, were inclined to give him a considerably longer reign, beginning in 914 or perhaps even 910. This earlier position is now hard to justify, but it did at least solve, or prevent, one major problem. For if Rægnald did not take over York until 919, we are left with the mystery of who was ruling York between the Battle of Tettenhall in 910 and Rægnald's conquest. The *Anglo-Saxon Chronicle* states that Rægnald 'won York'; so whom did he win it from?

The coinage, of course, does not help us, as the St Peter coins are anonymous, though the persistence of the design from c.905 might be taken to indicate some degree of continuity. The most obvious explanation is that York was in the hands of one or more Scandinavian kings whose names have not been passed down to us; after all, were it not for their deaths in the Battle of Tettenhall, we would not know of the existence of the kings Halfdan, Eowils, and Ivar, and it has been suggested that, before Rægnald, the political system in York was as much oligarchy as monarchy.[19] The St Peter coinage would thus be more civic than royal, issued by 'the leaders of the Viking community at York', whose low-key rule was 'terminated by the arrival of a powerful individual ruler who imposed his own name'.[20] This is the most likely explanation, but other possibilities can be entertained, and should be reviewed. One is that the Bernician ruling family of Eadwulf and his sons was exerting influence again over the old Deira.[21] The Battle of Corbridge could certainly be construed within such a scenario, as a campaign-winning engagement on Rægnald's part that sent the sons of Eadwulf back to their Bernician heartlands.

Another possibility is that, at least for some portion of the 910s or even earlier, the Anglo-Saxon rulers of Mercia, Ealdorman Æthelred and his wife Æthelflæd (daughter of Alfred), were in a position to exert political influence on some or all of Northumbria. In introducing the Battle of Tettenhall, Æthelweard's *Chronicle* states that 'the barbarians' (that is, the Vikings) broke the peace with Edward and with Æthelred, 'who then ruled the Northumbrian and Mercian areas'.[22] This is highly cryptic, to say the least.[23] Æthelred died in 911, but his authority in Mercia was taken over by his widow Æthelflæd, until her death in 918, and under that year the Mercian Register (copied into versions B and C of the *Anglo-Saxon Chronicle*) includes an equally tantalizing statement:

> The people of York [*Eforwicingas*] had promised her – and some had given pledges, some had confirmed it with oaths – that they would be under her direction [*on hyre rædenne beon*]. But very soon after they had agreed to this, she died twelve days before midsummer in Tamworth.[24]

All of this came to nothing, and on the death of his sister Æthelflæd, Edward the Elder promptly annexed Mercia: the Mercian Register records poignantly that her daughter Ælfwynn 'was deprived of all authority in Mercia and taken into Wessex'.[25] But why were the citizens of York acting in this way? Was this a fond memory of Æthelred's earlier authority, a desire to escape from the influence of the sons of Eadwulf, or of Edward the Elder, or a plea for Mercian protection in the face of imminent (pagan) conquest by Rægnald? At the end of the 910s the leaders of York may have found themselves in a three-way squeeze, caught between Bernician ambitions from the north, English ambitions from the south, and the approach of Rægnald from the west. In the event, as we have seen, Rægnald intervened decisively to restore Scandinavian rule and repel Anglo-Saxon threats.

A further proposal as to who ruled York, not just in the 910s but for much of the first half of the tenth century, has been argued forcefully by David Rollason.[26] Rollason points out, reasonably enough, that our textual sources do not give us much indication of how much time Scandinavian rulers actually spent in York – though of course textual sources do not give us much indication of anything in the first half of the tenth century. His proposal, therefore, is that in Viking Age York 'it was the archbishops who wielded the real power, using the military capabilities of the Viking kings when it suited them to do so'.[27] The archbishops of York, in this view, should really be regarded as 'prince-archbishops', supplying stability and continuity in the York kingdom, and controlling power and policy, with the here-today-gone-tomorrow Scandinavian kings as merely 'titular heads'.[28] Rollason's proposal would certainly be consonant with the complex Christian iconography found on the coins of Sigeferth and Cnut at the start of the tenth century, and would seem to make good sense for the long series of St Peter coins; it should also be noted that some archbishops of York had indeed issued coinage in the eighth and earlier ninth centuries. Moreover, as we shall see, at least one archbishop of York, Wulfstan I, is recorded as having firmly thrown in his lot with the Scandinavian kings of the city.

Some accommodation and co-operation between the archbishops and kings in Viking Age York, at least at certain times, seems indisputable, and both parties stood to gain from the relationship; but this does not mean it was an equal partnership, let alone that the archbishops held the upper hand, and there are a number of reasons for doubting Rollason's hypothesis in its stronger form. To begin with, one might observe that the evidence for early tenth-century archbishops of York spending time in the city is in fact much weaker than that for Scandinavian rulers, and it has even been suggested that what distinguishes the rule of the Viking kings from that of the earlier Anglian kings of Northumbria is that the Viking kings established a tradition of permanently residing in York.[29] Although the (arch)bishopric of York did not disappear under Viking onslaught, unlike some other northern sees, the evidence for its archbishops becomes highly exiguous. We know, for example, that one Æthelbald was consecrated archbishop in 900 (in London, interestingly, not York), and a later source indicates that he was still archbishop in 904, but the extent of his tenure is very obscure: the next reference we have to an archbishop of York does not come till 928, when one Hrothweard occupied the role; so we do not even know who the archbishop was in the decades when the St Peter coinage was being issued.[30] Indeed, strictly speaking, we don't even know if there was an archbishop of York during the years of the St Peter issue, and at the time when Athelstan conquered the city in 927: the twelfth-century *Chronicle of the Archbishops of York* (*Chronicon pontificum ecclesiae Eboracensis*) preserved no memory of any archbishops between Æthelbald and Hrothweard, and the re-instatement of an archbishop might have been a consequence of the West Saxon conquest.[31] It is only from 928 onwards that the archbishop of York appears regularly in the witness-lists of West Saxon charters, indicating his presence at royal councils.[32] Had the archbishops been such important actors in the north, we might reasonably have expected more to be recorded about them also in the Northumbrian/York annals preserved in the *History of the Kings* and in Roger of Wendover, especially for the period 900-930.

Equally tellingly, the archbishopric of York in the tenth century was financially poor, in comparison with other Anglo-Saxon sees; but considerable wealth would presumably be required to act as a power-broker or king-maker in the manner of a grand 'prince-archbishop'. The archbishops did not have access to the vast quantities of bullion required to introduce a silver coinage into Northumbria: the previous Northumbrian coinage had been brass *stycas*, and — notwithstanding the treasures that had been given to the Northumbrian church in the eighth century — the ninth-century kingdom of Northumbria has been described as 'bankrupt'.[33] The new wealth that was injected into late ninth- and early tenth-century York, out of which the new silver coins were manufactured, came from Viking loot, much of which was brought into England as Scandinavian plunder from Frankia (as well as stripped from English churches); it has even been suggested that the very re-introduction of coinage was undertaken 'perhaps for the purpose of distributing shares of loot'.[34] And, finally, if the Viking kings of York were weak, and really puppets of the archbishop, how were they able to take so much land away from the church and the Anglo-Saxon elite and give it to their followers (as we will see in later chapters that they did)? So both the absence of the archbishops from the documentary record in the early tenth century, and their lack of wealth, argue against Rollason's proposal in its stronger form.

Numismatically, too, there are good reasons for seeing the York coinage as secular rather than ecclesiastical. The Scandinavian coins of York express an ideology of royal power: the early coins accentuate the king's name and send out important public messages, while the resistance to influence from Anglo-Saxon practices seems very deliberate and meaningful. Control of the coinage in many ways equated to control of the economy, and it also generated income. To quote Mark Blackburn: 'Coinage was a major source of revenue for early medieval kings and, while there are many examples of rulers granting local minting rights to a church by way of endowment, it would be without precedent in Europe for control of all minting to be granted away by a state'.[35] Furthermore, and very importantly, there is one aspect in which the coins of Scandinavian York were distinctly sub-standard, and this was in terms of (Latin) literacy: texts are garbled, names misspelt, and letters poorly cut, and the nadir occurs, ironically, on the St Peter coins themselves, which have been described as 'grossly illiterate' (with EBORACE 'York' appearing bizarrely as BRACE, RACBE, ORACECB, and numerous other variants).[36] It would seem unlikely that the body of coinage most plausibly to be attributed to the church should be the one with the worst levels of literacy. We should also recall the presence of a Thor's hammer on some of the St Peter coins, an improbable feature of a supposed archiepiscopal coinage.

The one archbishop of York whose behaviour best fits Rollason's proposal, Wulfstan I, was appointed to the see in the reign of Athelstan, and so it is to that English king, and his Scandinavian opponents, that we should now turn.

Athelstan and his Brothers

Edward the Elder, Alfred's son and chosen heir, outlived his cousin and rival Æthelwold by over twenty years, and died in 924. The succession to Edward seems to have been disputed also, though not on the Æthelwoldian scale. Edward's eldest son, Athelstan, 'was chosen by the Mercians as king', but Ælfweard, a younger half-brother and perhaps Edward's favoured heir, was chosen by the West

Saxons. However, Ælfweard died very soon after his father, and so Athelstan succeeded to the combined kingdom of the Anglo-Saxons; he was consecrated as king in September 925.[37]

The identity of Rægnald's predecessor or predecessors as ruler(s) of York may be obscure, but that of his successor, ruling when Athelstan came to the throne, is certain; and he may well have been prepared for the position by Rægnald himself. Sihtric (Old Norse *Sigtryggr*), often known in historiography by his Irish nickname *caech* or *caoch* (probably 'one-eyed'), was another 'grandson of Ivar' who, like Rægnald and indeed his own successor Guthfrith, had been active in Ireland before proceeding to the York kingship.[38] The *Annals of Ulster* record that he entered Dublin in 917, and in 919 won a great victory against Niall Glundubh.[39] This landmark battle to the south of Dublin, which has been acclaimed as achieving 'the zenith of Norse power in the island', may be celebrated in a contemporary Old Norse praise-poem in honour of Sihtric, the anonymous *Darraðarljóð* (*Song of the Pennant*).[40] Although in the thirteenth-century prose source in which it is preserved (*Njal's Saga*) the poem is associated with the Battle of Clontarf in 1014, its contents fit better with what we know of the 919 battle, and the poem presents its hero as a vigorous 'young king [*ungr konungr*]', for whom 'many songs of victory' should be sung.[41] In 920 – that is, prior to Rægnald's death in 921 – the *Annals of Ulster* record that Sihtric left Dublin, and the following year Guthfrith (Old Norse *Guð(f)røðr*), yet another 'grandson of Ivar', entered the city (sometimes known in modern historiography as Gothfrith, to distinguish him from the earlier Guthfrith or Guthred, the late ninth-century convert king of Northumbria).[42] The implication seems to be that Sihtric left Dublin to join, and then succeed, Rægnald in York, while Guthfrith took Sihtric's place in Dublin.

We have at least one Viking hoard datable to Sihtric's reign at York, and of an intriguing composition. The so-called Goldsborough hoard was found in 1858 east of Knaresborough [WR] – in other words, right on the classic overland route between Dublin and York. The treasure in the hoard seems to be freshly arrived from Dublin, or at the very least put together in Ireland, as it contains (in whole or part) a number of silver Irish brooches, nearly 40 Arabic coins known as dirhems, and no York coins whatsoever. It has thus been diagnosed by James Graham-Campbell as representing 'warrior wealth', rather than the wealth of the mercantile city of York.[43] From its contents, the hoard has conventionally been dated internally to c.920, and has thus been linked to Sihtric's progress to York to claim the kingship; but recently it has been suggested that this dating is too early, and that c.925 may be more appropriate.[44]

In the reign of Sihtric, the York coinage reverts to the St Peter design, but with the addition of an aggressive-looking sword, as shown on the cover of this book. Sihtric also issued coins in his own name, but in the Five Boroughs rather than York, indicating that he wielded significant authority south of the Humber as well.[45] He makes his first appearance in the *Anglo-Saxon Chronicle* in 926 (version D), in an interesting development:

> In this year King Athelstan and Sihtric, king of the Northumbrians [*Norðhymbra cyng*], met together at Tamworth on 30 January and Athelstan gave him his sister in marriage.[46]

Athelstan had eight or nine full or half-sisters, and for a number of them he negotiated diplomatic marriages with important foreign rulers.[47] The sister who married Sihtric may have been called Eadgyth, but the marriage did not last long, as Sihtric died the following year. The *Annals of Ulster* state that his death occurred 'at an immature age' – an apparent confirmation of *Darraðarljóð*'s emphasis on the king's heroic youth in 919.[48] According to Roger of Wendover, writing in the thirteenth century, Sihtric's marriage had already failed before his death. The Scandinavian king, Roger claimed, 'gave up the heathen religion for the love of the maiden and received the faith of Christ. But not long afterwards he cast off the blessed maiden and, deserting his Christianity, restored the worship of idols, and after a short while ended his life miserably as an apostate'.[49] Eadgyth became a nun, to be remembered in later hagiography as St Edith of Polesworth (in Warwickshire).[50] The purposes of Sihtric and Athelstan in arranging the marriage in the first place are not hard to ascertain. For both of them a diplomatic *entente* between Northumbria and the expanding English state was desirable: Sihtric gained a powerful ally in case he was squeezed from the north, by the Scots or a resurgent Bernicia, while Athelstan was trying to stabilize his northern border, and consolidate his hold on Mercia and the Five Boroughs.

With terse under-statement, version D of the *Anglo-Saxon Chronicle* records for 927 that 'Sihtric died, and King Athelstan succeeded to the kingdom of the Northumbrians'. But according to version E of the *Chronicle*, there was another incident in 927 as well: 'King Athelstan drove out Guthfrith'.[51] Guthfrith is a shadowy figure in English sources, though less so in Irish ones, as we have already seen; the *Annals of Ulster*, for example, record him fighting alongside Rægnald at the Battle of Corbridge in 918.[52] He seems to have issued no coins, unless he was the last York king to oversee the anonymous St Peter coinage; and it is not clear whether his brief reign – if indeed he can be said to have reigned at all – took place immediately after Sihtric's death (in an act of succession) or after Athelstan's annexation of Northumbria (in an act of rebellion). The former might seem more logical, but William of Malmesbury, in the twelfth century, has a lively story about Guthfrith slipping away from Athelstan's grasp to lay siege to York until eventually, 'pursued by many misfortunes by land and sea', Guthfrith accepted the inevitable and submitted to the king.[53] Whichever it was, Guthfrith's

Northumbrian adventure did not last long: the *Annals of Ulster* record that he left Dublin and came back again 'within six months'.[54]

No battle is recorded by which Athelstan 'succeeded to the kingdom of the Northumbrians', and it may be that a mere show of military strength was enough.[55] Presumably Athelstan and his army marched north to York, though no text explicitly states this. William of Malmesbury does, however, record that Athelstan 'levelled with the ground the fortress [*castrum*] which the Danes had built long ago in York, in order to leave disloyalty no place of refuge; the booty found in the fortress – and very plentiful it was – he generously distributed to individuals'.[56] The location of this 'fortress' is unclear – unless by *castrum* William means the walls of York, which (as we will see in Chapter 6) the Scandinavian conquerors had rebuilt after 866.[57]

But that there was indeed Viking booty in and around York in 927 is confirmed by hoard evidence, which reveals very eloquently that Athelstan's 927 conquest represented a time of crisis for the Scandinavian elite. Two extremely important hoards appear to have been buried at precisely this time, and two further parcels of coins have also recently come to light. The first important hoard was found near Flaxton [NR], ten miles north-east of York, in 1807 (though it is also known as the Bossall hoard, after the ecclesiastical parish in which it was found).[58] The Bossall/Flaxton hoard contained a number of arm-rings and silver ingots, and about 270 coins, most of them York issues dating from the reigns of Rægnald and (especially) Sihtric. A date of deposition in c.927 seems very secure, and it was clearly wealth from York that was being buried. The find spot of the Bossall/Flaxton hoard was on the old Roman road from York to Malton [NR]: was it the property of a wealthy Scandinavian fleeing York?

The second hoard was found only in 2007. This is the so-called Vale of York hoard, discovered near Harrogate [WR] [Figure 6].[59] This was an even wealthier hoard than Bossall/Flaxton, containing over 600 coins, five silver arm-rings, assorted ingots and hack-silver, and (most impressively) a gold arm-ring – the only gold arm-ring to be found in any of the Viking Age hoards of Northumbria. The Vale of York hoard is also remarkable in having been found in its original receptacle: a sumptuous silver cup, manufactured in Carolingian Frankia in the early to mid ninth century, and probably of ecclesiastical provenance. The obvious explanation is that the cup was Viking loot from raids on Frankia some fifty or more years earlier, and other similar vessels have been recovered from Viking Age England; one wonders by what routes and human stories it had made its way to Yorkshire.[60]

The coin collection of the Vale of York hoard is made up of three components. There is a large quantity of Anglo-Saxon coins from the reigns of Alfred and Edward, seemingly a pre-existing treasure-collection. Then there is a sizeable group of coins from Scandinavian York, in the form of Sihtric's sworded

St Peter issue. Finally, there are over 100 Athelstan coins, including some minted in York. Most importantly, the Vale of York hoard contains a single Athelstan coin bearing the legend REX TOTIUS BRITANNIAE ('King of all Britain'). This type of coin seems to have been introduced in late 927 or early 928, and that there is only a solitary example in the Vale of York hoard may suggest that the hoard was buried very soon after the type was first issued; it thus gives us our best dating indication for the hoard's burial.[61]

The make-up of the Vale of York hoard is thus very intriguing. The unique presence of a gold arm-ring, allied with the exceptional Carolingian vessel, suggests that it was the property of a person or persons of very considerable wealth. The Athelstan coins indicate that the hoard was not deposited quite as early as Bossall/Flaxton, but certainly within the time-span of c.927-29. Taking the assemblage as a whole, we can construct a plausible (though not, of course, definitive) profile for its owner: some member of the Scandinavian aristocracy – unknown, but evidently very wealthy and thus very important – who had been previously settled in York or its vicinity during the years of Viking rule, but who was finding the new regime unpalatable, for whatever reason, and decided to get out.

In 2012, two further parcels of coins were found that complement these two major hoards (the two collections were discovered within a few weeks, and a few feet, of each other, so it is not clear if we are dealing with one hoard or two; they are currently known by the bland designation of the 'Near York' hoard).[62] The coins were found close to the find-spot of the Bossall/Flaxton hoard, near the Roman road from York to Malton. The first parcel comprised 34 Anglo-Saxon coins, 31 of them coins of Athelstan, including more of the 'King of all Britain' type. The second parcel, of the same size, contained more of such Athelstan coins, but also Viking coins of the earlier 920s, as well as four fragments of silver ingots. A deposition date in the late 920s or early 930s would seem most likely – further confirmation of the uncertainty and instability around York in the wake of Athelstan's take-over.

After recording Sihtric's death and Athelstan's annexation of Northumbria, the *Anglo-Saxon Chronicle* for 927 (version D) continues as follows:

> [Athelstan] brought under his rule all the kings who were in this island: first Hywel, king of the West Welsh, and Constantine, king of the Scots, and Owain, king of the people of Gwent, and Ealdred, son of Eadwulf from Bamburgh. And they established peace with pledge and oaths in the place which is called Eamont [in Cumbria], on 12 July, and renounced all idolatry and afterwards departed in peace.[63]

William of Malmesbury locates this meeting at nearby Dacre rather than Eamont, and identifies the Owain concerned as king of Strathclyde rather than Gwent.[64] We possess a Latin poem in honour of Athelstan, known as *Carta dirige gressus* after its opening words ('Letter, direct your steps'), which seems to date from very soon after the Eamont submission: this proclaims that England (*Saxonia*) is now 'made whole [*perfecta*]' and that 'King Athelstan lives / glorious through his deeds [*per facta gloriosus*]!'[65] There is one oddity about the poem, though, in the fourth stanza (as reconstructed by Michael Lapidge):

> He, with Sihtric having died [*Sictric defuncto*],
> in such circumstances arms for battle
> the army of the English
> throughout all Britain.[66]

If England is now made whole and the surrounding kings have just submitted to him, why should Athelstan arm for battle? One explanation, pertinent in the present context, could be that the poem dates from after the meeting at Eamont, but prior to Athelstan's chasing away of Guthfrith. The *Carta*'s note of *imperium*, of lordship over the whole of the country, is struck in other media too in the wake of the Eamont submission: as we have seen, Athelstan issued a coinage that styled him 'King of all Britain', and the same formulation is found in Athelstan's charters from this period.[67]

Athelstan's conquest of 927, then, is a very significant moment, not just in Northumbrian history but in English history more generally: the shape of Athelstan's realm has earned him the accolade of 'First King of England' – that is, of England as we now know it. The 927 conquest marks the point at which the Viking kingdom of York was suppressed for the first time, and (at least with retrospect) it signals the beginning of the end for Scandinavian rulers in Northumbria.

Athelstan's dominion over Northumbria, his incorporation of Northumbria into the English realm, lasted for twelve years, and various aspects of his rule in the north can be recaptured. For one thing, he made a 'clean sweep' of the preceding York coinage, attempting to replace the previous Scandinavian issues with a new series of designs, all produced according to the weight standard used in southern England.[68] Athelstan also introduced the Anglo-Saxon practice of naming moneyers on coins, as well as kings and mints.[69] All Athelstan's new coins at York were produced by a single moneyer named Regnald; his name is usually taken to be Frankish, but it is possible that it is Norse.

Athelstan himself seems to have been in York on two, maybe three occasions. One was in 927, when he secured his hold on Northumbria. Another may have been in 936 when, according to the historian Richer of Rheims, Athelstan received a Frankish embassy there.[70] And another is likely to have been in 934, in which year, as the *Anglo-Saxon Chronicle* records, 'King Athelstan went into Scotland with both a land force and a naval force, and ravaged much of it'.[71] The churches of Ripon [WR] and Beverley [ER] both remembered Athelstan as a benefactor, and his 934 campaign northwards is the most likely occasion for him to have visited these places, although no pre-Conquest source actually records such a visit.[72] He certainly made a pilgrimage to Chester-le-Street, as the community of St Cuthbert recalled: 'while King Æthelstan was leading a great army from the south to the northern region [of Britain], taking it to Scotland, he made a diversion to the church of St Cuthbert and gave royal gifts to him'.[73] These gifts included manuscripts, metalwork, and textiles, some of which survive; there can be no question that Athelstan had a particular devotion to the cult of St Cuthbert.[74]

We do not know that Athelstan visited York on his 934 campaign, but it would seem likely. On his way north, at Nottingham, he issued a charter that granted to the church of York a vast tract of territory; the details are recorded in the ornate Latin of Athelstan's draughtsman:

> I, Athelstan, king of the English, elevated by the right hand of the Almighty, which is Christ, to the throne of the whole kingdom of Britain, assign willingly in fear of God to Almighty God and the blessed Apostle Peter, at his church in the city of York [...] a certain portion of land of no small size, in the place which the inhabitants call Amounderness; that the bishop may [hold] it without the yoke of hateful servitude, with meadows, pastures, woods, streams, and all conveniences duly belonging to it, for as long as he may use the breathable air with his nostrils and the visible world with the glance of his eyes, and may leave it to sacred heirs after him, ever to his church in eternal inheritance. This aforesaid donation I have bought with no little money of my own.[75]

The charter is witnessed by no fewer than 58 members of the king's council, including a number of earls or ealdormen with Scandinavian names – local figures of authority, one assumes, in the southern Danelaw and perhaps the northern as well. The archbishop of York who received the grant was Wulfstan I, who a decade later was to be a sharp thorn in the side of Athelstan's successors.

In terms of motivation, Athelstan has usually been regarded as wishing to bestow favour on the church of York, in order to guarantee its loyalty (though if the archbishops had really been propping up the Viking kings for the last three or four decades, one might perhaps have expected a more punitive attitude on the part of the king). The territory of Amounderness itself, between the rivers Cocker and Ribble in what is now Lancashire, was a crucial region for the English church and state to control, since it faced Dublin across the Irish Sea and may have been an area both of strategic importance and Scandinavian influence – the Cuerdale hoard, for example, was found along one of its boundaries.[76]

The information that Athelstan bought Amounderness, rather than conquered it, 'with no little money of [his] own', is especially interesting; a later version of the charter adds that he bought it 'from the pagans [*a paganis*]'.[77] A couple of other charters reveal that, in the southern Danelaw, Athelstan promoted a deliberate policy of purchasing land from Scandinavian owners.[78] The place-name Amounderness means 'the headland of Ögmundr or Agmundr', a Scandinavian name, and an obvious comparison would be with the Yorkshire place-name Holderness [ER], usually construed as 'the headland of the *höldr*' (though this etymology is not without problems).[79] Intriguingly, an Agmund *hold* was killed in the Battle of Tettenhall in 910.[80] Might this combination of circumstances suggest, first, that units of land the size of Amounderness and Holderness were the sorts of territories held by Scandinavian nobles of the rank of *hold*, and, second, that the Agmundr after whom Amounderness was named had been killed twenty years prior to Athelstan's grant, at the Battle of Tettenhall? If so, then it must be assumed that Athelstan purchased the territory from Agmundr's heirs or descendants.

What were Athelstan's Scandinavian opponents doing all this time? Following his rapid expulsion from England in 927, Guthfrith had resumed the leadership of the Scandinavians of Dublin, and through the 930s the Dublin Vikings were engaged in a protracted conflict with those of Limerick.[81] Guthfrith died in 934, to be succeeded by his son Olaf (Old Norse *Óláfr*), and in 937 Olaf defeated his Limerick rival in battle. He was then free to turn his attention to York, the first of the great-grandsons of Ivar to do so.

A major alliance, surely some time in the making, was put together, comprising of Olaf Guthfrithson of Dublin, Constantine of Alba, and Owain of Strathclyde – all kings and kingdoms threatened or subdued by the northward expansion of Athelstan's England. The forces of these kings met those of Athelstan in late 937 at a place that the *Anglo-Saxon Chronicle* calls *Brunanburh*. The battle was a very bloody affair: half a century later, Æthelweard described it as a 'huge battle [*pugna immanis*]' and reported that 'it is still called the 'great battle' [*bellum magnum*] by the common people'.[82] Athelstan was victorious, though his main opponents all escaped with their lives, including, significantly, Olaf, who returned to Dublin – to bide his time.

Nobody knows for sure where *Brunanburh* was. The leading candidate is Bromborough in Cheshire, but other proposals have included Bromswold (Northamptonshire/Huntingdonshire), Brinsworth (Yorkshire [WR]), Bourne (Lincolnshire), Burnswark (Dumfriesshire), and somewhere near the River Went (Yorkshire again [WR]).[83] The identification with Bromborough is made on the basis of place-name evidence, as the agreement in form between the *Anglo-Saxon Chronicle*'s *Brunanburh* and the medieval forms of Bromborough is perfect.[84] There is also some plausibility in its proximity to the Irish Sea, for Olaf's journey from (and return to) Dublin (did Olaf's forces, one wonders, pass through the archbishop of York's Amounderness?). However, no account of the battle claims that it took place in the north-west, and John of Worcester specifies that Olaf's ships entered the Humber, which would suggest rather a location in the east of England, perhaps near the Northumbria/Mercia border.[85] Even the place-name evidence is inconclusive in certain regards: in some sources the site of the battle has a different name, including *Brunandun* (Æthelweard), *We(o)ndun* (Symeon of Durham and the *History of the Kings*), and *Vínheiðr* (*Egil's Saga*), so *Brunanburh* is not the only form that requires explanation. Bromborough's candidature is strong, but it is not an open-and-shut case.

The most important evidence concerning the Battle of Brunanburh is poetic. We possess poems in celebration of Athelstan's victory in no fewer than three languages: Old English, Latin, and Old Norse. The Old English poem is the most important: without warning, the sparse *Anglo-Saxon Chronicle* suddenly switches from prose to verse in 937, and includes as its sole account of the battle a 73-line poem – the first of a number of poems in the tenth- and eleventh-century *Chronicle*.[86] There is no way of knowing whether the poem was composed specially for the *Chronicle*, or whether it had an independent existence prior to its inclusion.[87] The poem gives an unexpected prominence to Athelstan's brother and heir, Edmund, and for that reason it has been suggested that the poem may be a composition from Edmund's reign rather than Athelstan's (since the *Chronicle* was not written year-by-year at the time of the events recorded); this is possible, but the prominence of Edmund could equally well be explained by the desire of Athelstan's regime to set up Edmund as his undisputed heir.[88]

'In this year King Athelstan, lord of nobles, dispenser of treasure to men, and his brother also, Edmund atheling, won by the sword's edge undying glory in battle around *Brunanburh*'.[89] The poem is a panegyric, not a battlefield despatch. It says little or nothing about tactics, but rather accentuates the virtuous prowess of Athelstan and Edmund, and the slaughter and humiliation forced on Constantine and Olaf. The two English brothers, the poem says, 'defend[ed] their land, their treasure, and their homes [*land ealgodon, / hord and hamas*]', before they 'returned together to their own country, the land of the West Saxons [*Wessexena land*], exulting in the battle'. For their opponents, on the other hand, there is death and shame: 'there lay many a man destroyed by the spears, many a northern warrior shot over his shield', so that the hostile kings 'had no need to gloat with the remnants of their armies'. Constantine 'left his young son on the field of slaughter', while Olaf has to retreat back to where he came from, consummately expelled: 'Then the Norsemen [*Norðmenn*], the sorry survivors from the spears, put out in their studded ships [...] to make for Dublin across the deep water, back to Ireland humbled at heart'. The poet concludes with an historical sweep, asserting that, never since the Angles and Saxons first came to Britain, 'was a greater slaughter of a host made by the edge of the sword'. But although the poem is triumphalist in its attitude towards Athelstan's defeated enemies, we should note that it is not expansionist or simplistically nationalistic: on the contrary, the poet steers a careful path in his depiction of West Saxons and Mercians acting together in an essentially defensive endeavour.[90]

William of Malmesbury, in his twelfth-century *History of the English Kings*, claims to draw on 'an ancient volume [*uolumine uetusto*]' for his important account of Athelstan's life, and for the Battle of Brunanburh William quotes a lengthy passage of poetry from this supposed source.[91] The antiquity and value of this poem has been debated: Michael Lapidge argued that it is in fact a twelfth-century composition, and not a genuine tenth-century source, but not all commentators have been persuaded, and it is possible that what William is quoting is an older poem (or prosimetrum, alternating verse and prose) which he has re-fashioned in various ways.[92] The verse passage that William includes in his *History* begins with the return of the Scandinavians, 'Europe's poisonous pest', after twelve years of just rule by Athelstan. Olaf appears, 'breathing grim, unlawful threats':

> To this raging fury, with the consent of the king of the Scots, the northern land [*borealis terra*] lends its support with no misgivings; and now they are swollen with pride, they frighten with their words the very air; the natives, the whole region yields to their presumption.

William's poem evokes the destruction that the invading forces inflict on Athelstan's land ('they ruined everything by continual raids, and laid waste the sad fields by spreading fire'), until the king finally arrives to cow and conquer his enemies. But the last lines of William's quotation are ominous for the future: 'Olaf escaped, alone out of what were lately so many thousands, a deposit left by death, the noble gift of Fortune, destined to shape events after Athelstan's time'.

As a third poetic voice on the battle, we might also consider the sole surviving portion of the Old Norse *Aðalsteinsdrápa* (*Poem in Praise of Athelstan*), an encomium by the Icelandic skald Egill Skalla-Grímsson (whom we shall meet again shortly, and whose brother, according to *Egil's Saga* and its verses, died fighting on Athelstan's side in the great battle). The genuineness of this poem has also been doubted, but no convictions of anachronism have been brought against it, and it can in fact be read as an acute and illuminating post-Brunanburh composition.[93] Its extant lines are as follows:

> Now the noble-born son of kings who towers over lands, makes battles stern, has brought down three princes [*þrjá jöfra*]. The land falls under the descendant of Ælle [*nið Ellu*]. Athelstan did more. All bend low before that kin-famous king. This we swear to, breaker of the fire of the wave [=prince].
> Now the highest reindeer road lies under bold Athelstan.[94]

The 'three princes' who have been vanquished are, of course, Olaf, Constantine, and Owain, and the two-line refrain recognizes the extension of Athelstan's authority into Britain's highland zone ('the highest reindeer road'). Most interesting is Egill's description of Athelstan as 'the descendant of Ælle'. Ælle, we should recall, was the Northumbrian king defeated in 866 when the Great Army captured York, and then killed the following year: in a stroke of fictive kinship, Egill's kenning pointedly casts Athelstan as the rightful inheritor of York.

The Battle of Brunanburh, then, received poetic celebration in a number of languages, and in the course of the Middle Ages it featured in many histories and chronicles, both prose and verse.[95] But in spite of such commemoration, one could argue that the battle itself was of much less importance than Athelstan's initial conquest of the north ten years earlier; in the short and medium term at least it had little lasting impact ('in essence', Clare Downham writes, 'the battle prevented Dublin-vikings from re-conquering Northumbria for only two years').[96] Possibly the battle had more long-term importance ideologically, in the idea of an enlarged England victorious over its assailants.[97]

In any case, Olaf Guthfrithson only had to wait for Athelstan's death, and then try again. The 'King of all Britain' died in 939, and was succeeded by two of his brothers in turn, Edmund (939-46) and Eadred (946-55). What happened next is most clearly told in the *History of the Kings*:

> King Olaf first came to York, and then, marching south, besieged Northampton. But accomplishing nothing there, he turned his army to Tamworth and ravaged everything round about it. When he reached Leicester on his return, King Edmund met him with an army. There was no severe fighting, for the two archbishops, Oda and Wulfstan, reconciled the kings to one another and put an end to the battle. When peace had thus been made, the Watling Street was the boundary of each kingdom. Edmund held the part to the south, Olaf the kingdom to the north [*ad aquilonalem regnum*].[98]

This was indeed, as Alfred Smyth put it, 'a moment of triumph' for the dynasty of Ivar, in which Olaf 'pushed the Scandinavian conquest to its greatest extent since the reign of Alfred'.[99] Watling Street was the line of the old boundary between West Saxon and Scandinavian rule established in the treaty between Alfred and Guthrum in the 880s; had forty years of effort by Alfred's descendants come to nothing?[100] The role of the two archbishops, of Canterbury and York, in effecting the agreement between Olaf and Edmund is of course eye-catching. It is not clear from the *History's* account whether Wulfstan was acting impartially, or as some sort of peace envoy from Olaf's side; the *Anglo-Saxon Chronicle's* version (in the D-text) is less ambiguous, though we should note that this account was probably added to the *Chronicle* some decades after the events described:

In this year Olaf took Tamworth by storm, and the losses were heavy on both sides, and the Danes were victorious and took away much booty with them. Wulfrun [an aristocratic woman] was taken captive in that raid. In this year King Edmund besieged King Olaf and Archbishop Wulfstan in Leicester, and he could have subdued them if they had not escaped by night from the borough. And after that Olaf secured King Edmund's friendship.[101]

The conduct of Archbishop Wulfstan has naturally excited much comment.[102] Was he a collaborator or a power-broker? Did he compromise his Christianity by allying himself with pagan or semi-pagan forces? What exactly did he think he was doing? The most plausible interpretation is to view him as a pragmatist, concerned to safeguard the possessions and independence of his church, and perhaps seeing co-operation with Olaf as the best means of doing this. Our extant sources adopt varying stances towards him: the *History of the Kings*, drawing on a northern set of annals, applauds him as a peace-maker, whereas the *Anglo-Saxon Chronicle*, written some time after the event and with a West Saxon perspective, regards him in much less favourable terms.

Whereas Sihtric *caech* had sought a marriage alliance with the West Saxon royal family (in Tamworth, the very town 'taken by storm' in 940), Olaf Guthfrithson allied himself instead, it seems, with the Anglo-Scandinavian aristocracy of the southern Danelaw – presumably to cement his support in that area. Roger of Wendover records that Olaf 'married Aldgyth, daughter of Earl Orm, with the support of whose aid and counsel he had obtained the aforesaid victory' (that is, his conquest of the midlands).[103] Orm is a Scandinavian name, but Aldgyth is an English one, and this implies that Aldgyth's mother was English. This is the only reference to Earl Orm in our sources, but the implication is that he was one of the ruling elite in the southern Danelaw, an influential figure whose assistance was invaluable to Olaf.[104]

Triumph is also the keynote of Olaf Guthfrithson's coinage, which is the most assertive of all the York issues.[105] Olaf issued a number of coin types, but the first is the most arresting: it shows an Odinic raven, with its wings spread wide, and the inscription reads ANLAF CVNVNC [Figure 5d]. The second word here is Old Norse *konungr* 'king', and its significance is considerable. The custom on coinage from Anglo-Saxon and Viking Age England was to use the Latin language for inscriptions, with an occasional use of Old English (as, for example, on some of Athelstan's coins, which use the Old English form EFORWIC for the name of the city). The use of the Old Norse language for such a medium is not only unparalleled but highly innovative, for (with the exception of a few runic inscriptions) the Old Norse language in England seems never to have been used for written purposes, and certainly not in the Roman alphabet; its existence was almost exclusively oral.[106] Olaf's raven coinage thus articulates an intensely 'Scandinavian' identity, both in terms of language and iconography – and even in weight too, for Olaf's coins revert to the pre-927 standard. What is more, the sheer quantity minted has led to the suggestion that Olaf was trying 'to oust English pennies from circulation':[107] this was a serious attempt to efface the Athelstan years, made by a forceful and successful ruler who seems to have understood well the political potential for coins to act as a mass medium; the raven pennies have been acclaimed as a form of 'victory-coinage'.[108]

Olaf's reign, though, in which he rolled back the frontiers of England, was short-lived. The *History of the Kings* again gives us the most coherent account:

> Olaf, when he had ravaged the church of St Bealdhere and burnt Tyninghame, soon perished. Therefore the men of York [*Eboracenses*] laid waste the island of Lindisfarne and killed many people. Then a son of Sihtric, Olaf by name, ruled over the Northumbrians.[109]

Tyninghame was an important Bernician church-site in East Lothian; the implication seems to be that the attack on Lindisfarne was in revenge for Olaf's death on campaign there.[110] Olaf was succeeded by his namesake, the son of Sihtric *caech*, better known by his obscure Irish nickname of Olaf *cuaran* ('sandal', or possibly 'hunchback').[111] It is confusing that the early to mid 940s are essentially a tale of two Olafs, and the confusion is made worse by the evident muddle that some of our sources get into in trying (and failing) to distinguish one from the other. As a result of this, a number of interpretations are possible, and some historians have suggested that the great conqueror of the central Danelaw was in fact this second Olaf, Olaf *cuaran*, and not Olaf Guthfrithson.[112] This is not, however, the canonical view, and nor does it agree well with the numismatic evidence.[113]

According to Frank Stenton's character sketch, Olaf *cuaran* was 'younger and milder than Olaf Guthfrithson and never equalled him as a Viking leader'.[114] Just as Athelstan had held together a kingdom which did not easily survive his death, so it was with Olaf Guthfrithson. Olaf's conquests were soon recovered by the kings of England, and for the Scandinavian kings of York and Dublin the rest of the 940s were something of an anticlimax. As the son of Sihtric *caech*, the young Olaf *cuaran* seems to have been in England when Northumbria fell into Athelstan's hands in 927, at which point he 'fled to Ireland'.[115] He succeeded Olaf Guthfrithson in 941, but did not hold on to his territories south of the Humber for long. Our most eloquent source is the second of the *Anglo-Saxon Chronicle*'s poems, under the year 942:

> In this year King Edmund, lord of the English, protector of men, the beloved performer of mighty deeds, overran Mercia, as bounded by Dore [WR], Whitwell

gate, and the broad stream, the River Humber; and five boroughs, Leicester and Lincoln, Nottingham and likewise Stamford, and also Derby. The Danes [*Dene*] were previously subjected by force under the Norsemen [*Norðmannum*], for a long time in bonds of captivity to the heathens [*on hæþenra hæfteclommum*], until the defender of warriors, the son of Edward, King Edmund, redeemed them, to his glory.[116]

This poem was given a defining explication by Allen Mawer in 1923.[117] Its significance turns on the difference between *Dene* and *Norðmenn*. The former, Mawer argued, are the (by now) long-term Anglo-Danish inhabitants of the Danelaw, whereas the latter are the York-Dublin forces of the two Olafs, both great-grandsons of Ivar. The *Dene* are settled and Christian, the *Norðmenn* aggressive and pagan – or at least, able to be presented as such – and the poem is thus a complementary artwork to place alongside Olaf Guthfrithson's raven pennies. The phrase 'for a long time [*lange þrage*]' is, however, puzzling, and needs to be taken either as poetic exaggeration, or conceivably as an allusion to baleful Hiberno-Norse influence going back as far as the time of Rægnald.

Edmund, then, very quickly gained the upper hand over Olaf *cuaran*. As a result, the *Anglo-Saxon Chronicle* tells us, 'King Edmund stood sponsor to King Olaf at baptism, and the same year, after a fairly big interval, he stood sponsor to King Rægnald at his confirmation'.[118] The enforced conversion of Viking kings had a long pedigree, going back in England to Alfred's terms over Guthrum in 878. The Rægnald referred to was a brother of Olaf Guthfrithson, and seems to have assumed joint rule in York with Olaf *cuaran*; in 944, they were both expelled at the same time: 'In this year King Edmund reduced all Northumbria under his rule, and drove out two kings, Olaf, Sihtric's son, and Rægnald, Guthfrith's son' (suggesting a thorough-going conquest).[119] Æthelweard adds that this expulsion was effected by 'Bishop Wulfstan and the ealdorman of the Mercians [*dux Myrciorum*]', but who this person was is completely opaque.[120] Moreover, there may even have been three kings current in York at around this time, for coins were minted in the name of a king called Sihtric – yet another figure whose identity is uncertain.[121]

Edmund died in 946, and was succeeded by his brother Eadred: 'In this year [947] King Eadred came to Tanshelf [WR], and there Archbishop Wulfstan and all the councillors of the Northumbrians [*ealle Norðhymbra witan*] pledged themselves to the king'.[122] It may have been at this point that Eadred, in an (unsuccessful) attempt to keep the loyalty of the archbishop, 'devoutly gave to the metropolitan church of York two large bells'.[123] However, 'within a short space they were false to it all, both pledge and oaths as well'.[124] Olaf *cuaran* seems to have come back to York for a second period of rule, from 949 (or 950) to 952, but when he was driven out on a second occasion (this time, according to the *Chronicle*, by the Northumbrians themselves), he decided to call it a day with his English ambitions, and directed himself instead to his rule in Dublin. And there he enjoyed a very long reign, as a founder of a dynasty and a patron of poets (in both Irish and Norse).[125] His end was pious: in 980, after the Battle of Tara, he gave up his throne and retired to Iona, where he died.

Olaf *cuaran* was thus the last of the Dublin kings to rule also in York. But between Olaf's first reign in York and his second, another figure had appeared in Northumbria, to whom we must now turn: Eric Bloodaxe.

The Last King: Eric Bloodaxe

So finally we come to the last Viking king of York, Eric Bloodaxe – though of course contemporaries at the time would not have realized that he was to be the last. He is also, ironically, the most famous in the present day, and this would certainly have surprised his contemporaries, so unexceptional were his achievements compared to some of his predecessors at York, such as Rægnald, or Sihtric *caech*, or Olaf Guthfrithson. Eric's fame is aided, no doubt, by his memorable nickname (Old Norse *Eiríkr blóðöx*), which may well be of contemporary or near-contemporary origin: it is first attested in a *lausavísa* ('loose verse') by the Norwegian poet Eyvindr Finnsson in the 960s.[126]

The sources for Eric Bloodaxe are both better and worse than for most of the Viking kings of York: worse, in that the dates of his reign – or rather reigns – are hard to establish for certain, and even his very identity has been disputed; but also better, in that we possess two (probably) contemporary poems in his honour, which enable us to recapture something of the atmosphere and ideas of his court: Egill Skalla-Grímsson's *Höfuðlausn* (*Head-Ransom*), and the anonymous (and posthumous) *Eiríksmál* (*Lay of Eric*).

Let us deal with the question of dates first. The *Anglo-Saxon Chronicle* entries relating to Eric (and Olaf *cuaran*'s second reign) are as follows:

> 948 (D): In this year King Eadred ravaged all Northumbria, because they had accepted [*genumen*] Eric as their king; and in that ravaging the glorious minster at Ripon [WR], which St Wilfrid had built, was burnt down. And when the king was on his way home, the army [which] was in York [*se here innan Heoforwic*] overtook the king's army at Castleford [WR], and they made a great slaughter there. Then the king became so angry that he wished to march back into the land and destroy it utterly. When the councillors of the Northumbrians [*Norðhymbra witan*] understood that, they deserted Eric and paid to King Eadred compensation for their act.
> 949 (E): In this year Olaf *cuaran* [*Anlaf Cwiran*] came into Northumbria.
> 952 (E): In this year the Northumbrians [*Norðhymbre*] drove out King Olaf, and received Eric, Harald's son.

954 (D and E): In this year the Northumbrians [*Norðhymbre*] drove out Eric, and Eadred succeeded to the kingdom of the Northumbrians.[127]

The *Chronicle*, then, states that Eric enjoyed two reigns in Northumbria, a first that ended in 948 and a second that ran from 952 to 954. In fact, it is impossible either to prove, or to improve, these dates definitively, though it has been pointed out that they are problematic in various ways. On the basis of Archbishop Wulfstan's attestation of Eadred's charters, and supposed confusion in the entries of the *Anglo-Saxon Chronicle*, Peter Sawyer has argued that Eric reigned only once in Northumbria, from 950 to 952.[128] There is some force in Sawyer's observations, but against them is version D of the *Chronicle*, which indicates two separate occasions on which Eric lost power in Northumbria.

There is also the complication of the *Life of St Cathroe*.[129] Cathroe was a royal cleric from Strathclyde who became abbot of the Frankish monastery of Metz. His *Life* was written in the late tenth century, and includes an account of a journey through northern Britain in which he is taken to a King Eric in York (*ad regem Erichium*), whose wife, supposedly, was a relative of the saint.[130] The problem is that, if the *Life* is reliable, internal references suggest that Cathroe's visit to York must have taken place sometime between 939 and 946 – too early, in other words, to agree satisfactorily with the *Anglo-Saxon Chronicle*'s chronology. Norse sagas do, however, claim that Eric assumed his rule in Northumbria as a sub-king of Athelstan, and a number of scholars have tentatively accepted this information, viewing the appointment perhaps as part of Athelstan's arrangements for the north after the Battle of Brunanburh.[131]

Coin evidence, unfortunately, is not able to help with the question of dating, at least in absolute terms, but coins bearing the inscription ERIC REX do seem to fall into two distinct groups, apparently supporting the view that Eric had (at least) two separate reigns in York.[132] The first issue is Anglo-Saxon in style, continuing a design used on the coins of Eadred and earlier West Saxon rulers, whereas the second is more Scandinavian in iconography: it re-instates the prominent sword found first on Sihtric *caech*'s coinage, and thus seems to hark back to an independent kingdom of York in aggressive fashion. Do these two issues indicate differing ideologies and approaches to foreign policy during the two periods of Eric's kingship?

Let us now turn to the question of identity. According to Norse sources, Eric Bloodaxe was the son of Harald Fairhair, the first over-king of a unified Norway. He succeeded his father, but soon acquired a reputation for tyranny and violence, killing a number of his brothers to secure his hold on the throne (the late twelfth-century Norwegian historian Theodoricus gives his nickname not as 'Bloodaxe' but as 'killer of brothers [*fratrum interfector*]').[133] He was therefore driven out of Norway by his younger brother Hákon. He took refuge first in

Orkney before becoming ruler in Northumbria – during which time, according to the sagas, he continued to raid widely in the British Isles.[134]

The crux is that English sources do not specify that the Eric who ruled at York came originally from Norway, or that he bore the soubriquet 'Bloodaxe'. Twentieth-century scholarship was happy to accept that Eric of York, as known from coins and the *Anglo-Saxon Chronicle*, was one and the same person as Eric Bloodaxe, exiled king of Norway, as known from Old Norse sagas, but this identification has recently been disputed by Clare Downham, and she has proposed instead that he may have been an otherwise unrecorded member of the York-Dublin dynasty of Ivar.[135] In the light of Downham's proposal, it is worth rehearsing the grounds for the traditional identification.

To begin with, the one item of genealogical information given in a contemporary English source is that, according to version E of the *Anglo-Saxon Chronicle*, Eric of York was the son of someone called Harald (*Yric Haroldes sunu*).[136] This agrees, of course, with what we know of Eric Bloodaxe, who was the son of Harald Fairhair. But no Eric son of Harald is known from Irish sources – indeed, no Scandinavian leader called Eric is known at all. This is significant: what we tend to see among the dynasty of Ivar is the repeated use of a limited set of names, and although there are a few Scandinavians called Harald attested in Irish sources, none would seem to fit chronologically as the father of Eric. (Downham's suggestion is that Eric may have been a son of the Harald who was a son of Sihtric *caech*; but this Harald died in 940, and Sihtric himself died in 927 'at an immature age', which would hardly allow enough time for an Eric son of Harald to grow up and rule York in the late 940s – or even earlier if one trusts the *Life of St Cathroe*, or Norse sagas.[137])

Norse sagas and historical writings agree that when Eric Bloodaxe was forced out of Norway he went to England, and a number of them contain substantial accounts of his reign in York – above all, *Egil's Saga*, much of which is structured around the conflict between Eric's family and Egill's family. But, as Downham rightly points out, none of these saga sources are earlier than the late twelfth century, and so to get at more contemporary evidence from the Norse side we have to turn to the evidence of two long poems preserved with *Egil's Saga*, Egill's *Höfuðlausn* and *Arinbjarnarkviða* (*Poem for Arinbjörn*). In the present context, the less studied *Arinbjarnarkviða* is the more important of the two. The poem is an elegy for Egill's friend Arinbjörn, but the early stanzas look back to Egill's adventure in York:

> Under the helmet of terror, the all-powerful lord of the people sat in the land. The king ruled in York [*í Jórvík*] with harsh thought for his sea-washed shores.
>   It was not safe, nor without terror, to look at the light of Eirik's eye, when serpent keen the eye of the all-powerful shone with terrifying light.

76

Yet I dared to bring my poem before the lord of the forest territory, so that the poem came frothing to every man's ear-mouth.[138]

One person at the court, Egill declares, stood by him, and that was Arinbjörn:

> There stood by me on the other side, better than many lords, my true friend, he whom I could trust, whose honour increases in every action.
> Arinbjörn who alone, first of men, brought me from the king's enmity, friend of the prince who in no way betrayed me in the court of the warlike prince.

Later, though, *Arinbjarnarkviða* presents a picture of Egill's friend at his home in Norway, generously giving away gifts:

> He is fierce to wealth, he who lives in Fjordane [*í Fjörðum*], he is bitter enemy to gold rings, he is the foe of rings, dangerous to rings, a treasure-killer.

The poem thus indicates that the King Eric who reigned at York, under a rule of terror, was accompanied at his court by at least one Norwegian magnate, and that this magnate later returned to his estates in Norway (in the time when Eric Bloodaxe's sons ruled the country) – strong contextual evidence for a Norwegian origin for Eric of York. *Arinbjarnarkviða* also characterizes the king as *Ynglings burr*: this probably means 'the son of a/the Ynglingr', alluding to Harald Fairhair's dynasty, the *Ynglingar* of Vestfold, though it may be that *Ynglingr* is just a *heiti*, or poetic synonym, for 'king'. As for *Höfuðlausn* itself, the poem that Egill recited before the king in York, this does not supply circumstantial evidence to the same extent, but it does rather pointedly imagine the wider audience for the poem as residing in Norway (and not in Ireland): Egill declares that 'Eric's deeds are known east over the sea'.[139]

The final strand of evidence to link Eric of York to Eric Bloodaxe is more indirect, but is still worth attending to. Various details indicate a connection between the dynasty of Harald Fairhair and mid tenth-century England, the most important of which pertain to Eric's brother Hákon. In addition to being known as Hákon *inn góði* 'the good', Hákon was also known by the nickname *Aðalsteinsfóstri* 'Athelstan's foster-son', and the name is first recorded in a verse from the 1030s by Sigvatr Þórðarson.[140] Old Norse kings' sagas preserve stories of Hákon's fosterage at Athelstan's court.[141] William of Malmesbury does not mention Hákon, but does record a diplomatic mission from Harald to Athelstan that may have supplied the context for Hákon's arrival:

> A certain Harald, king of the Norwegians, sent [Athelstan] a ship with gilded beak and a scarlet sail, the inside of which was hung round with a close-set row of gilded shields. The names of the envoys were Helgrim and Osfrith, and after a royal

reception in the city of York they wiped off the sweat of their journey with suitable rewards.[142]

Both the chronology and geography of this story are plausible, and the exchange makes diplomatic sense.[143] As a result of Hákon's English connection, various influences (including clerical) have been traced from mid tenth-century England to mid tenth-century Norway, and Norse sagas claim that Athelstan gave Hákon assistance in his move for the Norwegian throne.[144] Finally, a strange error in the *Anglo-Saxon Chronicle* for 1066 further indicates that the family of Harald Fairhair was known in England: in its account of the Battle of Stamford Bridge (to be discussed later, in Chapter 8) version D mistakenly gives the Norwegian king Harald the nickname *Harfagera* (Old Norse *hárfagri*) rather than, properly, *Hardrada* (Old Norse *harðráði* 'hard-rule') – a confusion that can only have arisen if the earlier Harald's nickname was already known.[145] We can therefore conclude that England would have been a very reasonable destination for an exiled son of Harald Fairhair to go to: the twist is that, unlike his younger brother Hákon, Eric did not seek sanctuary at the West Saxon court but rather re-appeared as king in Northumbria (unless, of course, one entertains the idea that Eric served as a sub-king for Athelstan).

The processes by which Eric gained the Northumbrian throne – if we leave aside the Athelstan hypothesis – are now irrecoverable. By the late 940s, were the *Norðhymbra witan*, and the *Eoforwicingas* and *Norðhymbre* more generally, fed up with Dublin kings, but not wishing to remain under southern English lordship? Is it possible that Eric was perceived as some sort of compromise candidate, and became king through invitation rather than conquest? Perhaps, as Eric John put it, Eric was 'exiled, available, charismatic and apparently just the man for York'.[146] Certainly it is striking that in these last years of Scandinavian rule we gain a clear sense of a local council making decisions as to who should or should not rule York; we seem no longer to be in the world of Rægnald or even Olaf Guthfrithson, in which the city is conquered by a war-leader, seemingly regardless of what its inhabitants might wish. The power lies no longer with the king as an autonomous actor.[147]

The richest, most interesting source for Eric's reign in York is Egill's praise-poem *Höfuðlausn*, not least because, regrettably, we possess no such poetry for any other Scandinavian king of York.[148] The attitudes, ideas, and content of the poem may thus give us a unique insight into how Eric wished to hear himself presented and praised, while the fact that the poem can be (roughly) dated and localized means that the potential for contextualization is high.[149] The poem's genuineness has, inevitably, been debated, but no anachronism has been demonstrated.[150] It is preserved in association with *Egil's Saga*, which gives an account of how Egill had to 'ransom his head' from his old enemy Eric by composing a poem in his honour. The saga's thirteenth-century narrative is of secondary value in terms of historical evidence, but it agrees broadly with what the poem *Arinbjarnarkviða* says.

Höfuðlausn presents two narratives, that of the king and that of the poet.[151] It begins and ends with the poet's story – his arrival at York ('I went west over the sea'), and his desire to gain the king's attention for his poem ('I ask for a hearing because I have brought praise'). Within this first-person framework, the main body of the poem celebrates Eric's qualities as king – his generosity, and above all his prowess in battle. But unlike many praise-poems, *Höfuðlausn* does not catalogue the patron's campaigns and victories with a roll-call of battles fought and enemies vanquished; indeed, the only specificity at all is a kenning that describes Eric as 'the destroyer of Scots [*fárbjóðr Skota*]'. Is this because Eric did not have many famous victories to boast of? As a way round this, Egill offers a sequence of representative tableaux, focusing on aspects of battle, or characteristic activities of the king; his basic literary mode is metonymy, in which the part stands for the whole, or a small detail communicates a bigger picture, though there are some wide-angle crowd scenes as well, with teeming multitudes and an emphasis on the noisiness of battle. For example:

> The din of swords on the rim of shields increased. War grew round the prince. The prince advanced. Then there was heard the river of swords resounding, flowing mightily, the chant of the storm of metal.

The recurrent stage properties of Viking battle poetry are much in evidence, such as weaponry and carrion-birds. The poet has a dazzling array of locutions for 'sword', for instance:

> Saddle of the whetstone [=sword] clashed on sun of battle [=sword]. The wound engraver [=sword] bit. That was the blood-snake [=sword]. I learned that Odin's oaks [=warriors] fell before the ice of the belt [=sword] in the game of iron [=battle].

Meanwhile, the so-called 'beasts of battle' are deployed to stress the slaughter that the king wreaks on his foes, guaranteeing that the carrion-birds that follow him will not go hungry:

> Battle-cranes [=eagles or ravens] flew over the rows of corpses. The beaks of the wound-seagulls [=ravens] did not lack blood. The wolf tore at wounds while the wave from the spear-point [=blood] splashed up towards the beaks of ravens.

There are over a dozen stanzas of this sort of thing. The overall effect is to present Eric as a great warrior, an 'artist of battle', to use one of Egill's memorable phrases.

But alongside the blood and slaughter there is also an emphasis on the king's generosity: the king 'throws out river-fire [gold], but holds his land in a tight grip'.

As the array of kennings for 'sword' suggests, *Höfuðlausn* is a flashy poem, a tour-de-force that draws attention to its own virtuosity. If it lacks substance in terms of the king's achievements – and it does – it compensates for this through its ostentatious diction and bravura effects. This can be apprehended also through attention to its metre. In the original, the 'sword' stanza quoted above is as follows:

Hlam heinsöðul
við hjaldrröðul,
beit bengrefill;
þat var blóðrefill.
Frá ek at felli
fyrir fetilsvelli
Óðins eiki
í járnleiki.

Like other skaldic poetry, *Höfuðlausn* observes familiar rules of alliteration (**H**lam, **h**ein-, **h**jaldr-). But on top of this it adds end-rhyme (-*söðul*, -*röðul*) – indeed, in several stanzas there is a rather demonstrative end-rhyme that extends across four lines. End-rhyme is very familiar to readers of English poetry, of course, but it was not a common feature of Norse verse: *Höfuðlausn* may well be the first extant poem in which it is used, and it has been suggested that Egill's inspiration for the practice may have been the rhymed Latin hymns current in Anglo-Saxon England.[152] So not only will the diction of *Höfuðlausn* have compelled attention through its density and imagination; to its original audience, the metre of the poem will also have sounded both ornate and innovative.

In terms of content, though, it is resolutely old-fashioned. Eric is depicted as an archetypal Viking warrior, fighting battles on the shoreline, wading through the dead, feeding the ravens. In the presentation of the king, there is not a hint of the complex politics, and hybrid cultural context, to be found in mid tenth-century York. The poem gives the impression that Eric's *Jórvík* is an enclave of old-style Viking values, not at all the progressive Anglo-Scandinavian trading centre that we know it was in actuality (and which we will explore in Chapter 6).[153] Is this, one wonders, one of the ways in which Eric was out of step with his constituents, one of the reasons why his rule in York did not work out as planned; or is this to read too much into what may, after all, simply be poetic convention?

We do not know why Eric lost his hold on the York kingship, for the final time, in (probably) 954. *Egil's Saga* creates a compelling, but no doubt highly imaginative, portrait of a weak and paranoid king, immured within his palace in the company of his chosen, loyal retainers. The *Anglo-Saxon Chronicle* is likely to be nearer the mark in the sense it gives of increasing pressure from the West Saxon dynasty; it was not desired that the northern conquests of Athelstan and his brothers should only be temporary. The *Chronicle* tells us that the Northumbrians 'drove out [*fordrifon*] Eric'; our fullest account of his death comes from Roger of Wendover's *Flowers of Histories*:

> King Eric was treacherously killed by Earl Maccus in a certain lonely place which is called Stainmore, with his son Haeric and his brother Rægnald, betrayed by Earl Oswulf; and then afterwards King Eadred ruled in these districts.[154]

A certain poignancy is imparted to Eric's demise: he is 'betrayed', and 'killed treacherously [*fraudulenter*]', in 'a certain lonely place'. The implication is that the unknown Earl Maccus was one of Eric's own retinue. *Maccus* is a Hiberno-Norse name, and a number of Scandinavian figures with that name can be identified in tenth-century sources; but it is not possible to say which, if any, was the Maccus who killed Eric.[155] Oswulf was the reeve of Bamburgh, the successor of the sons of Eadwulf. The reward for his part in Eric's death was the earldom of all of Northumbria, granted him by Eadred: a clear sign that he had acted in accordance with West Saxon desires. As for Stainmore [NR], remote and wind-swept on the boundary between Yorkshire and Westmorland, its location suggests that Eric was fleeing towards the west coast. Not necessarily Ireland, though: Stainmore is not on the way to the 'Aire Gap', the usual route between York and Dublin, but rather on the Roman road to Penrith, and so Eric seems to have been heading for Carlisle and the Solway Firth – perhaps with a view to returning to Orkney. Norse sagas imagine Eric's death as having occurred in a big battle, but Roger of Wendover's account – the only one to specify Stainmore – may be taken as suggesting a more minor skirmish, or perhaps an ambush.

According to Snorri Sturluson, it was to Orkney that Eric's widow and his sons withdrew, before proceeding to Denmark – and subsequently, a few years later, returning to Norway, where they defeated Eric's brother Hákon and reclaimed the throne. Notwithstanding the counter-indications of the *Life of St Cathroe*, Eric's wife Gunnhild may well have been a Danish noblewoman, and Norse sources claim a Danish mother for Eric himself.[156] And the kings' saga *Fagrskinna* (*Fair Parchment*) tells us that, after Eric's death, Gunnhild had a poem composed about him, and this is *Eiríksmál*, the second of our poems about Eric.[157] Unlike Egill's *Höfuðlausn*, *Eiríksmál* (self-evidently) was not composed or performed in York; but if one were to hypothesize, reasonably enough, that its poet had earlier been part of Eric's court in York, then its representative value would in fact be greater than that of *Höfuðlausn*, which is the production of an Icelandic skald merely passing through the city (and against his will).

Eiríksmál does not survive in its full form – we are lacking its conclusion – but it is so remarkable and powerful a poem that it is worth quoting in its entirety:

"What kind of dream is that," said Odin, "When I thought myself, a little before day, to be clearing Valhalla for a slain people? I woke the chosen warriors, commanded the valkyries to get up, to strew the benches, to wash the cups, to bring wine, as if a prince was coming. For me there is expectation of bold heroes from the world; so my heart is glad."

"What thunders there," said Bragi, "As if a thousand are moving, or too great a multitude? All the benches creak, as if Baldr is coming back to Odin's hall."

"You must not speak nonsense, wise Bragi," said Odin, "Since you know well what it is: the noise is because of Eric, the prince, who will here come into Odin's hall."

"Sigmundr and Sinfjötli, get up quickly and go to meet the king; invite him in – if it is Eric – I now have certain expectation of him."

"Why do you have expectation of Eric," said Sigmundr, "Rather than of other kings?" "Because," said Odin, "In many a land he has reddened the blade, and carried a bloody sword."

"Why then have you deprived him of victory, when he seemed to you to be bold?" "Because," said Odin, "The unknown cannot be known: the grey wolf gazes on the homes of the gods."

"Hail now, Eric," said Sigmundr, "Be welcome here and enter the hall, wise one. I wish to ask you this: what princes accompany you from the clash of swords?"

"There are five kings," said Eric. "I will tell you the names of them all; I am the sixth myself."[158]

As can be seen, in method and mood this poem could hardly be more different from Egill's *Höfuðlausn*. Whereas the earlier poem combined representative generalities with stylistic pyrotechnics, *Eiríksmál* reaches for the world of Norse mythology, and offers an imagined moment in the king's afterlife, a scene from a play complete with *dramatis personae* and formal speeches, all communicated in a style that is, on the whole, plain-spoken but potent. Eric has just arrived in Valhalla (Old Norse *Valhöll*), the hall of the dead where Odin gathers around him his chosen warriors in preparation for the apocalyptic battle of Ragnarok: the grey wolf that 'gazes on the homes of the gods' is Fenrir, ravenously waiting for his chance to break free and consume Odin himself. Valkyries are on hand to welcome the dead king, as are such legendary figures as Bragi (the first skald, perhaps metamorphosed into a god of poetry) and Sigmundr and Sinfjötli (key players from the Volsung cycle of legends). Eric's entrance is so grand, the sound of his approach so mighty, that at first there is some confusion: surely such a tumult could only be caused by the return of Baldr, Odin's dead son? But Odin knows it is Eric, and sets out his qualifications for entering Valhalla: 'in many a land he has reddened the blade, and carried a bloody sword'. The fragment ends as Eric himself crosses the threshold, accompanied by five other kings.

Eiríksmál is grappling with a perennial theological question, and offering a distinctive Viking Age answer. Why do bad things happen to good people; or more specifically, why do good kings lose battles and die? The solution proposed makes sense within the cosmological timeline of Norse myth: namely, good kings die because Odin wants to have them with him, to be among his chosen warriors (the *Einherjar*), since the time of the last battle is unknown, and could come at any moment. So Eric was killed in battle, the poem claims, not because he was a poor king or a poor warrior; on the contrary, it was precisely because he was such a great war-leader that Odin could not do without him, and for that reason he had to die.

There is a twist, however. *Eiríksmál* looks pretty obviously like a pagan poem. But saga sources claim that Eric was in fact a Christian convert during his time in England, and that his sons were later unpopular in Norway precisely because of their Christianity. We should recall that, while Eric's coins re-instate the aggressive sword of Sihtric *caech*, they do not revive Olaf Guthfrithson's Odinic raven. The relationship between paganism and Christianity in Viking Age Yorkshire will be discussed more fully in Chapter 5; for the moment we should just note the possibility that the mythology of *Eiríksmál* may be a form of cultural tradition, a set of inherited stories, rather than a lived belief. But whichever it is, the poem testifies eloquently to the vitality of Norse myth in the mid tenth century, and its utility in coping with death and disaster.

Who were the five kings who accompanied Eric into Valhalla? As we have seen, Roger of Wendover supplies two names. Snorri Sturluson offers a full five: this may be guesswork on Snorri's part, but is more probably explained by assuming that he knew the poem of *Eiríksmál* in its entirety, even though he chooses not to quote from it in his narrative. 'These are named: Guthormr and his two sons, Ívarr and Hárekr; Sigurðr and Rögnvaldr also fell there'.[159] The agreement between Snorri and Roger is good, though the English source describes Haeric/Hárekr as a son of Eric himself. But of these five kings themselves we know nothing more than what these two accounts tell us.[160]

Eric's contemporaries, as noted above, probably did not realize that his death at Stainmore marked the end of the Viking kingdom of York. Certainly his opponent King Eadred, who died the following year, in 955, did not expect a trouble-free existence for the kingdom of the English: his will includes a large bequest of money given for 'the benefit of his people [...] to the end that they may redeem themselves from famine and from a heathen army if they need'.[161] This is perhaps not surprising: Eadred himself had lost control of Northumbria on two previous occasions (once to Eric, once to Olaf *cuaran*), prior to Eric's final demise in 954.

As a footnote to the deaths of Eric and Eadred, we should note one further event, recorded in the *Anglo-Saxon Chronicle* for 956: 'In this year Archbishop Wulfstan died'.[162] So this enigmatic churchman, who had become archbishop of York in 930 or 931, outlived the Viking kings he had co-operated or collaborated with, and in his eventful career he saw multiple changes of rule in Northumbria. But towards the end he seems to have been brought under a tighter rein by the southern kings of England. In 952 Eadred had 'ordered Archbishop Wulfstan to be taken into the fortress of *Iudanbyrig*, because accusations had often been made to the king against him', and in 954 (seemingly after Eric's removal) he 'received back his bishopric, at Dorchester [on Thames]': in other words, the West Saxon kings were keeping a very close eye on him, and not allowing him to play a role in any sort of Northumbrian independence movement.[163]

After Eric's demise, the *History of the Kings* announces, with obvious hindsight, that 'here the kings of the Northumbrians [*reges Northanhymbrorum*] came to an end, and henceforward the province was administered by earls'.[164] The phrasing of this entry is interesting: it is not simply that the Scandinavian kings of York came to an end with Eric's death, but that the entire sequence of Northumbrian kings did, with the implication that the Scandinavian kings were part of a continuous line going back to pre-Viking and even pre-Christian times. So the passing of Eric marked not just the end of the Viking kings of York, but also of the whole tradition of monarchy in the north.

From the capture of York in 866 to the death of Eric in 954, the Viking kingdom of Northumbria had lasted less than a century. However, as the following three chapters will explore, its significance cannot be reduced simply to a narrative of political and military history. There is another, no less important story to be told, of emigration, settlement, and cultural exchange, and it is to this that we must now turn.

SCANDINAVIAN SETTLEMENT

Evidence for Settlement I: written sources

We should begin by re-quoting the *Anglo-Saxon Chronicle*'s key statement from 876, that in this year 'Halfdan shared out the land of the Northumbrians, and they proceeded to plough and to support themselves [*Healfdene Norþanhymbra lond gedǫlde ond ergende wæron ond hiera tilgende*]'.[1] This is the extent of the explicit notice given by the *Chronicle* to Scandinavian settlement in the north, though the entry for 896 may indicate further arrivals from the army that had plagued southern England for the previous three years ('in the summer of this year the Danish army divided, one force going into East Anglia and one into Northumbria').[2] Elsewhere the *Chronicle* uses the same verb, *gedælan* ('to share out') to describe the Scandinavian settlement of Mercia in 877 and of East Anglia in 880, and in the 880 entry the verb is also paired with *gesettan* ('to occupy, to settle').[3] This recurrent emphasis on 'sharing out' is interesting, and one further piece of lexical evidence that may cast light on the process of settlement is the Old Norse loanword *manslot* or *manna hlot* (found in texts from the southern Danelaw). This is among the earlier strata of Norse loans to be recorded in English sources, occurring first in a charter of 956, and the term seems to mean 'a share in ownership of land; a measure of land' (from Old Norse *mannshlutr* 'person's share').[4] Frank Stenton argued that 'the 'share' which it originally denoted may well have been the portion of land which fell to one of the rank and file of the Danish army at the time of its settlement'.[5] Stenton's interpretation is circumstantial – it cannot be demonstrated that the sharing out took place at the point of conquest in the 870s, though the agreement with the *Chronicle's* term *gedælan* is suggestive – but at the least we can say that the term attests to a (re-)distribution of land in areas of Scandinavian settlement during the period when Old Norse was spoken in England (and indeed, prior to 956, and thus during the period of Scandinavian rule in Northumbria).

As with the fall of York, later sources, often based upon the *Anglo-Saxon Chronicle*, offer a few extra glosses and expansions to the *Chronicle*'s own terse account. Asser, for example, offers the following: 'In the same year Halfdan, king of one part of the Northumbrians, shared out the whole province [*regionem*] between himself and his men, and together with his army cultivated the land' – a version that seems to nuance the *Chronicle*'s statement with regards to both the extent of Halfdan's dominion in Northumbria and his own acquisition of estates.[6] Roger of Wendover, in the thirteenth century, also makes the nature of Halfdan's division a little more explicit: 'Halfdan, king of the Danes, occupied Northumbria, and divided it among himself and his thegns, and had it cultivated by his army'.[7] The *History of St Cuthbert*, also expanding on the *Anglo-Saxon Chronicle*, explains that in the 870s the Great Army separated into three parts:

> One rebuilt York, cultivated the surrounding land and settled there. The second, however, which occupied the land of the Mercians, and the third, which invaded the land of the South Saxons, committed many crimes over the next three years and slew all those of royal stock excepting only Alfred.[8]

Showing its northern perspective, the *History* here offers a sort of 'harrying of the south' narrative, in which the northerly parts of England are settled and cultivated but the more southern ones plundered and despoiled.

The *History of St Cuthbert* also records or alludes to two later acts of land-distribution, between the Tees and the Wear, by the Scandinavian kings Guthred and Rægnald. Abbot Eadred of Carlisle, the *History* states, bought a number of estates 'from the aforesaid King Guthred, and from the Danish host [*Danorum exercitu*] which under him had divided the land among themselves'.[9] But some of these very estates were thirty years later seized by Rægnald, and re-awarded to Scandinavian thegns:

> [Rægnald] divided the estates of St Cuthbert, and one part toward the south, from the township which is called Castle Eden as far as Billingham, he gave to a certain powerful warrior of his who was called Scula. The other part, however, from Castle Eden as far as the river Wear, he gave to a certain one who was called Onlafbald.[10]

The picture offered here is very similar to that of the accounts for 876: military conquest leads to the wholesale acquisition of land, which is then given out by the conquering king to his supporters and soldiers.[11] The impression is not of a free-for-all land-grab (or estate-grab), though our textual sources are so reticent on this whole issue that we cannot say that this did not happen also; some arbitrary seizing of estates does seem to have taken place after the Norman Conquest, 200 years later.[12] By the time that northern England passed again into Anglo-Saxon hands (albeit temporarily), with Athelstan's conquest of 927, many or most of the pre-Viking estates of the Northumbrian monarchy, aristocracy, and church must have been irrecoverably re-allocated, scattered into the possession of a new Scandinavian elite.[13]

As the introductory example of the Middleton Cross in Chapter 1 showed, we do have images of some of this new Scandinavian elite, carved on stone monuments. Like Middleton, these sculptures offer us iconic images of the Viking lords of Northumbria, such as the seated figure at Nunburnholme [ER] [Figure 7] and the spear-bearing horsemen from Sockburn [Durham] [Figure 8]. Other good examples include those at Weston [WR], Baldersby [NR], and Gainford [Durham], in addition to the further instances at Middleton itself. Some of the warrior-figures are seated, some standing, some on horseback. The monuments on which they are depicted cannot be dated very narrowly, and most studies cautiously attribute them to some time in the first half of the tenth century; so these are unlikely to be representations of first-generation settlers (though in some cases this is not impossible). But they have considerable value in bringing us close to the new elite who assumed power and authority, and occupied the land, in the years of Scandinavian rule, and also to the martial image which they wished to project.[14] With few exceptions, pre-Viking sculpture did not depict secular figures, so these stones represent a radical change. They are not evidence for settlement in any numerically significant manner, but they are eloquent witnesses to the arrival of new local lords in Northumbria, and to a prominent warrior ideology.

In the study of Scandinavian settlement in northern England, it must be admitted that written sources do not get us very far, and we need to turn instead to archaeological finds and to place-names. But before we do so, there is one other type of evidence that needs some brief discussion, and that is genetic. As is well known, the so-called 'Y chromosome' passes directly down the male line, and 'mitochondrial DNA' (mtDNA) down the female line.[15] Since some genetic variability can be mapped, in theory a testing of modern DNA should be able to suggest the likely place of origin for a person's Y chromosome or mtDNA (depending on whether they are male or female), which should in turn be able to cast some light on population movements over time. Some obvious qualifications need to be made before proceeding, however. First, such DNA testing is likely to be more reliable at the population level, at which larger patterns are revealed, than at the individual level, at which results may be compromised or unreliable. Second, DNA testing is better at determining variations in space rather than time; it cannot easily tell us the date at which a variant moved (migrated) from one place to another. And third, such testing tells us only about population history, and nothing, scientifically speaking, about present identity: if one counts back a thousand years, allowing three generations per century, then we all possess over 1,000 million ancestors (many duplicated, of course), which means not only that everyone in a particular place or country is pretty certain to be related in some way to every previous population group ever to have settled in that place or country, but also that it would be absurd to pick out just one ancestor from those 1,000 million (the one that DNA testing happens to be able to track) as being especially influential or significant.[16]

Some interesting results have, however, emerged in the last decade or so, though none have been real surprises; in fact, the vindication of our textual and onomastic sources is one of the most worthwhile conclusions. So, for example, a celebrated series of studies suggested Celtic origins for 20-25% of the male settlers of Iceland, but more than twice that percentage for the female settlers.[17] In England, a study of the north-west seemed to confirm a significant Scandinavian input into the population of the region, derived ultimately from Norway.[18] But east of the Pennines there has been no equivalent demonstration, for one good reason: since the Anglo-Saxons came from northern Germany and southern Denmark, their genetic signature cannot be differentiated from later Danish settlers in the Viking Age.[19] DNA testing cannot tell a Dane from an Anglo-Saxon, though it can distinguish a Norwegian; but the settlement of eastern England in the ninth and tenth centuries was probably more a Danish phenomenon than a Norwegian one, so genetic history cannot, at least at present, answer the question of how heavy the Scandinavian impact on Yorkshire was. According to one important study, sample sites in Yorkshire, Norfolk, and the East Midlands – in other words, the area of the Danelaw – reveal that these are the parts of the country that show 'the highest degree of German/Danish input' (that is, Anglo-Saxon and Danish combined).[20] But this, as noted, is hardly a surprise.

Evidence for Settlement II: archaeology

We should turn now to the burial evidence for Scandinavian settlers in Yorkshire – an interesting body of material, but one that does not greatly illuminate questions of migration and settlement, as the diagnostically Scandinavian burials that have been discovered from Viking Age England are so few. Dawn Hadley has stated firmly that 'elaborate funerary display was a short-lived phenomenon among the Scandinavian settlers in England', and it is impossible to disagree with this judgement.[21] While the number of early Anglo-Saxon burials to have been found runs to the thousands (or at least, burials with early Anglo-Saxon grave-goods), identifiably Scandinavian burials can be counted only in tens: Viking graves in England have been very hard to find. This situation poses something of a puzzle, but convincing answers have been given.[22]

To begin with, we must ask by what criteria we would judge a burial to be diagnostically Scandinavian? Forms of burial in Viking Age Scandinavia were diverse, but the answer to this question must be that a demonstratively Scandinavian burial would show either the prominent presence of objects of a Scandinavian cultural type, or else the observance of a Scandinavian type of burial ritual (that is, of a type not otherwise practised in Anglo-Saxon England in the ninth and tenth century).[23] In the former category would come certain forms of jewellery or weaponry, and in the latter category, above all, mound-burial and cremation. If the Scandinavian settlers rapidly gave up the use of cremation and mound-burial, and also the practice of burial with grave-goods – and, as we will see, the evidence indicates that they did – then there would be nothing to indicate that any particular burial was Scandinavian rather than Anglo-Saxon (even if we assume that such ethnic distinctions can be easily made). Of course, the fact that such practices seem to have been discontinued raises immediately the question as to why this should have been the case. The most obvious reason would be conversion to Christianity: cremation was certainly a non-Christian form of burial, and while neither mound-burial nor burial with elaborate grave-goods are in themselves pagan, in the early medieval world such practices are much better attested in pagan cultures than Christian ones. So, for example, the graveyard of the tenth-century church at Wharram Percy [ER] has been wholly excavated, and no accompanied burials (that is, burials with grave-goods) were found.[24] And this is indeed the classic answer given to the puzzle of the paucity of Scandinavian burials: there are so few, it is argued, because the Scandinavians rapidly converted to Christianity, gave up their earlier burial practices, and were interred in churchyards.[25] Unfurnished burial became the norm. There seems little reason to dispute the fundamental correctness of this interpretation, though recent scholarship has wished to regard conversion and Christianization as not the only factor in play, and has given prominence equally to issues of power, politics, and social and ethnic identity.[26]

The conversion of the Vikings in England will be discussed in the next chapter; for now, we will restrict our attention to the few diagnostically Scandinavian burials that have been uncovered. Regionally, it is the north-west of England that boasts the most sites (as a result of its participation in the Irish Sea, Hiberno-Norse culture province), while the largest cemetery (involving cremations under mounds) is at Heath Wood, near Repton in Derbyshire.[27] The corpus of Yorkshire burials cannot compete in either quantity or spectacle, but over the years a significant number have been uncovered, as follows: Bedale [NR] (found in the early nineteenth century; a single female burial on the line of a Roman road), Kildale [NR] (mid nineteenth century; eight or nine burials, seemingly all male and accompanied with weapons, found under the church floor), Camp Hill, Carthorpe [NR] (mid nineteenth century; a single male, accompanied by weaponry), Pippin Castle, Scargill, near Harrogate [WR] (1901; a complex and poorly understood site, with assorted finds possibly from under tumuli and/or on the site of a lost chapel), Wensley [NR] (1915; a single male, accompanied by weaponry, in the churchyard), and Adwick-le-Street [WR] (2001; a single female, near a Roman road). This amounts to, as it were, the agreed corpus of Viking Age burials in Yorkshire.[28] A number of late Anglo-Saxon graveyards in both urban and rural contexts have also been extensively excavated, and these have thrown up occasional Scandinavian-style artefacts, as well as (at York Minster) substantial quantities of stone sculpture; but not – perhaps significantly – any weapon burials.[29] Further Scandinavian burials may be the two bodies discovered in 2005 in association with the so-called 'Ainsbrook hoard' (discussed in Chapter 2), which have been radiocarbon-dated to the tenth century; but these have not yet been published.[30] None of the Yorkshire burials are cremations, in contrast to examples west of the Pennines.[31]

Excluding 'Ainsbrook' as a possible further example, we can see that there are three or four sites which attest male burials with weaponry: Kildale (multiple burials), Camp Hill, and Wensley, with Pippin Castle a likely fourth example. In terms of weapon types, swords were found at Kildale, Camp Hill, and Wensley, as were spearheads; axe-heads were found at Kildale and Pippin Castle (and it should be recalled that at this period the axe was a distinctively Scandinavian weapon, as depicted on the Middleton Cross); knives or daggers at Kildale and Wensley (again, reminiscent of the knives or short swords depicted on the Middleton stones); and a scabbard and buckle at Kildale.[32] None of these burials can be easily dated by weapon morphology: the swords found at Wensley and Camp Hill are of a type which is given a conventional date of c.900, and may even be Anglo-Saxon in origin (as the type was introduced into Scandinavia from England), while the most easily identified sword from Kildale was of a type that had a lengthy currency.[33] All the Kildale swords are now lost (there seem to have been four in all), as are many of the finds from the nineteenth-century excavations, and thus further investigation is not possible.[34]

Other grave-goods were also found, for example a sickle at Wensley (symbolizing a more agricultural existence?) and weights and scales at Kildale (projecting a more mercantile identity, or used for sharing out Viking loot?). The finds from Pippin Castle (which have recently been reviewed by Angela Redmond) seem especially heterogeneous, and include two horse-shoes, assorted iron fragments, some flints, a fragment of whetstone, the humerus of an ox, and a piece of whalebone.[35] There was also a large boulder, with scratches on one of its sides: these have been read as a runic inscription SUNA 'son', and Redmond has suggested the boulder may be a rudimentary hogback tomb (a type of monument discussed later); but the standard studies of both hogbacks and runic inscriptions from Britain do not recognize the Pippin Castle boulder within their corpus.[36] What one is to make of this assemblage is very unclear, not least because the likely Viking Age remains seem to have become mixed up with material from later periods, such as twelfth- to fourteenth-century pottery.

All the male weapon burials were excavated in the nineteenth or early twentieth century, and on the whole both the excavation reports, and the conservation of finds, leave much to be desired (the bones from the Kildale burials, for example, 'were promptly put into one common grave').[37] We can, however, hazard that these burials are likely to date from fairly early in the history of Viking Age Yorkshire, before the abandonment of burial with grave-goods. But the lack of skeletal analysis means that we cannot say whether any of the males buried were, for example, warriors killed in battle, or – at the other extreme – aged members of a landed elite, whose death and burial post-dated any military activity they may have had by years or even decades. Such burials – like, in different ways, the Middleton Cross and other warrior sculptures – enable us to learn something of the culture of weaponry which the Scandinavian elite either participated in or liked to be associated with, and the role that weaponry played in commemoration and the posthumous projection of identity; but it can only be probable, rather than certain, that such burials represent first- or second-generation lordly settlers or their followers.[38]

The most remarkable Scandinavian burial to be found in recent years, and the only one so far to be excavated and published to a high standard, is in fact that of a female, not a male, uncovered at Adwick-le-Street, near Doncaster; and this burial in turn helps us to understand better the earliest recorded Scandinavian burial in Yorkshire, at Bedale.[39] Both Adwick-le-Street and Bedale were single female inhumations, and in both cases the women buried were wearing two diagnostically Scandinavian oval, 'tortoise' brooches, used to fasten the straps of their gowns [Figure 10]. Other goods found at Adwick-le-Street included a copper-alloy bowl, an iron knife, and an iron key or latch-lifter, while the Bedale woman was accompanied – bafflingly, unless the finders overlooked a male skeleton as well – by a spear.[40] There were no grave-goods at either site that might positively suggest the Christian faith (such as a cross), while the use of paired oval brooches indicates the wearing of what has been called (anachronistically but helpfully) the 'national costume' of Scandinavian women in the Viking Age, albeit one less common in Denmark than in Norway and Sweden.[41] The Adwick-le-Street brooches were quite 'battered and worn', and had lost their central bosses (probably during their lifetime of use, rather than after burial), and they were not a matching pair – unlike most oval brooches found in graves in Scandinavia.[42] Their style was that of the late ninth century. The Bedale brooches were a matching pair, dating from the late ninth or tenth century.[43]

The skeletal remains from Adwick-le-Street were especially revealing. The attrition on the woman's teeth indicates that her age at burial was at least 35-45, and quite possibly over 45. Modern chemical analysis of the strontium and oxygen isotopes in her tooth enamel has, moreover, been able to suggest a likely place of origin. Strontium in the soil, and oxygen in drinking water, are absorbed into the body in early childhood, and since the isotopes of these two elements vary from place to place, analysis can often reveal the geographical origins of a skeleton.[44] In

91

the case of the Adwick-le-Street woman, tests revealed two possibilities for her place of origin: conceivably north-east Scotland, but much more probably (on account of the oxygen signature) the Trondheim region of Norway. A very intriguing portrait therefore emerges of the woman buried at Adwick-le-Street, most probably a migrant from Norway: her costume and accoutrements indicate that she was a freeborn woman, probably married, with (for the Viking Age) a fairly long life behind her; but the poor state of her non-matching brooches suggests she was not among the highest elite. Whether she had settled in the Doncaster area, or was simply buried there, having died on a journey, cannot now be established (the burial was found next to a Romano-British trackway, and less than a mile from the Roman road Dere Street, now the A1). It is striking that the Bedale burial was also found on a Roman road, that between Catterick [NR] and Piercebridge [Durham].

The Bedale and Adwick-le-Street burials bring into sharp focus the question of female migrants and settlers, and also (through their oval brooches) enable us to move towards the second body of archaeological evidence to be discussed, namely jewellery. It has been pointed out that, of the small number of early Scandinavian burials from the Danelaw that have so far been sexed osteologically (as opposed to through grave-goods), nearly half are female.[45] The implication is that significant numbers of Scandinavian women (and, presumably, children) may have accompanied the major Viking armies into England on campaign, as well as crossing the sea in the years and decades after hostilities had ceased. Such an implication is, for example, readily supported by the range of finds recovered from the Great Army's camp at Torksey (where the army that had conquered York over-wintered in 872-73).[46]

Place- and personal name evidence, to be discussed later, suggests that Scandinavian women were indeed among those who remained in England, or came to England, after the Viking wars were over.[47] Textual sources also reveal that women and children were among the followers of the Viking armies that campaigned in England in the second half of the ninth century. In the *Anglo-Saxon Chronicle* entry for 893 we learn that when the English army captured the Viking fortress at Benfleet in Essex they took not only goods but 'women and also children', and that the Viking leader Hæsten's 'wife and two sons were brought to the king [Alfred]'; two years later it is recorded that 'the Danes had placed their women in safety in East Anglia' before they left their fortress there.[48] We should also recall the 'certain widow' in the *History of St Cuthbert*, from whom the young Guthred was purchased before he was elevated to the kingship of Northumbria.[49] Was she English or Scandinavian? The former is possible, in that the young Scandinavian might have been sold to her, and become a Christian when in her service.[50] But the latter would also seem plausible, and we might speculate that her late husband had perhaps been a member of the Great Army of 865, and/or one of the followers who benefited from Halfdan's sharing-out of the land; if so, this unnamed widow would be the earliest identifiable Scandinavian woman in England, at least according to textual sources.

The presence of female migrants is further revealed, and powerfully so, through the archaeological evidence of jewellery. This is a body of evidence that has, like others, truly exploded in recent years in both quantity and significance, as a consequence of metal-detectorists being encouraged to report their finds to the national Portable Antiquities Scheme.[51] In 1976, for example, Richard Hall was able to record only a single Scandinavian brooch that had been found in Yorkshire outside of a burial context, namely a trefoil brooch found at Low Dalby near Pickering [NR], which was reported in 1927.[52] Now, in excess of 30 Scandinavian brooches have been found in Yorkshire, and many times this number nationally; and more are being turned up every year. A comparable body of material, relating both to male and female costume, is represented by decorative strap-ends.[53]

This rapidly increasing body of jewellery evidence, with the potential to change our understanding of the Danelaw considerably, has recently been the subject of a full-length study by Jane Kershaw.[54] The cut-off date for Kershaw's corpus of material is December 2008 – she does not include items found after that date – but at the time of her census just over 500 Scandinavian-style brooches had been found in England. Kershaw subdivides her material into two main categories, which she labels 'Scandinavian' brooches and 'Anglo-Scandinavian' ones. Scandinavian brooches are those which are likely to have been manufactured in Scandinavia, and brought into England, whereas Anglo-Scandinavian ones are those manufactured in England. Contrary to what one might expect, the main differences between the Scandinavian and Anglo-Scandinavian series are not, in fact, in the areas of design and decoration – to the viewer, the two series are usually indistinguishable – but rather in the materials and techniques of manufacture. According to Kershaw's analysis, brooches made in Scandinavia tend to use brass, with tinning on the reverse, employ a double, H-shaped pin-lug and a hooked catchplate, and often have an attachment loop, so that objects can be suspended from the brooch. Brooches made in England, on the other hand, in both the Anglo-Saxon and Anglo-Scandinavian periods, do not normally use either brass or tinning, employ a single, transverse pin-lug and a C-shaped catchplate, and never have an attachment loop.[55] Such differences indicate varying traditions of craftsmanship in Scandinavia and England, and they mean that, if this distinction is a secure one, then we can normally tell where a particular brooch was made.

More will be said of the 'Anglo-Scandinavian' brooches in the next chapter; for now, we should focus on the 'Scandinavian' ones. The large oval brooches of the Bedale and Adwick-le-Street burials are, in fact, rather atypical, as most of the Scandinavian-style jewellery that has been found in England takes the form of smaller brooches, of a sort that do not further imply the wearing of distinctive

Scandinavian costume. Nonetheless, before we consider this smaller dress-jewellery, it is worth noting that, as a proportion of the total number of brooches found to date, Yorkshire is unusually well-represented in terms of oval brooches: in addition to the two from Bedale and the two from Adwick-le-Street, another has been found at Kilnwick [ER], re-used as decoration on a lead weight for weaving, and a fragment of another has recently come to light in the parish of Old Byland and Scawton [NR].[56]

The great majority of brooches found are much smaller, most commonly disc-shaped, though lozenge- and trefoil-shaped brooches also occur [Figure 11]. They are not, on the whole, elite objects in either value or craftsmanship. They were used by women as decorative fasteners for shawls or other clothing, and similar brooches were in use among the Anglo-Saxon population of England; so they need not signal, as the oval brooches do, the wearing of ostentatiously Scandinavian costume. They are decorated mostly in variants of the so-called Borre style and Jellinge style, which are the classic Scandinavian art-styles of the Viking expansion and diaspora: the Borre style (conventionally dated c.850-c.950) is distinguished by knot patterns and gripping beasts, while the Jellinge style (c.900-c.975) is marked by the interlace of ribbon animals.[57] It is easy to understand how such small brooches may have been lost more easily than the larger and more formal oval brooches – breaking or coming undone in the fields or on the paths – and most finds are thought to be 'casual losses from rural settlements'.[58] Although a sizeable corpus of brooches from Yorkshire has emerged, the county does not boast the same quantity of finds as Lincolnshire and East Anglia, and the reasons for this may be multiple: it may, of course, mean that fewer such brooches were being worn in the region in the Viking Age, or that the common circumstances of loss arose less frequently. But more likely variables are those of land, recovery, and reporting: metal-detectorists work most, and find most, on ploughland, whereas Yorkshire has a greater proportion of pastoral land than Lincolnshire and East Anglia; and there has also been a more robust tradition of detectorists reporting their finds in the southern Danelaw.

The various types of brooch, and decoration, have been helpfully itemized by Kershaw, and examples of most types have been found in Yorkshire: openwork lozenge brooches from Snape [NR] and Thorpe Bassett [NR]; trefoil brooches from Maltby [WR] and Low Dalby [NR]; Borre-style disc brooches from Appleton-le-Street [NR] and near Doncaster [WR]; Jellinge-style brooches from Skipsea [ER] and Wetwang [ER]; and an equal-armed brooch from Collingham [WR].[59] (Such a listing is merely representative, and not exhaustive.) With such a rapidly evolving corpus, any distribution patterns must be provisional, but it is conspicuous that the majority of finds come from the North and East Ridings, with relatively few from the West.

The quantity is important, of course, but what we want to get at here is the significance of these finds, especially for questions of migration. Kershaw's essential argument in this regard is that the range and distribution of the Scandinavian-produced brooches found in England indicate that they were not entering the country primarily as trade-goods: if that were the case, one would expect a more concentrated distribution, fanning out from places of import and sale (as happens with brooches manufactured in England), and probably a narrower range of types, brought in as merchants' wares from particular places of manufacture in Scandinavia. But instead, we find such Scandinavian brooches spread across most or all of the areas affected by Scandinavian settlement, with examples, sometimes few in number, from many or most of the types or subtypes being produced in the Scandinavian homelands. The better interpretation, then, is that these brooches are not entering England in the bags of merchants, but on the clothes of migrants – female migrants, not necessarily of the highest status; and this continually expanding body of material represents, in many ways, our best and most eloquent evidence for female migration. What is more, the chronology of these brooches, as far as it can be determined, is interesting: types ranging from the later ninth century through to the later tenth century have all been found in England, which suggests that migration was not a once-for-all event of the 870s, but rather a process extending across the whole period in which Scandinavian rulers held authority in England – and indeed beyond.

Evidence for Settlement III: place-names

Notwithstanding this remarkable, and ever-expanding, corpus of metalwork, it is, arguably, place-names that offer us our most extensive and important information about the nature and extent of Scandinavian settlement in the north and east of England: in Margaret Gelling's celebrated phrase, place-names act as 'signposts to the past' [Figure 9].[60] In short, the influence of the Old Norse language on Yorkshire place-names is immense – as also, of course, on place-names in Lincolnshire and other parts of the Danelaw. This place-name evidence has been much discussed, with debate being at times heated, and a number of reviews of the scholarship are available.[61] The traditional interpretation of the place-name evidence, which will largely be accepted here, is that it suggests strongly that a large number of Norse speakers settled in Yorkshire in the ninth and tenth centuries.

Some scholars have, however, queried the interpretation that large numbers of Scandinavian place-names (and Scandinavian-influenced place-names) must indicate large numbers of Scandinavian settlers.[62] So before we can proceed to a discussion of some of the main categories of Norse place-names in Yorkshire, the main objections to the standard interpretation of the place-name evidence should be considered.

Objection 1: could it be that the native Anglo-Saxons learned to speak Old Norse, so that many Norse place-names were given by Anglo-Saxons rather than Scandinavians? Old Norse and Old English were similar languages – indeed, in some ways they were more like different dialects than different languages – and it is highly likely that, at least for pragmatic purposes of communication, Anglo-Saxons and Scandinavians could understand one another when each spoke their own language.[63] This is not to say that some individuals may not have gained an active competence in the other language, but there is no evidence one can point to from Viking Age England for the use of interpreters, or for widespread bilingualism among one or both speech communities. Nor does one language seem to have enjoyed much greater prestige than the other. All this suggests that a model in which a large number of Anglo-Saxons, in the ninth and tenth centuries, switched to using Old Norse, as either a first or second language, is not likely to be correct. However, it is the case that gradually, over time, the Norse language ceased to be spoken in England, presumably as a result of a range of factors, such as inter-marriage and cultural erosion; and the demise of the Norse language will be discussed more fully later in this book. In Yorkshire this is most likely to have happened in the eleventh century, and as a result a large number of Norse words (and Norse pronunciations) passed into the English language. So place-names (especially minor names) which arose in the twelfth century or later, and which show Norse vocabulary or pronunciation (for example, minor stream-names in *beck*), should probably not be attributed to a Norse-speaking population. But nor do they indicate Anglo-Saxons speaking Norse during the Viking Age: rather, they testify to the profound influence which the Norse language had on English in the area, an influence which is best explained as a consequence of heavy Scandinavian settlement in the earlier period.

The next possible objection is related to the first, but pertains to personal names rather than language in general. *Objection 2: could it be that Anglo-Saxons adopted Norse personal names, so that place-names containing Norse personal names need not indicate Scandinavian settlement?* In other words, should we hesitate to interpret place-names such as Haxby [NR] and Slingsby [NR] ('Hákr's farm' and 'Slengr's farm') as indicating the habitation or possession of a Scandinavian: might Hákr and Slengr have been Anglo-Saxons whose parents gave them Norse names? The assumption behind this objection is that practices of name-giving in Viking Age England were much like those in twenty-first-century Britain, so that the popularity of different names, and different types of name, fluctuated according to fashion, and parents felt at liberty to give any names they chose to their children. But this assumption is almost certainly misplaced, as customs of name-giving in the medieval (and early modern) world were profoundly different from those in contemporary Britain.[64] Rather than being a free choice, and subject to the fluctuations of fashion, Anglo-Saxon and Viking name-giving seems to have been governed and constrained by family ties and other close connections (such as god-parenting): children were normally named after a relative or patron, so that a widespread decision on the part of Anglo-Saxon parents to throw off family names and networks, and to choose new-fangled Scandinavian names for their children, seems highly unlikely. Nor is there much empirical evidence to support such a suggestion: it is very hard to point to examples of Anglo-Saxon families where Norse names suddenly make an appearance without inter-marriage or other close affiliation.[65] This is not to deny that Norse names may sometimes have been given to children without Scandinavian connections; but it is unlikely that this was a significant factor in the appearance of a large number of Norse personal names in Viking Age Yorkshire.

Even if one grants that it was mostly Scandinavians who used Old Norse, and that Norse personal names usually indicate people of Scandinavian ancestry or affiliation, a further objection to the standard interpretation of the place-name evidence is still possible. *Objection 3: might the large number of Norse place-names be attributable to a small elite, rather than a large number of settlers?* In some respects this is a variant, or even a combination, of Objections 1 and 2. In recent decades 'elite emulation' (or 'elite transfer') has often been appealed to, in historical and (especially) archaeological debates, as a way of accounting for cultural changes without invoking the idea of invasion or migration.[66] As an explanation for certain events and developments in the early medieval world, particularly in terms of material culture, it is no doubt compelling, but elite emulation is unpersuasive as the primary motivation for Scandinavian place-names in England. For one thing, language is not the same as material culture, and does not operate and evolve according to the same rules, so the extension of what is fundamentally an archaeological model to historical linguistics may be problematic.[67] Nor does the meagre burial evidence from Viking Age England give us much encouragement for postulating widespread Anglo-Saxon emulation of a Scandinavian elite. More specifically, as we have just seen, the linguistic and onomastic results of Viking Age contact are not plausibly explained by the supposed cause of emulation – whether one thinks of that emulation in terms of Anglo-Saxons adopting the Old Norse language, or adopting Old Norse personal names, or somehow accepting and replicating Old Norse place-names (and place-name patterns) handed down *de haut en bas*. Historical linguists have demonstrated that the linguistic impact of Norse in England is hard to explain by reference to a small number of elite speakers: the influence of Old Norse on the English language, in terms of vocabulary, grammar, and pronunciation, is too substantial for this to have been the case.[68] The same is true of the Norse impact on place-names in England: their number, diversity, and vitality is too great to be attributed to only a limited body of Norse language-users, as we will see more fully when we review some of these place-names below.

Although the Norman Conquest may come to mind as a possible parallel in support of this objection, it does not, in fact, supply a persuasive comparison. The Norman elite did indeed make up only a small minority of the post-Conquest population in England; but their influence on English place-names was in fact modest, and on minor names it was insignificant. The French language did of course supply a great quantity of words to English in the later Middle Ages: but this linguistic transfer was on the whole restricted to vocabulary (grammar was untouched), and in many respects it was as much a consequence of the Europe-wide cultural prestige of French in the thirteenth and fourteenth centuries as it was a direct result of the Norman Conquest.[69]

Furthermore, there is a great contrast between the occurrence of Norse personal names in England and, later, that of Norman names (and related Biblical and saints' names). The sheer range of Norse personal names attested in Viking Age England indicates that what we are dealing with is a vibrant, living tradition of name-giving, and not simply a closed corpus, limited in number and lacking in evolution. New permutations of Norse names, unattested in Scandinavia itself, arose in northern and eastern England – of female names as well as male names.[70] While Norman and Biblical names did come to dominate name-giving in England in the later Middle Ages (at the time of the rise of hereditary surnames), the repertoire of Norman names recorded is many times smaller than the vast corpus of Norse names a few centuries earlier: in other words, it is the number of different Norse names that is significant, even more than the number of different people bearing Norse names. This suggests a very sizeable population of families giving their children Norse names, using, as it were, a language and grammar of name-giving of which they themselves are 'native speakers'.

As can been seen, then, while all of the objections raised against the standard interpretation of the place-name evidence have some coherence to them, they are unlikely to be fundamentally correct as the main means of explaining – or explaining away – Scandinavian place-names in England. The place-name (and personal name) evidence suggests a great number of Norse speakers in the area of the Danelaw, which suggests in turn a very sizeable migration during the settlement period. What 'very sizeable' means is, of course, extremely hard to say, and we should certainly not imagine that the Scandinavian settlers formed any sort of majority over the pre-resident Anglo-Saxons. But it is worth remembering that at exactly the same time when Halfdan was sharing out Northumbria among his followers, Scandinavian migrants were also making their way to Iceland, a considerably less fertile, less hospitable, and less accessible destination. It has been estimated that something in the order of 10-20,000 migrants made the journey to Iceland, and that within a few decades this population had expanded to perhaps 60-

80,000.[71] One would not, on the face of it, expect fewer migrants to have travelled to England than to Iceland, though estimates of the number of Norse migrants must remain only that – estimates, and highly speculative ones too.

But how far do the Old Norse place-names in England represent the establishment of new settlements and the colonization of new land, how far simply the re-naming of older settlements and estates – albeit by a sizeable Norse-speaking population? As we will see below, the evidence suggests elements of both processes, but something should be said in general terms to begin with. One feature of pre-Viking England seems to have been the existence of large or multi-vill estates, sometimes termed 'multiple estates': large possessions with a *caput* or estate-centre which was serviced and supported by surrounding and tributary estates.[72] Much of the evidence for supposed multiple estates is late (with Domesday Book often the earliest source for their reconstruction), and the model as a whole has been criticized on the grounds that some of its assumptions are non-falsifiable.[73] Nonetheless, it is generally agreed that the Scandinavian conquest of northern England did see the break-up of many or most of the large estates that may have existed (whether or not they fully matched the 'multiple estate' model), estates which had previously been in the control of the church, or the crown, or the aristocracy.[74] Such large estates were broken up, and parcelled out, into smaller units, often in private ownership rather than strict dependence – a development which can be subsumed under the broader label of 'manorialization', an important process in the late Anglo-Saxon landscape.[75] Scholars who have taken a minimalist view of Scandinavian settlement in England have often pointed to this fragmentation of estates as the fundamental mechanism by which Scandinavian place-names arose, and have attributed them (in Glanville Jones' words) to 'a small number of privileged newcomers who were allowed by their leader to impose a degree of intermediate authority over old established hamlets'.[76] As discussed above, the place-name material does not really allow for such a minimization of numbers – as the historian Patrick Wormald wrote, 'a mere change of landlords will not account for all the evidence', and one might in any case wonder whether the peasantry really would stay put when their lords had been driven off and their estates plundered – but nonetheless it is important to bear in mind this model of the break-up of estates as one of the basic processes by which land passed into Scandinavian hands in Viking Age England.[77]

It is also clear that this Viking Age privatization of land-holding led to a market in the buying and selling of land, as testified by a number of tenth-century charters.[78] Such a market is also implied in the *Anglo-Saxon Chronicle*'s account of the dispersal of the 896 army (partly quoted above): 'the Danish army divided, one force going into East Anglia and one into Northumbria; and those that were moneyless [*feohlease*] got themselves ships and went across the sea to the Seine'.[79] By the 890s, then, it seems that new arrivals in the Danelaw, if they did not possess family or lordly connections, required capital to buy themselves into land. Two northern hoards of the 870s, from Gainford [Durham] and Lower Dunsforth [WR], may well represent the *feoh* of members of Halfdan's army: these relatively modest hoards are composed exclusively of Anglo-Saxon silver pennies from south of the Humber (four at Gainford, and fifteen, or possibly more, at Lower Dunsforth), and it makes more sense to see these as imported Viking possessions than as the wealth of native Northumbrians.[80]

The break-up of large estates need not involve the colonization of new land – though it may do so – but it may well lead to new settlements, functioning as the centres of the new, smaller, independent estates, and generally 'filling in' the occupied landscape.[81] Moroever, while it is now doubted whether there was much 'virgin' land going spare in Viking Age England, land that had never previously been cultivated, it is certainly possible that one consequence of Scandinavian settlement was an intensification of land-working, with a return to cultivation of some land which had perhaps been farmed in the Romano-British period, but had reverted since then to non-cultivation.[82] As Margaret Gelling has pointed out, 'virgin' land is an unhelpful term in this discussion, and 'disused' or 'under-exploited' would be better: the issue is not whether or not an area of land had ever been cultivated before the arrival of the Vikings, but rather whether it was being intensively cultivated at the time.[83] We should not, however, discount the possibility of some genuinely virgin land being cleared for occupation: place-names in *þveit* 'clearing' would be an obvious group of names to consider, though there is not such a quantity of these to be found in Yorkshire as there is in Cumbria.[84] In the course of the two centuries after the Norman Conquest, a better recorded period, it has been calculated that the amount of arable land under cultivation in England increased by 35%, through changes in agricultural practice, intensification of land-use, and an associated 'drive to the margins'; and there is good evidence that such processes were in train from the ninth century onwards.[85]

We can now turn from the general to the particular, and review the main types of Old Norse place-names in Yorkshire. In terms of settlement names, there are three main categories: names in *–tun*, names in *–by*, and names in *–thorp*. A fourth category would be miscellaneous settlement names not falling into any of the previous three. Of course, it is not the case that we can correlate Scandinavian settlement with Norse place-names in any simple, one-to-one fashion, as if Scandinavians only lived in places with Old Norse names and Anglo-Saxons in places with Old English names; that is not likely to be how it happened, though place-names that incorporate personal names are indeed likely to indicate the habitation or possession of a specific individual.

The Old English word *tūn* ('estate, settlement') was an important and productive place-name element in the mid and later Anglo-Saxon period, denoting a settlement or estate of some consequence.[86] We find that the first element of Old

English *tūn* names is often an adjective or noun (for example Weston 'west *tun*' [WR], or Poppleton 'pebble *tun*' [WR]), but sometimes a personal name (for example, Ebberston 'Eadbriht's *tun*' [NR]); the assumption is that the person commemorated in the name was a significant occupier or possessor of the estate, perhaps its first recipient when it was granted out by the king. As a result of the Scandinavian conquest of the north, this second type seems to have increased very greatly in frequency, with an Old Norse personal name being the first element (for example, Staxton 'Stakkr's *tun*' [ER] and Towton 'Tófi's *tun*' [WR]), and this group of names has traditionally been labelled 'Grimston hybrids' in the scholarship on Scandinavian place-names: 'Grimston' because *Grímr* is a common Old Norse personal name occurring in these names, and 'hybrids' because the names have been construed as a combination of an Old Norse personal name and an Old English generic (*tūn*). These 'Grimston hybrids' are important, and more will be said about them in a moment.

We also find, though less frequently, *tun*-names with an Old Norse word as their first element (or specific): for example, Brayton 'broad *tun*' [WR], Carlton 'peasants' *tun*' [WR], and (Cold) Coniston 'king's *tun*' [WR]. In the great majority of cases, the Old Norse specific, or defining element, has a corresponding (cognate) word in the Old English language, and so the usual assumption is that this group of names, which have been labelled 'Carlton hybrids', are originally Old English names which have been Scandinavianized in their first element by the adaptation to, or substitution of, the cognate Old Norse word. So, it is hypothesized, the Old Norse first element *breiðr* ('broad') in Brayton was originally Old English *brād*, *karl* in Carlton was Old English *ceorl*, *konungr* in Coniston was Old English *cyning*, and so on.

If we were to take the Carltons as our guide, then the obvious conclusion would be that the Grimstons were also, originally, Old English names in *–tūn*, in which Old Norse substitution or adaptation has occurred in the first element; and this has been the common view of these names. There are a number of problems with this view, however. One is that a defining feature of the Carltons is that the Old Norse specific was (probably) cognate with the preceding Old English specific, but this cannot have been the case for the Grimstons, where the specific is an Old Norse personal name. And a more fundamental problem with the customary interpretation has been pointed out by David Parsons, which is how odd it would be if only Old English settlement names in *–tūn* should have been treated in this way (that is, with the substitution of an Old Norse personal name in the first element) and not other classes of Old English settlement name, such as those in *–hām*.[87] There are no 'Grimsham' hybrids, as it were, and what this suggests is that the Grimstons may not after all be adaptations of pre-existing Old English names in *–tūn*; rather, they may be wholly new names (albeit for pre-

101

existing settlements), with *tūn* having been adopted into the Norse place-name lexicon with a meaning of 'English village or estate' (or more fully, 'English village or estate transferred into the possession of a new, Scandinavian lord'). This would mean that the Grimstons, linguistically speaking, are wholly Old Norse names, and not in fact 'hybrids', with one element from Norse and one from English.

Regardless of these linguistic niceties, it remains the case that the Grimstons are the most likely category of name to indicate the Scandinavian take-over of English villages and estates. This take-over should primarily be thought of at the level of lordship – it does not mean that all the English residents and workers were driven out – though of course it is important to remember that an elite male is not likely to have settled on his own, as the only Dane in the village. As the better-documented settlement of Iceland indicates, and other migrations as well, elite males are likely to have brought with them a household of relatives and dependents, and perhaps also to have stimulated side-by-side settlement by other members of their kin-group.[88] That the great majority of Grimstons were pre-existing English settlements, and not new developments in the Viking Age, is indicated by a number of varied factors, all of which suggest a prosperous and well-established site: for example, their position on fertile soils, the frequency with which they became parishes, their relative wealth in Domesday Book, and their low rate of depopulation and desertion in the later Middle Ages.[89]

An obvious question is whose name is preserved as the first element in the Grimstons. Were Stakkr, Tófi, and the rest, the first Scandinavian recipients of these settlements? Does the corpus of Grimstons give us, in effect, a muster-roll for the officers of Halfdan's army? There is little external evidence that can cast light on this question, to confirm whether these names and settlements should be dated to the 870s, or to a later period, though it has been demonstrated that personal name types that develop after 1000 are not normally found in Scandinavian settlement names in England.[90] A possible counter-indication may be the small number of *tuns* where the personal name in the first element corresponds to the name of the person recorded in Domesday Book as possessing the estate in 1066.[91] If such *tuns* are not eleventh-century settlements – thus indicating the longevity of *tun* as a place-name-forming element – then this might suggest that the personal names in such place-names were unstable, and liable to replacement as possessor succeeded possessor. But the fact that this group of names is so small (relative to the enormous quantity of *tuns* recorded in Domesday Book) must indicate, in fact, that such replacement was exceptional rather than the norm, and indeed it cannot even be certain that the person named in Domesday Book and the person commemorated in the place-name were one and the same: since the elite of Anglo-Saxon England were very often named after their ancestors, it may possibly be an ancestor of the 1066 tenant who is commemorated in the place-name. There is only one possible Domesday example in this category from Yorkshire: in 1066 land at

Stainton [East Staincliffe wapentake, WR] was held by a man named Steinn, but this may well be a coincidence.[92] Stainton is a common Danelaw place-name (there are at least a dozen examples), which arose through the Scandinavianization of an originally Old English *stān-tūn* ('stone settlement', so possibly 'quarry'); in other words, the name is probably a Carlton hybrid and not a Grimston.[93] In terms of historical identification, a more intriguing and persuasive case, in that it features an unusual personal name, is that of Toulston [WR], 'Toglauss' *tun*'. The *Anglo-Saxon Chronicle* records that an earl with that name was killed in a battle at Tempsford in Bedfordshire in 917: some connection with the person commemorated in the place-name is plausible, though it may perhaps be a relative or descendant rather than the same person.[94] A further possibility is a connection between the Skurfa killed at the Battle of Tettenhall in 910 and Scruton [NR], 'Skurfa's *tun*', but the same personal name also occurs in the place-name Sheraton [Durham], and so this may be less likely, unless one imagines the same man holding both estates.[95]

On probability, the Scandinavians named in the Grimstons were most likely the early recipients of the estates after the Viking conquest.[96] What the analogue of Iceland suggests (where we have the twelfth- or thirteenth-century *Landnámabók*, or *Book of Settlements*) is that settlement names are likely to be named after – or at least, at a later period were thought to be named after – the very individuals who founded or first occupied the settlement.[97] This is no more than one would expect, of course, though a speculative permutation for some of the Grimstons might be that the name preserved is not always that of the Scandinavian founding father of 876, but sometimes that of a re-founding father – perhaps the lord who oversaw a village's transformation into a planned, nucleated settlement, or who built a new church.

In her standard study, Gillian Fellows-Jensen counts 42 Grimstons in Yorkshire that are recorded in Domesday Book.[98] These are widely distributed across the more fertile parts of the county, and with fewer in the West Riding than in the North and East. They also preserve a wide variety of Norse personal names, as follows (with the names being those suggested by Fellows-Jensen in her 1972 survey):

North Riding: Burneston (Brýningr), Burniston (Brýningr), Catton (Káti or Katti), Foston (Fótr), Fryton (Friði), Garriston (Gjarðarr), Grimston (Grímr), Kirby Sigston (Siggr), Moulton (Múli), Nawton (Nagli), Oulston (Ulfr), Scruton (Skurfa), Wigginton (Víkingr), Youlton (Jóli), *Þurulfestun* [lost] (Þórulfr)
East Riding: Low Catton (Káti or Katti), Flixton (Flík or Flikkr), Folkton (Folki), Foston on the Wolds (Fótr), *Fostun* [lost] (Fótr), Ganton (Galmr), Grimston (Grímr), Grimston Garth (Grímr), Hanging Grimston (Grímr),

Hilston (Hildulfr), Muston (Músi), Nafferton (Náttfari), North Grimston (Grímr), Rowlston (Róðulfr or Rólfr), Ruston Parva (Róarr), Scampston (Skammr or Skammel), Staxton (Stakkr)

West Riding: Barkston (Börkr), Brotherton (Bróðir), Fewston (Fótr), Flockton (Flóki), Grimston (Grímr), Royston (Róarr), Saxton (Saxi), Thurlstone (Þórulfr), Toulston (Toglauss), Towton (Tófi)

Of course, alternative explanations for some of these are possible (for example, the first element of Brotherton might be the common noun 'brother' rather than the name Bróðir, or the personal name in Garriston might be Gerðr or Gyrðr). There are also other candidates that might be added to the list, such as Flaxton and Claxton [both NR], two settlements north-east of York, close to the find-spot of the Bossall/Flaxton hoard: the etymology of Flaxton might be either 'flax settlement' or 'Flak's settlement', while Claxton appears as *Claxtorp* ('Klakkr's *thorp*') in Domesday Book, but as Claxton ('Klakkr's *tun*') in all later sources.[99] It is also to be suspected that 'Grimston' itself is a generic name, indicating a poorer quality settlement, rather than that there was an unusually large number of Scandinavian settlers called Grímr.[100] But in spite of the inevitable uncertainties, Fellows-Jensen's count is likely to give us a broadly reliable figure.

On the whole, as has been said, the Grimstons indicate prosperous settlements, so we should certainly point to them as being, as a category, among the places occupied or owned by the Scandinavian rural or landed elite. But the count of 42 Grimstons (or thereabouts) in Yorkshire is in fact quite a modest number (out of the total number of Old Norse place-names in the county), and it suggests that, in Yorkshire, we should not assume that English estates taken over by Scandinavians are confined only to those bearing Grimston names. That this is the case may be further suggested by the evidence of stone sculpture (a body of material which will be discussed more fully in subsequent chapters). The early tenth century, as we will see, saw a remarkable renaissance of stone sculpture in northern England, as many crosses and other monuments were erected in new, Scandinavian styles, presumably for new, Scandinavian patrons. But quite a lot of these sculptures are to be found in villages (in churches) which have Old English rather than Old Norse names – Middleton, with its famous warrior crosses, would be a good example. Forty years ago, Gillian Fellows-Jensen calculated that (according to the sculptures known at the time of her research) some 96 settlements existed in which sculptures in a Scandinavian style had been preserved: of these, 58 of the settlements bore English or British names, 15 bore pre-existing English or British names which had been Scandinavianized in some way, and only 23 bore names which were purely Scandinavian.[101]

Before we proceed to interpretation of these figures, a few methodological reflections are required. First, we should heed the warning that in place-name studies it is the general patterns that are important, rather than individual examples; we cannot use the distribution of English and Scandinavian names simply on a case-by-case basis, to say that Scandinavians settled at this site but not at that. Second, and similarly, we should recognize that, in any individual case, we cannot be certain that the patron of a particular monument was of Scandinavian origin – though it would seem extreme to deny the validity of the general paradigm. And third, we should note that it is not possible, chronologically, to correlate or calibrate finely the production of the sculpture and the coining of the Grimston names, though a suggested dating bracket for both between the late ninth century and early tenth would not be controversial. Nonetheless, and in spite of these qualifications, what the co-plotting of settlement names and Viking Age sculpture does seem to suggest, as a general principle at least, is that the early tenth-century Scandinavian elite was not confined to settlements bearing Scandinavian names; otherwise, one would have to argue that, for some unknown reason, settlements with continuing English names were excepted from the division of Northumbria by Halfdan and subsequent rulers, and remained in the possession of an English elite – an assumption which would also transgress the principle that one should not identify settlements as English or Norse simply according to the language of their name. Moreover, the sculptures tend to be found in prosperous and high-status settlements (which is just what one would expect, as the patronage of sculpture was a costly business) – settlements on a par with the wealth and status of the Grimstons.[102] All this combines to suggest, then, that while the Grimstons do indeed represent the category of place-names best indicative of elite Scandinavian take-over, this take-over was not restricted to settlements now bearing Grimston names. Why some settlements should have been re-named and not others is an interesting question, though in some cases medieval forms reveal that, while a settlement boasting Viking Age sculpture may be known by an English name in the present day, a Scandinavianized variant of the name was in fact current in the Middle Ages (so, for example, Stonegrave [NR] is recorded in Domesday Book in both an English and a Scandinavian form, *Stan-* and *Stein-*).[103] Since we only know of linguistic forms from documentary evidence (from the eleventh century and later), and since such documents are written in English or Latin but not in Norse, we may in any case suspect that our textual sources under-report the frequency of Scandinavian place-names, and especially of Scandinavianized variants of originally English names.[104]

The next category of names we must consider are those in –*by* 'farmstead, settlement, village'.[105] These are much more numerous in Yorkshire than the Grimstons: no fewer than 210 *by*-names are recorded in Domesday Book for Yorkshire, plus another 69 in later sources.[106] They are found most densely in the Vale of York and the North Riding.[107] Linguistically, the composition of Yorkshire's *by*-names is very interesting: Gillian Fellows-Jensen calculated that the ratio of Old Norse first elements to Old English was 92:8; and where a personal name forms the first element (which is the case in over half the examples), the Old Norse to Old English ratio rises further to 94:6.[108] The *by*-names thus boast an impressive cast of Scandinavian occupiers and owners, such as Ásgautr (Osgodby [ER]), Áslákr (Aislaby [NR]), Brandr (Brandsby [NR]), Dragmáll (Dromonby [NR]), Eymundr (Amotherby [NR]), Feitr (Faceby [NR]), Helgi (Hellaby [WR]), Ormr (Ormesby [NR]), Rauðr (Roxby [NR]), Róðmundr (Romanby [NR]), Styrr (Stearsby [NR]), Uglubárðr (Ugglebarnby [NR]), Þóraldr (Thoralby [NR]), and Þormóðr (Thormanby [NR]); and a few of the personal names are female, such as Gunnhildr (Gunby [ER]) and Hjalp (Helperby [NR]). There is also a healthy range of Old Norse words (appellatives) recorded as the first element of those *by*-names that do not include a personal name: for example, *brunnr* 'stream, spring' (Burnby [ER]), *ferja* 'ferry' (North Ferriby [ER]), *kona* 'woman' (Whenby [NR]), *kvern* 'mill' (Quarmby [WR]), *lundr* 'copse' (Lumby [WR]), *malmr* 'sandy field' (Melmerby [Halikeld wapentake, NR]), *mikill* 'great' (Mickleby [NR]), *skítr* 'dung' (Skidby [ER]), *skógr* 'wood' (Skewsby [NR]), *veðr* 'wether-sheep' (Wetherby [WR]), and *øfri* 'upper' (Earby [WR]). So the *by*-names demonstrate lexical and anthroponymic variety in their first elements. (The recurrent combination *kirkja* + *by* 'church *by*', will be discussed in the next chapter.)

What is more, some *by*-names preserve traces of diagnostically Old Norse grammatical inflexions, such as the genitive singular *–ar* preserved in Bellerby [NR] ('Belgr's *by*') and Helperby [NR] ('Hjalp's *by*'). The conclusion, therefore, must be that the *by*-names 'arose in a predominantly Norse-speaking environment'.[109] Lesley Abrams and David Parsons further observe, in their incisive review of these names, that settlements with *by*-names are typically less prosperous, and of lower status, than those with *tun*-names (both Grimstons and 'English' *tun*s, as it were), and therefore that 'they are unlikely on the whole to represent either the takeover of thriving English villages or the spoils seized by members of a (small, élite) conquering army'.[110] The *by*-names thus appear to give us evidence of substantial Scandinavian settlement at a level somewhat lower than that represented by the Grimstons and comparable settlements.

A very difficult question to answer, though, is whether, as a class, *by*-names indicate new settlements or not. The answer, probably, is that some do and some don't.[111] A number of the *by*s, like the *tun*s, are evidently new or alternative Norse names for pre-existing English settlements (most famously, Whitby [NR] was earlier *Streoneshalh*), and in a few cases there is even variation between *by* and *tun* in the early forms (for example, Coniston [ER] ('king's *tun*') is recorded as *Coningesbi* in Domesday Book).[112] But the element is not fundamentally a synonym for *tun*, and instead it is used frequently for isolated or dispersed settlements. Some of these, perhaps even many, may well be new places with new names, and the likelihood is that the *by*-names cover a variety of settlement histories, including the transfer of established estates, the break-up of old estates and the 'manorial' creation of new, smaller estates, and even, possibly, the opening-up of uncultivated land.[113]

In some ways it is easier to appreciate the characteristics of the *by*s if we contrast them with the *thorp*s. There are just over 150 *thorp*s in Yorkshire in Domesday Book.[114] Again, over half of the examples have a personal name as their first element, and the proportion of Old Norse personal names to Old English is 90:10. *Thorp*s have always been recognized as being, on the whole, lesser settlements than other place-name types, including *tun*s and *by*s: they often exist in simplex form (that is, the place-name is just 'Thorpe'), they have a high frequency of desertion in the later Middle Ages, and they have rarely grown into major settlements. A recent study of *thorp*-names in England, by Paul Cullen, Richard Jones, and David Parsons, has, however, made some startling, but nonetheless persuasive, claims as to what may have been distinctive and defining features of *thorp*s in the early Middle Ages.[115] In the 1960s and early 1970s Kenneth Cameron, in an influential series of studies, argued that both *by*s and *thorp*s were likely to be new settlements on new sites, and thus evidence for the ways in which the Scandinavian settlers colonized previously uncultivated land (or, we should say, under-exploited land); and he proposed that, as the *by*s were on better soil than the *thorp*s, the *thorp*s were likely to be secondary, dependent settlements.[116] Cullen, Jones, and Parsons have, however, turned Cameron's formulation on its head: modern soil taxonomies suggest that, on the whole, *thorp*s occupy superior sites to *by*s, not inferior ones, and that, furthermore, the characteristic soils on which the two place-name types are found are contrastive and complementary: the *thorp*s tend to be sited on soils more suitable for arable farming, the *by*s on soils more suitable for livestock. It may be for this reason that *thorp*s are especially prominent in the East Riding, and *by*s in the North Riding.[117] On top of this, there is usually a difference in the settlement morphology of the two sites (that is, in the typical shapes they assume in terms of street lay-out and so on): *thorp*s tend to be compact, nucleated settlements (and thus, ostensibly, deliberately planned), whereas *by*s are more often dispersed and 'polyfocal' (and thus, ostensibly, of more organic growth). The conclusions to which such findings point are clear: many *thorp*s appear to have been planned settlements for the purposes of arable farming, usually dependent on a more important manorial centre, and possibly linked with the revolutionary development of open-field farming that seems to have begun in the ninth century. *By*s, on the other hand, are not likely to have had quite such a unity of purpose or genesis, though they may often have had an association with livestock farming rather than arable. The great place-name scholar Eilert Ekwall, for example, believed that the *by*-names represented settlements occupied not by one but by several Scandinavian settlers and their households – an assumption that accords well with the dispersed nature of many of the *by*s.[118] Other scholars have also argued for a correlation, under certain circumstances, between Scandinavian immigration and dispersed settlement.[119]

We should hesitate, though, to see the origins of the *thorps*, let alone the innovation of open-field farming, as a singularly Scandinavian achievement.[120] Although there is little or no archaeological evidence for *thorps* being any older than 850 at the earliest, and most seem to have grown up, very rapidly, in the tenth and eleventh centuries, nonetheless it is very striking that a mapping of *thorps* does not respect the supposed line of the Danelaw: there is no distinction between 'English' and 'Scandinavian' territory. This agricultural revolution, then, if that is what the *thorp*-names indicate, seems to have been a shared one, and indeed even the place-name element may have been shared between Old English and Old Norse. But the high frequency of Norse personal names as the first element in *thorp*-names remains significant: in keeping with the evidence of the Grimstons and the *by*s, the Danelaw *thorps* may well indicate a greater, or more accelerated, tendency towards the individual ownership of small estates.

All three of our main types of settlement names, then, seem to reveal a transformation in patterns of land-holding, in which land was passing out of royal, or aristocratic, or ecclesiastical control into private possession on a much smaller scale, and Norse personal names very frequently form the first element for all three types of names. All three types of names appear to have arisen at a relatively early date (that is, well before the Norman Conquest), and among a Scandinavian speech community. As to whether these places with Scandinavian names represent new settlements or not, the best interpretation at present is that, on the whole, the Grimstons are likely to be older, well-established Anglo-Saxon settlements and the *thorps* are likely to be new developments, while the *by*s sit somewhere in the middle and cover a variety of possibilities.

Grimstons, *by*s, and *thorps* have been the three categories of names which have received most attention from scholars, but they by no means add up to form the full corpus of Scandinavian, or Scandinavian-influenced, settlement names in England, and in Yorkshire: a considerable number of settlements bear Old Norse names outside of these three categories. Fellows-Jensen, in her corpus of Scandinavian settlement names recorded in Domesday Book, counted a further 30 settlements named after some sort of habitation, and 104 named after a topographical feature.[121] The habitative category would include examples such as Lofthouse [WR] (< *lofthús* 'house with a loft'), Scorborough [ER] (< *skógar-búð* 'hut in a wood'), Upsall [NR] (< *upsalir* 'high dwellings'). The most common sub-types in the topographical category are settlements named after rivers and other features associated with water (for example, Ellerbeck [NR] (< *elri-bekkr* 'alders stream'), Nunburnholme [ER] (< *brunnum* 'at the streams', with *Nun-* a later addition), and the several settlements named Holme (< *holmr* 'higher ground among marshes, water-meadow') and Wath (< *vað* 'ford')); settlements named after hills and valleys (for example, Howe [NR] (< *haugr* 'mound, barrow, hill'), Sedbergh [WR] (< *set-berg* 'flat-topped hill'), and Thixendale [ER] ('Sigsteinn's valley')); and settlements named after woods and clearings (for example, Aiskew [NR] (< *eiki-skógr* 'oak wood'), Langthwaite [WR] (< *lang-þveit* 'long clearing'), and Rookwith [NR] (< *hrókr-viðr* 'rook wood')). In most of these cases the assumption must be that the topographical name arose from a feature of the landscape, and was extended or transferred to a nearby settlement.[122] Whether the settlements bearing Norse topographical names were newly established, or were pre-existing English settlements that were re-named, must be decided on a case-by-case basis.

So far this discussion has only attended to settlement names given in the Old Norse language. But there are other types of place-names that, if anything, testify even more strongly to the quantity and distribution of Norse speakers in Viking Age England – and thus are vital evidence for migration and settlement. The first of these is the very great number of pre-existing Old English names that have been 'Scandinavianized' in some way by Old Norse speakers. This phenomenon of Scandinavianization was touched on above in the context of Scandinavian-style stone sculpture occurring in villages with English names, but it merits further discussion. Although Old English and Old Norse were closely related languages, there were important differences between them, not least in phonology: for example, Old English had the sound *sh* where Old Norse had *sk*, *ch* where Old Norse had *k*, *d* where Old Norse had *ð*, *ā* where Old Norse had *ei*, *ēa* where Old Norse had *au*, and so on. Many such differences were systematic and predictable, and so in effect were regular distinctions in pronunciation and accent, just like (for example) the long and short *a* in southern and northern Modern English *bath* or *grass*.[123]

The consequence of this is that, in the mouths of Norse speakers, many English place-names underwent adaptation – either because the English name contained a sound not found in Norse, or because Norse speakers evidently perceived the correspondences between English pronunciation and their own. So, for example, the place-name Rawcliff Bank [NR] derives from Old English *rēad-clif* 'red cliff', and this English form is recorded in at least one source.[124] But later forms show that the first element of the name was Scandinavianized to the cognate Old Norse *rauðr*, and the modern form of the name descends from this Scandinavianized variant. The place-name Rawcliff(e)/Roecliffe occurs four other times in Yorkshire: it is only in the case of Rawcliff Bank that we possess written evidence for both the English and Scandinavianized forms, but we can assume with certainty that the same process of Scandinavianization has occurred in every case.[125] Countless other examples could be cited.[126] For instance, in Brayton [WR], as we have already seen, Old English *brād* 'broad' has been replaced by cognate Old

Norse *breiðr*; in Stainborough [WR], *stān* has been replaced by *steinn*; in Skirlaugh [ER], *scīr* 'bright' has been replaced by *skírr*; and so on.[127]

In all of these examples the Scandinavianized form contains a comprehensible Old Norse word, because a Norse term existed that was cognate with the original English one (*rauðr*, *breiðr*, *steinn*, *skírr*); we are back in the territory of the 'Carlton hybrids'. But in many cases where no Norse cognate existed, the process of Scandinavianization still occurred – as it must have done inevitably, as what it represents is an incoming speech community adapting names into more congenial sound patterns, better able to be articulated. The result in these cases, however, would either not be a comprehensible Norse word, or (by chance) an unrelated Norse word of doubtful suitability: for example, Lothersdale [WR] shows the substitution of Norse *ð* for English *d* (in Old English *loddere* 'beggar'), East Keswick [WR] shows the substitution of Norse *k* for English *ch* (in Old English *cēse* 'cheese'), and East and West Scrafton [NR] shows the substitution of Norse *sk* for English *sh* (in *scræf* 'cave').[128] Skipton [WR] gives a good example of how the resultant name might be inappropriate rather than simply meaningless: substitution of Norse *sk* for English *sh* (and shortening of the vowel) has caused an original 'sheep settlement' (Old English *scīp*) to become 'ship settlement' (Old Norse *skip*).[129] There is an abundance of Scandinavianized names in Yorkshire (as elsewhere in the Danelaw), and they serve as an unusually good window (or hearing loop) onto the Norse accents and speech habits to be heard in Viking Age England. We should therefore remind ourselves that, for such Scandinavianized variants to have entered into the written records of the region, they must have been widely used and widely accepted; there were, presumably, many more Scandinavianized forms that existed only as spoken variants and were never recorded in writing. Scandinavianized names supply a striking indication, then, of the strength and influence of the Old Norse speech community in Viking Age Yorkshire; for Old Norse speakers to have affected permanently the pronunciation of many English place-names, one assumes that they must have been numerous and (near-)ubiquitous.

Let us move on, finally, to the significance of place-names that are not settlement names at all, often grouped under the label of 'minor names': field-names, topographical names, and river-names. (Street names will be discussed in Chapter 6.) There has been a good deal of excellent research on the field-names of the Danelaw, though relatively little of this has been focused on Yorkshire.[130] Field-names are important because they are likely to have arisen in a 'bottom-up' fashion, through the name-giving practices of the local agricultural population rather than through the 'top-down' administrative labelling of a small elite. Field-names are thus able to give us access to the language, or at least the vocabulary, of a particular locality, and if that language should be heavily Old Norse, or Norse-influenced, then it would seem to indicate the common use of Norse among the farmers and workers in that area.[131] The snag is that field-names tend to be recorded late, usually not before the twelfth or thirteenth century at the earliest, at which point Old Norse will not have still been a living language in England; so we must use the field-names as a pointer to reconstruct the language of the area at whatever earlier point the lexicon of field-names came into existence. A corpus of Yorkshire field-names is readily available in A.H. Smith's English Place-Name Society volumes, though only for the West Riding did Smith organize this material geographically. For the heavily Scandinavianized North and East Ridings Smith notes that Norse elements are common in the field-names of the region, including (but not limited to): *deill* 'portion of land', *engr* 'meadow, pasture', *flöt* 'level ground', *garðr* 'enclosure', *gata* 'road', *haugr* 'mound, barrow, hill', *höfuð* 'head', *holmr* 'higher ground among marshes, water-meadow', *kelda* 'spring', *leirr* 'mud', *lundr* 'copse', *marr* 'pool', *vrá* 'corner, nook', and *þveit* 'clearing'.[132] The heavy Norse influence on the field-naming vocabulary of the region is clear enough.

A study of the names of minor topographical features – hills, crags, woods, and so on – would reveal the same pervasiveness of Norse-derived vocabulary, at least in some parts of the county. Such Norse-derived minor names are innumerable, and can probably be appreciated better from large-scale Ordnance Survey maps than from the English Place-Name Society county volumes. Again, the point is not that these names must have been given by Norse speakers in the Viking Age – though some of them may well have been – but rather that they bear forceful witness to the Norse influence exerted on vocabulary and name-giving in Yorkshire, an influence that does in turn bear witness to the major population of Norse speakers that must have existed at one time. But one category that may possibly indicate early Scandinavian land-taking is an interesting group of names whose second element is *dalr* ('dale', perhaps sometimes replacing earlier Old English *dæl*, of identical meaning) and whose first element is a Norse personal name. Examples include Blakes Dale ('Bleikr's dale') and Thixendale ('Sigsteinn's dale') in the East Riding, Garsdale ('Garðr's dale') in the West Riding, and a whole raft of names in the North Riding: Apedale (Ápi), Aysdale (Ási), Bransdale (Brandr), Fangdale (Fangi), Gundale (Gunni), Raisdale (Røyðr), and Rosedale (Russi).[133] These names possibly indicate Scandinavian lords assuming authority over a wider extent of land than simply a single, closely delimited settlement. Just occasionally we have a pairing of names at the same place between dale-names and other types: Commondale and Coldman Hargos [NR] were earlier *Colemandale* and *Colemanergas* ('shielings'), both preserving the Hiberno-Norse name Colman.[134]

River-names form something of a special case of topographical names. The names of rivers and streams possess remarkable linguistic 'inertia', and historically have been very slow to change: for this reason many rivers in England, especially major ones, still bear Celtic names – or even pre-Celtic, non-Indo-European ones.[135] So it is all the more notable that a considerable number of water-courses in Yorkshire bear Norse names, for example the Brennand, the Rawthey, and the Skell in the West Riding ('the burning one', 'the red river', and 'the resounding one'), and the Bain, the Greta, and the Seph in the North Riding ('the straight one', 'the rocky river', and 'the calm one').[136] In addition, there is a host of names whose second element is 'beck' (Old Norse *bekkr*) and whose first element is Norse too, for example Arkle Beck, Costa Beck, and Thordesay Beck, all in the North Riding ('Arnkell's beck', 'the choice river', and 'Þórdís' river'). For Norse river-names to be established, a necessary precondition would seem to be a widespread and substantial population of Norse speakers; like field-names, river-names do not fit easily into a model of name-giving which foregrounds elite agency.

With field-names, and topographical names such as river-names, we have, as noted, left settlement names behind, and such names are not in themselves onomastic evidence for settlement. But indirectly, as has been said, they are exceptionally important, as pointers to a substantial Norse-speaking population in early medieval Yorkshire. The place-name evidence is vast, and of enormous value for any study of Viking Age England. Here, it has been interrogated to see what it reveals of migration and settlement; in the next two chapters, we will investigate more what it can tell us about cultural and social history.

CONTACT AND CONVERSION

Peoples and Languages

In cultural terms, a concentration on the Scandinavians in Yorkshire is only half of the picture: what the region witnessed in the Viking Age was a pervasive, and creative, meeting of cultures, between English and Scandinavian. In this chapter we will therefore focus on questions of contact and cultural exchange. We will consider some of the evidence for ethnic diversity in Viking Age Yorkshire, and examine how the contact between cultures and peoples may have played out in the spheres of language, art, and identity: how the population of Viking Age Yorkshire spoke and listened, how they expressed themselves, and how they thought of themselves (and other people thought of them). And we will look closely at the conversion of the Vikings in England: the religious and ecclesiastical sphere was, of course, one of the most important contexts for the contact and interaction between the incoming Scandinavians and the pre-resident Anglo-Saxons.

In general, there is likely to have been a good deal of give-and-take between the English and Scandinavian communities in Viking Age Yorkshire, as in the Danelaw more broadly. Some features of both Scandinavian and English culture persisted, and some perished; the Scandinavians took on certain aspects of English culture, and vice versa; and new, 'hybrid' forms evolved, unique products of Anglo-Scandinavian contact, which had not previously existed in either culture. But as we will see, this does not mean that the two peoples quickly became indistinguishable, fully assimilated into a new 'Anglo-Scandinavian' culture; rather, some markers of Scandinavian culture and identity seem to have endured (as also of English), which were no doubt reinforced through the tenth century by further new arrivals from Scandinavia.

As we approach the question of culture contact, however, it is important not to think of either the Scandinavian side or the English side as unitary and homogenous. In terms of people, religion, and culture – and indeed in its very genesis – pre-Viking Northumbria was already an amalgam, the mixed product of Britons (Celts) and Anglo-Saxons.[1] The British kingdom of Elmet, in west

Yorkshire, persisted into the seventh century, and references to Britons occur in Northumbrian legal texts as late as the early eleventh century.[2] Our earliest Northumbrian poet, Caedmon of Whitby (late seventh century), bears a Celtic name, as do the early Northumbrian saints Cedd and Chad, while the Lindisfarne Gospels, the apogee of early Northumbrian art, proclaim their dual heritage on every decorated page. Nor were the Scandinavian settlers of a single origin, and although there were some cultural traits that were shared across the so-called 'Viking diaspora', others were more restricted and regional.[3]

The varied nature of the Scandinavian settlers in Northumbria is well demonstrated by a particular group of 'ethnic' place-names. Yorkshire boasts no fewer than four settlements named Normanby ('the *by* of the Northmen or Norwegians'), one Normanton, three Danbys ('the *by* of the Danes'), two Denbys and one Denaby (with apparently the Old English form *Dene* rather than the Norse *Danir*), and one Danthorpe.[4] The usual explanation for these names is that they identify groups who were atypical of their location rather than typical: in other words, not many Norwegians were to be encountered in the vicinity of a Normanby, and hence the ethnicity of the occupants stood out. There may be some truth in this, at least for some names, but alternative explanations can easily be imagined: for example, the Danbys and Normanbys might function more as a generic type of name, a set formula ('settlement established/taken over by Danes/Norwegians'), and less as individual names arising independently from local observation. The existence of three Inglebys in Yorkshire ('the *by* of the English') indicates that it cannot have been the case that the ethnicity itself was a rarity in the area; perhaps the Inglebys were noteworthy because places named in *by* were not customarily in English possession.

But names such as Danby and Normanby do at least indicate a perceived distinction between Danes and Norwegians, and that both were present in Viking Age Yorkshire; it is unlikely that the Norse speakers who used the terms *Danir* and *Norðmenn* regarded them as synonymous. The questions naturally arise as to what were the relative proportions of Danes and Norwegians in the Scandinavian settlement, whether we can now distinguish one from another at this distance of time, and if so, whether their distribution can be mapped. The standard view, ever since the nineteenth century, has been that the settlement of the east of England was effected primarily by Danes, and that of the north-west by Norwegians, often arriving via Ireland or the Scottish isles.[5] There seems little reason to doubt that this is fundamentally correct, not least on the grounds of geographical proximity. Denmark was, during the Viking Age, by some measure the most populous and powerful part of Scandinavia, and hence the most likely origin for migrants to the east of England – though the presence of a strong Norwegian element east of the Pennines has also long been recognized. The distribution in Scandinavia of the brooch types found in England indicates that migrants to the Danelaw had

114

geographically diverse origins, though parallels with Denmark are most prominent for the small brooches, and with Norway for the more limited body of oval brooches.[6]

Philologists and place-name scholars have long identified a body of so-called 'test-words' which are held to be indicative of the Old West Norse language (Norwegian) but not Old East Norse (Danish), and vice versa, though over the years the diagnostic validity of some of these words has been queried.[7] Top of the list as a Danish test-word must be the settlement generic *by*: place-names in *–by* are usually considered to be a sign of Danish rather than Norwegian influence, as Modern English forms in *–by* more plausibly derive from Old East Norse *–bý* than from Old West Norse *–bær*.[8] Supposed Norwegian test-words include *þveit* 'clearing', *búð* 'booth' (as opposed to Old East Norse *bóth*), and *brekka* 'slope' (as opposed to Old East Norse *brink*). Also attributed to Norwegian influence, as indicating Vikings coming from the west, are elements that have been borrowed into Norse from Goidelic Celtic, such as *ærgi* 'shieling, hill-pasture' and *cros* 'cross' (Goidelic being the branch of the Celtic languages represented by Irish, Gaelic, and Manx, in contradistinction to the Brittonic Celtic of Welsh, Cornish, and Breton). We cannot, of course, interpret the distribution of such test-words in any simple fashion, assuming that a Danish generic indicates a Danish settlement and a Norwegian generic a Norwegian one; rather, what we are observing is the relative proportion and distribution of the contributing elements to the onomasticon or name-hoard of Viking Age England. Some personal names are also thought to be more typical of Danish origin, such as Friði, Tófi, and Tólir (in Firby [ER], Towton [WR], and Tollesby [NR]), and some of Norwegian, such as Belgr, Hákr, and Hjalp (in Bellerby [NR], Haxby [NR], and Helperby [NR]); here, we may more willingly correlate onomastic provenance and settlement history.[9] Taken altogether, the distribution of Danish and Norwegian test-words and names in Yorkshire does suggest – as one might in any case have expected – a heavier Norwegian influence the further west (or north-west) in the county one goes.[10]

The Danbys, Normanbys, and Inglebys listed above do not, in fact, exhaust the category of ethnic place-names in Viking Age Yorkshire. Also to be found are two Irtons and one Irby ('the *tun/ by* of the Irish'), and two Birkbys ('the *by* of the Britons'), as well as some unique names: Ferrensby [WR] ('the *by* of the *Færeyingr* [man from the Faroe Islands]'), and Flotmanby [ER], where the first element is *flotmenn* ('sea-men, pirates'), an Old English term for the Vikings.[11] A number of names indicate Frisian affinities: Firsby [WR] seems to be 'the *by* of the Frisians', a name complemented by Ferry/Water Fryston [WR] and Monk Fryston [WR], 'the *tun* of the Frisians'.[12] It is possible that these *tun*-names are pre-Viking in origin (we know, for example, that Frisian merchants were present in eighth-century York), but a Viking Age origin is also highly plausible: from the mid ninth century onwards there had been a Scandinavian presence in Frisia, and the *History of St*

Cuthbert describes Ubba, at the time of the capture of York in 866, as 'duke of the Frisians [*dux Fresciorum*]'.[13]

To complete this ethnic census of Viking Age Yorkshire, we should also attend further to personal names, and note the small but significant presence of persons bearing Continental Germanic names: such names occurring as the first element of place-names include Arnold, Fulcard, and possibly Folcward (in a lost *Arnodestorp* [NR], Foggathorpe [ER], and Fockerby [WR]).[14] To complement this place-name evidence, we should recall the observation made in Chapter 2 that the Viking kings of York seem to have imported Frankish moneyers to implement their coinage programme; although the pre-Athelstan York coinage did not bear moneyers' names, in the mid tenth century we do find Continental Germanic names such as Durant and Ingelgar.[15]

The Irish, or at least Goidelic, element in Viking Age Yorkshire should be considered in more detail. Onomastically, this element can be observed in personal names, in vocabulary, and even, possibly, in syntax. To take the last point first: a small number of so-called 'inversion compounds' have been suggested in Yorkshire, in the North Riding and the north-west of the West Riding.[16] Inversion compounds follow the Celtic sequence of generic followed by specific, rather than the usual Germanic sequence of specific followed by generic (so, 'settlement-Thorstein's' rather than 'Thorstein's settlement'), and they often show a combination of Goidelic and Scandinavian vocabulary and personal names in their elements; their origin seems to lie in the linguistic contact between Norse speakers and Goidelic speakers in the early Middle Ages, in Ireland or more probably the Western Isles.[17] The suggested Yorkshire examples – *Stainpapan* [WR] ('Papan's stone'?), *Hillegrime* [WR] ('Grímr's hill'?) and four others – are all lost names, and all have been viewed with some scepticism.[18]

More certain is the evidence of personal names and place-name elements, though again it is probably better to identify such names and elements as generally Celtic or Goidelic rather than specifically Irish, as the influence and the persons may have been reaching northern England from Scotland and the Western Isles, or even the Isle of Man, as well as from Ireland.[19] Place-name elements, as noted already, include *cros* 'cross' and the important *ærgi* 'shieling, hill-pasture'. Goidelic personal names preserved in Yorkshire place-names include Dubgilla (in Duggleby [ER]), Fíach (in Feizor [WR]), Máelmuire (in Melmerby [Hang West wapentake, NR]), and many others.[20] 'Goidelic' names overlap as a category with 'Norwegian' names, and their distribution pattern shows a particular density in the Craven area of the West Riding, and in Wensleydale and Swaledale in the North Riding. Such a distribution, like the distribution of 'Norwegian' names more broadly, suggests overland movement across the Pennines, though it is also the case, of course, that York and the Irish Sea region were linked by sea as well as land: the presence of, for example, a number of *ærgi* place-names in the East

116

Riding suggests that we should not regard all Goidelic traces as simply an eastward extension from the more Celticized north-west.[21]

There is also, of course, a strong Irish signature in the material culture of Viking Age Yorkshire. Irish influence can be discerned on stone sculpture in certain parts of the county, a form of evidence to be discussed later in this chapter.[22] Among the small items that have been found by metal-detectorists, ringed pins in particular (found in considerable abundance) are taken to reflect Irish culture, as the only evidence we have for their manufacture comes from Dublin; and at least one type of strap-end also has a likely origin in the Irish Sea region.[23] Many of the early tenth-century hoards also reveal Irish connections: broad-band silver arm-rings (found in the hoards of Cuerdale, Goldsborough, and the Vale of York) are a diagnostic Irish feature, and the Cuerdale hoard also contained, to date, the only so-called 'bullion-rings' to be found outside of Ireland.[24] Another hoard that illustrates perfectly this Hiberno-Norse axis is that found recently at Bedale [NR], in 2012 [Figure 12].[25] This also contained a silver arm-ring, as well as a gold-inlaid sword pommel, silver neck-rings, a penannular brooch converted to hack-silver, and over 30 silver ingots. There were no coins.

An obvious question, therefore, is how well these indicators of cultural and settlement history can be correlated with the datable facts of political history. Rægnald's conquest of 919 initiated thirty years of especially close political ties between the Viking kingdoms of York and Dublin, and we know from the *History of Saint Cuthbert* that (as one would have expected) Hiberno-Norse kings such as Rægnald rewarded their followers with estates in Northumbria. Should most traces of Irish (or Goidelic) cultural influence therefore be dated to after 919, or should we imagine that the York-Dublin connection merely served to strengthen existing influences? It is very clear that links between York and Dublin pre-dated the arrival of the grandsons of Ivar, as proven spectacularly by the contents of the Cuerdale hoard (c.905-10), which combined metalwork from Ireland with coins from York. This is also suggested by the rule in York of the obscure Sigeferth, if the king who issued coins in York (c.895-900) is, as seems likely, the same figure as the earl who left Dublin with his followers in 893 and the *piraticus* who raided south from Northumbria in the same year. Indeed, the leaders of the Great Army that conquered Northumbria had Irish connections from the very beginning, being part of the mighty 'dynasty of Ivar', and David Dumville has argued that we should recognize the 'essential continuity' in political leadership that existed among the Scandinavians in Northumbria from the mid ninth century through to the mid tenth.[26] It may therefore be a mistake to date Irish influence primarily (let alone exclusively) to the period after 919, as is often done, for example, in stone sculpture studies; fundamental Irish connections pre-dated the arrival of Rægnald and his followers.[27]

The 942 poem in the *Anglo-Saxon Chronicle* (quoted in Chapter 3) did, however, wish to claim that there was a clash of cultures between the settled, Christian Danes of Halfdan's settlement, and the new, aggressive (and, moreover, pagan) Hiberno-Norse, a clash which only West Saxon conquest could resolve. Did Rægnald and successive kings re-allocate Yorkshire estates to their supporters, so that relations were strained between the newly-endowed elite and those who had been settled for nearly half a century? Did non-elite migration follow eastwards in the wake of Rægnald's conquest (as it seems to have followed westwards in the wake of Halfdan's), or were the settlement consequences of Rægnald's conquest more like those of Cnut's in the early eleventh century, involving only a small military elite? If we are trying to identify place-names that reflect the consequences of the cross-Pennine, York-Dublin axis of the first half of the tenth century, then our best candidates are likely to be those place-names containing a Goidelic personal name, and perhaps also place-names in *ærgi*.[28] Irby and the two Irtons also remain suggestive place-names. Moreover, the evidence for Goidelic name-giving and culture persists into the eleventh century, as we will see in a later chapter, and indicates that the connection between Ireland and Scandinavian Yorkshire was an enduring and important one; it did not cease with the break between the kingships of York and Dublin.[29]

In terms of language contact, though, it is the interactions between Old Norse and Old English – or rather, between their speakers – that must claim our attention. Evidence and logic suggest that both Old English and Old Norse were widely spoken for a lengthy period of time in Viking Age Yorkshire; the region was a bilingual one in the sense that two languages were spoken side-by-side.[30] The two languages were structurally close, owing to their ancestry and evolution. They shared a great deal of vocabulary, which often differed only (if at all) in regular sound correspondences, though differences in inflexional morphology (that is, grammatical endings) were much greater. As a consequence of such similarity, and as noted in the previous chapter, speakers of the two languages were probably mutually intelligible, at least for pragmatic purposes.[31] Such intelligibility is likely to have both facilitated social interaction and, at the same time, maintained difference and group identities; neither the English nor the Scandinavians were obliged to give up their own language and learn the others'.

Both the linguistic and social situations were thus radically different from those in the fifth and sixth centuries, when the immigrant Anglo-Saxons came into contact with the native, Celtic-speaking Britons. Old English and Brittonic were in no way mutually intelligible, and it was the subaltern Britons who switched to the language of their conquerors – and did so permanently. It is certainly possible that, in the ninth and tenth centuries, some of the English acquired more than a passive competence in Old Norse, but a substantial language shift is not plausible, not least because English continued to be spoken throughout the period, and it was,

118

eventually, to be the speakers of Norse who gave up their language – a shift that was probably completed sometime in the eleventh century (or conceivably a little later in some parts). We might speculate in particular that acquisition of a more active competence in Old Norse may have been the case in mixed households, where an English woman had married a Scandinavian man. If this was the case, and if the children of such a marriage grew up with Norse as a native language (in spite of, or in addition to, English being their mother's tongue), then we need actually to posit an increase in the number of Norse speakers over time, rather than a decrease.

In the previous chapter we noted the common phenomenon whereby English place-names were 'Scandinavianized' in their phonological form: the adaptation of *Scīptūn* to Skipton, and so on. The regularity of such adaptations is one of our best evidences for mutual intelligibility between speakers of the two languages, as it indicates that (for example) Norse speakers perceived that their *sk* corresponded with English *sh*, their *ei* with English long *ā*, and so on.[32] In some cases, as we have seen, our records reveal that two variants of the same name (an original English one, and a Scandinavianized one) co-existed side-by-side, thus giving us a glimpse of the two speech communities that were present in Viking Age Yorkshire: as already noted, the place-name Stonegrave [NR], for example, is sometimes recorded in the English form *Stān-*, sometimes in the Norse form *Stein-*.[33] This co-existence of variant pronunciations must have been a common feature of Danelaw speech, and the persistence of the original English form implies again that there was not a widespread shift to Norse on the part of the English population. Such co-existence also suggests that the two languages may have enjoyed roughly equal prestige, or at least that Old Norse did not enjoy much greater prestige than Old English on account of the Scandinavian conquest – which in any case only survived in untroubled form till 927. There are no indications that the conquests of Athelstan and his successors had any profound effect on the spoken language of the northern Danelaw, and the Norse language did not suffer any sudden decline after the termination of Scandinavian rule in York.

So far we have only been talking about spoken language. The situation with regards to written language was somewhat different, for a variation in function seems to have existed between the two languages. The language of literacy in pre-Viking Northumbria was Latin. In the south of England, and largely as a result of King Alfred's initiatives, Old English came to be used increasingly as a written language in the late ninth century and the first half of the tenth century. But this Alfredian movement did not reach Northumbria until later in the tenth century, after the West Saxon conquest; the few examples of historical writing from mid tenth-century Northumbria, as noted earlier, are still in Latin, not Old English (the annals preserved in the *History of the Kings* and Roger of Wendover, and the *History of St Cuthbert*, if it has a tenth-century core).[34] One of the consequences of this is that Old Norse remained an oral language, and it did not come to be written down in the Viking kingdom of York: there was no pre-existing tradition of vernacular manuscript literacy in the Roman alphabet either in Viking Age Scandinavia (for Old Norse) or in Northumbria (for Old English), and so it is no surprise that Old Norse did not develop as a written language. By the time a vernacular language did start to be written down in manuscripts in the north of England, that language was Old English, following the incorporation of the region into the kingdom of England. The only certain exception to this rule – that Old Norse was never written in the Roman alphabet in the Viking kingdom of York – is the raven-coinage of Olaf Guthfrithson, which proclaims Olaf as CVNVNC, 'king', in the Old Norse language.[35] Although it is only one word, this use of Old Norse is unambiguous and highly significant – one powerful indication out of several of Olaf's apparent desire to set up his northern kingdom as a serious rival to the West Saxons' southern one.

The Scandinavians did, of course, possess a tradition of literacy in runes (carved on stone and wood) rather than in the Roman alphabet (written in manuscripts), though the majority of the runic inscriptions from Scandinavia post-date the Viking settlements in England. But the corpus of Old Norse runic inscriptions from England is meagre.[36] The north-west of England boasts the greatest number (though still well within single figures), whereas at the time of writing only one certain Norse inscription is known from Yorkshire – and that is fragmentary and unreadable. This is from Skelton in Cleveland [NR], and occurs on an eleventh-century church sundial [Figure 17]. The extant and legible part of the inscription reads, in Norse runes, **ibil:ok**.[37] The last two runes clearly indicate Old Norse *ok* 'and', but the preceding text is wholly cryptic. What is provocative about the Skelton inscription is first, how late it is (eleventh-century), and second, the fact it is accompanied by an (equally inscrutable) inscription in the Roman alphabet, which may conceivably be in Old Norse rather than Old English or Latin.[38] If it is, then it is the only known example of Old Norse being used in a Roman inscription, and it dates from as much as a century after the end of Scandinavian rule in York; so it is puzzling indeed. A few other inscriptions, or apparent inscriptions, have been ventured as further examples of the use of Norse runes in Yorkshire, but none have been found convincing: a rune-inscribed slate from Settle [WR] is almost certainly a modern copy, a lost stone from Thornaby-on-Tees [NR] may or may not have carried an (un-interpretable) inscription, and the runes on the boulder from Pippin Castle near Harrogate [WR] (if that is what they are) are unparalleled in their size and roughness.[39]

The lack of written texts in Old Norse and Old English means that we have a crippling shortage of evidence in any attempts to reconstruct the linguistic history of the Danelaw. Everything is off-stage, as it were, and we receive only a very partial picture of both the nature of the Old Norse language as it existed in Northumbria, and the effect of the two languages on one another; our best evidence for the Old Norse language in England – its phonology, morphology, and vocabulary – comes to us from the fossilized forms of place-names. When the curtain rises again, and written texts from the north begin to be a little more common, what we see are the products of language contact, not the process itself.[40] So, for example, the Old English glosses added to the Lindisfarne Gospels in the late tenth century contain a number of loanwoards from Old Norse, indicating how Northumbrian Old English had been influenced by the speech of the Scandinavians.[41] Another eleventh-century sundial, from Aldbrough in Holderness [ER], reads as follows: 'Ulf ordered the church to be erected for himself [HANVM] and for Gunnwaru's soul' [Figure 18].[42] This reveals that the Norse pronoun *hanum* 'him' had been borrowed into the local form of English: there is no evidence for this from elsewhere in the Danelaw, although the third person plural pronouns in Modern English (*they*, *them*, and *their*) are Norse-derived. It also seems very likely that the quotidian interaction of the two closely related languages, Norse and English, contributed to the erosion and re-structuring of the main aspect in which the two languages were most dissimilar, namely their inflexional endings (so, for example, the word 'stone' had different plural endings in Old English and Old Norse – English *stānas* versus Norse *steinar* – even though we know from place-names that the two speech communities had no difficulty in construing the phonological correspondence *ā* – *ei* in the stem of the word). The loss of inflexions in English (and the associated system of grammatical gender) is the most important change to have occurred between Old English and Modern English. This change happened in the late Anglo-Saxon and early post-Conquest period, and it happened earliest in the north of England. The presence of Old Norse speakers in the north may not have been the cause of this fundamental change in the nature of English, but it seems indisputable that they re-inforced and accelerated whatever changes had begun.[43]

Thus there was indeed give-and-take between Scandinavians and Anglo-Saxons in the linguistic sphere, as there was in many aspects of culture. Contact between the two speech communities affected their languages considerably; but it did not, at least in the Viking Age, lead to the development of a single 'Anglo-Scandinavian' language. What finally emerged in the north of England, in the later medieval period, was recognizably English; but it was a heavily Scandinavianized English, bearing a massive imprint from the immigrant language, in terms of vocabulary, phonology, and even grammatical re-structuring.

Conversion and Christianization

From the ninth century onwards, the Vikings rapidly acquired the reputation of being the destroyers of churches and the enemies of Christianity. But as the evidence (or non-evidence) of burials surveyed in the previous chapter suggests, as well as the stone sculptures mentioned so far in this book, there are ample indications that the Scandinavians in England became in time – and, it may be, in quite quick time – observers of Christian practices and patrons of the church. In this section we will therefore consider the movement of the Scandinavians in Northumbria from paganism to Christianity.

Historians often distinguish two phases in a community's adoption of Christianity: the initial profession of acceptance, often marked by baptism, and the more gradual changes in practice and worldview. These two phases have been variously termed conversion and Christianization, or 'conversion moment' and 'conversion period'.[44]

We should begin with paganism, though. Norse paganism was, of course, polytheistic, with the most important gods being Odin, Thor, Freyr, and the goddess Freyja.[45] But it was not systematic, and it possessed neither a single orthodoxy nor the institutional structures required to impose one; in this, it was radically unlike Christianity, and later accounts of Norse myth which present a consistent and tidy narrative (beginning with Snorri Sturluson's *Edda* in the thirteenth century) are likely to have been over-systematized by a misleading analogy with Christianity. In the Viking Age, beliefs and rituals varied from period to period and place to place, and on the whole mythological stories were fluid.[46] Christianity was beginning to be felt in Scandinavia, of course, but the widespread conversion of the region post-dated the settlements in England: although there had been some Christian contacts in the early ninth century, the conversion period really begins in Denmark in the mid tenth century, in Norway in the later tenth century, and in Sweden in the eleventh century.[47]

Different gods had different associations and cults. Some were closely connected with fertility and agriculture – Freyr, Freyja, and Thor, among others – but the gods of warfare were Tyr and above all Odin, the 'Allfather' of the Norse pantheon. Odin was the god of warriors and aristocrats – and also of poets – and Neil Price has argued that "Becoming a Viking' may not therefore have been simply a rapid route to wealth or improved status [...] It could also have constituted a profoundly religious act'.[48]

This is worth bearing in mind as we think about Viking attacks on western Europe, and on England in particular. Vikings attacked churches and monasteries because of their wealth, both in terms of treasure and, potentially, clerics to sell as slaves. But to attend only to the material dimension of such raids is not enough: contemporary perceptions that such attacks were religiously motivated, or at least were to be best understood in terms of religious conflict and religious meaning, should also be respected. From the start, one of the favoured Anglo-Saxon terms for the Vikings was 'heathen' (Old English *hæðen*, Latin *paganus*), as if their heathenism was among the most conspicuous things about the Vikings; and similar usages can be found among the other peoples on the receiving end of Viking attack.[49] As we saw in Chapter 2, Christian writers such as Alcuin reached either for an apocalyptic model to make sense of their persecution at the hands of the Scandinavian raiders (with the Vikings as a sign of the end of the world) or else for a covenantal one (with the Vikings as the scourge of God's elect); and Christian commentators were well aware of Jeremiah's Old Testament warning that a pagan evil would come forth from the north.[50] A number of late ninth-century Anglo-Saxon wills state that a bequest is made to a church or monastery 'for as long as baptism may endure in the island of the English people' – a clause which suggests an anxiety that Christianity in England might be entirely wiped out.[51]

There can be no doubt about the great harm that the Vikings did to the English church in the north and east of the country.[52] This harm and destruction took place both during the period of raiding, in the late eighth and early ninth century, and also during the period of conquest and settlement, in the later ninth century. As noted in Chapter 2, Viking Age graves in Norway have yielded many items of ecclesiastical treasure, plundered from the churches of Britain and Ireland, ranging from precious book-clasps to even bishops' crosiers.[53] Many pieces, no doubt, were chopped up, shared out, and melted down. And the tribulations of the subsequent period of conquest were even more severe for the churches of northern and eastern England: according to the *History of St Cuthbert*, the Vikings of the Great Army 'demolished and despoiled the churches' in the areas they conquered, while Symeon of Durham wrote that they 'destroyed monasteries and churches far and wide with sword and fire, and when they departed they left nothing except roofless walls'.[54] It is true that some churches had earlier faced pressures of 'secularization' in the pre-Viking period, from kings and aristocrats, but this was on nothing like the scale experienced in the ninth century.[55]

The evidence for ecclesiastical disruption is considerable. Churches and monasteries were vacated or abandoned, temporarily or even permanently, with the continuation of normal ecclesiastical life seemingly impossible. In all the Anglo-Saxon kingdoms conquered by the Scandinavians, there were some bishoprics – otherwise to be reckoned as 'among the most durable institutions in medieval Europe', in the words of Patrick Wormald – that simply disappeared, never to re-emerge (Hexham in Northumbria, Leicester in Mercia, *Dommoc* in East Anglia).[56] York was the only episcopal see in the whole of the area of the Danelaw neither to disappear nor to be moved, and we should remind ourselves that we have no idea who the archbishop of York was, or even if there was one, between 904 and 928.[57] The one piece of evidence for continuity of learning at York is the Latin annals which lie behind certain entries in Roger of Wendover's *Flowers of Histories* and other sources. These demonstrate that there must have been at least one cleric still active with a knowledge of Latin, and it is worth noting again that, as far as we can judge, this York chronicle did not adopt a hostile attitude towards the city's Scandinavian kings – unlike, say, the *Anglo-Saxon*

Chronicle, or the *History of St Cuthbert*.[58] But it is not much to show for the church that had earlier produced Alcuin.

For what also disappeared, very significantly, were books. In the pre-Viking period, books and documents were the exclusive property of the clergy, both monastic and secular, and so the destruction or abandonment of churches, and the theft of their treasures, had a fatal effect on the libraries of northern and eastern England, so that almost nothing survives. As King Alfred lamented, some were burnt; others were plundered as treasure; and at least one deluxe manuscript (now known as the Stockholm Codex Aureus) was seized and held up for ransom.[59] As Alfred Smyth has observed, 'it only took one Northman – with a different and more regressive set of cultural values – to torch an undefended monastic library which had taken two and a half centuries to accumulate, or to slay a monastic scholar who carried that accumulated wisdom in his or her head'.[60] The quantity of surviving pre-Viking manuscripts that can be attributed to areas of Scandinavian conquest is absolutely tiny. This is certainly true of York: Alcuin's famous library, once one of the finest in Europe, has almost entirely disappeared, and no manuscript can be proved to survive which was present in York at the time of Viking conquest.[61] To quote Wormald again, 'the evaporation of almost the entire literate tradition of the pre-Viking Danelaw can only be the responsibility of the Vikings'.[62]

It was not just the threat or experience of violence, and the theft or destruction of treasures, that incapacitated the church in Northumbria. It also lost land, and lots of it. We saw in the previous chapter that the Scandinavian settlement of the 870s and later saw the break-up of major estates, in which great quantities of high-quality land passed into the possession of new Scandinavian lords. The re-distribution of land and revenues affected the church just as much as it did the Northumbrian monarchy and aristocracy, and Martin Carver has memorably described this spoliation and re-distribution as 'a 9th-century dissolution of the monasteries'.[63] Even if ecclesiastical communities had not physically vacated their churches, or been driven out or enslaved, it is likely that, without the resources of land and income, they must have been seriously reduced and compromised in their activities.[64]

Nonetheless, in recent years scholars have rightly wished to stress the evidence that does exist for some forms of ecclesiastical continuity in the Danelaw, to counteract the more general impression of institutional collapse in Scandinavian-conquered regions.[65] So, for example, it has been pointed out that a number of churches that were important in the pre-Viking period continued to be so, and that their land-holdings, as far as they can be reconstructed, may not have changed all that much. In Yorkshire it has been argued that a number of important churches, including Beverley [ER], Dewsbury [WR], Leeds [WR], Masham [NR], Northallerton [NR], Otley [WR], and Ripon [WR], survived the Scandinavian settlements in a relatively undamaged state; and the main evidence for this claim includes the extensiveness of their later land-holdings and parochial authority, and/or the presence at the same site of both pre- and post-Viking stone sculpture.[66] Such major churches may even have fared better in Yorkshire than they did in neighbouring Lincolnshire.[67] This revisionism is valuable, and cumulatively it is incontrovertible; but the evidence is not always unambiguous. Some of the methodological reservations that have been raised against the 'multiple estate' model (as discussed in the previous chapter) apply here also, in that church holdings in the pre-Viking period (especially for so-called 'mother-churches') are reconstructed by scholars from post-Viking evidence, and there is a certain danger of circularity. Our lack of Viking Age sources also means that it is, in fact, impossible to prove genuine, unbroken continuity: the best that can be demonstrated is an agreement in function and importance for certain churches before and after the watershed of the Scandinavian settlement, not that such churches continued undisturbed through the decades of change in the late ninth and early tenth centuries. The presence of, say, eighth-century sculpture and tenth-century sculpture at the same site does not in itself demonstrate that ecclesiastical life at that site negotiated the tumultuous ninth century without incident or interruption. What we might be seeing is re-establishment rather than continuity, a picking-up of the pieces after a period of turmoil; we should recall that the impact of the Vikings on Northumbria, the shock that they delivered to the social system, was so profound as to bring an end to a coin economy for thirty years. As Lesley Abrams has written, 'in much of the Danelaw, ecclesiastical activity between 880 and 920 is invisible in the surviving sources', and the loss of manuscripts remains a poignant indication of disruption, a mark of discontinuity to set alongside the break in the use of coins.[68]

So even if churches did survive, it will not have been in an undamaged state; and whatever clergy remained will have found themselves in the midst of a sizeable new population of pagans. A few place-names bear witness to this period of paganism, most importantly Roseberry Topping [NR], a stark and dramatic hill whose modern name conceals its origin as *Othenesberg* 'Odin's hill' [Figure 19].[69] The Anglo-Saxon homilist Ælfric, writing in the late tenth century, observed that the worship of Odin was associated with 'high hills [*heagum beorgum*]'; Roseberry Topping provides a compelling example.[70]

The few potentially pagan inhumations to be found in Yorkshire were discussed in the previous chapter, but it is also worth pondering the significant number of minor place-names which have a Scandinavian personal name as their first element and the Norse word *haugr* as their second. Old Norse *haugr* meant 'burial mound; artificial mound; hill' (and indeed, so frequent was the practice of raising mounds over the dead in early Scandinavia that Old Norse even possessed a related verb, *heygja*, meaning 'to bury in a mound').[71] There are quite a lot of examples from Yorkshire of *haugr* names that have a Scandinavian personal name as their first element, especially in the North Riding: a selection would be Kilgram Grange (earlier *Kelgrimhou*, 'Kelfgrímr or Ketilgrímr's mound'), Sunley Hill (earlier *Sunnolvehou*, 'Sunnólfr's mound'), and Ulshaw Bridge (earlier *Ulveshowe*, 'Úlfr's mound').[72] In some cases these names may have been applied, folklorically, to natural hills or to earlier barrows.[73] But in other cases there seems no reason to doubt that *haugr* does indeed mean 'burial mound' (whether for the mound over an inhumation or cremation). In a number of cases, moreover, there is a correspondence with the name of the nearby settlement: in the West Riding we find the paired names of Grimesthorpe and *Grimehou* ('Grímr's *thorp* and mound'), and *Haggenby* and *Haggandehou* ('Höggvandi's *by* and mound'), seemingly indicating (in A.H. Smith's assessment) 'the home and burial place of a heathen Viking'.[74] Neil Price has observed that, in the early Scandinavian world, 'the named landmarks that resulted [from mound burial] played a part in the cognitive landscape of the community'.[75] Many of these Yorkshire names are now lost – that is, they have not persisted into the present time, and the location designated is unknown – but they may offer a glimpse of a 'cognitive landscape' labelled and perceived in terms of the burial mounds of important local figures.

In terms of archaeological finds, apparent ritual deposits from the Viking Age have been found in the River Hull at Skerne [ER], including a sword, iron tools, and skeletons of horses, cattle, sheep, and dogs.[76] More widely, Yorkshire, like other parts of the Danelaw, has yielded a number of silver pendants in the shape of Thor's hammer.[77] In recent years metal-detectorists have turned up Thor's hammers (in whole or part) at Leconfield [ER], Wetwang [ER], and Copgrove [WR] [Figure 21], while the site of the 'Ainsbrook' hoard produced a Thor's hammer seemingly re-fashioned from part of a copper alloy balance.[78] The Cuerdale hoard also contained a Thor's hammer, and the Goldsborough hoard may have done so (it is hard to tell if the object concerned is a Thor's hammer or an upside-down cross).[79] The image of Thor's hammer, as we have seen, also occurs on some York coinage.

The *History of St Cuthbert* preserves a particularly colourful story of the pagan antagonism of one of Rægnald's followers, called 'Onlafbald' (mentioned at the start of Chapter 4 as one of the thegns he endowed with land):

> This son of the devil was an enemy, in whatever ways he was able, of God and St Cuthbert. Thus one day, while filled with an unclean spirit, he entered the church of the holy confessor in a rage, and with Bishop Cuthheard and the whole congregation standing [there] he said, 'What can this dead man Cuthbert, whose threats are mentioned every day, do to me? I swear by my powerful gods Thor and Odin that from this hour I will be the bitterest enemy to you all.'[80]

Cuthbert's persecutor, needless to say, soon receives a miraculous come-uppance, and experiences a sudden painful death. But the significance of the story lies in the fact that Norse paganism in Northumbria was remembered as being actively inimical to Christianity, and that the leading gods were well known to clerical writers.

As we saw in the previous chapter, Scandinavian settlement in England was not a once-for-all event. The second quarter of the tenth century saw the arrival in Northumbria of Rægnald's Dublin-based Vikings such as Onlafbald, conspicuous by their paganism and, for that very reason (if the 942 poem in the *Anglo-Saxon Chronicle* can be believed as well as the *History of St Cuthbert*), a tribulation both to the native English and the settled migrants of the Danelaw. There was also continued migration into England, and continued traffic across the North Sea, throughout the tenth century, while the early eleventh century, and the conquests of Swein and Cnut, brought a new wave of invaders: so it is unlikely that there was ever a time in Viking Age Yorkshire when pagan Scandinavians were not in evidence to some degree.

Moreover, even though the conquerors and settlers in Northumbria did in time come to embrace Christianity, this does not necessarily mean that Viking Age Scandinavians wore their religion lightly – as Onlafbald's aggression in the *History of St Cuthbert* also implies. Indeed, the fact that, for their enemies, the Vikings represented a distinctively pagan horror, and the remarkable persistence and preservation of pagan lore in Scandinavia compared to the rest of Europe, suggests that Viking belief may have been unusually deep-rooted.[81] Even in the early eleventh century, one archbishop of York, Wulfstan II, can be found repeatedly fulminating against 'heathen' practices.[82] Although Wulfstan had an expansive idea of 'heathenism' (Old English *hæðendom*) that included all forms of conduct that fell short of appropriate Christian behaviour (for Wulfstan, the term covered not only devil-worship, but also the non-payment of tithes), nonetheless it is clear that knowledge of the Norse gods was still a live issue, as was the observance of superstitious practices of augury and nature-worship.

The role of missionaries is the aspect of the conversion of the Vikings in England about which we are most ignorant. No missionary narratives were preserved for the Danelaw as they were, for example, for early Anglo-Saxon England or mainland Scandinavia. But there must have been priests present to carry out baptisms, and to give instruction, either drawn from the surviving churches or specially sent into the mission field.[83] The fact that Scandinavian pagans continued to come and go in Northumbria, especially in the first half of the tenth century, means that it is not easy to put a timescale on the period of conversion, and it may well be that we should be thinking in terms of generations, and therefore decades – which would mean, as Lesley Abrams has pointed out, that the supposedly rapid conversion of the Danelaw was not really 'rapid' at all.[84]

The first signs of evangelization seem to show through in the 890s – already a quarter of a century after the fall of York. A letter survives from Pope Formosus to the bishops of England, dating from the early to mid 890s, in which the pope reports that he has heard that 'the abominable rites of the pagans have sprouted again' in England, and that for a time the bishops 'kept silent "like dogs unable to bark"'.[85] Now, however, the bishops and their clergy 'have at length awakened, and have begun to renew the seed of the word of God'. From the same period we have Asser's statement that King Alfred was in the habit of giving gifts to churches and clerics in Northumbria (among other places outside of Wessex).[86] We also know of at least a couple of named Scandinavian converts from this time. One was King Guthred who, it will be recalled, was acclaimed as king in Northumbria by the Bishop of Lindisfarne, and was buried in York Minster in 895 (the one certain date that we have for his biography). The other, very interestingly, is a young man called Oda. Byrhtferth of Ramsey's *Life of St Oswald*, written in the early eleventh century, records of Oda that 'certain people say that his father was one of those Danes who came with the ship-army of Ubba and Ivar: for that reason his father did not wholly seek to serve Christ'.[87] In his youth, though, Oda was brought up in the household of 'a certain venerable thegn, one who believed faithfully in God, by the name of Æthelhelm', and at the same time 'he studied a number of books with a certain man of religion'.[88] In due course, Oda became bishop of Ramsbury in Wiltshire, sometime in the mid 920s, and in 937, according to one later writer, he was present with King Athelstan at the Battle of Brunanburh.[89] A few years afterwards, he was elevated to being archbishop of Canterbury, a position he held until his death in 958; he was thus the archbishop of Canterbury who, according to the *History of the Kings*, negotiated with Wulfstan I of York to achieve a peace between Olaf Guthfrithson and King Edmund, and so we should savour the irony of the son of a member of the Great Army negotiating on behalf of the king of England with another English archbishop representing a pagan Viking king.[90] The chronology of Oda's career suggests that he was born well before the end of the ninth century, perhaps in the 880s. He is therefore the earliest second-generation Scandinavian migrant, born in England, whom we can identify by name, and also one of the first whom we know to have become literate; he can thus be set alongside the young man 'of Viking parentage' whom Asser, writing in the 890s, records having met in King Alfred's monastic foundation at Athelney in Somerset, 'living there in the monastic habit – and he was assuredly not the last of them to do so'.[91] Oda's was clearly a remarkable career trajectory for the son of a member of Ivar's army.[92] Furthermore, Oda's brother (whose name we don't know) also became a priest, and this brother's son (Oda's nephew) was Oswald, later to become archbishop of York and one of the key reformers of the second half of the tenth century – which explains the interest in Oda on the part of Oswald's biographer.[93]

So-called 'top-down' conversion is one of the dominant models for the process in the early Middle Ages, in which kings converted and then their subjects followed suit. Guthred's acclamation by Bishop Eardulf does not quite fit into this model, but it is significant that our first real evidence of conversion is at the level of the king. The early Scandinavian coinage of York, issued from about 895 onwards, fully supports this indication that the city's Viking rulers had either converted or at least opened themselves to Christian influences: as we saw in Chapter 2, the coins are characterized by a sophisticated repertoire of Christian iconography – a range of images and ideas which the Scandinavian kings must have derived from somewhere (or rather, someone).[94] Conversion brought many political advantages to Germanic kings, above all entry into the European Christian establishment, and access to networks of exchange (material as well as cultural) and the technology of literacy.[95] Clearly this was an *entrée*, and an access, which some of the early Viking kings of York, such as Guthred, earnestly desired; it was noted in Chapter 2 that one of the other developments in Guthred's reign may have been the establishment of diplomatic relations with West Saxon and Welsh rulers.

But the attraction of conversion was clearly not felt by all the later kings of York. A peculiarity of the Viking kingdom in Northumbria is that, owing to the late conversion of the Scandinavians of Dublin, new kings arriving from Ireland were often pagan, and the process of conversion needed to be begun anew – or not, as the case may be.[96] Rægnald (919-21) seems never to have converted, and he came to be remembered as the pagan terror of the *History of St Cuthbert*. Sihtric *caech* (921-27) did convert, and married Athelstan's sister; but Roger of Wendover later reported him as an apostate who 'restored the worship of idols'.[97] The triumphant Olaf Guthfrithson (939-41) issued an aggressive coinage sporting an Odinic raven. Olaf *cuaran* succeeded Olaf Guthfrithson in 941, but was not baptised until 943, after submission to King Edmund, and in the same year Edmund also stood sponsor to Rægnald Guthfrithson.[98] Even the religious status of the last king of York, Eric Bloodaxe, is uncertain: the poem *Eiríksmál* commemorates his death through a scene from Norse mythology.

Here, then, is a situation radically unlike the usual model of top-down conversion in the early Middle Ages. In tenth-century Yorkshire, following the arrival of the grandsons of Ivar, it was more likely to be the king who was still pagan, and not his subjects. For a perspective that is more grass-roots, if not quite 'bottom-up', we might consider the significance of place-names in 'Kir(k)by' (Old Norse *kirkju-bý*). There are more than twenty of these in Yorkshire, such as Kirby Hill [NR], Kirby Misperton [NR], and Kirkby Malzeard [WR].[99] In many or most cases the distinguishing affix is a later development: in Domesday Book (usually their first occurrence), these settlements are just called *Kirkju-bý* (*Chirchebi* in Domesday spelling). The standard interpretation is that these names mean 'settlement with a church' – in other words, the term was used by the incoming

Scandinavians to designate settlements that were distinguished by the presence of a pre-existing church (perhaps in stone?). There is likely to be some truth in this, but Thomas Pickles has pointed out that it cannot be the whole truth, as we know of many settlements with churches that did not come to be so labelled; he has therefore suggested an alternative interpretation, which is that the term means 'settlement owned by the church', and that it indicated a site or estate that continued to be owned by, or to owe dues to, a more important mother-church.[100] Again, this is likely to be correct in some regards, but similarly it cannot be the whole picture, as not all the estates belonging to mother-churches were labelled thus, and it is not very common for the first element of –by names to be an abstract noun ('the (institutional) church') rather than a concrete one (so perhaps the name should be glossed as 'settlement belonging to a (particular) mother-church'). It may be that we should not be looking for perfect consistency or a single meaning for the term, and the important thing to note for present purposes is that Kirkby names indicate sites that were judged to have some special ecclesiastical significance. They thus provide us with some on-the-ground evidence for the encounter between the Scandinavian settlers, and their descendants, and the pre-existing church.

All of which brings us to stone sculpture, of which Richard Bailey has justly stated that 'no other documentary or archaeological material brings us so close to the meeting point of pagan and Christian belief'.[101] This is one of the reasons why this book began, at the start of Chapter 1, with the example of the Middleton Cross, as an eloquent point of entry into the history and culture of Viking Age Yorkshire. The carving of stone monuments was one of the main ecclesiastical art-forms of pre-Viking England, and especially so in Northumbria.[102] Crosses and other stone monuments were used as liturgical stations, shrines, church furniture, and memorials to the dead. The essential point about pre-Viking stone sculpture is that it was, with very few possible exceptions, an exclusively ecclesiastical art-form, and usually associated with major churches and monasteries; it was not a widespread art-form, nor generally used for secular commemoration. The great monuments of pre-Viking Northumbria include Acca's Cross in Hexham, the Ruthwell Cross in Dumfriesshire, and the Bewcastle Cross in Cumbria, and when originally set up, many of the sculptures were colourfully painted, possessing a brightness that their modern drab appearance gives no hint of.

Such three-dimensional carving in stone was not practised in Scandinavia, though there was a tradition of two-dimensional carving in the picture-stones of Gotland, and (above all) commemorative runic inscriptions – though we should remember that, as noted earlier, the majority of rune-stones date from after the period of the Viking settlements in England.[103] There can therefore be no question whatsoever that the production of literally hundreds of stone monuments in Viking Age Yorkshire represents the adoption by the incoming Scandinavians of a pre-

130

existing Anglo-Saxon tradition – and an ecclesiastical tradition at that. This is not to say that there must have been Anglo-Saxon carvers continuing in Viking-period Northumbria, ready to teach their skills to new apprentices and cultivate the new elite as potential patrons; we cannot go that far, and it may be that – as in other areas of culture – there was a hiatus in production prior to the re-establishment (with changes) of the old practice. But the very idea of erecting stone crosses was Anglo-Saxon, not Scandinavian.

The precise number is hard to count, as so many monuments now exist only as fragments, but something in the order of 500 pieces of Viking Age sculpture survive from Yorkshire, from well over a hundred different sites – a huge quantity, far in excess of the number of pre-Viking monuments.[104] So the production of stone sculpture was not only adopted by the Scandinavians: it was adopted enthusiastically, and extended in various ways. In fact, an emphasis on the Anglo-Saxon origins (or at least inspiration) of Viking Age sculpture can be misleading, as it foregrounds continuity. It is equally important to stress that there is a profound discontinuity in terms of function and distribution – amounting, in many ways, to the invention of a new art-form.[105] No longer was stone sculpture the preserve of major ecclesiastical centres, and no longer was its function primarily liturgical. As the example of the Middleton Cross indicates, the new function of sculpture was usually secular and funerary: grave monuments to the new elite, albeit still at church sites. Whole new forms were devised, most importantly the hogback, a low, house-shaped monument that was invented and flourished in tenth-century Yorkshire [Figure 22].[106]

The regional distribution of stone sculpture will be investigated further in the next chapter, to see what it can reveal about local communities in Viking Age Yorkshire; at present, the focus is on what we can learn about the process of Christianization. What the sculpture shows is that the new elite in Viking Age Yorkshire learned from pre-Viking traditions but adapted them to their own purpose, and in so doing they marked a decisive shift in power and meaning from the ecclesiastical to the secular. The new crosses and hogbacks were erected in churchyards (though very few have been found *in situ*, most were later re-used as building material), and thus they were undoubtedly Christian monuments, at least in some way: they are indeed, as Richard Bailey claimed, the best and most widespread form of evidence for the movement from paganism to Christianity. But their widespread distribution, at countless small parish churches, indicates that they are no longer the product and property of monasteries or major churches alone. Rather, they should be read as part of the same process of social change as the break-up of large estates, both ecclesiastical and aristocratic, into multiple smaller ones, as discussed in the previous chapter: what the sculptures reveal is a new generation of local, secular lords, recently endowed with land and resources, who are choosing both to act as church patrons and to be commemorated with stone

131

monuments. In many cases, as part of this process of 'secularization' or 'manorialization', local lords may have been founding the first ever churches on their estates – in other words, helping to create the system of small parishes that has come down to the present day.[107] At many sites, we have only a handful of Viking Age monuments, and David Stocker has plausibly argued that these represent 'the founding monuments in a new generation of parochial graveyards', 'a single elite family burying in their own 'proto-parish' church'.[108]

These monuments cannot be dated closely. Only a few have been recovered from archaeologically datable strata, and as a consequence scholars have suggested a broad dating band of the first half of the tenth century, extending in some cases into the second half of the century and occasionally beyond.[109] The chronology of art-styles in the Scandinavian homelands is well established (Borre, Jellinge, Mammen, Ringerike, Urnes), and is of some assistance in dating within a century or half-century.[110] But it is also well recognized that art-styles in Viking Age Britain may not have evolved according to quite the same timetable as in Scandinavia itself, while the alteration and adaptation of Scandinavian styles in England means that the categories themselves may not always be apt labels (especially for the Borre and, above all, the Jellinge styles).[111] The pseudo-Jellinge serpent on the reverse of the Middleton Cross, it may be recalled, has been described as 'almost inconceivably incompetent', as well as (more charitably) 'endearingly incompetent' and simply 'a poor attempt at the Jellinge style', but such pan-Scandinavian appraisals may be insufficiently sensitive to local, overseas developments.[112]

A different criterion that has been used for attempting a more narrow dating is the presence of Irish (or at least Irish Sea) influences, most importantly in the preference for so-called ring-headed crosses: this form certainly has an Irish Sea origin, though its flourishing in tenth-century Yorkshire really marks it out as a distinctive style of the Vikings in England.[113] The question is whether one attributes Irish Sea influence to political or mercantile links in general (which existed between York and Dublin from the last third of the ninth century onwards) or more specifically to the conquest and settlement in Yorkshire of a powerful Hiberno-Norse elite (beginning with Rægnald's conquest in 919). The latter might seem reasonable, but it probably results in too narrow a dating bracket, and so the former should be remembered as well. (This is, of course, the same question we reviewed at the start of this chapter with regards to linguistic influence from Goidelic Celtic.) It would also seem too much of a paradox to suggest that most of our monuments should be dated to the Hiberno-Norse period, as these decades are also the ones that give us our best evidence for a resurgent paganism – though it is a commonplace among archaeologists that the most vigorous articulations of paganism are often made in a period of imminent conversion, when arguments are antagonistic and belief-systems are threatened. We should most probably imagine varying speeds of conversion and Christianization among the Scandinavian migrant groups in Northumbria, with some moving to a settled Christian existence sooner than others.

There is one further, very important contribution that the stone sculpture can make to our understanding of the conversion period in Northumbria, and that is in terms of enabling us, potentially at least, to access some of the forms of religious belief that were current in the region. A small proportion of our Viking Age sculptures are decorated with scenes from Norse mythology and legend – something in the order of 5% of the extant monuments, at 10% of the known sites.[114] There is nothing in Northumbria to compare with the great Gosforth Cross from Cumbria, but mythological images that have been identified include the god Tyr on hogbacks at Sockburn [Durham] and Lythe [NR], putting his hand in the mouth of the wolf Fenrir [Figure 20], Heimdallr at Ovingham [Northumberland], blowing his horn, and an apparent Ragnarok scene from Skipwith [ER].[115] A number of possible Odin figures have been suggested at Billingham [Durham], Kirklevington [NR], and Sherburn [ER], but all are debatable.[116] More certain is the identification of two popular legendary stories (that is, stories featuring human heroes rather than gods): scenes from the life of Sigurd the dragon-slayer are depicted at Kirby Hill [Birdforth wapentake, NR], Nunburnholme [ER], Ripon [WR], and York [Figure 23], while the escape of the smith Weland, in a bird-like flying machine of his own making, is depicted on four or five Yorkshire stones (two from Leeds [WR], one from Bedale [NR], and either one or two from Sherburn [ER]).[117] Poetry confirms the popularity of these stories in Viking Age Northumbria: *Eiríksmál* features Sigmundr and Sinfjötli, two of the chcracters from the Volsung cycle, among its actors, while the Eddic poem *Völundarkviða*, the main treatment of the Weland legend in Old Norse verse, may have a Northumbrian origin.[118]

The presence of mythological and legendary scenes on Christian crosses poses fascinating questions, and three main interpretations or approaches have been offered, all of which have some value to them. The first approach is to query, in effect, whether these are Christian monuments at all, or at least to problematize the form of Christianity they evince. In this interpretation, the sculptures provide evidence for the elasticity of the Scandinavians' religious beliefs, which were easily able to accommodate the White Christ into their polytheistic pantheon; a famous analogue from a later Icelandic source is the example of Helgi the Lean, whose faith, according to *Landnámabók* (*The Book of Settlements*) 'was very much mixed: he believed in Christ but invoked Thor when it came to voyages and difficult times'.[119] To more rigorous Christian commentators, Helgi's Christianity would not have seemed Christianity at all, but rather a form of paganism; but to his heathen Icelandic contemporaries, it will have been Helgi's devotion to Christ that was unusual, rather than his fondness for Thor (and he named his settlement in

Iceland *Kristnes*, 'Christ's Headland'): in other words, Helgi's beliefs would have marked him out to his contemporaries as a progressive figure, and not a reactionary one (as a stricter Christian view would suggest). In late ninth- and early tenth-century Northumbria there may have been many individuals with beliefs like Helgi's, and one could argue that the stone sculptures are evidence for this sort of co-existence or mixing of beliefs, perhaps slightly further along the continuum of Christianization from the example of Helgi himself. Moreover, David Stocker has suggested that such a 'hybrid religion' can tell us something about the archbishops and church of York.[120] The example of Wulfstan I in the 940s indicates how much at least one of the archbishops was prepared to co-operate and collaborate with the (sometimes pagan) Scandinavian kings that ruled in York; the sculptures could thus be read as testimony not to the failure of the church of York in achieving only a partial conversion, but rather to its success in reaching an effective accommodation with the new rulers of the region, even at the cost, possibly, of theological compromise.

The objections that might be made to this first interpretation are several, though none are conclusive. One is that truly mythological subjects (as opposed to legendary ones, such as Sigurd and Weland) occur only on a very small number of stones; the great majority are unimpeachably Christian, albeit often with secular decoration. Another is that the commissioning and carving of stone crosses was an expensive art-form, associated with the church; and so it might be thought inherently unlikely that patrons would pay for, and sculptors carve, monuments that reveal a religious confusion, though of course one might say that the confusion exists only from a stringently Christian perspective. A third is that the monuments might in fact be making a point about the superiority of Christianity over paganism, rather than a fusion between the two: Christ will be triumphant, whereas the old gods will perish at Ragnarok.[121]

This brings us, then, to the second main interpretation that has been advanced, which is that the mythological and legendary crosses demonstrate not religious confusion or artistic naïvete, but rather considerable theological sophistication. It may be that the scenes and figures chosen from Norse myth and legend were precisely those which in some way echoed, or fore-shadowed, or paralleled, tropes and elements from Christian teaching. So, for example, Sigurd eating the dragon's blood might be held to parallel the feast of the Eucharist.[122] The prominence of Weland the smith might be associated with some early medieval conceptions of Christ and his father Joseph as metal-workers rather than carpenters.[123] This type of interpretation has been called 'figurative thinking'; its basis lies in the figurative or allegorical mode of reading which the early Church Fathers developed for reading the Old Testament as a prefiguration of the New.[124] It thus presupposes a learned and sophisticated culture in Viking Age Yorkshire, both in terms of the makers of the crosses and (one assumes) their audience. Such a figurative way of thinking, coloured by patristic learning, has been vigorously advocated for some of the masterpieces of early Northumbrian sculpture, such as the Ruthwell Cross; the assumption is that the same mode is operative in these later Viking Age works.

This is a well-established and influential interpretation, but there are reasons to query it. A crucial piece of evidence is a text written in Wessex in the late 990s, Ælfric's Preface to his translation into English of the Book of Genesis.[125] In this piece, the homilist Ælfric expresses his reluctance to undertake any further translations of the Old Testament, on the grounds that a lay audience is liable to misinterpret what they read or hear read. To be specific, the laity (and even, Ælfric says, some of the clergy) lack the knowledge and learning to distinguish the 'spiritual meaning' from the 'bare narrative', and thus are likely to read the Old Testament purely on the literal level, and not on the figurative or allegorical. This is an interesting reservation. It suggests strongly that a competence in figurative interpretation was not at all widespread in late tenth-century Wessex, neither among the clergy nor prosperous lay-people. And if this was the case among circles known to Ælfric, in late tenth-century Wessex – the time and place of the Benedictine Reform – one must conclude that such competence was much less likely to be in evidence in early or mid tenth-century Yorkshire, among clerics in a damaged and impoverished church, and a newly converted (or semi-converted) Scandinavian population. This is not to exclude the possibility that some of our sculptures are informed by figurative thinking, but Ælfric's Preface to Genesis does suggest strongly that we cannot presuppose a familiarity with such thinking. Nor are cost and effort in themselves guarantees of subtlety and sophistication; in some environments, theological subtlety and sophistication may simply not have been available, at whatever price. The best or most persuasive parallels might be between the Norse Ragnarok and the Christian Apocalypse, though even here one could read the monuments in terms of cultural translation rather than a figurative relationship.[126]

This brings us, then, to our third way of thinking about these sculptures, which is that these scenes do not in fact possess any religious significance – pagan, Christian, or syncretic – but rather are expressions of a cultural inheritance, a secular desire to hold on to Scandinavian traditions in a new environment.[127] When the Scandinavians encountered stone sculpture in England, they found an art-form decorated not only with Anglo-Saxon ornament, but also with stories which were of cultural value to their makers and audience (mostly Biblical and hagiographical stories). This was a practice that the Scandinavians in England copied when they themselves began to act as commissioners and consumers of sculpture, but with a different set of stories: not normally stories about their old gods (as they were now Christian, such stories might be thought unsuitable), but stories about their heroes at least. Rosemary Cramp has claimed that 'the Vikings introduced a secularization of taste in art, as they also secularized landholdings', and the Sigurd and Weland sculptures could easily be cited to support such a view.[128] Even the truly pagan scenes, however, such as the Tyr hogbacks at Sockburn and Lythe, can be accommodated into this view, and what we would be seeing is not a lived belief but rather a form of 'cultural paganism', a holding-on to the Norse story-world.[129] The poem *Eiríksmál* again forms a helpful parallel here, suggesting that Norse myth might still have an important function to play even among the converted.

Before we leave this subject it is, however, important to stress again that the sculptures depicting Norse myth and legend are only a small, if significant, minority of the corpus – though that minority becomes somewhat larger if we add in the warrior-crosses to make a category of markedly Scandinavian scenes. Many of the tenth-century Yorkshire sculptures show Christian figures and scenes instead, such as the Crucifixion (for example, at Kirklevington [NR]), the Virgin and Child (for example, at Sutton upon Derwent [ER]), and assorted clerics or saints (for example, the cross at Stonegrave [NR], which is carved with two ecclesiastical figures, each carrying a book).[130] It is also important to re-iterate the obvious point that many of the crosses are, literally, crosses, in which the Christian cross-head is the most prominent feature.

The stone sculpture, then, provides eloquent witness to the process of conversion and Christianization among the Scandinavians in Yorkshire, though as we have seen, there is ample scope for debate as to how exactly that process unfolded. The sculpture also exemplifies in superlative fashion the contact of cultures between English and Scandinavian, and the potential for new forms both of belief and expression to evolve out of that contact. So that is the final, very important question we should consider in this chapter: how far did the two peoples and cultures assimilate to one another in Viking Age Yorkshire, and how far did they remain distinct?

Assimilation and Identity

This is a question that has stimulated debate since at least the twelfth century. William of Malmesbury claimed that, by the time of Edward the Elder, 'the Northumbrians [...] had already grown into one nation [*unam gentem*] with the Danes'.[131] John of Worcester, on the other hand, tells the story of a Scandinavian raid on the mouth of the Humber in 993: he records that 'a large number of local inhabitants' assembled to fight the raiders, but the leaders of the group took to flight and betrayed their followers 'because they were Danish on their father's side'.[132] For the first of these twelfth-century writers, then, the English and Scandinavians had become merged and indistinguishable by the early tenth century; for the second writer, distinct ancestries, Scandinavian and English, could still be traced at the end of the tenth century, and such ancestries were meaningful in governing individuals' identity and behaviour.

A similar diversity of opinion can be found in modern scholarship, and, as one route into the issue, it is worth continuing with the evidence of stone sculpture. The most obvious way in which the Scandinavians came to be assimilated into the pre-existing culture is in religion, in their conversion to Christianity – though as we have seen, the evidence on this suggests that conversion and Christianization were not instantaneous or rapid. There is, of course, nothing unusual about the fact that the Scandinavians converted: for the peoples of northern Europe, that is, after all, the story of the first millennium.[133] What is unusual is the manner in which the Scandinavians held on to stories from their pre-Christian past, to a degree not paralleled elsewhere in Europe (and above all in Iceland). This in itself suggests that certain cultural traditions were not easily jettisoned, and other, less eye-catching features of the stone sculpture teach the same lesson. In terms of ornament and decoration, the sculptures of Viking Age Yorkshire show both the continuance of Anglo-Saxon patterns and also the incorporation of Scandinavian ones.

Some monuments also show images or elements drawn from both cultures. It has been pointed out, for example, that Anglo-Saxon women, unlike Scandinavian, did not wear necklaces, yet the Virgin Mary carved on the Sutton upon Derwent cross is wearing a necklace – so we can see that an image derived from Anglo-Saxon Christian art has here evolved under Scandinavian influence (indeed, influence drawn from life, not from inherited iconography).[134] The Crucifixion depicted on a cross from Kirkdale [NR] shows Christ sporting a Scandinavian-style forked beard.[135] The Nunburnholme Cross [Figure 7], one of the great monuments from Viking Age Yorkshire, is especially complex and puzzling, and our difficulties in reading it are not helped by the fact that a central portion is missing, and the two parts that do survive have been misaligned in their reconstruction.[136] Briefly, what seems to have happened with the Nunburnholme Cross is that a first sculptor began work on an elegant and sophisticated Christian monument in either the late ninth or early tenth century, looking back to the traditions of Anglian art ('there is little Viking taste in any of the First Sculptor's work', James Lang wrote). But this first sculptor left his work incomplete, and after an unknown interval a second, less skilled sculptor finished the monument; it is this second sculptor who carved both the seated warrior-lord and the Sigurd scene. (Later still, a third sculptor, probably after the Norman Conquest, added a centaur.) The possibilities for speculation are thus almost endless. Was there a large or a short gap between the first sculptor and the second? Was the first sculptor, for whatever reason, taken off the job, and replaced by an inferior practitioner? Either way, the second sculptor's work made the monument's imagery more secular, through the addition of the warrior-lord and the Sigurd scene; the first sculptor's work is wholly Christian in its iconography. In both cases, furthermore, these secular additions involved carving over work by the first sculptor in part or whole. But the monument cannot be read solely in terms of the secularization of a pre-existing Christian monument: for the second sculptor also carved a Virgin and Child, and figures holding books. The Nunburnholme Cross is thus a superb exemplification of cultural contact and exchange, however opaque its interpretation remains.

The monument type most frequently acclaimed as a new hybrid creation, the direct result of Anglo-Scandinavian contact, is the hogback. This has no clear predecessors on either the Anglo-Saxon side or the Scandinavian, but Viking Age Yorkshire is its demonstrable place of origin and centre of distribution.[137] Comparably, but on a smaller scale, a number of sites, including Carthorpe [NR], Snape with Thorp [NR], and Yapham [ER], have yielded miniature metal bells, of unknown function (possibly female necklace ornaments) [Figure 13].[138] These so-called 'Norse bells' have been found elsewhere in Scandinavian-settled parts of the British Isles, and in Iceland, but they are not attested in mainland Scandinavia itself, and hence they seem a distinctively hybrid, or at least colonial, innovation.

It is revealing to compare the stone sculpture evidence with the jewellery. We saw in the previous chapter that the large number of Scandinavian-style brooches uncovered by metal-detectorists in recent years has both confirmed the presence of a substantial population of female migrants among the settlers in England, and also revealed that Scandinavian-style jewellery continued to be worn through the tenth century; it did not disappear after the first decades of settlement. Indeed, signs of repair on the Scandinavian brooches found in England are quite common, and a high proportion are described as 'worn' in their condition: this argues further against their rapid abandonment, and suggests perhaps that women's jewellery in the Danelaw may have performed an enduring function as cultural heirlooms, possibly even over several generations of use.[139] Jane Kershaw, the leading scholar of this material, has accordingly concluded that the jewellery evidence at least argues against 'high levels of cultural assimilation', and that the brooches continued to broadcast a message of difference, of Scandinavian identity.[140]

However, we should also bring into the picture here Kershaw's category of 'Anglo-Scandinavian' brooches; that is, brooches which display Scandinavian form and ornament – which look Scandinavian – but are revealed through their manufacture to have been produced in England. Such Anglo-Scandinavian brooches, perhaps surprisingly, show very little evidence for the mixing of art-styles, in which elements of English and Scandinavian design are combined, or for the creation in England of new brooch types not found in Scandinavia.[141] Anglo-Scandinavian brooch traditions, Kershaw concludes, are 'conservative', and thus form a rather striking contrast to aspects of the stone sculpture.[142]

The production and dissemination of Anglo-Scandinavian brooch types seems at present more a phenomenon of the southern Danelaw than the northern. Over 230 examples have been recovered of the so-called 'East Anglian Series' of Borre-style brooches, clearly manufactured at particular sites in Norfolk, but very few (to date) have been found in Yorkshire.[143] There are some other Anglo-Scandinavian brooches from Yorkshire – for example, a trefoil brooch from Cottingham [ER], Borre-style brooches from Wharram-le-Street [ER] and Deighton near Northallerton [NR], and brooches in the Terslev variant of the Borre style from Bawtry [WR] and Beverley [ER] – but in Yorkshire such 'Anglo-Scandinavian' brooches are outnumbered in Kershaw's database by the imported 'Scandinavian' brooches by roughly a factor of two.[144] Relative proportions of Scandinavian to Anglo-Scandinavian brooches are thus interesting (though later finds may, of course, change the picture): although Yorkshire has produced considerably fewer brooches in total than Lincolnshire or East Anglia, the proportion of 'Scandinavian' brooches to 'Anglo-Scandinavian' is higher in Yorkshire than the other areas.

Kershaw's argument is that the Anglo-Scandinavian brooches 'tell us something of the response of indigenous women, perhaps as well as that of second-generation settlers or those of mixed descent'; in short, that 'Anglo-Scandinavian dress items were fashionable'.[145] The adoption by native Anglo-Saxon women of Scandinavian-style jewellery may well be the best explanation for the extraordinary popularity of the 'East Anglian Series', especially in Norfolk, but present evidence does not suggest the same sort of booming market for Anglo-Scandinavian brooches north of the Humber. So the brooch evidence from Yorkshire, as opposed to East Anglia, does not (yet) suggest a widespread adoption of Scandinavian-style jewellery by the native population.

So it is worth thinking further about the other constituency suggested by Kershaw – second-generation inhabitants of the northern Danelaw, whether of Scandinavian parentage or mixed descent – and to add in a further group as well, namely English women who married Scandinavian men, and who may have desired, or been required, to accommodate to a more Scandinavian culture. To begin with, we should recall that purely Scandinavian jewellery does not seem to have been either manufactured in England or imported on a commercial scale, which means that, on the whole, such jewellery was not to be obtained in Viking Age England except through gift and inheritance. So any desire for further Scandinavian-style jewellery, whether to replace losses, or to give to wives or children, had to be met through the acquisition of Anglo-Scandinavian brooches (that is, brooches in the Scandinavian style but manufactured in England). From the manufacturing point of view, then, it may be more plausible, at least in the northern Danelaw, to see the Anglo-Scandinavian brooches as being a response to demand from a settled Scandinavian (or Anglo-Scandinavian) population, rather than as goods produced primarily for an Anglo-Saxon audience who wanted a touch of Scandinavian chic.

For 'fashion', in any simple or ephemeral sense, may not be a very helpful term here, or have much explanatory power. Scandinavian political authority in the southern Danelaw had been overturned by the end of Edward the Elder's reign; in the Viking kingdom of York, the beginning of the end came in 927, in the reign of Edward's successor, Athelstan, though the drama required a further three decades to play out. But the production and display of Anglo-Scandinavian brooches persisted throughout the tenth century, and indeed the Jellinge style only came into currency as the tenth century unfolded. So while an appeal to fashion may make some sense in the first years or decades after the Scandinavian conquests, such an explanation does not account for the longevity of Scandinavian-style jewellery, which seems to point instead to a substantial population for whom Scandinavian ornament was a normal part of their costume, as an expression of enduring choices, preferences, and commitments. That such ornament is associated with women rather than men is intelligible, as archaeologists have observed that in the medieval period women often seem to have acted as preservers and transmitters of collective or ethnic culture.[146]

Another type of portable object provides, in turn, an interesting comparison with the jewellery evidence. Steven Ashby's recent work on bone and antler combs in Northumbria and Scandinavia has revealed significant patterns in the manufacture and decoration of such objects.[147] Early medieval combs were important status and display items, not simply utilitarian objects, and in the pre-Viking period both Northumbria and Scandinavia had their own traditions of comb manufacture. In the late ninth and early tenth centuries, Scandinavian-made combs (Ashby's 'Type 5') are found widely in the Viking diaspora, including Northumbria, and such combs complement the situation with jewellery, where the evidence suggests migrant entry into England for Scandinavian-made material.[148] In the tenth century, however, Scandinavian-style short, deep combs (Ashby's 'Type 6') are found on both sides of the North Sea, and from form and decoration alone it is impossible to say whether they were made in Northumbria or Scandinavia; a Northumbrian provenance for the majority of the Type 6 combs found in England may be suggested by the fact that the rivets are iron (as in English and Irish practice) and not copper alloy (as in Norwegian and Swedish), though the picture is complicated by the use of iron rivets in Denmark also. In other words, unless we attribute all such combs to Danish practices and practitioners, then we may be seeing tenth-century craftsmen, trained in English traditions, attempting to make combs that are identical in appearance to Scandinavian combs of the same period. From the late tenth century onwards, Northumbrian and Scandinavian combs go their own ways again in terms of form and style.

This is not the whole picture, however. Ashby's 'Type 7' is found in northern England and in Ireland (especially Dublin), but only rarely in Scandinavia, which suggests it may have been a type distinctive to the Scandinavian-settled areas of the British Isles. Moreover, English-style combs ('Type 3') continued to be manufactured in tenth-century Northumbria, suggesting an enduring market for such objects – which indicates, as does the jewellery evidence, that tenth-century Northumbrian society did not witness a blanket assimilation of English and Scandinavian cultures, and that the signalling of differences continued to be important.

Where does all this leave us with regards to the important question of identity – how people thought of themselves and how others thought of them? Was there a continuing sense of Scandinavian (and English) identity within the northern Danelaw, or did a new, unitary 'Anglo-Scandinavian' identity emerge, shared by most or all of the inhabitants of Yorkshire? 'Anglo-Scandinavian' is of course a modern term, not one recorded in any medieval source; so perhaps, if there was a new, unitary identity, it was expressed in different language, in terms of 'northernness' – a northernness that had been re-shaped through Viking conquest and culture. This may possibly be so, and more will be said in Chapter 7 about the idea of the north in late Anglo-Saxon England; but the important thing to note at this stage is that, if a shared identity and culture did emerge in tenth-century Yorkshire, it was one which accommodated, and co-existed, and overlapped, with distinctively Scandinavian identities and cultures as well. For there can be no question that, as we have seen, certain Scandinavian cultural traits or practices persisted in a recognizable form throughout the tenth century – and even beyond, as we will see in later chapters. So while there may be good evidence for acculturation and assimilation in some spheres, there is equally good evidence for continued difference in others; the diverse peoples of Viking Age Yorkshire did not just melt and meld into an undifferentiated mass.

The best evidence for Scandinavian assimilation to English practices, as noted, is religious, and the patronage of stone sculpture shows how the new Scandinavian elite adopted a native habit – with, however, a new twist. This new Scandinavian patronage led to new forms of decoration, both in terms of ornament and images, so that even in this area of greatest assimilation a distinctive Scandinavian stamp was impressed, and stone sculpture also provides us with our best type of a new, hybrid cultural form: the hogback.

But other forms of material culture, as we have just seen, signal continuing difference rather than assimilation: the increasingly large corpus of female jewellery reveals that Scandinavian art-styles persisted, and Kershaw's so-called 'Anglo-Scandinavian' types may give us our best evidence for English assimilation to Scandinavian practices, as well as suggesting a continuing investment in the idea of a distinctively Scandinavian culture – including, perhaps, for daughters or granddaughters of mixed marriages.

As for language, it is likely that this was one of the most important markers of identity in Viking Age England – indeed, perhaps even the most important – but of course language is invisible in the archaeological record, and from our sources it cannot be dated and located with the same precision as material culture. In his homily *On False Gods* (*De Falsis Diis*), the homilist Ælfric made an implicit equation between the Danish people and the Danish language (with Old English *Denisc* 'Danish' standing for 'Scandinavian' in general), when he wrote that the classical god Mercury 'was honoured among all heathens, and by another name he is called Odin in Danish', while Jove 'among certain peoples [*þeodum*] is called Thor, whom the Danish people love most of all'.[149] Ælfric is here articulating a belief in what has been termed 'ethnolinguistic' identity: in other words, Danes speak Danish, and Danish is spoken by Danes. Of course, Ælfric's view must be an over-simplification, but it is still important evidence for a perceived connection between language and cultural identity. And there can be no doubt of the reality of the distinction between the English language and the Norse language in Viking Age England, above all in vocabulary and phonology: the accents of speech may well have been the most enduringly distinctive marker of a Scandinavian or English heritage. Similarly, personal names and nicknames seem to have been recognizably either English or Norse, and not an indistinguishable mixture.[150] A 1044 charter, for example, granting land in Dorset, introduces its recipient – who has a Norse name – with the statement that 'according to the custom of his own people from infancy [he] has borne the name Orc'.[151] The mid eleventh-century *Life of King Edward* (*Vita Ædwardi Regis*) refers to 'Siward, earl of the Northumbrians, called in the Danish tongue 'Digri', that is 'The Strong''.[152] So the difference between Norse and English may have been particularly felt in the area of personal naming.

This observation gains added resonance when we consider the vitality of Norse personal names in England. As noted in Chapter 4, there is little positive evidence for the general adoption of Norse personal names by the English population, and the mechanism by which Norse and English names came to co-exist in the same family is likely to have been inter-marriage, not fashion. But Norse personal names in northern England enjoyed an extraordinary persistence and creativity, with many new names, and permutations of names, being recorded in England which are not recorded in the Scandinavian homelands.[153] Some of these will have arisen originally as by-names or nicknames (such as *Sprækr* 'lively' and *Gamalbarn* 'old boy'), whereas others will have come into being through the creative combination of pre-existing name elements (such as *Arnbrandr* and *Hundigrímr*). This vibrancy of Norse personal names suggests strongly that important values of tradition and identity were invested in the culture of naming.

Both Old English and Old Norse, as languages, transcended political boundaries; they did not correlate with kingdoms or states. The language spoken by all Scandinavians in the Viking Age was known as the *Dönsk tunga*, 'the Danish tongue' – it was a pan-Scandinavian language that unified those who spoke it. (Why it should have been labelled *Dönsk* is disputed; it may be that the name arose from outsiders, such as Ælfric, who used 'Danish' as a catch-all term for all Scandinavians.[154]) Similarly *Englisc* ('English') brought with it a cultural or even ethnic unity, but not a political one, at least in origin. Pre-existing any sort of kingdom or nation of the English, the English language was, as it were, pan-Anglo-Saxon, unifying those who spoke it, and differentiating them from those who did not. King Alfred, in the 'us-and-them' context of the early Viking Age, called it 'the language that we can all understand'.[155] According to one reading of West Saxon ambitions, such linguistic unity among the Anglo-Saxons may have been helpful in paving the way for political unity too, but we should not automatically correlate language and kingdom.[156]

These examples of language and naming remind us that some of the most important markers of culture may simply be invisible in the archaeological record. Hairstyle is another good example.[157] In the late eighth century, as we saw in Chapter 2, Alcuin was lamenting that the Northumbrian aristocracy had wanted to copy pagan – that is, Scandinavian – hairstyles, and saw this as a sign of moral laxity.[158] The idea of the reprehensibility of adopting Scandinavian styles proved surprisingly long-lived, at least among learned and zealous clerics. Two centuries later, at a time of renewed Viking attacks in southern England, Ælfric wrote to one 'brother Edward' to complain that 'you do wrong in abandoning the English practices which your fathers followed, and in loving the practices [*þeawas*] of heathen men who begrudge you life, and in so doing show by such evil habits [*unþeawum*] that you despise your race [*cynn*] and your ancestors, since in insult to them you dress in Danish fashion with bared necks and blinded eyes'.[159] Ælfric's letter seems to offer a glimpse of potentially a whole repertoire of cultural forms which might be easily labelled and judged as either 'English' (ancestral, Christian) or 'Danish' (foreign, pagan). With respect to the specific hairstyle proscribed in the letter (long at the front, short at the back), it is striking that the Bayeux Tapestry depicts some Normans sporting precisely such a hairstyle, but not the Anglo-Saxons – which may suggest that the style was judged to be a recognizably Scandinavian one, and thus appropriate for those Normans (Northmen) who wished to proclaim their Scandinavian heritage.[160] There may also be a hint that such a preoccupation with hairstyle and personal appearance was foppish and degenerate: a famous story in the later chronicler John of Wallingford (who died in 1214) tells how the Scandinavians in England were popular with English women, to the chagrin of their menfolk, because they took a bath once a week, on Saturdays.[161] (And the Old Norse word for Saturday is indeed *Laugardagr* – 'bath-day'.) As for beards, it is notable that the portrait of Rægnald on his York coins, one of the warrior-crosses from Middleton, and the Kirkdale Christ, all show a forked form, suggesting that this may have been a favoured style for Scandinavians in the early tenth century. So, hairstyles and beards may have been among the most conspicuous markers of cultural identity in Viking Age England, much more prominent than the bells, brooches, and strap-ends that have survived for our scrutiny.

In 1002, King Æthelred the Unready, in a notorious decision, 'ordered to be slain all the Danish men who were in England [*ealle þa deniscan men þe on Angelcynne wæron*]', on St Brice's Day, 13 November.[162] The point to discuss here is not whether or not Æthelred's plan could possibly have been carried out on any sort of large scale (the strongest evidence that some Danes really were massacred comes from Oxford, rather than anywhere within the Danelaw).[163] Rather, the important point is simply that Æthelred and his councillors seem to have regarded it as not at all difficult to identify who was a Dane and who wasn't; the presupposition behind the policy is that there was a genuine, and readily apprehensible, difference between the two peoples in England. Of course, the identities that people ascribe to themselves may be very different to those ascribed to them by others, and ethnically-based policies have often wished to claim that such demarcation is unproblematic. But the St Brice's Day resolution does suggest that in Viking Age England the difference between English and Scandinavian was not felt to be quite as shifting or elusive as some recent scholarship has argued.[164]

For taken all together, there is more than enough evidence to suggest that, while assimilation and acculturation may have taken place in some cultural spheres, in others the difference between Scandinavian and English was a real and meaningful one, and one that persisted at least through the tenth century. The difference between the two peoples was not black-and-white – as we have seen, the Scandinavians in Viking Age Yorkshire were in some respects Anglicized and the English were Scandinavianized – but it does seem that a distinctive Scandinavian culture and identity persisted, and was actively preserved. Indeed, the region as a whole assumed something of a Scandinavian stamp and colouring, which continued, as we will see in later chapters, long after the demise of the Viking kings of York, and the region's incorporation into the kingdom of England.

Whether that sense of cultural or ethnic identity was a salient factor in political attitudes and actions is, however, a different question altogether, and it may well be that political identity was focused and expressed more in terms of a northern or Northumbrian identity that was able to accommodate within itself both Scandinavian and English. There is no evidence in tenth-century Yorkshire of politics splitting between Scandinavians and English on ethnic lines; indeed, on those occasions where we can detect a correlation in our sources between ethnicity and politics, it is in terms of an apparent tension between the settled (Anglo-)

Scandinavians of the region and the more pagan and aggressive Hiberno-Norse – a tension that can be seen in the 942 poem in the *Anglo-Saxon Chronicle* ('the Danes were previously subjected by force under the Norsemen'), and perhaps also in the diplomatic relations with Æthelflæd of Mercia recorded in 918. As we will see more clearly in Chapter 7, the political fault-line in tenth- and eleventh-century Yorkshire seems to have lain between north and south, not English and Scandinavian.

TOWN AND COUNTRY

YORK AND ITS HINTERLANDS

York

At the centre of Scandinavian rule in Northumbria was the city of York. Indeed, the preferred modern designation, 'the Viking kingdom of York', indicates that, in many ways, the city and the kingdom were one and the same. All roads led to York, literally: the city was the hub of an extensive Roman road network.[1] York was, of course, the only city in Northumbria. It was the centre of government, the centre of trade, the centre of the church. It was the only mint north of the Humber, and by far the most populous habitation north of the Thames.

Archaeologically, we know more about York than any other city in medieval England, thanks to the excavations and publications of York Archaeological Trust – especially, for the Viking period, through the famous Coppergate dig of the 1970s, led by Richard Hall.[2] But in considering the nature and significance of the city in the Viking period, it is important that we are not simply led by the archaeological evidence, considering only those aspects of the city which excavation has been able to illuminate. Rather, there are certain key questions which this chapter will ask, and attempt to answer – sometimes from archaeological evidence, sometimes from textual sources, and sometimes (it must be admitted) from informed speculation. How did York function as a political centre in the tenth century, and what was the relationship between the kings and other powerful parties – the aristocracy, the merchants, the church? Was the prevailing culture of the city Scandinavian or not? And – very importantly – what was the relationship between the city of York and the rest of the kingdom of Northumbria (that is, modern Yorkshire): did the city dictate and determine the nature of life and culture in the regions and hinterlands of the county, or was country life unaffected by doings in the metropolis? In a thought-provoking observation, Lesley Abrams has suggested that 'the sons of Scandinavian lords in

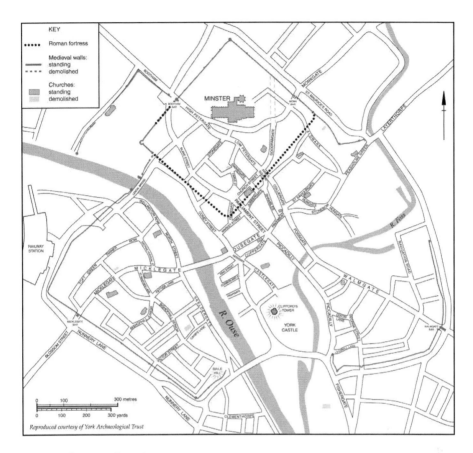

Map 2 The city of York

tenth-century Yorkshire could have travelled to centres of power like York and Dublin for a time and acquired some life-changing experience before taking over the management of their family estates'; in other words, through courts and towns such as York, local lords may have 'engaged with the wider world', so that 'culture could flow back to rural society'.[3]

A well-known passage in Byrhtferth of Ramsey's early eleventh-century *Life of St Oswald* introduces York as follows:

> There is a city called York [*ciuitas Eboraca*], the metropolis of all the Northumbrians, which was once splendidly constructed and stoutly provided with walls. It is now decrepit with age; yet it boasts a large population – no fewer than thirty thousand men and women (excepting children and teenagers) are counted as the populace of that city. It is inexpressibly filled and enriched by the treasures of

147

merchants, who come there from everywhere, and most of all from the people of Denmark [*ex Danorum gente*].[4]

Scholars have often dismissed Byrhtferth's figure of 30,000 as a wild over-estimate, but Byrhtferth was late Anglo-Saxon England's most distinguished mathematician, so it may be unwise to reject his evidence out of hand.[5] The period of Scandinavian rule witnessed substantial migration to the city, and very considerable growth: modern estimates suggest a population of perhaps 10-15,000, whereas the population of the pre-Viking city may only have been 10% of this figure.[6]

York was of course a Roman city, Eboracum, with its twin centres being the Roman fortress to the east of the River Ouse, and the *colonia* or civilian settlement to the west, both enclosed by fortifications.[7] But the city was depopulated after the end of Roman rule, in the fifth and sixth centuries, and only re-appears in the historical record in 627, when, according to Bede, the Northumbrian King Edwin was baptized and built the first Anglo-Saxon minster.[8] This was on the site of the old Roman *principia* or headquarters building, at the centre of the fortress. But although the church of York was to become very eminent, especially in the time of Alcuin in the eighth century, our best archaeological evidence for occupation and expansion in the Anglian period occurs down-river, in the Fishergate area, which was the site of the Anglo-Saxon *wic* or trading centre.[9] It was, apparently, the Vikings, and not the Anglo-Saxons, who grew the city outwards, beyond the extent of the Roman fortress, especially to the south, south-east, and south-west, and recent excavations have continued to reveal the extent of the Viking Age city, which spread out well beyond the area of Roman occupation and indeed beyond the line of the later medieval city walls.[10]

Viking Age York must therefore have been a city in which Roman stone and Roman structures were prominent features, whether still standing, plundered for re-building, or lying tumbled and prone, like the great columns of the former basilica.[11] The significance of the first element in the York street name Stonegate (Old Norse *stein-gata*) is that it indicates a paved, Roman street; it was in fact the Roman *via praetoria*, connecting the *principia* with the main gate of the fortress. Another revealing street name in this context is Stonebow. Although the medieval forms of the name indicate Old Norse phonology (*steinbogi* 'stone arch'), it is impossible that the architectural feature referred to, built in stone, can have been a Viking Age construction, and it may be that an earlier Old English *stānboga* lies behind the Scandinavian name (the Old English word occurs, for example, in the poem *Beowulf*). The name seems clearly to indicate the presence of a Roman arch as a prominent feature, and it has been suggested that such arches were sometimes removed piece by piece from surviving Roman structures, to be re-built in local churches, such as St Mary Bishophill Junior in York, and Kirk Hammerton [WR], west of the city.[12]

(a)   (b)

Figure 1 The Middleton Cross [NR]: (a) front (b) back.

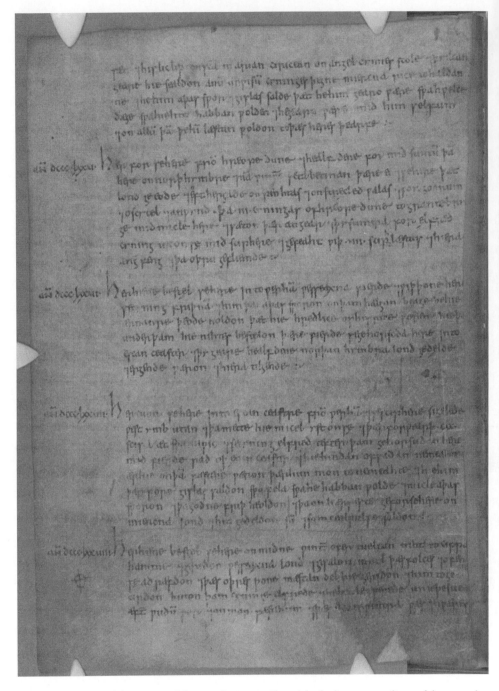

Figure 2 Folio 14v of the A-text of the *Anglo-Saxon Chronicle*: the bottom two lines of the central entry (for 876) record the settlement of Northumbria by Halfdan and his army.

Figure 3 Cross-shaft from St Mary Bishophill Junior, York, probably depicting two early ninth-century citizens of York.

Figure 4 Grave-marker from Lindisfarne, apparently showing Viking warriors.

Figure 5 (a) Coin of Cnut (c.900-05) (b) swordless St Peter coin (c.905-19) (c) Rægnald 'Bow / hammer' type (c.919-21) (d) Olaf Guthfrithson 'Raven' type (c.939-41)

The Vale of York hoard

gure 6 The Vale of York hoard, found near Harrogate [WR] and dating from the late 920s.

Figure 7 The Nunburnholme Cross [ER].

Figure 8 Warriors on horseback on a hogback from Sockburn [Durham].

Figure 9 Some Old Norse place-names north of York [all NR]:
(a) Haxby and Wigginton ('Hákr's *by*' and 'Víkingr's *tun*')
(b) Brandsby and Whenby ('Brandr's *by*' and 'the women's *by*')
(c) Coneysthorpe ('the king's *thorpe*')
(d) Airyholme near Hovingham ('the hill-pastures').

Figure 10 Oval brooches from a Scandinavian woman's burial at Adwick-le-Street [WR].

(a)   (b)

(c)   (d)

Figure 11 Small Scandinavian brooches found in Yorkshire: (a) Terslev/Borre-style brooch from Whitley [WR] (b) Jellinge-style brooch from Skipsea [ER] (c) trefoil brooch from Selby [WR] (d) openwork lozenge brooch from Thorpe Bassett [ER].

Figure 12 The Bedale hoard [NR].

Figure 13 'Norse bell' from Yapham [ER].   Figure 14 Gold finger-ring from Whorlton [NR].

Figure 15 Viking Age weights from near Stamford Bridge [ER].
Figure 16 Late Viking Age stirrup strap mount from Kilham [ER].

Figure 17 Inscribed sundial from Skelton in Cleveland [NR].

Figure 18 Inscribed sundial from Aldbrough [ER].

Figure 19 Roseberry Topping [NR], originally *Othenesberg* 'Odin's hill'.

Figure 20 The god Tyr on a hogback from Sockburn [Durham].

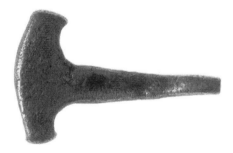

Figure 21 Thor's hammer from Copgrove [WR].

Figure 22 Hogbacks at Brompton near Northallerton [NR].

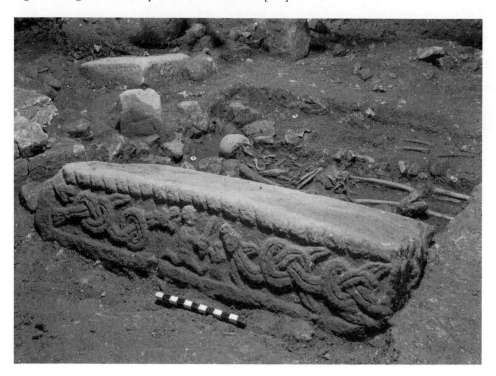

Figure 23 Grave-marker from the cemetery under York Minster, depicting the hero Sigurd.

Coppergate, York

Reconstruction of Viking Age Coppergate, York, by Andy Liddell.

Figure 25 Reconstruction of the beach market at Lythe [NR], by Peter Snowball.

Figure 26 St Gregory's Minster, Kirkdale [NR].

Figure 27 Inscribed sundial at Kirkdale.

Figure 28 Modern memorials in Stamford Bridge [ER], commemorating the battle there in 1066.

The street names of York have been very well studied.[13] As is well known, Scandinavian elements are prominent in such names, most obviously in the use of *gate* as the standard term for 'street' (from Old Norse *gata* 'street'). However, some of the names in *–gate* are obviously post-Norman Conquest in origin, as they refer to later structures or persons (such as Castlegate and Friargate), so it cannot be assumed that all street names with a Scandinavian element are of Viking Age origin: a brief discussion of dating is therefore required at this point. Few of the street names of York are recorded before the twelfth century, and so we cannot use the date of first record as the date of origin (as there were, evidently, streets in York before the twelfth century); tests of a linguistic or cultural nature are required instead. Such tests cannot reveal a precise date of origin for most names, but cumulatively they do suggest strongly that many of York's street names came into existence in a period when Old Norse was still being widely spoken in the city. So, for instance, the name Hartergate (now Friargate) preserves a distinctive Old Norse genitive singular inflexion (*Hjartargata* 'Hjörtr's street'), and thus the name can only have been given in the Old Norse language, and not through the borrowing of Norse words or names into English. Bootham was originally a dative plural *búðum* 'at the booths', probably referring to market stalls set up just outside the city walls. Similarly, there are strong phonological indicators in the medieval forms of some names, including Coney Street (Old Norse *konungr* 'king') and the lost Footlessgale (*fótlauss-geil* 'footless lane'). We do not know for sure the date at which the Old Norse language ceased to be commonly spoken in York (and in Yorkshire), but some time in the eleventh century would be a reasonable estimate. We can conclude, then, that the majority of the Scandinavian street names of York probably came into existence in the tenth or early eleventh century.

The heavy Scandinavian influence on the street names of York does not mean, of course, that all streets with Scandinavian names must have been laid out for the first time in the Viking period, though many unquestionably were, as the city grew in size and population. What we may also be observing, as with settlement names more widely, is a period of Scandinavian re-naming, which defined the nomenclature of the city for subsequent centuries. Stonegate is an obvious example of a pre-Viking street which acquired its enduring name in the Scandinavian period, though in fact the medieval forms of Stonegate record both Norse and English variants in the phonology of the first element (*steinn* and *stān*), thereby reminding us of the co-existence of the two languages in the city.

The evolution of the street system of Viking Age York has been carefully if tentatively traced.[14] Both the historical development of the streets of central York, and their names, reveal plainly that the Scandinavian centuries were the defining period for the city. Where, then, was the seat of authority? The early kings of Deira may have taken over the use of the Roman *principia*, as suggested by the use of that site for the first Anglo-Saxon cathedral.[15] But there is no evidence for royal occupation of the *principia* area in the Scandinavian period – it may by this time have become an exclusively ecclesiastical complex – and the best candidate for the palace of the Viking kings is the site now known as King's Court or King's Square. The modern form of the name, King's Court, is first recorded only in the sixteenth century; prior to that point, the name of the site was the Old Norse *Konungsgarðr*, of identical meaning.[16] The name *Konungsgarðr* is not itself recorded before the thirteenth century, but the poet Egill Skalla-Grímsson, in his *Arinbjarnakviða* from the early 960s, does refer to the 'court [*garðr*]' of Eric Bloodaxe at York, and also to his 'house [*hús*]'.[17] Post-Conquest royal residences in York were located elsewhere, so the likelihood seems high that the place-name preserves the memory of the earlier, Viking kings. The area has not been extensively excavated, but it has been pointed out that, at King's Court, various streets converged on one of the gatehouses of the Roman fortress, and thus we may be justified in picturing King's Court – the *konungsgarðr* – as the place where Egill 'saved his head' with his praise-poem *Höfuðlausn*.[18]

The evidence that enables us to re-construct the governmental administration of the Viking kings of York is, with one major exception, highly exiguous. This is partly due to the lack of documentary record, and the fact that Viking Northumbria was an oral society: it has been suggested that, in the areas of Scandinavian conquest and settlement, administration and land-holding were more reliant on the spoken word than the written, in contrast to the tendency in the rest of England.[19] The Viking kings of York, that is to say, did not use the technology of writing to govern; but this does not mean that they did not run an efficient state.

They were clearly able to draw on and organize resources sufficiently to re-build or strengthen the walls of York. A number of our sources comment on this, though they are not wholly consistent and the state of the fortifications in the Scandinavian period remains somewhat unclear.[20] We know from various sources (both textual and archaeological) of the speed and success with which Viking armies in England were able to construct fortifications (embankments and palisades), not least for use as their 'winter-camps'.[21] Written in the 890s, Asser's account of the fall of York in 866 includes the statement that 'in those days the city did not yet have firm and secure walls'; the implication must be that it was the Scandinavian conquerors who had subsequently been responsible for strengthening the city's defences, sometime between 866 and the composition of Asser's work twenty-five years later.[22] Similarly, the *History of St Cuthbert* records that Halfdan's army 'rebuilt York [*Eboracam ciuitatem reedificauit*]'.[23] At some point, presumably in the Scandinavian period, the expansion of the city involved the abandonment of the southern and western walls of the Roman fortress; this in turn necessitated the building of new walls that ran to the banks of the rivers Ouse and Foss, in order to maintain the city's defences. This resulted in a very large enclosed area, bigger than those at the great Scandinavian trading centres of Birka and

Hedeby.[24] We may recall from Chapter 3 that, according to William of Malmesbury, when Athelstan captured the city in 927, he 'levelled with the ground the fortress [*castrum*] which the Danes had built long ago'.[25] It is not clear whether, by *castrum*, William means the old Roman fortress, the new city walls, or some sort of inner fortification; whichever it may be, the detail attests to the construction capabilities of the Viking kings.[26]

The fact that the streets of the city are not all laid out in a neat grid-pattern, unlike many West Saxon *burh*s or planned towns of the period, may suggest an element of organic, almost haphazard, evolution. Nonetheless, some features of the Viking Age street-system can only have come into existence through a strong central authority, most obviously the re-routing of the main approach to the city from the south-east (now Micklegate, Old Norse *mikil-gata* 'great street').[27] Once within the walls of the Roman *colonia* or civilian settlement, on the west bank of the Ouse, this road diverges from the route of the Roman *via principalis* (which continued straight on over the Ouse to the gate of the fortress), to cross the river at a point some way south of the earlier Roman river-crossing. This suggests that the Roman bridge further up-river was no longer standing, and that a new bridge was constructed in the period when the 'great street' was established and named (on the site of what is now Ouse Bridge).[28]

The building and upkeep of fortifications and of bridges were two of the so-called *trinoda necessitas*, the threefold 'common burdens', which Anglo-Saxon kings imposed on their subjects.[29] The third was military service. As noted in Chapter 2, it is striking that Anglo-Saxon sources continue to refer to the Scandinavians settled in Northumbria as an army (Old English *here*, Latin *exercitus*) well into the tenth century. This may partly be a fossilized usage in our English sources (especially in the *Anglo-Saxon Chronicle*), but the frequency with which armies continued to raid southwards from Northumbria in the early tenth century suggests that some reality lay behind it. If so, and if the building of the new bridge was done under Scandinavian rule, then this would complete the set of three, and would suggest that the Scandinavian kings of York may well have been able to impose the three 'common burdens' on their subjects.

The supreme administrative achievement of the Scandinavian kings, however, and the one which we can know most about, was their institution and control of the city's coinage.[30] As has been explored in Chapters 2 and 3, this was a very major operation, though the poor levels of literacy on the coins suggest again that the bureaucratic machinery of York was not founded on an extensive use of the written word. The power of the Scandinavian kings, of course, was based not only on military conquest but also on wealth. It was the kings of York and their followers who caused the expansion of the city, as they 'stimulated the Danelaw economy' through the injection of massive amounts of capital, especially in the form of silver loot, much of it brought from Frankia.[31] This is one reason for doubting the hypothesis that the real power in York lay with the archbishops, and that it was they who were responsible for issuing coins: one of the most important uses to which this new influx of Viking silver was put was, as we have seen, the re-introduction of coinage, and of minting in the city.

There was a lot of wealth circulating in Viking Age York, initially brought in as Viking treasure, later re-cast as silver coins, and subsequently generated through trade and exchange. As a sign of such wealth, we might note the two gold arm-rings which have recently come to light. Most Viking Age jewellery is silver, and silver arm-rings functioned both as display objects and a form of portable wealth: significant numbers of silver arm-rings have been found in the north of England, of which two of the finest were uncovered near Selby [WR] in the nineteenth century.[32] By contrast, gold arm-rings are a very rare phenomenon in the Viking Age, though gold finger-rings – requiring much less metal – are not so exceptional: examples found in Yorkshire include those from Maunby [NR] and Whorlton [NR], as well as three from York itself [Figure 14].[33] Until a decade ago, however, no complete gold arm-rings were known from Northumbria. But in 2004, one came to light in very unexpected circumstances, as part of the estate of a York builder; how he acquired the object is completely unknown.[34] Then only three years later, a second example – though not so large and heavy – was discovered as part of the Vale of York hoard [Figure 6].[35] The important point is that both of these recent finds are from the York region: it was the city of York that possessed the wealthy elite who must have been the owners and wearers of such outstanding objects. The wealth of Viking York is also stressed by William of Malmesbury, who records that when Athelstan conquered the city and razed the *castrum* in 927, he found 'booty' there which was 'very plentiful'.[36]

Numismatists and archaeologists distinguish between three different types of economy that were operative, and often co-existent, in the Viking Age.[37] In a commodity economy, it is goods that are the units of exchange, from textiles to livestock. In a bullion-weight economy, it is silver that is exchanged, in the shape both of coins and of other forms of silver (and occasionally gold) bullion, such as ingots, arm-rings, and chopped up pieces of metal (hack-silver): the silver is weighed out, and often tested for its purity, through 'pecking' or 'nicking'. Finally, in a strict coin economy, other forms of silver (including imported coins) are excluded, and the coins only require counting out and not weighing, as one can be confident that they are guaranteed coin of the realm, minted to the same weight-standard.

We should probably assume that both a commodity economy and a bullion-weight economy persisted in some places throughout the Viking Age in Yorkshire, especially in more rural regions; and powerful exemplifications of the bullion-weight economy are provided by coin-less hoards, such as the Bedale hoard of 2012 [Figure 12], or the Bowes Moor hoard of 1982 [both NR], which contained 21 items of bullion, most of them ingots.[38] But the shift to a coin economy for trade centred on York can be dated with some accuracy. So-called mixed hoards (that is, those comprising both coins of the realm and other forms of silver, including foreign coins) are still held to indicate a bullion-weight economy, whereas hoards exclusively composed of state coins suggest that a shift to a coin economy is in progress or has occurred. The last substantial mixed hoards are the Bossall/Flaxton hoard (north-east of York, and dated c.927) and the Vale of York hoard (found near Harrogate, and dated c.927-29); and the earlier in profile of the two parcels in the 'Near York' hoard is also mixed (found near the Bossall/Flaxton hoard, and dated to the late 920s or possibly early 930s). So it looks as if Athelstan's 927 conquest of Northumbria was the crucial event, and no mixed hoards have been found that date from after Olaf Guthfrithson's re-establishment of Scandinavian rule in York in 939: Anglo-Saxon rule brought an end to the bullion-weight economy of Yorkshire (or at least, of York and its hinterlands), and it was not re-introduced when Scandinavian kings returned a decade or so later.[39] In any case, we should probably assume that a coin economy prevailed sooner within the city of York itself than elsewhere in the region, as suggested by the substantial hoard found at Walmgate (deposited c.915), all the coins of which were York issues.[40] Since York was the sole mint in Viking Age Northumbria, those living within the city and its environs are likely to have been more accustomed to the everyday use of coinage than those in more remote parts: it is striking, for example, that single finds of coins issued by the early king Cnut (c.900-05) have nearly all been discovered within a 20-mile radius of York, as if it was within the orbit of the city itself, and its immediate hinterland, that most coins were circulating.[41] As noted in Chapter 1, very few single finds of York Viking coins have so far come to light west of the Pennines, and it is single finds rather than hoards that give us the best evidence for the day-to-day use of coins.

This brings us to trade – along with military conquest, the main reason for York's pivotal role in the Viking Age. It was trade, stimulated initially by loot, that caused the development of the city, and the growth of a large population who – unusually for the early Middle Ages – were making their livings not primarily through agriculture. The role of the Vikings in urban growth is now very well recognized, both in Scandinavia and overseas; York is the supreme example from the British Isles, with Lincoln and Dublin also of importance.[42] Egill's *Höfuðlausn*, our sole extant poem from Viking Age York, alludes playfully to the city's status as a trading emporium in its opening stanzas: 'I went west over the sea,' Egill declares, 'I loaded the cabin of my ship with a cargo of praise' and 'I carried mead of Odin [=poetry] to the fields of England'.[43] Other Scandinavian travellers to York may have brought furs, or amber; Egill brings poetry, a deluxe import indeed. Egill came by ship, as did, no doubt, many of the merchants bound for York, but the city was well connected by overland routes as well: Roman roads led west over the Pennines, to Chester and the Irish Sea, and to Carlisle and the Solway Firth. A number of balance-scales, and accompanying weights, have been recovered from the city – an essential tool for commercial transactions, especially before the establishment of a pure coin economy.[44]

Other textual sources of the period also attest to York's fame as a mercantile centre. Byrhtferth's *Life of St Oswald* was quoted earlier; another pertinent reference comes in Roger of Wendover's *Flowers of Histories*:

> About the same time merchants coming from York landed in the isle of Thanet, and were at once taken prisoner by the islanders and robbed of all their goods; whence King Edgar, moved by anger, was so furious with these pillagers that he despoiled all of them of their possessions and even deprived some of life.[45]

In Roger this incident is dated to 974, but it is no doubt the same event as that ascribed (probably more reliably) to the year 969 in the *Anglo-Saxon Chronicle*, which records tersely that 'King Edgar ordered all Thanet to be ravaged', without supplying the motivation.[46] Trade was important to tenth- and eleventh-century kings: they received revenues from it, and acted to protect it.[47] The passages from Byrhtferth and Roger of Wendover also indicate that York's eminence as a centre of trade continued after the kings of England had supplanted Scandinavian rulers in the mid tenth century; it may, of course, have been one of the reasons why, together with the Vale of York's strategic importance, the West Saxons kings so desired to annex Northumbria in the first place.[48]

York's power as a trading centre seems to have been founded on exceptionally high levels of manufacturing in the city; it was not simply an entrepôt where goods were shipped in and out. York's manufacturing history in the Viking Age has been revealed by archaeological investigation, above all the excavations conducted between 1976 and 1981 at 16-22 Coppergate – the famed 'Viking dig'.[49] The waterlogged, oxygen-free soil of Coppergate preserved a variety of organic objects in unusually good condition, and these favourable soil conditions arose partly through the deposition of vast quantities of waste (organic and otherwise) in deep pits.[50] The foundations of wooden buildings were found too, as we shall see in a moment, but it is these pits or middens that substantially preserved and supplied the many thousands of small objects which the Coppergate dig revealed. The Coppergate excavations do not stand alone, however, and archaeology has revealed evidence for Viking Age activity at over 70 sites across the city.[51]

Ailsa Mainman and Nicola Rogers, in their survey of 'Craft and Economy in Anglo-Scandinavian York', identify nine industries which were practised in York, at Coppergate and elsewhere.[52] These are: iron working; non-ferrous metal working (copper alloy, lead alloy, silver, even gold); wood working; leather working; bone and antler working; amber working; glass working; jet working;

and textile working. It is the presence of waste products and unfinished pieces in the archaeological record which proves that we are looking at manufacture, on an intensive scale, and not simply domestic consumption. The range and quantity of objects recovered is astonishing: beads, brooches, belt-buckles, shoes, scabbards, combs, comb-cases, ice-skates, bowls, knives, keys, padlocks, pins (both metal and bone), linen smoothers, rings, tweezers, spoons, fish hooks, board games, playing pieces, pan pipes, and even a decorated bow from a wooden saddle. There is a particularly intriguing collection of objects pertaining to coining – three lead pieces stamped with coin-impressions, and two iron coin-dies for striking coins, of St Peter and Athelstan issues – though whether this means that Coppergate was actually the site of a mint is disputable; a safer description may be that site was involved in 'minting-related activity' (and a further explanation may simply be that these objects came to Coppergate in order to be melted down by iron and lead workers).[53] As for pottery, its manufacture was revolutionized in the Viking Age by the invention of the potter's wheel and improvements in kiln design. Pottery of a distinctive local type seems to have been manufactured in or near York in the earlier Viking period (so-called York ware is dated to the second half of the ninth century and the first half of the tenth), but other types from the Southumbrian Danelaw later became more popular (so-called Torksey ware and Stamford ware).[54] It may be that Torksey ware came to be made locally too, as a result of migration to York by Lincolnshire potters.

At Coppergate, the craft material was recovered from four 'tenements': narrow strips of land running down to the River Foss, with buildings at the front and yards at the back (and it is these tenements that have been reconstructed at the celebrated Jorvik Viking Centre) [Figure 24]. The street was a Viking Age creation: it was divided into plots in the decades around 900, but the first substantial buildings seem not to have been erected until the second quarter of the tenth century (the dating is determined through dendrochronology), so we should note that intensification of activity at Coppergate did not begin until some decades after the establishment of Scandinavian rule in the city (and indeed, perhaps not until the city first came under English control in the time of Athelstan). The buildings of Coppergate were initially single-storey structures with post-and-wattle walls, but in the later 950s, three of the four were rebuilt more ambitiously with planked walls and an underground cellar, presumably used for the storage of goods (and on one plot there was a third phase of building, in the first half of the eleventh century).[55] On some tenements a separate workshop appears to have been added at the back, even though there seems in fact to have been somewhat less craft activity on the site in this second phase.[56] The different tenements were not used exclusively for different crafts; rather, each of the four plots has thrown up evidence for a range of different crafts being practised. It is hard to know how to interpret this: it might indicate seasonal variation, or a rapid turn-over of occupants, or multi-skilled craftsmen, or some other scenario.[57] We should probably assume that people lived on these sites, though no sleeping areas have been identified with certainty, and whether the domestic occupants were the same people as the craftsmen (who might perhaps have rented work-space) is unclear.[58] Three of the four tenements produced substantial evidence for wood turning through the use of a lathe: over 300 wooden cores from cups or bowls were recovered from Coppergate, and the first element of the street name is indeed Old Norse *koppari* 'wood-worker, cup-maker'; the Coppergate excavations were thus, incidentally, a stunning vindication of the value of place-name evidence.[59] Other York street names that seem to refer to the siting of particular crafts in the Scandinavian period are Skeldergate (from Old Norse *skjaldari* 'shield-maker') and the now lost Ketmongergate (from Old Norse *kjöt-mangari* 'meat-seller').

But York was also a port, and not just a factory: it did see the import of wares from overseas.[60] Items arriving from Scandinavia included amber, walrus ivory, honestones, and clubmoss for textile dyeing (plus poetry, if we believe Egill). From Germany came pottery, textiles, and quernstones; from Shetland, bowls made from steatite or soapstone; from Ireland, ringed pins. The city was also connected to more far-flung networks of trade, and received some exotic goods, no doubt via middlemen, from Russia and the Arab world. Byzantine silk seems to have been imported in some quantity, telling us something about the colourful clothes of the city's elite.[61]

Nonetheless, the domestic market seems to have been more important than the international, and the supply of raw materials from the locality must have generated far more traffic in York's narrow streets. This is an aspect of the city that neither archaeological nor textual sources have so far been able to illuminate in great detail, but we can assume with some certainty that timber, wool, iron ore, and deer antler were among the more important materials being brought in – in addition to the food required to feed the city. Most of the raw materials are likely to have come from the city's hinterlands – from rural Yorkshire – but on the whole we can only speculate on the working relationships that may have existed between urban merchants and craftsmen on the one hand, and rural suppliers on the other.[62] Richard Hall imagines the scene: 'In they came, food from farms and estates within a day or two's journey, and the more specialized items, such as jet, or lead, from whatever productive sources looked to York as their most accessible or profitable market. Transport may have been overland, on foot, horseback or with ox-carts; the rivers also provided easy access. Out in return went the finished goods made from these imported raw materials, or perhaps some of the luxuries brought to Jorvik from much further afield.'[63] Some striking insights have been attained, however: for example, while huge quantities of coppiced roundwood must have been required for wattle walls and walkways in the city, analysis of tree-rings reveals no consistency in the coppicing cycle, which suggests, perhaps surprisingly, that coppicing was occasional and demand-led, rather than systematically managed.[64]

As this example shows, the Coppergate excavations have also revealed a very great deal about everyday life in the city, especially through the ever more refined techniques of environmental archaeology – above all, about the diet of Coppergate's Viking Age residents, and the flora and fauna to be found at their habitations.[65] Vast quantities of human faeces were retrieved from the cesspits of Coppergate, to be painstakingly analysed. The tenth-century population of York, we learn, consumed wheat, rye, barley, and oats; a greater variety of fruit than of vegetables; meat from cattle above all, but also from sheep and pigs; lots of shellfish; and, unsurprisingly, fish, initially from the rivers but later – perhaps once the rivers of York had become polluted through industry – increasingly from the sea.[66] Additionally, bones from a wide range of birds were recovered from Coppergate, from obvious domestic fowl like chicken and geese to (in much smaller numbers) wild birds such as grouse, guillemot, and plover. Bee-keeping was important, as honey was the main source of sugar.[67] From Coppergate's middens we even know what the Viking Age equivalent was of toilet paper (answer: moss and textile fragments). This may, in fact, have been much in demand, as the residents of Scandinavian York had a chronic problem with intestinal worms, as well as lice and fleas. Life in Coppergate, we can be sure, brought with it a fair amount of squalor and stench.

Although we naturally think of York as one of the great centres of the Viking world, it is important to remember that, as a coastal city evolving rapidly through massive immigration, York is likely to have been a progressive meeting-place, and melting-pot, of cultures and identities; if we want to find traditional Scandinavian culture, untouched and unchanging, we may be better off looking to the more conservative countryside. Only a relatively small amount of the manufacturing products of Viking Age York (as opposed to the heirlooms or imports) can be regarded as purely Scandinavian in terms of methods or affiliations.[68] Amber working stands out almost uniquely as a major new craft, introduced from Scandinavia and widely practised in the city.[69] The well-excavated buildings of Coppergate and elsewhere (including, recently, Hungate) are not diagnostically Scandinavian in form and construction – though this does not mean that they are diagnostically English either, but just that the two were not to be distinguished.[70] Some textiles show distinctive Scandinavian methods of manufacture, but most don't.[71] The brooches recovered from York fall into Jane Kershaw's 'Anglo-Scandinavian' category, and English styles were popular too, while a trefoil brooch mould found at Blake Street shows a highly unusual combination of a Scandinavian form with Anglo-Saxon motifs.[72] In leather working, elements of Anglo-Saxon craftsmanship persisted alongside new practices and preferences from Scandinavia.[73] In leather, bone, and metalwork it can sometimes be hard to tell where the English Trewhiddle style ends and the Scandinavian Jellinge style begins.[74] In stone sculpture too, as we will see, elements from both cultures were combined.

All this evidence for Anglo-Scandinavian interaction does not necessarily mean that Anglo-Saxon craftsmen must have carried on in York over the transition of the 860s and 870s, and then taught their skills to the new arrivals; we should recall the powerful signs of economic discontinuity in early Viking York, namely the abrupt end of the coin economy, and the abandonment of the Fishergate trading site. A more likely explanation is that Anglo-Saxon craftsmen were among those who migrated to York once the new regime was established, to form part of the new community of the cosmopolitan city; there is no reason why we should attribute York's population boom solely to Scandinavian immigration. And similarly, we should not imagine that the products of York were being consumed solely by those with Scandinavian ancestry or affiliations: the city's craftsmen and traders were no doubt happy to cater to an English market as well.

On the other hand, a different form of evidence, street names, does signal a pronounced Scandinavian flavour to the culture of the city. York's street names are full of Norse words and personal names, far beyond the use of *–gate* as the main suffix. The first element of Blossom Street, for example, is not 'blossom' at all, but Old Norse *plógsveinn* 'ploughman', as early forms reveal. The first element of Feasegate is Old Norse *fé-hús* 'animal-house', and that of the now lost Lounlithgate was Old Norse *laun-hlið* 'secluded gateway'. Cargate (now King Street) is from Old Norse *kjarr* 'marsh'. Haver Lane (earlier *Havergate*) contains either Old Norse *hafr* 'goat' or *hafri* 'oats'. Hellekeld, the name of a former property in King's Court (backing onto Pump Court), derives from Old Norse *helga-kelda* 'holy spring'. Similarly, Old Norse personal names are well represented – the names, presumably, of owners or occupants at a formative stage of name-giving. Goodramgate, for example, shows some variation in its medieval forms, and it is not clear whether the first element is the man's name *Guðrum* or the woman's name *Guðrún* – but whichever it is, both names are Old Norse. Blake Street may possibly be '*Bleiki*'s street', though a derivation 'bleaching street' has also been suggested. The first element of Knavesmire is likely to be the Old Norse personal name *Knörr*, and that of Ogleforth the personal name *Ugla* (if it is not simply the Old Norse noun *ugla* 'owl'). For only one of York's medieval street names has an Old English personal name been suggested: Walmgate may be derived from *Walba*, a shortened form of Old English *Wealhbeorht* or *Waldbeorht*; but it is equally possible that the name derives from Old Norse *Valbi*, a shortened form of *Valbjörn* or *Valbrandr*. Even though most of these street names are only recorded in the twelfth century, it is unlikely that the persons commemorated are of twelfth-century date, as the more extensive documentation from that period means that we know the names of York's leading twelfth-century citizens; and the persons named in these street names are not among them.[75]

As with the place-names of Yorkshire more generally, there is also a significant number of street names that indicate Irish or Goidelic influence – an influence to be best attributed to the period of Scandinavian rule. The best-known of these names is the now lost *Divelinestaynes* or Dublinstones, a quay-side site on the River Ouse where, one assumes, Dublin ships were loaded and unloaded. Also suggestive of Irish connections are the names (also lost) of *Galmanho* and *Galmanlithe*, which contain the personal name *Galmann*, probably an Old Norse borrowing of the Irish *Colman*. Patrick's Pool speaks for itself. And there were two medieval streets in York called Bretgate (one now lost, the other now called Jubbergate), the first element of which alludes to a distinctive community of Britons (using Old Norse *Bretar*) – most probably a community with links across to Cumbria and thus the Irish Sea region, though conceivably more 'local' Celts.

In language and personal names, then, York does seem to have been a strongly Scandinavian city. The persons whose names are commemorated in these street names are likely to have been among the city's elite, as also were the moneyers (who were the king's agents in controlling the coinage, and should not be confused with the artisans who did the actual melting and hammering). So far, buildings archaeology in York has not yielded up the homes of any of the wealthy and powerful; Coppergate's celebrated tenements belong further down the social scale. To get closer to the culture of York's resident tenth-century elite we need to turn instead to funerary monuments.

Stone sculpture has been recovered from over ten sites in York, most importantly from underneath the Minster itself. Excavations in the late 1960s and early 1970s, undertaken as part of a process to strengthen the Minster's foundations, uncovered a pre-Conquest cemetery containing over 100 burials (though the pre-Conquest church itself was not found, implying that it probably does not lie under the present Minster) [Figure 23].[76] A variety of burial practices were encountered: burial in coffins (both wooden and stone), under hogbacks and other grave-markers, with pillow-stones, on wooden biers, and on beds of charcoal, and altogether nearly 50 items of stone sculpture were recovered.[77] The cemetery directly underlay the footings of the Norman church, and thus indicated an early or mid eleventh-century date for the burials. However, a number of the stone monuments had clearly been re-used, having been cut down in size, and stylistic affinities are mostly with earlier tenth-century work; so the Minster cemetery gives us a corpus of tenth-century sculpture from the city – indeed, presumably from the tenth-century Minster cemetery – albeit re-used in an eleventh-century context. These are the only examples of Viking Age stone sculpture to have been found archaeologically *in situ* over burials, and thus their diagnostic value, even in a context of re-use, is very considerable.

These are the monuments of the *Jórvík* elite, and they are generally of high quality – a reflection, no doubt, of the wealth concentrated in York.[78] One recurrent type is the recumbent slab or grave-cover, shaped out of re-cycled building blocks from the Roman fortress. Other examples have been found elsewhere in York, suggesting it was a city-wide fashion, with slabs being produced to a set type.[79] Another feature of the York sculptures is their combination – though not exactly fusion – of English and Scandinavian traditions: as their main student, James Lang, has observed, the stone carvers of tenth-century York 'had one eye turned to the new animal ornament which appealed to new Anglo-Scandinavian patrons whilst looking back over their shoulder to the Anglian sources of their medium and its ornamental repertoire'.[80]

Viking Age sculpture has been recovered from a number of parish churches in York also. The most significant and prolific are St Mary Castlegate, St Mary Bishophill Junior, and St Mary Bishophill Senior, with the last-named yielding over twenty pieces. The two Bishophill churches are located within the walls to the west of the Ouse – that is, the area of the old Roman *colonia*. It has been argued that, in the pre-Viking period, this part of York formed both an important urban nucleus and something of a monastic precinct: in the later Middle Ages, Holy Trinity Priory was an extremely wealthy monastery, and may possibly have been so in the earlier period too (though it should be noted that the etymology of the name 'Bishophill' is not as transparent as it seems, and so does not constitute positive evidence).[81] But if the area did form an ecclesiastical complex, the properties of the monastery there, like those of many other churches throughout the region, are likely to have been fragmented and secularized in the Viking period, and the quantity of stone sculpture from the three churches mentioned have been taken as reflecting the new, mercantile wealth of Viking Age York: in other words, the church of St Mary Bishophill Senior – to take the leading example – may have been patronized by the merchants of the tenth-century city, as they and their families were buried there.[82] A small number of contemporary burials have in fact been excavated from the churchyard of St Mary Bishophill Junior, including two with Scandinavian grave-goods: one (either male or female) wore a silver arm-ring, while the other (certainly male) held in his hand a York St Peter coin of the pre-Rægnald period.[83] This is as close as we can hope to come to the citizens of Viking Age *Jórvík*.

Rural Communities

We should now look beyond the city of York, to consider life in the Yorkshire countryside in the Viking Age, and the relationships that may have existed between York and the rural areas. Some settlement may have fanned out from York, with migrants passing through the city as a sort of tenth-century Ellis

160

Island.[84] This does not in itself prove that York was anything more than a gateway to the regions, but in fact it has been argued that 'it is only with the Viking takeover that it is proper to speak of a true hinterland for York'.[85] In other words, the relationship between city and countryside in the earlier Anglian period is hard to reconstruct, and may have been relatively unimportant; whereas with the expansion of York in the Viking period, a variety of relations were strengthened or created — political, economic, cultural, and social. Furthermore, a range of hinterlands is possible, on a sliding scale: from the satellite or service settlements within a day's journey of the city (some of which have since been swallowed up into York itself), to those much further away in both distance and time, but still connected nonetheless in some significant manner. Equally, though, we should entertain the possibility that there were some parts of Viking Age Yorkshire that were more or less unaffected by events and activities in the city.

Let us begin with political and administrative connections. A number of rural estates in Yorkshire have Old Norse *konungr* 'king' as their first element, indicating that these were royal possessions: Coneysthorpe in the North Riding, Coniston in the East Riding (*Coningesbi* in its earliest form), and Coneythorpe, Conisbrough, Conistone, and Cold Coniston in the West Riding.[86] It is possible that some of these names are Scandinavianizations of earlier names with Old English *cyning* (especially Conisborough), and even if this is not the case, there is no guarantee that the estates received their Old Norse names before 954; but it is plausible that at least some of these settlements were so named because they were counted among the rural estates of the Viking kings of York, and managed for their benefit. It is unimaginable that the kings of York did not possess extensive rural estates, and in the next chapter it will be suggested that many of these royal estates, after 954, passed into the hands of the earls who were appointed by the West Saxon kings to govern Northumbria.

But did the administrative reach of the Viking kings of York extend further than rural land-holding? It was noted in Chapter 1 that, in the mid eleventh century, the newly-instituted shire of Yorkshire is named in the *Anglo-Saxon Chronicle* and other contemporary sources as *Eoforwicscir*. The city-name is thus given in the Old English form *Eoforwic*, rather than the Old Norse *Jórvík*, and this linguistic choice is best explained by the fact that the administrative unit of Yorkshire was the creation of an English-speaking government. But even if the shire of Yorkshire is a mid eleventh-century institution, we should pause to wonder about the term *riding*; it is not necessarily the case that the shire and the ridings came into existence at the same time.

The word *riding* is derived from Old Norse *þriðjungr* 'a third part, a thirding', with later loss of initial *th-* following a similar consonant. The only other part of the country to show a similar division into ridings is the former kingdom of Lindsey, in Lincolnshire, an area that was also marked by heavy Scandinavian settlement, though a fondness for such numerical subdivisions is also shown by medieval Iceland's organization into *fjórðungar* 'fourth parts, farthings'. So the grounds for thinking that, etymologically at least, the term is of Scandinavian origin seem good, and the Old Norse origin of the term contrasts provocatively with the Old English provenance of *Eoforwicscir*. Nonetheless, questions arise when one asks at what point in time the division into ridings took place. The word first occurs, with reference to Yorkshire, in Domesday Book, where the three Ridings, North, East, and West, are so named; but it is not possible to argue from negative evidence here, and to suggest that the ridings may have come into existence only shortly before their first record, as there are no pre-eleventh-century sources in which one might reasonably have expected the ridings to be mentioned (unlike for the shire, which could well have been mentioned in the *Anglo-Saxon Chronicle* at an earlier date, had it existed).

Outside of the division of Yorkshire, it is possible that the Old Norse word *þriðjungr* is found once as a loanword in Old English, in the form *ðirdung*, in the late tenth-century gloss made to the so-called Durham Ritual by the scribe Aldred (who also glossed the Lindisfarne Gospels) – though only with the meaning 'a third part', not 'a third part of Yorkshire'.[87] The occurrence of this loanword in the Durham Ritual (if its interpretation is correct) indicates that the Norse term was current and familiar in late tenth-century Northumbria. The date at which Lindsey was divided into ridings is also unclear: Peter Sawyer has proposed the reign of Cnut in the early eleventh century – at the same time, he argues, as the shire of Lincolnshire itself was created – but Stenton earlier asserted that 'there is every reason to believe that the ridings of Lindsey and Yorkshire go back to the first establishment of the Danelaw', and in this he has been followed by some other historians.[88]

The boundaries of the three ridings of Yorkshire converge on the city of York.[89] The administrative county of Yorkshire itself seems to have come into existence in the middle of the eleventh century, and so one might argue (as Sawyer does for Lincolnshire) that the ridings cannot logically pre-exist the shire. But if the subdivision into ridings only occurred at or after the creation of the shire, and as the county name itself is English, at least in eleventh-century sources, then it seems very surprising that an Old Norse word should be used for the subdivisions of the shire: the use of the term suggests an origin at a time when Old Norse place-names were being created in Yorkshire, by a Norse-speaking authority. At least two possible hypotheses could explain this. One is that Old Norse must still have been the language of authority in mid eleventh-century Yorkshire, though the English form of the shire-name (and other evidence) would suggest this is unlikely. The other hypothesis, then, is that the subdivision into ridings must have pre-dated the creation of the county, as Stenton believed, and to have occurred at a time of Norse rule and Norse language – in other words, in the last quarter of the ninth century or the first half of the tenth century, unless perhaps the division into ridings was a first step after the West Saxon conquest of 954. As a parallel, we should recall the subdivision of Iceland into quarters, by a comparable group of Scandinavian settlers: this seems to have taken place in the 960s.[90] If this logic holds good, then the division into ridings would be a product of the Viking kingdom centred on York (and the thirds would be thirds of the kingdom); and the shire of Yorkshire, when it came into formal existence in the mid eleventh century, took over, and corresponded with, the boundaries and subdivisions of the Viking kingdom (which itself largely corresponded with the former kingdom of Deira). This would indicate in turn that there was some degree of centralization and organization for the kingdom of York – a further argument against the proposal that the Viking kings of York possessed little authority.

How far the kings or York were able, or desired, to impose a strict coin economy across their territory is less certain. We saw earlier how, according to the hoard evidence, the shift from a bullion or mixed economy to a pure coin one seems to have occurred in the late 920s or early 930s, and possibly somewhat earlier in the city of York itself. But in recent years metal-detectorists have been turning up a considerable quantity of Viking Age weights from rural locations in the North and (especially) East Riding [Figure 15].[91] These weights (which would have been used with balance-scales) seem to be evidence of a significant bullion economy, widespread across the Scandinavian parts of the county, in which the unit of transaction was weight in silver rather than coin of the realm; so we must either assume that all these weights pre-date the rise of a coin economy, or conclude that the hoard evidence does not give us the full narrative. The recovery, outside of major hoards, of individual silver ingots, and other forms of hack-silver, tells the same story: an important early find came from near Easingwold [NR], while an increasing number have more recently come to light through detectorist activity, for example at Melsonby [NR], Boynton [ER], and near Driffield [ER].[92]

Easier to gauge is the cultural or artistic reach of York. Stone sculpture gives us our best evidence for this, on account of the size of the corpus and the rootedness of its geographical distribution (on the whole, most sculptures seem not to have moved much, and often were carved near to their find-spot). The discovery of the Viking Age cemetery under York Minster revolutionized understanding of the relationships and development of Yorkshire stone sculpture. Previously, for example, it had been thought that regional monuments such as the Middleton Cross occupied influential positions in the evolution of forms and designs; subsequently, it was realized that sculptures such as those at Middleton, and others in Ryedale, were decidedly provincial, and represented a copying or adaptation, by less skilled sculptors, of styles developed in York.[93] The Ryedale crosses are marked by long, single-panelled faces and ribbon-like animal ornament, and both of these features are found with greater aplomb on York stones.[94] In

James Lang's view, York was 'the design source of much of the sculpture spread throughout Yorkshire'.[95] Usually, the source should be thought of in terms of artistic exemplars or inspiration, but sometimes we can observe physical exports: a grave-slab from the northerly site of Gainford [Durham], out of keeping with most other Tees valley sculpture, is actually an outlying example of a common York type, and seems to have been shipped or transported all the way from York to Gainford.[96]

This view can be over-stated, however. For one thing, the direction of influence was not all from the city to the hinterlands. The whole genre of the hogback – Viking Age Yorkshire's main innovation in the repertoire of sculptural forms – seems to have been a provincial invention, which later caught on in York, as elsewhere: its origin was probably at Brompton, near Northallerton [NR].[97] The relationship between the influential Nunburnholme Cross [ER] and sculpture in York is far from clear.[98] Even the Ryedale school, in which metropolitan influences are most apparent, boasts features that are not derived from the city, such as a distinctive type of cross-head and, of course, the prominence of warrior-figures on the sculptures.[99] So a pure model of core versus periphery, with artistic influence flowing in a one-way direction from the former to the latter, and being ever debased as it goes, is far too reductive. In addition to this, certain York styles, such as the grave-slabs, were just not much copied out in the regions, while some important areas of sculptural production in the north and west of the county, further away from York than Ryedale, were largely unaffected by the styles of the city, and instead looked west over the Pennines towards Cumbria and Ireland.[100]

What these more provincial areas of sculpture enable us to do, then, is to identify particular 'schools' of carving, even individual workshops – which in effect means that we are identifying local artistic and intellectual communities.[101] As Richard Bailey has written, 'the crosses and slabs give us access to the Viking-Age history of numerous small towns and villages which have otherwise left no record in any contemporary source', and the clustering of sculptures means that we can often move beyond an atomistic approach to such histories.[102] Not always, however: even within the ambit of well-established schools, sculptural production was by no means homogenous, and many unique or hard-to-parallel monuments exist. An excellent example would be the Stonegrave Cross [NR], found at a site which is just to the south of the main Ryedale group, and which is recorded in documentary sources as being a monastery in the pre-Viking period. The Viking Age cross there depicts a figure at prayer holding a book, and a cleric adorned with a book-satchel, and it shares few characteristics with the nearby Ryedale school; it has been suggested that a distinctive religious community, perhaps with links to Celtic culture, may have persisted or been re-established there in the tenth century.[103]

So we should be aware of the individuality of sites such as Stonegrave. But in addition to that based in Ryedale, important sculptural schools or workshops that have been identified include those in Allertonshire, especially around Brompton [NR]; at Burnsall in upper Wharfedale [WR]; and at Lythe on the coast [NR]. Brompton, as noted earlier, is the likely place of origin for the hogback tradition, and some eleven examples derive from there; the presence of end-beasts in the shape of naturalistic bears is a distinctive feature of the Brompton collection [Figure 22]. Another important site within the Allertonshire school is Sockburn [Durham], whose sculptures are distinguished by their warrior-figures and mythological content.[104] The sculpture of the Allertonshire school as a whole shows considerable Irish affiliations, an interesting correlation with the Scandinavian place-names of the area.[105] The sculpture from Burnsall in Wharfedale also has connections with the Irish Sea region. Thirteen Viking Age pieces, including three hogbacks, have been found at Burnsall, making it the most prolific site in the Dales. But much of its sculpture is quite plain, with many faces and panels undecorated, and Elizabeth Coatsworth characterizes Burnsall as 'a local workshop aware of the fashionable trend but out of the mainstream'.[106] The Burnsall sculptures also show continuing Anglian influence, with ring-heads by no means as ubiquitous as further north and east in the county.

Lythe is a very different case, and a very intriguing one, which merits extended discussion. The site has produced nearly 50 pieces of sculpture of Viking Age date, from over 30 different monuments, including some 17 hogbacks. Lythe sits above the long strand of Sandsend, the plausible site of a 'beach market', a type well attested elsewhere in Viking Age Britain [Figure 25].[107] It thus forms the most persuasive rural example of David Stocker's proposed category of merchants' churches (like St Mary Bishophill Senior in York); that is, local churches that came to be patronized by a Scandinavian mercantile elite.[108] The interesting complication with Lythe is its relationship with Whitby, which lies only three miles south along the coast, and is clearly visible. Whitby is almost certainly to be identified with Bede's *Streoneshalh*, location of the epochal synod of 664 and burial place of King Edwin; it was a very important early Anglo-Saxon monastery, producing a great deal of stone sculpture, though the visible building remains are of the post-Conquest re-foundation. According to a twelfth-century text preserved in the *Whitby Cartulary*, the Anglo-Saxon monastery was destroyed 'by the most cruel pirates Ivar and Ubba [*crudelissimis piratis*]', and as an ironic testament to Viking rapacity, an arm from a shattered Anglo-Saxon stone cross seems to have been chiselled out and re-used as a mould for making silver ingots; a second ingot mould has also been found at the site.[109] The harbour below the monastery stands at the mouth of the River Esk, and Esk Dale is marked very heavily by Scandinavian place-names. In the tenth century, jet from the area was exported widely (it is found, for example, in York and on the Isle of Man), while the nearby quarries of Aislaby continued to supply stone as they had in the pre-Viking period.[110]

The settlement around the harbour was re-named as Whitby (Old Norse *hvíta-bý*, probably 'white settlement', rather than '*Hvíti*'s settlement', from the stone of the cliffs), and the ecclesiastical site up on the headland, where a secular church emerged out of the ruins of the monastery, came to be known by the time of Domesday Book as *Prestebi* ('the priests' settlement').[111] The oddity is that Viking Age Whitby/*Prestebi* has yielded only two items of tenth-century sculpture, in great contrast both to the earlier history of the site and to contemporary developments at Lythe.[112] Lythe is probably a Scandinavian place-name too (Old Norse *hlíð* 'slope'), but the church there preserves a couple of scraps of pre-Viking architectural sculpture, and thus it must have been an ecclesiastical site in the Anglian period (it is dedicated to the Northumbrian saint St Oswald, and may possibly have been a dependent cell of the monastery of *Streoneshalh*).[113] So clearly the Viking period sees a shift in orientation, or a differentiation in purpose, between the churches of Lythe and *Prestebi*: the former comes to function as the main focus for patronage and burial for the merchants of the area, while the latter becomes perhaps a private church, with burial there restricted only to a few founding members of the proprietorial family.[114] As can be judged, then, the tenth-century history of the Lythe/Whitby area permits us a sense of some of the complex micro-developments that are likely to have played out in many localities across Viking Age Yorkshire.[115]

What about the settlements themselves, buildings rather than monuments? As we saw in Chapter 4, the evidence of place-names, and of portable metalwork, gives us insights into the nature and distribution of Scandinavian settlements, nucleated and dispersed. The indications are that many Yorkshire villages were laid out or re-planned, into their enduring form, in the Viking period, and at the same time many parish churches and churchyards were built and established.[116] But finding the archaeological remains of Viking Age settlements has, outside of York itself, proved extremely difficult.[117] The very importance of the Viking period for settlement development is one reason for this: if the tenth century was the key period in which many settlements assumed their current form, at least at their centre, then it follows that many Viking villages are likely to lie buried underneath modern ones, and it is only when a site was subsequently depopulated and abandoned in the later medieval period that archaeological investigation is possible.[118] Another reason, though, is uncertainty over what precisely a Scandinavian building might look like; or at least, an awareness that it may be difficult to isolate diagnostic, typological features that can be used to differentiate Scandinavian-style buildings of the tenth century from Anglo-Saxon ones. One possible candidate is the bow-sided hall or longhouse, which has been found at a number of sites in eastern England, including Thwing [ER], and which stands in a close relationship with the distinctive form of the hogback.[119] But this is not certain, and it remains the case that, in definitive and agreed terms, 'distinctive Scandinavian building forms have not been found'.[120]

A number of individual sites should be mentioned, however, some of which are more persuasive than others as examples of Scandinavian settlements. Two upland sites that were excavated in the 1970s are Gauber High Pasture, Ribblehead [WR] and Simy Folds in Upper Teesdale [Durham]; a third comparable site, further afield, is Bryant's Gill in Kentmere in Cumbria.[121] All three sites revealed long rectangular buildings on stone foundations, together with smaller outbuildings, and the assumption is that these were homesteads where mixed farming was practised. But few small finds were recovered, and it cannot be said that the dating indications resoundingly support the identification of these sites as Scandinavian farms. Charcoal from Simy Folds has been carbon-dated to the second half of the eighth century, and the same is true for Bryant's Gill — too early for a Scandinavian provenance for the buildings themselves. The case for Ribblehead is stronger, as four Northumbrian *stycas* of the mid ninth century were retrieved, from locations which indicated that the buildings are likely to date from after their time of minting rather than before; so we can at least be confident that the site was occupied during the later ninth century and later. Whether Ribblehead should be regarded as a Scandinavian site or a late Northumbrian one is open to dispute, though the discovery of a small bell there may suggest the presence of Norse material culture. There has certainly been some desire to count these sites as Scandinavian rural settlements — and 'desire' may be the operative word for Simy Folds especially — if only because, until recently, no better candidate has presented itself.[122]

We now have far greater information and understanding about another site — or rather, group of related sites — explored in the last twenty years, at Cottam (Old English *cotum* 'at the cottages') and Cowlam (probably Old Norse *kollum* 'at the hill-tops') in the Yorkshire Wolds [both ER].[123] A combination of metal-detecting, field-walking, and excavation has revealed that in the later eighth and ninth centuries there were three 'Middle Saxon' settlements close to one another, two at Cottam (Cottam A and Cottam B) and one at Cowlam. All three were abandoned in (probably) the late ninth century, but at Cottam B the settlement was re-located to a new site, 100 metres to the north-east. The most striking feature of the new, early tenth-century farmstead at Cottam B was its elaborate gateway, perhaps suggesting the social assertiveness of the *nouveau riche*. Some of the finds from the new farm have a strong Scandinavian signature: a Jellinge-style brooch, a Borre-style buckle, Torksey pottery, and two diagnostic 'Norse bells', and the view of the excavator, Julian Richards, is that 'the new occupants may well have been Scandinavian colonists'.[124] In turn, though, the gated farmstead was only occupied for fifty years or so, before occupation shifted again, to the village of

Cowlam, and, possibly, the village of Cottam too, both of which became deserted in the later Middle Ages. Excavation at the deserted village of Cowlam suggests it was established as a planned settlement in the tenth century, probably at the same time as the new farmstead at Cottam B; but whereas the village of Cowlam thrived (at least in this period), the nearby settlement of Cottam B was abandoned.

Consideration of Cowlam and Cottam also brings Wharram Percy [ER] into the picture (probably Old Norse *hvarfum* 'at the bends (of the river)'; 'Percy' is a later manorial affix). Wharram Percy is of course a famous site, the flagship for the study of deserted medieval villages, and it has received an unparalleled degree of excavation and attention.[125] The site has yielded Viking Age artefacts, such as a Borre-style strap-end, and what has become clear is that the Scandinavian period was the crucial time for Wharram Percy's development as a village.[126] Sometime in the period c.850-950 a dam and water-mill were created, and in the tenth century a burial ground was established and a wooden church built. At about the same time the settlement as a whole was re-organized and laid out as a nucleated, planned village, with two facing rows of so-called tofts and, later, crofts (that is, houses on the street-front with strips of land behind).

Cottam and Wharram Percy thus bring us back to the question of agriculture. A number of scholars have argued that the Viking period saw the intensification of land-use on the Wolds, with land coming back into agricultural use that had been earlier been farmed in the Romano-British period but abandoned in the Anglian.[127] Certainly, there are no grounds for doubting a fundamental discontinuity on the Wolds between the Romano-British period and the Anglo-Saxon, but archaeological evidence from such sites as Wharram Percy and Cowlam/Cottam indicates that at least some higher land was being exploited again from the eighth century, especially for sheep grazing.[128] But it is also clear, on the basis of place-name evidence, settlement morphology, and small finds archaeology, that the ninth, tenth, and eleventh centuries saw an increased density of population and a 'massive expansion in cultivation' – though this need not mean that virgin or marginal land, never before farmed, was being cultivated for the very first time.[129] The tenth century was the 'village moment' on the Wolds, as Scandinavian conquest established new patterns of lordship, and it seems to have involved land that had lain fallow since the Romano-British period being once more being taken under the plough. To quote the conclusions of Julian Richards on the settlement history of the Wolds:

> During the middle Anglo-Saxon period the first permanent settlements were established [...] These served as sheep stations, hunting lodges, craft-working centres and foci for administration, and some developed as periodic market centres. Many were dependencies of major estate centres, on the Wolds and in the Vales, and may have acquired specialist functions of resource provision. With the

disruption of land holding following from the Scandinavian settlement, they were often separated from their estate centres and became nucleated villages under new local lords.[130]

In Chapter 4, the major place-name types were explored, of Grimstons, *by*s, and *thorp*s: the first, we saw, seems to indicate pre-existing English villages taken over and perhaps re-organized by Scandinavian lords; the second, a variety of settlement forms, including dispersed settlements engaged in pastoral farming; and the third, planned settlements focused on arable farming. With regard to the *thorp*s, we saw that the shift to open-field farming cannot simply be attributed to Scandinavian invention, though it is contemporaneous with the rise of Scandinavian lordship.[131] Another place-name element that indicates Scandinavian farming practices is *ærgi*. As noted in the previous chapter, the term *ærgi* was borrowed from Goidelic into Norse (probably from Gaelic *áirge*), and it became a widely used element in the Norse place-names of northern England. The basic meaning of the word is 'shieling, hill-pasture', indicating the agricultural practice of transhumance, the movement of livestock to higher pastures during the summer season.[132] But there were other, native Norse words with much the same meaning, namely *sætr* and *skáli*; the distinctive meaning of *ærgi* seems to have been 'home-shieling, pasture near to the farm', as opposed to shielings on higher (and inferior) land, and this explains why several places in *ærgi* subsequently became independent farms or settlements.[133] Yorkshire examples include Aireyholme (a farm near Great Ayton [NR]), Airyholme (a farm near Hovingham [NR]), Argam [ER], Arram (in Hunmanby parish [ER]), Arram (in Leconfield parish [ER]), and Eryholme [NR]. Another distinctive feature of *ærgi* names is that the place-name form seems often to have been in the dative plural, *ærgum* 'at the home-shielings', though a few examples also occur combined with a personal name, such as Golcar (probably 'Guðlaugr's shielings' [WR]). As ever, it is hard to say for sure whether the *ærgi* names represent new sites, or rather the re-naming of pre-existing Anglian sites, with perhaps an intensification of use.

It is worth pursuing place-names a little further, and with a different purpose from that in Chapter 4. For Old Norse place-names in England not only give us evidence for Scandinavian settlement; they also supply us with windows onto the lives lived by the settlers and their descendants, offering otherwise unobtainable glimpses of life and culture in Viking Age Yorkshire. Names for roads (or places named after road-features) demonstrate this well, offering a combination of perception, use, ownership, and lived experience: Norse examples in Yorkshire include Braygate Street ('broad road' [NR]), Roppa ('red path' [NR]), Staingate ('stone-paved road' [WR]), Figham ('cattle track' [ER]), Gunnergate Lane ('Gunnarr's road' [NR]), and Slape Wath ('slippery ford' [NR]), in addition to several instances of *leið-gríma* 'way-mark', seemingly indicating a navigational blaze on a tree.[134] Alternatively, we could attend to recreation, and to Norse place-name evidence for hunting (Hunmanby [ER] 'the settlement of the houndsmen', and probably also Galtres [NR] 'boar-thicket', later an important post-Conquest hunting forest), and for horse-racing and horse-fights (examples include Hesketh [NR and WR] and Heskitt [WR], from Old Norse *hesta-skeið* 'horse race-track', and Follifoot [two in WR], from Old English *fola-(ge)feoht* 'horse-fight; place where horse-fights took place').[135] Superstition and folklore are predictably rewarding: several 'holy wells' are recorded (from Old Norse *helga-kelda*), *Drechowe* 'dragon's mound' is a lost name in the North Riding, and other supernatural creatures attested in Norse place-names include the mound-haunting *skratti* ('goblin; wizard; devil') in Scrathowes [NR] and Scratters [ER], and the *skyrsi* 'monster' lurking at Skirse Gill and Skirsgill [both WR].[136] The etymology of Trollers Gill [WR] is, as A.H. Smith notes, 'the troll's arse', denoting 'a great bank in the ravine'.[137]

Place-names recording legal practices can illuminate an important aspect of Scandinavian culture. So, for example, it has been suggested that the etymology of Wetwang [ER] is not the obvious one of 'wet field', but rather the Old Norse legal term *véttvangr* 'field of summons for a trial'.[138] The suffix Bierlow, recorded in a number of West Riding names (such as Brampton Bierlow), is from Old Norse *býjar-lög* 'law of the village'; the term also survives in Modern English as 'by-law'.[139] A Norse term that continued as a productive element in the post-Conquest period is *vönd-deill*, later Middle English *wandale* 'share of common arable land'.[140] But unquestionably the most important institutional names are those containing the crucial Norse word *þing* 'legal assembly'. Although it is now lost, Viking Age Yorkshire boasted at least one example of the celebrated *þingvöllr* type of name ('assembly-plain'), found in many places in the Viking world, including the Isle of Man (Tinwald), Shetland (Tingwall), and Iceland (Þingvellir).[141] Recorded in twelfth-century documents, a site named *Tingwal* or *Thingwala* lay close to Whitby, in a heavily Scandinavianized part of the county.[142] Other names containing *þing* include Fingay Hill [NR] and Fingerfield [WR] (both *þing-haugr*, 'assembly mound') and Morthen [WR] (*mór-þing* 'moorland assembly').[143]

Consideration of legal meeting-places brings us more broadly to the question of local administrative structures. The North Riding and the West Riding were divided into units known as wapentakes, whereas in the East Riding the units were usually known as hundreds (though in one case, Domesday Book refers to the same East Riding unit as both a hundred and a wapentake).[144] Hundreds and wapentakes constituted the main local courts in pre-Conquest England, and they also had a function in taxation and other assessments. The hundredal unit is English, and seems to have been introduced in many parts of the country by the West Saxon kings in the course of the tenth century, so the use of the term in the East Riding suggests that the system may have been introduced into the north at some point after 954 (or possibly after Athelstan's conquest of 927).[145] On the other hand, the term 'wapentake' is Old Norse, *vápnatak* meaning 'the taking up of weapons', though it is unclear whether this refers to the taking up of weapons at the end of a completed assembly, or the brandishing of weapons during an assembly to signal assent. A further complication is that the Domesday hundreds of the East Riding were later amalgamated (re-amalgamated?) into larger wapentakes. The question of the origins of the wapentakes is thus not dissimilar to that of the origins of the ridings, and of course the two must go together, as the wapentakes correlate with the ridings, and do not straddle riding-boundaries. It might be argued that the hundreds and wapentakes of Yorkshire are a West Saxon imposition; but in that case one would need to explain why the hundredal system was not used throughout. Alternatively, and more plausibly, one could regard the wapentakes as a Scandinavian importation, pure and simple; but in that case one would need to explain why the East Riding is subdivided into hundreds. Clearly, a compromise position would be to assume some sort of mixed origin or development, perhaps with West Saxon re-organization following upon an earlier Scandinavian practice.[146] Other, related Scandinavian units of subdivision and assessment which were introduced into the Danelaw area include the 'ploughland' (or 'carucate'), roughly equivalent with the native English 'hide', and its eighth part, the 'oxgang' (or 'bovate').[147] Moreover, it has been observed that much of Domesday Book's survey of Yorkshire 'makes sense only in terms of an Anglo-Scandinavian reckoning by twelves rather than tens, and of the 'long hundred' of 120'.[148]

All wapentakes and hundreds had designated assembly-places, often focused on a prominent mound or hill, and many of those in Yorkshire bore Norse names, such as *Maneshou* wapentake in Ryedale [NR] ('Man or Manni's mound') and *Toreshou* hundred on the Wolds [ER] (probably 'Þórir's mound').[149] It is possible that the persons specified in hundred and wapentake names (such as Manni and Þórir) were the figures of authority within the wapentake; alternatively, if the assembly-mound was man-made rather than natural, they might be the figures believed to be buried in the mound.

Returning to place-names, we can conclude by looking at some terms of rank. Below the king, at the top of the Scandinavian social scale, came the earl, though Old Norse *jarl* seems only to be recorded in minor names from Yorkshire.[150] Next came the *hold* (Old Norse *höldr*): Holderness [ER], as we saw in Chapter 3, may indicate the territory of a *hold* in the early tenth century, and the term is also recorded in *Holdelythe* [NR], a district in Ryedale.[151] Further down came the *bóndi* and the *drengr*. *Bóndi* ('free farmer') occurs as an affix in Bond Burstwick [ER], and also in a considerable number of minor names, such as Bond Ings ('meadow' [WR]), Bondgate ('street' [WR, several examples]), and *Bondflat* ('level ground; division of a common field' [NR]).[152] *Drengr* is a term much recorded in Norse skaldic poetry and runic inscriptions from Scandinavia, and it is

171

borrowed into Old English.[153] Its laudatory sense is 'brave, youthful man', but in England the term also develops an administrative sense, indicating a prosperous, leading tenant of the thegnly class.[154] Yorkshire place-names containing the term include Dringhouses and Dringthorpe [both WR], Dringhoe (*haugr* 'mound, hill' [ER]), and *Drengate* ('street' [ER]).[155] Although not strictly a term of rank, it is also worth noting here the occurrence of the Old Norse term *gildi* 'guild; guild-member', in the compound *gildi-hús* 'guild-house'. Examples are surprisingly common from Yorkshire (for instance, Gildersdale [ER] and Gildersome [WR]), indicating an important aspect of social organization in Danelaw communities.[156]

Slavery was a standard feature of Scandinavian society in the Viking Age, and northern England was no exception.[157] The usual Old Norse word for '(male) slave' was *þræll*, and this term is borrowed into Old English in the late Anglo-Saxon period; like its female counterpart, *þírr*, it appears in late Northumbrian glosses on the Gospels, where the Norse-derived terms are used to render Latin *servus* and *ancilla*.[158] There are not many traces of slavery in the place-name evidence, though *Thrillekeld* [ER] is a direct parallel to the Cumbrian place-name Threlkeld ('thralls' well').[159] More in evidence is the related *leysingi*, the Old Norse term for a freedman, a slave who has been manumitted. The term was also used as a by-name, and place-name examples include two Lazenbys [both NR] and one Lazencroft, earlier *Lesingthorpe* [WR].[160] Freedmen may well have formed a numerous and important social class in the Scandinavianized society of the north, and it has been suggested that they were a key group of people involved in the opening up and (re-)cultivation of neglected land – taking on a difficult task for their own benefit, while still owing dues back to their former masters, who would benefit from their industry.[161]

This review of terms of rank brings us finally to a somewhat exhausted debate on the so-called 'free peasantry' of the northern Danelaw. The great Anglo-Saxon historian Frank Stenton argued that areas of Scandinavian settlement boasted a higher proportion of free peasants than other parts of England, and the main evidence on which he based his claim was the prevalence of freemen and sokemen in those areas in Domesday Book.[162] Sokemen have been defined as 'a caste of upper peasantry, clinging tenaciously to certain rights and freedoms', and normally they did not owe service to their local lord of the manor; the term is preserved, for example, in the place-name Socken Wood [ER].[163] Such independent, higher-ranking peasants, Stenton claimed, were the descendants of the settlers from the Viking Great Army, and their more remote lord was the descendant of their ancestors' erstwhile army commander, perhaps of the rank of *hold*; this social structure, inter-connected but also devolved, was held to enshrine a distinctively Scandinavian commitment to liberty. Stenton's hypothesis, it must be said, was quite fiercely assailed by some other historians. R.H.C. Davis (followed by Peter Sawyer) countered that the correspondence between Domesday sokemen and Scandinavian settlement was not in fact all that perfect: for while Lincolnshire had lots of sokemen and lots of Scandinavian place-names, Yorkshire had lots of the latter but not the former, and East Anglia lots of the former but not the latter.[164] However, it is important to remember that the Yorkshire Domesday is simply less systematic and less forthcoming than the Lincolnshire Domesday – it is not just sokemen that it says less about – while the current abundance of metal-detected jewellery has removed one of the main planks of Davis' argument, that East Anglia did not see significant Scandinavian settlement.[165] More recently, Dawn Hadley has demonstrated that we must be cautious not to attribute all the differences and oddities of the northern Danelaw to the impact of the Scandinavians: some may well have been regional differences that pre-existed the Viking settlement, and it is generally agreed that the type of estate known as a 'soke' (where constituent elements can be widely dispersed, each owing service to the remote estate centre, rather than a local manor) predates the Viking Age, even though it may have been adapted and re-named through Scandinavian settlement.[166]

Nonetheless, much of Stenton's essential insight remains, even if some of his grounds might be queried. It may well be over-simple to see the freemen and sokemen as the direct descendants of the original settlers, and the structure of estates as fossilizing the hierarchies of the Scandinavian *here*, but there can be no doubt that the Viking shake-up of estates did lead to more land being held in more hands, and that there was something of a difference between northern and southern society. In the south, there was often a correlation between manor and village, so that the two were co-extensive, and heavy burdens were placed on the 'manorialized' peasants of the village; but in the north, there were often several manorial holdings in any individual settlement or vill, holdings which were smaller and both owed and possessed less burdensome rights.[167] The line between the lower gentry and the upper peasantry was also more blurred. 'Individually', Stenton wrote of the free peasants of the north, 'they were men of small estate, possessing only one or two plough oxen and farming on an average some twenty to thirty acres. But they were certainly independent of anything that can be called manorial discipline'.[168]

In this chapter, we have reviewed some of the main circumstances of life in Viking Age Yorkshire, both within the city of York and in the surrounding regions, and have tried to tease out some of the ways in which town and country were (or were not) connected to one another. What, then, changed when the West Saxon kings permanently established their rule in Northumbria, and brought the region into the English state? That is the question which the next chapter will explore.

YORKSHIRE UNDER THE WEST SAXON KINGS

Northumbria and England

In following the political history of Viking Age Northumbria, at the end of Chapter 3 we paused in 954, with the death of Eric Bloodaxe, the last Viking king of York. We will now resume that political narrative.

When it came to the late Anglo-Saxon state, to what has been called 'the united kingdom of England', Northumbria was different.[1] It was remote from the southern centres of power, and culturally distinctive; and it had never belonged naturally with the kingdoms and territories south of the Humber. This sense of northern difference was not an invention of the Vikings, or of the Viking Age. While the archbishop of Canterbury enjoyed ecclesiastical authority in the north, and Bede had a vision of the *gens Anglorum* as forming one people, Northumbria had never been part of the *imperium* or authority enjoyed by those early Anglo-Saxon kings acclaimed by Bede as exerting over-kingship beyond their own territories (except when the ruler concerned was himself Northumbrian). In other words, there was a distinction to be made in early Anglo-Saxon England between Northumbria on the one hand, and all the other kingdoms south of the Humber on the other: the River Humber itself formed a major division. There was little in the pre-Viking history of the north to justify an assumption, in the tenth century, 'that it would seem natural, even to the English-born section of the inhabitants, to be governed by a southern king'.[2]

So the work that needed to be done in the north after 954 was not only political, but also cultural and even intellectual. The West Saxon take-over meant that the north's incorporation into the kingdom of England needed to be thought through and negotiated, both in the north and in the south, to make sense of (and, possibly, to safeguard) Northumbria's position in the new, unified Albion of Athelstan and his heirs. If it is, in origin, a mid tenth-century work, then the *History of St Cuthbert* is one text that engages in precisely such a process, as it is greatly preoccupied with the relationship between St Cuthbert (and his community and lands) and the West Saxon dynasty represented by Alfred, Athelstan, and Edmund.[3] Another text that may have had a similar purpose is the 'Northern Recension' of the *Anglo-Saxon Chronicle* (surviving now as versions D and E), which appears to have been put together in the second half of the tenth century, quite probably for one of the archbishops of York, and which endeavoured to connect Northumbria's pre-Viking past with the new, West Saxon-led kingdom of England.[4] The diplomatic formulae of Northumbrian charters in the later tenth century also show the extension of West Saxon administrative language into the north.[5]

These are all, of course, elite texts, and it can hardly be over-stressed that in many ways the incorporation of Northumbria into the English kingdom was a long, drawn-out affair; indeed, it has been described as 'one of the most sensitive and intransigent political issues of the tenth and eleventh centuries'.[6] This point can be grasped if we re-consider the late creation of 'Yorkshire' as a county. As we saw in Chapter 1, the first textual evidence for the name and administrative entity of Yorkshire dates from the 1060s – over a century after the expulsion of the last Scandinavian king of York. But what the shire system signified, as it was rolled out across the territories north of the Thames, was the incorporation of parts of the country into the administration of the English (or originally West Saxon) state. Anglo-Saxon shires were used for tax gathering, military organization, and judicial processes, among other things.[7] That it may have taken a hundred years for the kings of England to implement the shire system north of the Humber indicates the relative weakness of their power there, at least in terms of administrative control.

Other shires in the most heavily Scandinavianized parts of the country seem also to have come into existence at a relatively late date. It has been argued that both Lincolnshire and East Anglia may only have been 'shired' in the reign of Cnut (1016-35).[8] Various pieces of evidence, as assembled by the historian Dorothy Whitelock in a classic study, show the king's administrative grip tightening north of the Humber a little later than this, above all in the reign of Edward the Confessor, and not least, as we shall see, through the appointment of the Wessex-based Tostig as earl of Northumbria in 1055.[9] So, for example, the sheriff, or 'shire-reeve' was an important royal official in late Anglo-Saxon England, and the first recorded sheriff of Yorkshire was one Gamal son of Osbern, who is addressed alongside the earl of Northumbria in a writ of William the Conqueror, dating between 1067 and 1069. Domesday Book does, however, reveal that Gamal was a major figure in Yorkshire in the time of King Edward, and this may indicate that he was appointed sheriff prior to 1066.[10] Domesday Book also reveals that the citizens of Torksey in Lincolnshire had a particular responsibility, that 'if the king's messengers should come thither, the men of the same town should conduct them to York with their ships and other means of navigation'.[11] This suggests, of course, that such messengers may have been fairly frequent by the time of King Edward.

175

The shire of Yorkshire thus seems to have been instituted in the later years of Edward's reign, with all the closer control which this implies, and (as we saw in Chapter 1) the first recorded occurrence of the name 'Yorkshire' does indeed come in one of Edward's writs, dated between 1060 and 1065.

Late Anglo-Saxon England's north-south divide can also be observed in the very usage of the term 'north'. There seems to have been no more agreement in the early medieval period than in the present day as to where exactly 'the north' may be said to begin. Edward the Elder's second law-code distinguished between 'the eastern [and] northern kingdoms [*east ... norð*]', with the latter seemingly referring to Northumbria, while a legal tract of uncertain date, preserved among texts associated with Wulfstan II of York (1002-23), was titled *Norðleoda laga* 'The Law of the North People'.[12] These examples suggest the equation of 'the north' with Northumbria, but the various versions of the *Anglo-Saxon Chronicle* imply instead, not surprisingly, that the definition of 'northernness' was partly a matter of perspective. When, as we will see, in 1016 the kingdom of England was, for a brief time, formally divided, Mercia and Northumbria were collectively designated in the D-text as the *norðdæl* 'the northern part'.[13] The same perspective is repeated in the D-text in 1051, when the phrase 'all this northern province [*ealne þisne norðende*]' is used to refer to the earldoms of Northumbria and Mercia combined.[14] Such entries may suggest that, for the northerly compilers of the D-text, Mercia was to be counted as part of a 'greater north' when it formed a political unit with Northumbria, but when this was not the case, it was not so regarded; we will observe such a perspective again in the next chapter, when we come to the 1065 rebellion against Tostig. On the other hand, an amusing contrast emerges in the manner in which the D and E versions record the death in 1049 of Eadnoth, bishop of Dorchester-on-Thames in Oxfordshire. (At this time Dorchester was a huge diocese, stretching from the Thames to the Humber, and after the Norman Conquest it was to be re-located to Lincoln.[15]) The D-text of the *Chronicle*, reasonably enough, commemorates Eadnoth as the bishop of Oxfordshire, whereas the E-text, here drawing on a Canterbury exemplar, describes him as 'bishop to the north [*be norðan*]', as if anywhere and everywhere above the Thames was to be regarded as 'the north'.[16]

Northumbria was different, then, and the difference between north and south was felt on both sides. With this in view, let us begin our political narrative, in 954. It may be recalled that the twelfth-century *History of the Kings* – which drew on earlier northern annals – marked the passing of Eric Bloodaxe by observing, somewhat poignantly, that 'Here the kings of the Northumbrians came to an end, and henceforward the province was administered by earls.'[17] It has been suggested that some of the Scandinavian elite, especially perhaps in the upper echelons of power and government, may have left Northumbria after 954, never to return.[18] But there is no evidence that local lords were forcibly deprived of their

176

land in 954 (or indeed, had earlier been deprived in 927, at the time of Athelstan's conquest), as had happened to much of the Northumbrian elite in the 860s and 870s, and was to happen again in the 1070s. Nor is there much evidence for the political settlement of West Saxon and Mercian nobles in the north, though an important Mercian magnate named Wulfric Spot at some point acquired substantial estates in southern Yorkshire, and between the Mersey and the Ribble in the west.[19] It is just possible that a royal land-grant in York may be commemorated in the medieval street-name Booklane Lane: later this became Bookbinders Alley (and later still Minster Gates); but its late medieval form *Buklandlaine* indicates that the etymology may in fact be Old English *bōc-land* 'land held by royal charter'.[20]

A couple of narrative texts from the second half of the tenth century cast additional light on the experience of the Northumbrian elite after the West Saxon conquest, as well as offering further southern perspectives on the north, and on northerners. One is Wulfstan of Winchester's late tenth-century *Life of St Æthelwold* (*Vita Sancti Æthelwoldi*). This text narrates how King Eadred endowed the reformer Æthelwold with the monastery of Abingdon (now in Oxfordshire), and visited the monastery with 'not a few of his Northumbrian thegns', who happened to be in his entourage at the time. A great feast was laid on, with 'lavish draughts of mead'; the consequence, according to this southern source, was that 'the Northumbrians became drunk, as they tend to, and very cheerful they were when they left at evening'.[21]

Eadred's Northumbrian guests may not have been spending time in his company through their own volition. The Abingdon incident must have taken place in, or soon after, 954, and another text, the poem *The Battle of Maldon*, reveals that members of the Northumbrian elite were held as hostages in the south as late as the 990s. These were courtly hostages, no doubt treated well; but they were hostages nonetheless, held for political purposes to guard against Northumbrian separatism. The battle at Maldon was fought in 991 between the forces of Essex under Ealdorman Byrhtnoth and the Danish army that was attacking the south-east; and it was an emphatic defeat for the English. The poem that was subsequently composed was designed to commemorate the dead of Maldon, and it devotes eight lines to the distinguished conduct of a Northumbrian nobleman named Æscferth: 'the hostage eagerly began to help them; / he was from a hardy family from Northumbria [*on Norðhymbron heardes cynnes*] [...] he did not draw back at all in that battle-game'.[22] This is an interesting passage: as well as suggesting that Northumbrian hostages were not an unusual feature of elite southern retinues of the time, it also offers a more respectful attitude to the northern nobility than that found in Wulfstan's *Life of St Æthelwold*.

Although most of the Northumbrian elite may have held on to their estates, the lands of the Northumbrian kings must, nonetheless, have passed into West Saxon royal control. Domesday Book allows us to identify estates which were 'comital' in the eleventh century – that is to say, in the possession of earls, who received such lands from the king as part of their appointment; they were not part of the earls' hereditary property.[23] The Domesday survey reveals that by far the biggest land-holder in Yorkshire on the eve of the Norman Conquest was Morcar, the earl of southern Northumbria at the time.[24] This can only have been through royal patronage, as Morcar's family did not have long-standing connections with the region; and so we need to explain how the king of England had acquired such extensive estates north of the Humber with which to endow his earls. The probable answer must be that many of the comital estates of 1066 had been the possessions of the Viking kings of York, and had been acquired wholesale in 954. One other estate that may have been confiscated by the West Saxon kings was that of Amounderness, in the north-west. It will be recalled that Athelstan gave this great tract of land to the church of York in 934 (early in the episcopate of Wulfstan I); however, by 1066 it was in the possession of the earl of Northumbria, and one explanation would be that the territory was re-allocated as a punishment for Wulfstan I's disloyalty.[25]

The example of Amounderness may cast light on a bigger issue, namely the distribution of property in and around the city of York between the king, the earl, and the archbishop. York itself, of course, continued to flourish after the West Saxon take-over; indeed, the famous passage from Byrhtferth's *Life of St Oswald*, quoted in the previous chapter, describes the city as it was in the early eleventh century, not during the period of the Viking kings ('inexpressibly filled and enriched by the treasures of merchants, who come there from everywhere, and most of all from the people of Denmark').[26] The city was affected by a fire in 1032, but this does not seem to have been a serious check on its prosperity.[27] In the second half of the tenth century, and the first half of the eleventh, York was the second or third most important mint in England, after London and possibly Lincoln.[28] The last century of Anglo-Saxon England witnessed the growth in size and significance of a number of cities, and the development of influential urban elites; York was no exception.[29]

For documentary insight into the structure of York in the last century of Anglo-Saxon England, we need to turn to three early Norman texts that cast retrospective light on the city. The most important, of course, is Domesday Book: the record for the county of Yorkshire begins with an extensive entry on the city of York.[30] The other two texts are the *Rights and Laws* of the Norman archbishop (probably dating from the 1080s) and a letter from the Chapter of York to the Chapter of Southwell in Nottinghamshire, concerning the customs of York Minster (dating from 1106).[31] By using these three sources, plus later medieval title deeds, Sarah Rees Jones has been able to reconstruct in convincing detail the distribution of property in the city between the king, the earl, and the archbishop on the eve of the Conquest.[32] What she shows is that, in the mid eleventh century, the king possessed the whole area between the Ouse and the Foss south of the old Roman fortress – in other words, the Viking Age commercial city, revealed to us most vividly through the Coppergate excavations – as well as dominating the main approach roads into York, around Micklegate to the west and Fishergate to the south. But unlike the archbishop and canons of York Minster, and also the earl of Northumbria, in the eleventh century the king did not hold extensive rural estates outside the city, encircling its walls; and this suggests that, at this point at least, there was no intention to maintain and service a permanent royal residence in the city.

The question, of course, is how far back this distribution of property goes. Rees Jones herself subscribes to the view that, in the tenth century, it was the archbishops who were the real rulers of *Jórvík*, and so she proposes that the tripartite division of the city, between archbishop, earl, and king, may have occurred as late as the second quarter of the eleventh century, with the archbishops holding all the land and power themselves up to that point. Such a date would accord well with the suggestion that the shiring of Yorkshire was a late event, but otherwise it seems too late, and it is hard to imagine how such a massive stripping of wealth from the Minster could have taken place in the eleventh century without howls of archiepiscopal protest echoing through our sources: as we will see shortly, the late Anglo-Saxon archbishops of York were energetic guardians of their estates and revenues. And as was observed in Chapter 3, there are, in any case, good reasons for doubting the initial hypothesis that York was ruled by 'prince-archbishops' during the tenth century, namely, to recap: the severe disruption suffered by Northumbria in the two or three decades after 866; the lack of positive evidence for archbishops being present in York, and the more extensive evidence for Viking kings ruling in York and maintaining a residence there; the lack of archiepiscopal wealth, contrasted with the mammoth amounts of silver that the Viking conquerors introduced; and the indicators that associate York's coinage with the Viking kings rather than the archbishops.

Taking all this into account, one might therefore suggest that the distribution of property in and around the city in the mid eleventh century can be better explained by an alternative hypothesis and chronology of events (though other explanations do, of course, remain possible). First, and as previous chapters have explored, the Viking conquest of 866 led to the new kings of York seizing land and power from the church, as also from the Northumbrian monarchy and aristocracy; and in the decades that followed, the city expanded greatly under the rule of the Viking kings, especially (as Coppergate reveals) as a centre of trade and manufacturing. And then, second, the West Saxon conquest of the tenth century, culminating in 954, led to the kings of England retaining control of the city's approach roads and mercantile district (we should recall Edgar's anger at the mistreatment of York merchants in Kent), but re-allocating other estates in order to establish a base in the city for a strong earldom, as their preferred form of government in the north. It is also possible that, at this point, the Minster both gained and lost estates (and it is here that the example of Amounderness is suggestive); as we will see, Eadred and his successors had no intention of allowing the church of York to continue on its separate (and separatist) way, and the archbishops were kept on a much tighter leash after 954.

Earls and Archbishops

The office of earl, then, was, crucial in the West Saxon kings' plans for regional government in the north, as it was throughout late Anglo-Saxon England.[33] Dorothy Whitelock showed conclusively that one of the main methods by which the Wessex kings endeavoured to bind Northumbria into the kingdom of England was through the appointment of earls – and also archbishops of York – with strong southern connections.[34] At times, the whole of Northumbria (that is, both Deira and Bernicia) was under the authority of a single earl, while at others, it was split between two, along the division between the two ancient kingdoms. These earldoms were governed from the centres of Bamburgh and York, and the Bootham and Marygate area of York (just outside the city walls to the north-west) was later known as *Earlsburgh*, indicating that this was probably the part of the city where the earl's hall lay; this supposition is strengthened by the fact that one of the earls of Northumbria had a church built there in the eleventh century.[35]

With some inevitable uncertainties, the earls of Northumbria between 954 and 1066 can be readily chronicled – a sign of the increased abundance of sources for this period, compared with the earlier decades of Scandinavian rule.[36] The first was Oswulf, high-reeve of Bamburgh, who had been instrumental in Eric Bloodaxe's ambush and death at Stainmore, and whose authority was now extended southwards over all of Northumbria. In the mid 960s the earldom was divided, though, and the *Anglo-Saxon Chronicle* records that a nobleman called Oslac (Old Norse *Áslakr*), whose family connections seem to have been with the eastern Danelaw, was appointed to the southern region centred on York.[37] By this point the king of England was Edgar, son of Edmund, and his reign (959-75) was later remembered as something of a golden age, in terms of both peace and piety. In the present context, one of Edgar's law-codes (IV Edgar) is especially important, as it recognizes that different laws should be allowed to obtain 'among the Danes' from those observed among the English. The tone of deference on Edgar's part, and the degree of (semi-)independence allowed, are remarkable: 'it is my will that secular rights be in force among the Danes according to as good laws as they can best decide on', the code states, and 'the Danes are to decide by law what punishment they wish to apply in that matter', and above all, 'it is my will that there should be in force among the Danes such good laws as they best decide on, and I have ever allowed them this and will allow it as long as my life lasts, because of your loyalty, which you have always shown me'.[38] It cannot be the case that Edgar's code imagines neighbours living in the same place following different laws according to whether they were Scandinavian or English; rather 'among the Danes' must have more of a geographical sense than an ethnic one, indicating the Scandinavian-settled parts of England and (importantly) recognizing that the historical experience of settlement had led to a different culture in those parts, one which could best be characterized in terms of a Scandinavian stamp and inheritance – and which could not simply be coerced into line with the rest of the kingdom.[39] Earl Oslac is named in the code as the person responsible for the enforcement of Edgar's laws in the north, along with all the *here* ('army; host') within his earldom – an interesting choice of word for the settled population of Scandinavian Northumbria.

We also possess a charter, dated 963, in which Edgar grants land at Sherburn-in-Elmet [WR] to Oslac.[40] This was an important estate, which not long afterwards passed into the possession of York Minster. In another charter of the same year, Edgar gave land at Newbald [ER] to another prominent Yorkshire thegn, named Gunner (Old Norse *Gunnarr*), and four years earlier he had given land at Howden and Drax [both ER] to a woman called Quen.[41] These charters of 959 and 963 are the earliest we possess from the region of Yorkshire, and, in their recording of estate boundaries, such charters offer a wealth of information about landscape and landmarks in the late Anglo-Saxon period ('from Seaxferth's burial mound north to the ditch', goes part of the Newbald bounds; 'along the ditch to the small stream; along the small stream by the headland of the fields to the street; from the street east right on up to a forest on the north of 'Faryisdal''; and so on).[42] According to a thirteenth-century source, John of Wallingford, Edgar held a royal council in York during his reign; perhaps this took place in 963, and the Sherburn and Newbald charters were among the outcomes.[43]

Edgar's reign also saw the flourishing of Benedictine monasticism, when monasteries were either founded or re-founded in accordance with the strict observation of the Rule of St Benedict, with a stress on discipline and chastity.[44] But the movement was effectively confined to the south and west of England; no new Benedictine monasteries were founded north of the Humber, though at some point the monastery of Peterborough seems to have come into possession of Quen's estate at Howden.[45] Such reformed Benedictine monasteries became the most important – though not the only – site for the composition and copying of written works in both Latin and Old English, and a great number of our localizable manuscripts from the tenth and eleventh centuries have been identified as products of Benedictine centres; this is one reason why texts from the north of England are so much scarcer than those from the south. Indeed, there are very few texts (especially vernacular texts) that we can confidently attribute to late Anglo-Saxon

Yorkshire (as opposed to wider Northumbria): one such may be the glosses added to the so-called Rushworth or Macregol Gospels by two scribes named Owun and Farmon, the latter of whom identifies himself in a colophon as *preoste æt harawuda* – probably Harewood [WR] near Leeds, though this localization has been disputed.[46]

When Edgar died in 975, however, there was a reaction against the monastic movement which he had sponsored, and, as part of the fall-out, Oslac was deprived of his earldom. The D-text of the *Anglo-Saxon Chronicle* states simply that 'the famous Earl Oslac was exiled from England', but other versions of the *Chronicle* commemorate Oslac's misfortune in old-fashioned verse which depicts him as an heroic exile, unjustly banished after his lord's death: 'the valiant man Oslac was driven from the country, over the tossing waves, the gannet's bath, the tumult of waters, the homeland of the whale; a grey-haired man, wise and skilled in speech, he was bereft of his lands'.[47]

The beneficiary, and possibly also the agent, of Oslac's downfall was his successor, Earl Thored. Thored, like Oslac, is a Norse name (*Þórðr*), which suggests Danelaw connections like his predecessor. If Oslac's expulsion and Thored's rise are connected, then this does indeed indicate, in Whitelock's words, 'troubled times in Yorkshire'.[48] A memorandum of Archbishop Oswald of York, concerning archiepiscopal estates and dating between 975 and 992, complains that when Thored 'came in', St Peter (that is, York Minster) 'was afterwards robbed' of certain properties.[49] Alongside this we can place a charter from Thored himself, in which he endowed the community of St Cuthbert (at this time at Chester-le-Street) with a number of estates quite close to York: Smeaton, Crayke, and Sutton-on-the-Forest [all NR].[50] Oswald's complaint may therefore have been justified: Thored may have deprived York Minster of properties and income, and given at least some of them to the community of Cuthbert, the other major ecclesiastical power in the north. But Thored was not just a powerful local magnate. He was also, of course, the king's authority in Northumbria, and two pieces of evidence indicate a close connection with the government of Æthelred the Unready (who came to the throne in 978). The first is that the *Anglo-Saxon Chronicle*, for the year 992, records that the king appointed Thored as one of the leaders of an unsuccessful attempt to defeat in a sea-battle the Scandinavian raiding fleet that was attacking the south of England.[51] The second is more personal: according to the twelfth-century witness of Aelred of Rievaulx, Æthelred's first wife was a daughter of Earl Thored, and such a marriage might reflect the continuing desire of the West Saxon kings to stabilize the political relationship with Northumbria.[52] As for Æthelred himself, there is evidence that he visited York at some point in his reign, in the form of a charter preserved in the *History of St Cuthbert*, witnessed by leading figures 'who were there that day in York with the King'.[53] Like Edgar, he issued a law code (III Æthelred, issued at Wantage) which recognized the distinctively

Scandinavian character of northern England.[54] But he was also the king who ordered the so-called 'St Brice's Day massacre' of 1002, discussed at the end of Chapter 5.

Thored's successor was Ælfhelm, who was in post by 993.[55] As his Anglo-Saxon name suggests, Ælfhelm was of English descent, and his links were with a powerful family in the midlands. Curiously, both his mother and his daughter were women of importance, in very different ways, in the history of Anglo-Scandinavian relations: his mother was the noblewoman Wulfrun, who was taken captive by Olaf Guthfrithson in Tamworth in 940, on his great advance into Mercia after Athelstan's death; and his daughter was Ælfgifu of Northampton, whom the Danish conqueror Cnut was later to take as wife or concubine and whose sons with Cnut were Swein (with whom she ruled Norway in the early 1030s) and Harold 'Harefoot' (king of England 1040-42).[56] Ælfhelm's brother was the Wulfric Spot mentioned earlier in this chapter, a powerful magnate who founded the Benedictine monastery of Burton upon Trent in Staffordshire.[57] Thanks to the survival of Wulfric's will, we are able to reconstruct the history of this important family in some detail; we learn, for example, that Wulfric granted to his brother Ælfhelm the major estate of Conisbrough [WR] in south Yorkshire.[58]

But Ælfhelm did not remain in favour with Æthelred. In 1006, in the words of Simon Keynes, 'something approaching a palace revolution' seems to have taken place at the king's court, and Ælfhelm was among those who were ousted: he was killed, and two of his sons were blinded.[59] The earldom of Northumbria, north and south of the Tees, was at this point re-united, and passed to Uhtred of Bamburgh.[60] Uhtred, like Thored previously, also seems to have had family connections with Æthelred, as his third wife was Æthelred's daughter.

It was during the time of Uhtred's earldom that the Anglo-Saxon kingdom of England, and the West Saxon house of Alfred, experienced its first defeat, as the country was conquered by the Danish king, Swein Forkbeard. But before we come to that period of drama, we should track backwards for a moment, to trace the post-954 archbishops of York in the same way as we have traced the earls of Northumbria. Just as the earls of Northumbria were, on the whole, figures with a close link and loyalty to the southern establishment, so too were the archbishops appointed after 954. We should recall that the last archbishop of York prior to the West Saxon take-over had been the troublesome separatist Wulfstan I; after 954, the southern powers were careful to ensure that no archbishop of York was elevated from within Northumbria, although several (like the earls) had connections with the eastern Danelaw. During this period, York was often held in plurality with a southern diocese, both for reasons of wealth (as York was not an especially prosperous see) and political loyalty.[61]

The first of the new archbishops was Oscytel, who remained bishop of Dorchester even after he became archbishop of York. Oscytel (Old Norse *Ásketill*) was connected to the Anglo-Danish family which had produced Archbishop Oda of Canterbury (whose father, it may be recalled from Chapter 5, had come to England as part of the Great Army of 865).[62] We have strong evidence, in the form of two charters from 956 and 958, that, at the start of Oscytel's episcopate, the West Saxon kings Eadwig and Edgar made a concerted effort to build up the wealth and properties of the church of York; and the most important estate which we know to have been added to the church's holdings at this time was that of Southwell in Nottinghamshire.[63] (And it is apposite to note here that, at times, certain midland shires, including Nottinghamshire, also came under the authority of the earls of Northumbria.[64]) The so-called 'Oswald memorandum' also records 'lands which Archbishop Oscytel obtained in Northumbria with his [own] money': these included Everingham [ER] ('from Oswulf's father, when he was at point of death') and one of the several places in Yorkshire named Appleton ('which he bought for 24 pounds from Deorwulf').[65] More startling is the revelation that Oscytel acquired some properties for the church as a result of ecclesiastical penalties: 'Helperby [NR] was given to him in compensation for illicit cohabitation – there were two brothers who had one wife'.[66]

Oscytel died in 971. He was succeeded briefly, for a mere matter of months, by an unknown Eadwold, who soon resigned the see (according to Symeon of Durham) in the desire for a quieter life.[67] That Eadwold may have been nudged out of office is perhaps suggested by the identity of his successor, namely the big-hitting Oswald: bishop of Worcester since 961, nephew of Oda, and one of the three Benedictine reformers promoted to leading positions by Edgar (the other two being Dunstan, appointed archbishop of Canterbury in 960, and Æthelwold, appointed bishop of Winchester in 963).[68] Trained in reformed monasticism at Fleury in France, Oswald remained bishop of Worcester throughout his time as archbishop of York, and he was also very committed to the Benedictine monastery he had founded at Ramsey in Cambridgeshire; it was a Ramsey author, Byrhtferth, who composed the crucial *Life* of Oswald after his death.[69] The textual evidence for Oswald's activities at Worcester (and indeed Ramsey) is vastly greater than that for his activities at York, for which the most important source is the 'Oswald memorandum', already mentioned; but even this is preserved in a Worcester manuscript, not a York one.[70] The memorandum records the estates which the church of York had lost in the anti-monastic reaction after Edgar's death (and Thored's appointment as earl in Northumbria), especially those belonging to Otley, Ripon, and Sherburn-in-Elmet [all WR], as well as those acquired by Oscytel.

Oswald was a very significant actor in the Anglo-Saxon reform movement, and he was immediately culted as a saint after his death in 992; but very little is known about his career at York. He was succeeded as both archbishop of York and bishop of Worcester by a certain Ealdwulf, who had previously been abbot of the reformed monastery at Peterborough. Ealdwulf was not commemorated as a prominent cleric, but his own successor in 1002 was a massive figure, indubitably one of the most important persons in the late Anglo-Saxon church and state. This was Wulfstan II, sometimes known by his pen-name of *Lupus* or 'Wolf' (and numbered as Wulfstan II to distinguish him from the traitorous Wulfstan I of the mid tenth century, though sometimes, confusingly, he is labelled as Wulfstan I in scholarship on the church of Worcester). Like Oscytel, Wulfstan seems to have had family connections with the eastern Danelaw, and like Ealdwulf, he may have been an abbot before becoming an (arch)bishop – but if so, we do not know of which monastery.[71] Wulfstan first comes into view in the historical record in 996, when the *Anglo-Saxon Chronicle* records his appointment as bishop of London.[72] In 1002 he became archbishop of York and bishop of Worcester, though he seems to have given up the latter position in 1016. It is a sobering thought that one of Wulfstan's first experiences as archbishop, close to the centre of the king's council, may have been his involvement in the sanctioning of the St Brice's Day massacre of November 1002.[73]

Like Oscytel and Oswald before him, we have strong evidence that Wulfstan was a tenacious guardian and administrator of the church's properties. One manuscript that is associated with Wufstan is the so-called York Gospels, a sumptuous gospelbook (in Latin) which was probably made in Canterbury and presented to Wulfstan as a gift.[74] A number of vernacular documents have been added at the end of the manuscript, and these include a set of surveys of the archiepiscopal estates associated with Sherburn-in-Elmet, Otley, and Ripon: the surveys provide an interesting indication of the extent of (some of) the archbishop of York's holdings, and also reveal that some of the estates seized by Earl Thored were, by the early 1020s (the date of the surveys), back in the possession of the church.[75]

But it is not primarily as an administrator that Wulfstan is remembered, energetic though he may have been in this regard. Rather, he compels attention as a preacher, a legislator, and a political theorist.[76] As a preacher, Wulfstan stands out as one of the two most important writers of homilies in the late Anglo-Saxon church, alongside his contemporary Ælfric (a Winchester-trained monk at Cerne Abbas in Dorset, and later abbot of Eynsham in Oxfordshire). A definitive enumeration of Wulfstan's sermons cannot be given, as he seems never to have collected them together, and it seems likely that other writers copied his style; but we possess something in the order of 30-40 homilies composed by him, many written in a heightened, exhortatory style. The York Gospels contain three short sermons by Wulfstan entitled 'Sermon of the Wolf', 'On Christendom', and 'On Heathendom', and these are even annotated (though not written) in Wulfstan's own handwriting, as are a number of other manuscripts – which gives us an unusually direct encounter with a named figure from late Anglo-Saxon Yorkshire.[77]

The events by which Wulfstan came to act as a legislator cannot now be recovered, but he acted as the main composer of Æthelred's laws from probably 1008 onwards. In both law and sermon, Wulfstan was concerned with what Patrick Wormald has called 'the holiness of society', and he used the same style for both: his homilies can seem legal-minded in their preoccupations, and his laws homiletic.[78] Wulfstan's laws contain the first occurrence of a considerable number of legal loanwords from Old Norse, and indeed the very word 'law' is a loan from Norse; as noted in Chapter 1, the term 'Danelaw' (*Dena lagu*) seems to be a Wulfstanian coinage.[79]

We will come to Wulfstan's role as a political theorist shortly. But for now we should move on from thinking about individual Northumbrian personnel, secular and ecclesiastical, and consider national events in the time of Wulfstan's episcopate.

As the *Anglo-Saxon Chronicle* records, Viking raids on the south of England had resumed in the 980s, and this second wave of attacks is often designated the 'Second Viking Age' in England (the first being, of course, that of the Great Army). In the 990s the attacks became increasingly serious: the notorious 'Danegeld' was first paid in 991, and increasingly large amounts were handed over in the last decade of the old millennium and the first decade of the new, so that, altogether, a staggering quantity of portable wealth passed from English to Scandinavian hands during this period.[80] What is more – and unlike during the First Viking Age – the assault on England was led by the king of Denmark, Swein Forkbeard: it was transparent that military conquest was desired, and not just the milking of Anglo-Saxon England's great resources of wealth. The most compelling narrative of this period is that offered by the *Anglo-Saxon Chronicle*, but we should remember that (as noted in Chapter 1) this account was written with hindsight, not on a year-by-year basis. Nonetheless, the scornful and despondent tone of the Chronicler gives an unforgettable impression of how the failings of Æthelred's government were viewed by at least one disillusioned commentator of the time. Take, for example, this passage from the entry for 1010:

> And when they [i.e. the Scandinavian army] were in the east, the English army was kept in the west, and when they were in the south, our army was in the north. Then all the councillors were summoned to the king, and it was then to be decided how this country should be defended. But even if anything was then decided, it did not last even a month. Finally there was no leader who would collect an army, but each fled as best he could, and in the end no shire would even help the next.[81]

Another commentator on the events, and atmosphere, of these years was Archbishop Wulfstan, who preached a sermon titled *The Sermon of the Wolf to the English* (*Sermo Lupi ad Anglos*), not to be confused with the shorter 'Sermon of the Wolf' to be found in the York Gospels. The title, as recorded in one of its manuscripts, may be in Latin, but the sermon itself is in English, and an extraordinary and powerful English at that, as Wulfstan upbraids his people for their sins and failings, of which the Scandinavian attacks are both the cause and (in a covenantal view) the effect:

> Things have not gone well now for a long time at home or abroad, but there has been devastation and persecution in every district again and again, and the English have been for a long time now completely defeated and too greatly disheartened through God's anger; and the pirates so strong with God's consent that often in battle one puts to flight ten, and sometimes less, sometimes more, all because of our sins [...] Often two seamen, or maybe three, drive the droves of Christian men from sea to sea, out through this people, huddled together, as a public shame to us all, if we could seriously and rightly feel any shame. But all the insult which we often suffer we repay with honouring those who insult us; we pay them continually and they humiliate us daily; they ravage and they burn, plunder and rob and carry on board; and lo, what else is there in all these events except God's anger clear and visible over this people?[82]

Wulfstan's sermon ends plaintively: 'God help us. Amen.'

The climax came in 1013, as the *Anglo-Saxon Chronicle* records in less impassioned language:

> Before the month of August, King Swein came with his fleet to Sandwich, and then went very quickly round East Anglia into the mouth of the Humber, and so up along the Trent until he reached Gainsborough. And then at once Earl Uhtred and all the Northumbrians submitted to him, as did all the people of Lindsey, and then all the people belonging to the district of the Five Boroughs, and quickly afterwards all the Danish settlers [*here*] north of Watling Street.[83]

Watling Street was the line of the old boundary between Alfred and Guthrum in the late ninth century, and in modern scholarship is often taken to mark the boundary of the 'Danelaw'. We should hesitate, though, to attribute the north's submission to Swein purely to ethnic sympathies: though this may have played a part (as suggested, perhaps, by the *Chronicle*'s use of the term *here*), it is likely that the move was motivated more by a desire for cleavage from the south – or at least, a lack of desire to cleave to the south at all costs – than by any active preference for a political association with Scandinavia. Nonetheless, Swein restrained his army from raiding until after they had crossed Watling Street on their way south; but after that, 'they did the greatest damage that any army could do'.[84] Oxford and Winchester soon submitted, as did the west of England, and although London did not fall militarily to Swein's forces, its citizens recognized the inevitable outcome and eventually submitted also, 'for they were afraid that he would destroy them'.[85] Swein's conquest was complete, and 'all the nation [*þeodscipe*] regarded him as full king'. But Æthelred was still alive, and thus he was forced to go into exile, crossing the Channel to the court of Richard, Duke of Normandy, the brother of his wife Emma.

Swein's triumph, however, did not last long, and within a few months he had died, on 3 February 1013, the first Scandinavian king of all England. According to Geffrei Gaimar's early twelfth-century *History of the English*, Swein was first buried in York Minster, though a decade or so later his remains were moved to Norway.[86] Swein's forces acclaimed his son Cnut as king, but the English *witan* or council 'determined to send for King Æthelred, and they said that no lord was dearer to them than their natural lord if he would govern them more justly than he did before'.[87] It has been suggested by one scholar that the meeting at which this resolution was passed may have been held in York, and that Wulfstan's *Sermon of the Wolf to the English* was originally composed to be delivered at it. In return, Æthelred sent the message 'that he would be a gracious lord to them, and reform all the things which they all hated'. And so he 'came home to his own people and he was gladly received by them all'.

This was all very well, but it did not take account of Cnut. After returning to Denmark for a short period, Cnut mounted a sustained assault on the kingdom of England, to regain what his father had won. Æthelred died in 1016 ('he had held his kingdom with great toil and difficulties as long as his life lasted', the *Anglo-Saxon Chronicle* comments), and that year saw a series of battles and pursuits between Cnut and Æthelred's son Edmund 'Ironside' (grandson of the Northumbrian Earl Thored).[88] The definitive encounter was at Ashingdon in Essex: 'there Cnut had the victory and won for himself all the English people [*ealle þeoda Angelcynnes*]', the *Chronicle* states; 'and all the nobility of England was there destroyed'.[89]

Yorkshire and the north were not at the heart of these conflicts, which were fought out in the south of England. But among a catalogue of battles, an Old Norse praise-poem addressed to Cnut declares that 'you angrily caused the English people to experience sorrow in broad Hemingbrough [*í breiðri / borg Hemminga*]'.[90] Such a battle is not mentioned in any other source, but Hemingbrough [ER] was a comital estate of the earls of Northumbria, and there is no reason to disbelieve the skald's encomium.[91] Edmund Ironside travelled north in 1016 to recruit Earl Uhtred, and together they campaigned southwards, until Uhtred learned that Cnut's army was now in Northumbria: then 'he left his ravaging and hastened northwards, and submitted then out of necessity, and with him all the Northumbrians [*ealle Norðhymbra*]'.[92] So in 1016, as in 1013, Northumbria submitted to the Danish conqueror earlier than any other part of the kingdom. But this did not save Uhtred himself, who was killed by a certain Thurbrand, a figure to whom we shall return later.[93]

Edmund Ironside was defeated at the Battle of Ashingdon, but not killed. The terms agreed with Cnut were that Edmund should rule over Wessex, and Cnut over Mercia (in addition to already possessing Northumbria); the D-version of the *Chronicle*, as we have seen, describes Cnut's portion as the *norðdæl* or 'northern part'.[94] But Edmund died before the end of the year, and at that point Cnut became king of all England.

Church and Elite in the Eleventh Century

Cnut's conquest of England in 1016 has traditionally been over-shadowed in historiography by the far more famous conquest of 1066. But the fifty years between Cnut's conquest and William's form a fascinating, and unusually well documented, period, in which there were many important new developments – in society and politics, in the church, and in literature and culture.[95] It is certainly true that, for the history of Yorkshire, we begin to be presented with a previously unparalleled wealth of sources, both textual and material.

We should begin with the church, and with the figure of Wulfstan – Æthelred's law-maker and the preacher of the *Sermon of the Wolf to the English*. Perhaps surprisingly, in the light of the roles he had played under Æthelred, Wulfstan was not a casualty of Cnut's conquest. Instead, it seems that the veteran churchman and the young Danish conqueror chose to work purposefully together, and as a result Wulfstan has been hailed as one of the key architects of the transition between Æthelred's regime and that of Cnut.[96] In 1020, Wulfstan is recorded by the *Anglo-Saxon Chronicle* as accompanying Cnut to Ashingdon, to dedicate a memorial church at the site of the king's victory.[97] The text of Cnut's so-called 'First Letter' to the English people, in which he pledged to be 'a gracious lord and a faithful observer of God's rights and just secular law', is only preserved among the additions made to Wulfstan's York Gospels, and indeed the letter is at least partly written in Wulfstan's characteristic style.[98] And Wulfstan was certainly the author and compiler of Cnut's two-part law-code (the first part ecclesiastical, the second part secular), which was the largest and most compendious of all Anglo-Saxon law-codes, and was to prove enduringly influential through both the eleventh and twelfth centuries. Also in these years Wulfstan composed a ground-breaking work of political theory now known as the *Institutes of Polity*, which offered a blueprint of the ideal ordering of church and state.[99]

As all this activity and influence suggests, Wulfstan must have spent much of his time at the king's court, though the estate surveys in the York Gospels (and other evidence) indicate that he did not neglect his archiepiscopal responsibilities at home.[100] When he died in 1023, he was buried at Ely, in Cambridgeshire, where he had been a benefactor and may have had family connections.[101]

The historical importance of the next two archbishops of York, and the textual traces they have left, are inevitably much slighter than that of the gigantic figure of Wulfstan. But his immediate successor, Ælfric (nicknamed *Puttoc* 'kite' in some sources), deserves notice as the longest-serving archbishop of York since Wulfhere in the ninth century (1023-51).[102] Originally a monk of Winchester (and not to be confused with the homilist of the same name), Ælfric seems also to have had some connections with Cnut: he was the recipient of a surviving 1033 charter in which the king granted him the large Yorkshire estate of Patrington [ER], and he was subsequently a supporter of Cnut's son, Harthacnut.[103] Ælfric was succeeded by Cynesige (1051-60), whose background is uncertain: some sources claim him as a royal priest, others as a monk of Peterborough.[104] But it is likely to have been either Ælfric or Cynesige who was responsible for the production of the text known as *The Northumbrian Priests' Law*.[105] This is an invaluable source, the bulk of which is concerned with penalties for ecclesiastical and liturgical offences committed by or against priests ('If a priest refuses anyone baptism or confession [...] If a priest misdirect the people regarding a festival or a fast [...]' and so on), though its later clauses also reveal some details of secular social structure in Northumbria. Monetary penalties in the code are specified in terms of *ora*, a northern measurement of Norse origin.[106]

Cynesige's successor was Ealdred, another major political figure – more international than Wulfstan, though less significant as a writer – who was in time to be the archbishop who crowned William the Conqueror as king of England.[107] Previously a monk at Winchester and then abbot of Tavistock, in 1046 Ealdred became bishop of Worcester, a see that he renounced after he was appointed archbishop of York in 1060. In his pre-York years, Ealdred had a remarkable diplomatic, and even military, career; William of Malmesbury later appraised him as 'a man wily in secular affairs, but not without piety'.[108] In 1049 he was involved in the defence of the Welsh border against an attack from the Welsh and Irish, and in 1051 he was appointed by Edward the Confessor to lead an abortive raid against the Godwineson family.[109] In the previous year, 1050, Edward had sent him to Rome on a diplomatic mission to the pope (and he visited Rome again in 1061), and in 1054 he was sent to Germany to try to bring home Edward 'the Exile', son of Edmund Ironside: the *Anglo-Saxon Chronicle* records that Ealdred 'went overseas to Cologne on the king's business, and there was received with great honour by the emperor [Henry III], and he stayed there for nearly a year, and the bishop of Cologne and the emperor both gave him entertainment'.[110] As we can sense from this entry, such diplomatic missions were grand affairs, an impression confirmed by Ealdred's next journey, in 1058, to Jerusalem via Hungary: the *Chronicle* declares that 'he went to Jerusalem in such state [*weorðscipe*] as none had done before him'.[111] It is no wonder that Ealdred has been described as 'the most widely travelled bishop of the Anglo-Saxon age'.[112] That we know so much about Ealdred's movements is partly explained by the fact that, as may be recalled from Chapter 1, he was probably responsible for the compilation of the D-text of the *Anglo-Saxon Chronicle*, or at least for one important stage in its compilation, and it is D that records all these details of Ealdred's travels; he also plays a prominent role in the twelfth-century *Chronicle of the Archbishops of York*.[113] Ealdred's internationalism left its mark: his year in Cologne, in particular, seems to have been important for the introduction of German liturgy into English church practice.[114]

We should not, of course, focus our ecclesiastical attention exclusively on the archbishop of York. But before we move on to consider lesser, local churches (which proliferated greatly in the late Anglo-Saxon period), we should also pay some attention to the two most important churches in Yorkshire after York Minster itself, namely Ripon and Beverley, both of which seem to have become 'archiepiscopal minsters' in the late Anglo-Saxon period (that is, under the control of the archbishop); these three major churches are, for example, the subject of a short text on church sanctuary from the early eleventh century (*Norðhymbra cyricfrið*).[115] The histories of Ripon and Beverley are, in many ways, similar, and have recently been reviewed by David Woodman.[116] Both churches were defined by association with a charismatic bishop, later saint, from the golden age of Northumbrian Christianity (St Wilfrid of Ripon, and St John of Beverley). Both may have suffered in the Viking campaigns and settlements of the ninth century, and begun a process of consolidation and re-development after the West Saxon conquest of the north (a process that may be observable from archaeological excavations at the two sites).[117] And both, as noted, enjoyed an increasingly close association with the archbishops of York in the later tenth and eleventh centuries: the *Life of St Oswald* tells of the saint's interest in the church at Ripon, and in its key figure, Wilfrid; meanwhile at Beverley, both Ælfric and Ealdred, in the eleventh century, concerned themselves with the cult of St John, and Cynesige oversaw the building of a new tower.[118] The histories of the two churches were not identical, however: Beverley, for instance, seems to have had better grounds for the supposed association with Athelstan which both churches later claimed, while the D-text of the *Anglo-Saxon Chronicle* records in 948 that 'King Eadred ravaged all Northumbria, because they had accepted Eric [Bloodaxe] as their king; and in that ravaging the glorious minster at Ripon, which St Wilfrid had built, was burnt down'.[119] In other words, the West Saxon dynasty may have supported the church of Beverley from the beginning, but treated that of Ripon in more punitive fashion (though the *Chronicle* entry does not quite state that it was Eadred who burned down Ripon Minster); as a consequence, Beverley retained control of the relics of its blessed saint, John, whereas some – though not, it seems, all – of Wilfrid's were taken away to Canterbury.[120]

Had the church of Ripon allied itself more closely than Beverley with the Scandinavian rulers of Northumbria? One form of evidence in support of this suggestion may be sculptural: Viking Age sculpture has been found at the church at Ripon but not at Beverley, and one of the Ripon pieces is a cross-head which may depict the legend of Sigurd the dragon-slayer; evidently, Scandinavian tastes were in vogue in early tenth-century Ripon, and Scandinavian patronage in evidence.[121] But this does not mean that the church at Beverley may not also have achieved a working relationship with the Scandinavian rulers of Northumbria, just that we lack positive evidence (and indeed, unlike Ripon, no certain pre-Viking sculpture survives from Beverley either). Traces of Scandinavian culture have certainly been found in Beverley: the street names of the town show influence from Old Norse, and an Anglo-Scandinavian Terslev-style brooch was uncovered in excavations near the Minster.[122]

As we saw in previous chapters, the Scandinavian settlement of the ninth and tenth centuries was one of the crucial forces in the establishment of new churches and churchyards lower down the scale from these major minsters. As large estates were broken up and re-distributed, the new, local lords often chose to build churches as well as to re-structure their settlements (in the development of nucleated villages). Many of these early churches may have been in wood, but the period of roughly 950-1100 has been described as a 'Great Re-building', when local churches were built or re-built in stone, and the network of ecclesiastical parishes took enduring shape.[123] This was a nation-wide phenomenon, but it may have been more pronounced in the north of England than in the south, on account of the proliferation of small estates and local lords that the Viking conquest had effected.[124] Nor was it simply a rural movement: many urban churches and parishes took shape at this time too.[125] An incomplete inscription found at the church of St Mary Castlegate, York, reads: '[...ard] and Grim and Æse raised (this) church in the name of the holy Lord Christ, and to (or of) St Mary and St Martin and St [?Cuthbert] and All Saints. It was consecrated in the [...] year in the life of –'.[126] Of the three recorded personal names, Grim and Æse are Old Norse (*Grímr* and *Ási*), while the first, damaged name '[...]ard' may have been so too: what this inscription records is the building, or more likely re-building, in stone of a local urban church by three patrons of apparently Scandinavian ancestry.

Wharram Percy [ER] supplies a classic example from rural Yorkshire. Excavation has shown that, in the early or mid eleventh century, a stone church was built at Wharram for the first time; but it had been preceded in the tenth century by burials at the site and (possibly) a wooden church.[127] More widely, a number of churches in the county show surviving stone towers of a probable eleventh-century date, including Appleton-le-Street [NR], Bardsey [WR],

Hovingham [NR], Kirk Hammerton [WR], Middleton [NR], Monk Fryston [WR], Skipwith [ER], Wharram-le-Street [ER], and St Mary Bishophill Junior in York (indeed, the tower of St Mary Bishophill Junior is the most important and impressive Anglo-Saxon structure still to be seen in York).[128] Some, but not all, of these churches were pre-Viking in foundation.[129] But it is also striking that a number of these churches boast items of Scandinavian stone sculpture, and the church of Hovingham gives us a clear example of a certain sort of ecclesiastical trajectory through the course of the ninth to eleventh centuries. A large and sophisticated early ninth-century architectural frieze, depicting the Virgin Mary and associated Biblical figures, testifies to Hovingham's importance in the pre-Viking period, a witness that is supported by indications that Hovingham may have been the centre of a major estate.[130] But then the next pieces of evidence are a couple of tenth-century cross-heads, one with a Hiberno-Norse ring-head and the other with Scandinavian-style ornament; and this would seem to indicate the passing of church and estate into the possession of a new lord or lords with Scandinavian tastes.[131] Then finally, in the eleventh century, we see the building of a new and impressive stone tower.[132]

A number of Yorkshire cemeteries of the later Anglo-Saxon period (ninth to eleventh centuries) have been extensively excavated, including Crayke [NR] and Addingham [WR].[133] Unlike Wharram Percy, both of these were important ecclesiastical sites in the pre-Viking period, but another new, local churchyard of the tenth or early eleventh century that has been excavated – though not yet properly published – is that at Kellington [WR], where the foundation of the churchyard was followed in the eleventh century by a timber church and then a stone one.[134] A few sources may also give us some information about the interiors of churches in the late Anglo-Saxon period, the most important of which is the list of church-furnishings and manuscripts at Sherburn-in-Elmet [WR] added at the end of the York Gospels:

> These are the church treasures at Sherburn: namely, two gospel books, and two crosses, and one *Aspiciens* [an antiphonary], and one *Ad te leuaui* [a gradual], and two epistolaries, and one sacramentary, and one hymnal, and one psalter, and one chalice, and one paten, and two mass vestments, and three chasubles, and two altar cloths and two altar covers, and four hand-bells and six hanging bells.[135]

Sherburn was not typical, because it was an archiepiscopal estate, though the list of manuscripts agrees well with prescriptions concerning the books that a parish priest ought (ideally) to possess.[136] Also less than representative (though nonetheless noteworthy) are the glazed floor-tiles recovered from All Saints Pavement, York, an important church in the tenth and eleventh centuries.[137] But such items do give us a sense of the objects and decoration that might be encountered in at least some prosperous churches. This is also a convenient place to note that one well-known object at York Minster, the so-called 'Horn of Ulf', cannot be, as is traditionally claimed, a gift to the minster by a local Scandinavian lord in the Anglo-Saxon period: its art-style suggests a date of c.1080, though there probably was a benefactor called Ulf who gave land and gifts to the Minster around the time of the Conquest.[138]

For an indication of the more difficult, and probably more typical, circumstances under which priests might be operating in the eleventh century, we can turn again to *The Northumbrian Priests' Law*: this lays down penalties, for example, for priests celebrating mass without a consecrated altar, or with only a wooden chalice, or without wine, which suggests that none of these irregularities may have been unusual.[139] The code also forbids priests from putting 'unsuitable things in the church', from insulting and fighting other priests, and from wearing weapons in church, all of which gives a further impression, of the secular worldliness of certain clerics. 'If a priest practises drunkenness', the code states laconically, 'or becomes a gleeman or a tavern-minstrel, he is to compensate for it'.

One well-known church of this period is Kirkdale [NR] [Figure 26]. Here, a famous inscription around a sundial states: 'Orm Gamal's son bought St Gregory's church when it was completely ruined and collapsed, and he had it built anew from the ground to Christ and St Gregory, in the days of King Edward, and in the days of Earl Tostig' [Figure 27].[140] The dates of Edward and Tostig give the inscription a dating bracket of 1055-65 for Orm's re-building of his church, and substantial parts of its eleventh-century structure still survive.[141] The practice of erecting dedicatory sundials seems also to have been something of a vogue among eleventh-century patrons in the area, and other examples can be found at Great Edstone [NR] and Old Byland [NR], as well as at Aldbrough [ER] and Skelton in Cleveland [NR], as we saw in Chapter 5.[142] Although the name Kirkdale is Norse (first recorded in 1202; the site appears in Domesday Book as *Chirchebi*), findings from archaeological excavations, and the presence of high-status pre-Viking sculpture, indicate that the site was an important church or monastery in the earlier period.[143] The existence of tenth-century Scandinavian-style sculpture at Kirkdale creates the suspicion that Orm's claim that the church was 'completely ruined and collapsed' may be something of a re-founder's over-statement, and it has been suggested that Orm may have been trying to (re-)establish a religious community at Kirkdale, and not simply re-build a parish church, possibly with some assistance from Archbishop Ealdred of York.[144] Kirkdale's proto-Romanesque architecture indicates that Orm was a well-connected man, in touch with, and even in the vanguard of, new developments in ecclesiastical culture.

The person of Orm Gamalson gives us an appropriate hinge at which to move our focus away from the ecclesiastical and towards the secular. Recent research has demonstrated forcefully that we should not think of Orm as some minor local lord, but rather as a wealthy and powerful magnate, whose holdings and influence were regional and not merely parochial.[145] Domesday Book indicates that Orm held land and manors in a dozen places, mostly in the Ryedale area, with his estate-centre probably at Kirkbymoorside [NR], not far from Kirkdale. It is at least possible – though not certain – that he was lord of Wharram Percy in the mid eleventh century, and also the patron responsible for the building of Hovingham's church tower.

There are two possible means by which Orm and his family may have gained their power and estates. The first, of course, is that the family's holdings may have dated back to the late ninth century, to the re-distribution of land among Halfdan's leading supporters. But the second possibility is that Orm's family may have come to prominence as a result of Cnut's conquest in the early eleventh century, as a result of either being newly arrived in England, or else rewarded by Cnut for their support. Most of our evidence for the bestowing of estates by Cnut on his Scandinavian supporters pertains to the south and west of England; but we can be sure that Cnut's conquest will have shaken up the bases and balances of regional power in the north of England as well.[146]

We saw earlier in this chapter that Earl Uhtred of Northumbria was killed in 1016. Cnut replaced him as earl with a Norwegian, Eiríkr Hákonarson, who was the head of the powerful earls of Lade in the Trondheim area of Norway, and married to Cnut's half-sister.[147] Eiríkr had assisted Cnut in his conquest of England, and we possess praise-poetry that celebrates his heroic deeds ('Valiant Eiríkr often made the troop of the English diminish and caused their deaths').[148] Our last documentary record to Eiríkr dates from 1023, but the next reference to an earl of Northumbria does not appear until 1033, when we find the office occupied by a previously unknown figure named Siward (Old Norse *Sigvarðr*), known by his Norse nickname *inn digri* 'the Stout' or 'the Strong'.[149] Siward's origins are unknown, but it is evident that he was a trusted intimate of Cnut's, and the best hypothesis is that he was a Danish aristocrat, probably related to the king.[150] Siward is a figure around whom colourful legends of a Scandinavian character later gathered, not least in a twelfth-century text known as the *The Deeds of the Ancestors of Earl Waltheof* (*Gesta antecessorum comitis Waldevi*), in which Siward's father is called Beorn *Beresune* and has bear's ears, and Siward himself possesses a raven-banner, fights two dragons, and meets a mysterious Odinic figure.[151] For these and other reasons, Stenton characterized Siward rather dismissively as 'a Danish warrior of a primitive type'.[152]

But Siward successfully held the earldom of Northumbria for over twenty years – possibly over thirty, if he succeeded Eiríkr as early as 1023. He married Ælfflæd, the daughter of Ealdred, earl of Bernicia, and from 1041 onwards Siward's earldom embraced all of Northumbria, both north and south (and we might also note here that one of his wife's sisters married Orm Gamalson, patron of

Kirkdale).[153] His main responsibility seems to have been the defence of Northumbria's northern borders against the increasingly militant Scots, into whose territory he advanced in 1054, when he 'proceeded with a large force to Scotland, both with a naval force and with a land force, and fought there with the Scots and routed the king Macbeth'.[154] The D-text of the *Anglo-Saxon Chronicle* records that, in this campaign, 'his son Osbeorn and his sister's son Siward and some of his housecarls, and also some of the king's, were killed', while the C-text simply states that 'many fell on his side both among Danes and English'.

We have little or no information about Siward's activities within Yorkshire itself, though it has been suggested that the place-name 'Siward's Howe', on Heslington Hill in York, may indicate the site of meetings presided over by Siward as earl.[155] Our fullest information concerning Siward's association with York comes in the record of his death in the *Anglo-Saxon Chronicle*, the year after his Scottish expedition: 'In this year Earl Siward died at York, and he lies at Galmanho in the minster which he himself had built and consecrated in the name of God and Olaf'.[156] *Galmanho* was in the Bootham area of York, the part later known as *Earlsburgh*, but it is the dedication of Siward's church that is arresting. The Olaf commemorated was Óláfr Haraldsson, king of Norway from 1015 until 1028, when he was driven out in the process of Cnut's annexation of the country; but he returned two years later, and was defeated and killed in the Battle of Stiklestad, after which he was regarded almost immediately as a saint – indeed, as Scandinavia's first native saint, the *rex perpetuus* or 'perpetual king' of Norway.[157] In promoting the cult of St Olaf, Siward was thus at the forefront of a new, Scandinavian-oriented piety, one which took root in England in the course of the eleventh century.[158]

Seething and simmering through the years of Siward's earldom, however, was an extraordinary story of family enmity, often referred to as 'the Northumbrian bloodfeud', a story that is preserved in a late eleventh- or early twelfth-century Durham text known as *On the Siege of Durham* (*De Obsessione Dunelmi*), and which has been the subject of a book-length study by Richard Fletcher.[159] Uhtred's killer in 1016, we may recall, was a figure named Thurbrand or Thorbrand, and *On the Siege of Durham* narrates an essential part of the back-story, telling us that 'Uhtred married Sige, the daughter of Styr, son of Ulf, a wealthy and prominent man; her father gave her to him on the condition that he would kill Styr's leading enemy Thurbrand'.[160] The *History of St Cuthbert* remembers Styr as a generous patron of the church of Durham.[161]

But it was, in fact, to be Thurbrand who killed Uhtred:

When Cnut had laid hands upon the whole kingdom of England, he sent to the earl [Uhtred] ordering him to come to him as his new lord. He did so, having accepted safe conduct for his journey and return. On the appointed day, he entered the king's presence at *Wiheal* [possibly Wighill (WR)] to discuss terms of peace; through the treachery of a powerful king's thegn, Thurbrand, known as Hold, the king's soldiers who had hidden behind a curtain spread across the width of the hall, suddenly sprang out in mail and slaughtered the earl and forty of his chief men who had entered with him.[162]

This killing provoked an inter-family conflict which persisted for three generations and over fifty years. Uhtred's son, Ealdred (who, as we have seen, was Siward's father-in-law), killed Thurbrand, his father's killer. Then Thurbrand's son, Carl or Karli, and his antagonist, Ealdred, 'tried to ambush each other at every opportunity but were finally brought to agreement by the intervention of friends'. Indeed, they even became sworn brothers and embarked on a pilgrimage to Rome together, before stormy weather at sea forced them to turn back. And then:

> Carl received the earl [Ealdred] into his home with befitting magnificence. But after this show of conviviality, while he [Carl] was escorting him [Ealdred] – suspecting no evil – apparently to show him honour, he [Carl] killed him in a wood called Risewood [Rise (ER)].[163]

This was not the end of the feud. More than thirty years later Ealdred's grandson (and Siward's son), Waltheof, perpetrated an act of reprisal:

> [Waltheof] sent a large band of young men and avenged the killing of his grandfather with the utmost slaughter. For when the sons of Carl were feasting together at their elder brother's house at Settrington [ER], not far from York, the men who had been sent caught them unawares and savagely killed them together [...] Having massacred the sons and grandsons of Carl, they returned home bringing with them much booty of various kinds.[164]

As far as we know, the massacre at Settrington, in 1073 or 1074, was the end of this extraordinary chain of bloodshed. But although the narrative can be read as a simple tale of families at war, that is not the whole story. In early medieval culture, feud was not a symptom of uncontrollable violence, nor a theatre for purely private vendettas; on the contrary, it was a means by which one kin-group or power-group could further their political ends at the expense of their rivals, and successful players of the game were those who were expert at knowing exactly when, and against whom, to strike.[165] What we can therefore see is that, for the first two generations at least, the conflict that *On the Siege of Durham* records is a competition for power in eleventh-century Northumbria between a grand family in Deiran Yorkshire (Thurbrand's kin) and the grandest of families in Bernician Northumberland (Uhtred's kin, the earls of Bamburgh).[166] The context for the conflict was Cnut's conquest, and the potential it had unleashed for the re-shaping of power structures in the north. By the time of the last act in the drama, Waltheof's killing of the sons and grandsons of Carl, the picture had changed somewhat: first, by Earl Siward's marriage to the daughter of Earl Ealdred (thereby uniting Deiran and Bernician power in one family); and second, of course, by the Norman Conquest. But it cannot be coincidence that Waltheof acted to avenge his grandfather only a year or two after he was appointed earl of Bernician Northumbria by William the Conqueror: clearly he was acting both to settle old scores and secure his position in the north.

Also worth noting are the personal names in these two families. Thurbrand's family, based in Yorkshire, bear Norse names, whereas Uhtred's family, in Northumberland, bear English ones. We should not, however, see bloodfeud as some sort of distinctively Scandinavian style of conflict, even though the later Icelandic sagas do give us our fullest and best feud narratives from the Middle Ages. But Thurbrand's ancestors, we can assume, were among the leading Scandinavian elite of pre-Conquest Yorkshire, and later in the eleventh century a building in York, which was evidently a major landmark, was known as 'Thurbrand's house' (either after Thurbrand himself, or after his grandson of the same name).[167] In the light of the title *hold* accorded him in *On the Siege of Durham*, it has even been suggested, rather speculatively, that he may have been the city's political leader.[168] (The text *Norðleoda laga*, 'The Law of the North People', equates the wergild of a *hold* with that of the king's high-reeve.[169]) Whether or not this is the case, Thurbrand and his descendants held extensive estates in the Wolds and the Vale of Pickering, as Stuart Wrathmell has demonstrated; and Orm Gamalson may possibly have been related to him.[170]

The text that gives us the greatest information about the mid eleventh-century elite, at least of a certain sort, is, of course, Domesday Book. But the information that the Domesday survey of Yorkshire gives us is, as we saw in Chapter 1, as partial as it is extensive. It is in no way to be regarded as an exhaustive statement of lordship and resources in 1066, and the format of its entries varies greatly.[171] But Domesday Book does enable us to perceive various tiers or types of lords in mid eleventh-century Yorkshire, as the Domesday survey sought to record both the people who held land in 1086 (at the time of the survey), and also their so-called *antecessores* or antecedents, those who held the corresponding land in 1066 (at the time of Edward the Confessor's death, or shortly before). At the top of the scale in Yorkshire in 1066 were the king, the earl, and the archbishop of York, and then below them major local magnates such as Orm Gamalson, or the Bárðr who held extensive estates in the West Riding. Not everyone within this class should necessarily be classified on regional terms as 'Yorkshire thegns': extensive Yorkshire estates, and a house in York, were held, for example, by an important figure named Merleswein or Mærle-Sveinn, who was the Sheriff of Lincolnshire in Edward's reign, and who possessed substantial estates in Cornwall,

Devon, and Somerset, as well as Lincolnshire and Yorkshire.[172] At the bottom of the scale were many individual 'lordlings', who held their own manor or estate and no more, and who may or may not have been subservient to an overlord (often unnoted in Domesday Book). So, for example, although Orm may well have been the overlord of Wharram Percy, the resident lordling will have been either the Karli or Lagmann who are recorded as holding property there in 1066.[173] Many of the entries in the Yorkshire Domesday reveal that the vill concerned was home to more than one lord: these were minor land-holders indeed.

The complication is that Domesday Book does not distinguish between individuals of the same name. This means that if, for instance, we find that three separate holdings, in three separate places, were possessed by someone called Thorulf, we cannot know for sure if this indicates three separate Thorulfs, each with minor holdings, or one wealthier Thorulf, with property in three locations. (This is a genuine example: the name Thorulf is indeed associated with three places in Yorkshire in Domesday Book, namely Dunsley [NR], Sheriff Hutton [NR], and *Fornetorp* in Thwing [ER]. The likelihood must be that these are three different individuals.[174]) Naturally, the probability increases that it is the same person who is being referred to when the personal name that they bear is a rare one, or the land they hold is in proximate places, such as Uglubárðr (holding land in Croome and Kirby Grindalythe [both ER], and possibly, one might speculate, a relation of the Uglubárðr who gave his name to Ugglebarnby [NR]), or Ingiríðr (a woman, holding land in Hawold and Huggate [both ER]).[175] Identification is also helped by the fact that, as we will see in the next chapter, the new Norman lords after the Conquest were normally, or at least initially, endowed with land not on a regional or geographical basis, but rather through the transfer *en bloc* of estates held by pre-Conquest antecedents, wherever they were located; so land that was in a single pair of hands in 1086 may also have been so in 1066. Nonetheless, quite a lot of names occur only once, in one place, in the 1066 record, thus revealing to us a class of minor lords or prosperous free peasants: examples include Reiði in Little Hatfield [ER], Búi in Anley [WR], and the interestingly named Mylnu-Grímr, 'Grímr of the mill', also in Croome.[176] But with a popular, widely distributed name like Thorkell or Thorketill, the possibilities are countless, and disentangling individuals may be impossible.

What is striking, of course, is the persistence of Norse names among the land-holding elite of 1066 – a full two centuries after the arrival of the Great Army, whose members are likely to have been the ancestors of many of these eleventh-century land-holders. In a remarkable piece of research, David Parsons has taken Domesday Book's unparalleled record of mid eleventh-century naming patterns, and calculated, on a county by county basis, the relative proportion of Norse names to English names in each county.[177] So, for example, in Staffordshire the proportion is 37:63; in Kent it goes down to 15:85. In other words, in the recorded corpus of names for Staffordshire in Domesday Book, for every 37 different Norse names recorded, there are 63 different Old English names (and these calculations must be made on the basis of different names, as otherwise one land-holder in twenty different places would have to be counted twenty times). What is compelling about Parsons' figures is the manner in which the Norse proportion goes up as one heads north and east, further into the northern Danelaw. In Derbyshire the proportions are 51:49, with Norse names just in the majority; in Lincolnshire, 62:38; and in Yorkshire, 70:30. In other words, over two-thirds of the names of land-holders in Yorkshire in 1066 were Old Norse, the highest proportion for any county. When one considers that Parsons' count must, of necessity, include non-resident land-holders from further south (such as the king himself), then it is clear that the local population of land-holders must have been even more dominantly Norse in their personal names. Furthermore, Parsons' general figure of 70:30 for the county as a whole conceals some pronounced regional variations: the West Riding, especially to the south-west, shows a greater proportion of Old English names, whereas in Ryedale in the North Riding, over 90% of Domesday land-holders had Norse names.[178]

Other sources complement these Domesday figures. Among the moneyers recorded on York coins in the late tenth and early eleventh centuries, three-quarters bear Norse names.[179] And copied at the back of the early eleventh-century York Gospels is a fascinating list which begins 'These are the *festermen* of Ælfric [...]'.[180] The legal concept of *festermen* was a Scandinavian one: such figures acted as surety in a case at law or some other transaction, and the Ælfric concerned is almost certainly the archbishop of York from 1023-51.[181] Some 70 *festermen* are listed in the York Gospels, thus constituting a valuable sample of the mid eleventh-century Yorkshire elite, and many seem to have come from the area around Sherburn-in-Elmet [WR]; Sherburn was, as we have seen, an archiepiscopal estate. Six of the *festermen* are identified as priests: interestingly, all six have Norse names, suggesting that the church in eleventh-century Yorkshire may have been heavily staffed by men of Scandinavian descent. In total, two-thirds of Ælfric's *festermen* bear Norse names, while a quarter have English names, and the remainder are either ambiguous or fall into another category.

It is important to go back to some of the points made in Chapter 4, to appreciate what these numbers mean. As we saw there, naming in the early medieval period (and certainly in the Viking Age) was largely governed and conditioned by family connections; it was not a free choice. So these eleventh-century indicators do not mean that English and Norse names had simply been mixed together in the northern Danelaw, in a certain proportion, to create a collective bran-tub out of which any family could draw any name. Rather, individual families preserved individual traditions of naming: some families, no doubt for reasons of ancestry and cultural heritage, continued to prefer English names, while others (the majority at the gentry level) maintained a tradition of Norse names. It is true that, in the eleventh century, it is possible to find English and Norse names co-existing in the same family, and after two centuries of interaction this is hardly surprising. But it is not the norm.[182] In the list of Ælfric's *festermen*, for example, there are three individuals for whom patronymics are given (*Þorcetel Unbainasuna, Raganald Asbeornnas suna*, and *Halwærð Sæfugalasuna*): in all three cases we see that fathers with Norse names have sons (*festermen*) with Norse names. We also have examples from the eleventh century of the classic pattern by which names were passed on from grandfather to grandson (that is, men named their sons after their own fathers): the father of Orm Gamalson, as we will see, was very probably called Gamal Ormson, and Orm himself may well have had a son called Gamal, while Thurbrand *hold* had a son called Carl, who had a son called Thurbrand. Peter Sawyer has pointed out that, in all the pages of the Lincolnshire Domesday, we only find one case in which the names of both the father and the grandfather of a particular land-holder are given: but the individual concerned was a certain Svartbrand, who was the son of Ulf, who was the son of Svartbrand.[183] It is also worth noting that, within the eleventh-century culture of Norse nomenclature, Irish or Goidelic names persisted as a distinctive sub-group, seemingly indicating both a harking back to Celtic origins and also continuing contacts with the Irish Sea world.[184] The distribution of Goidelic personal names in Domesday Book agrees conspicuously with their occurrence in place-names, and shows a particular density in the western Dales.

Scandinavian styles in material culture also continued into the later tenth and eleventh centuries, though not as forcefully as in the area of personal names. So, for example, Anglo-Scandinavian brooches in the Jellinge style continued to be made in York into the later tenth century, before an important shift occurred in the eleventh century.[185] After the turn of the millennium, there is a clear decline in the prominence of female jewellery, and a rise in the importance of (male) equestrian equipment, in the form of stirrup mounts and terminals and bridle fittings.[186] These have been found widely by metal-detectorists, especially in the East Riding: examples include those from Boroughbridge and Darrington [both WR], and Dunnington, Kilham [Figure 16], Melbourne, North Dalton, Skipsea, Skirpenbeck, and Thwing [all ER].[187] Although found in the traditional heartlands of the Danelaw, such equestrian items are in fact distributed across all of England, and it seems very likely that we should attribute their appearance to Cnut's conquest and its consequences.[188] The use of stirrups is thought to have been introduced into England from Denmark; Cnut's armies campaigned across much of the country during 1015-16, and his supporters and followers settled widely in southern and western regions.[189] We should assume, therefore, that the use of stirrups was adopted more widely by the eleventh-century elite, and came to form part of the material kit of male aristocrats and gentry.

Many of these equestrian items are decorated in the so-called Ringerike and Urnes styles which, together with the Mammen style, represent the three Scandinavian art-styles of the later Viking Age, supplanting the earlier Borre and Jellinge styles.[190] The Mammen style (conventionally dated c.960-c.1025) is a development of the Jellinge style, with more prominent spirals and tendrils; the Ringerike style (c.1000-c.1075) accentuated further certain features of the Mammen style and gave greater prominence to a central 'great beast'; and the Urnes style (c.1050-c.1125) was distinguished by elegant, interwoven animals. Ringerike/Urnes metalwork finds in England have been mapped comparatively against those in the Borre style, and the contrastive distributions are very revealing: while Borre finds cluster persuasively in the east of England (Yorkshire, Lincolnshire, East Anglia), Ringerike/Urnes finds are not restricted to such traditional areas of Scandinavian settlement, and are also found widely in the central and west midlands, and in the south of England.[191] The city of York has so far yielded a few objects in the Ringerike style, but little or nothing in Mammen or Urnes.[192]

Only a very few instances of these later styles are attested in Yorkshire stone sculpture. So, for example, a grave-cover from Levisham [NR] has been proposed – but also disputed – as an example of Mammen style, and possible Mammen-like tendrils have been perceived on a few pieces from the West Riding.[193] A grave-cover from Otley is generally accepted as the most persuasive example of the Ringerike style to be found in northern sculpture.[194] A fragment from Holy Trinity, Micklegate, York, has been suggested as a possible example of the Urnes style, but this is by no means agreed.[195]

There are thus no grounds for doubting the accepted view that it was the first half of the tenth century (and, perhaps, a bit earlier) that was the boom period for the production of Scandinavian stone sculpture in northern England, though we should note that the re-use of earlier grave-slabs in the York Minster cemetery, in the late tenth and early eleventh centuries, implies that Anglo-Scandinavian sculpture could still be desirable as a form of funerary monument.[196] But it is hard to escape the conclusion that, by the turn of the millennium, and with the exception of the equestrian equipment consequent on Cnut's conquest, there was little distinctively Scandinavian art being produced in northern England. Moreover, some southern English styles were beginning to take hold in the north, such as the so-called Winchester style of ornamentation, heavy in the use of acanthus leaves.[197]

The evidence we have just considered, of personal names and material culture, clearly tells us something important about questions of assimilation and identity in the eleventh century – questions which were raised for the ninth and tenth centuries at the end of Chapter 5. The remarkable persistence of Norse personal names, in contrast to the waning of a strong Scandinavian signature in sculpture and jewellery, suggests that some expressions of identity were felt to be more ancestral, and non-negotiable, than others; the thinness of attestations of the Ringerike, Mammen, and Urnes styles may also indicate a weakening in the oversea ties between northern England and the Scandinavian homelands (though some other points of evidence might be a counter-indication to this, such as the spread of St Olaf's cult across the North Sea, or the pronounced and well-informed interest that the D-text of the *Anglo-Saxon Chronicle* takes in events in Norway in the late 1040s).[198]

An important related question would therefore be whether the Old Norse language was still spoken in eleventh-century Yorkshire, or whether the language had died out with the shift of generations, so that even families with a strong tradition of Norse nomenclature were now English-speaking. Unfortunately, our positive evidence on this question is minimal.[199] The fact that eleventh-century inscriptions, such as that at Kirkdale, are in Old English, is of little consequence, as Old Norse (as we saw in Chapter 5) was never used as a written language in Viking Age England; so it would be perfectly possible for the same person to speak in Old Norse but commission inscriptions in Old English (or Latin).[200] It has been suggested that the lost York street name Footlessgale (from Norse *fótlauss-geil* 'footless lane') refers to 'the crippled poor' at St Leonard's Hospital, which was (re-)founded in the late eleventh century, and so the name must post-date the foundation; but this is speculative and uncertain, not least because the hospital may have had a tenth-century pre-existence.[201] A more significant piece of evidence is the extant portion of a Norse praise-poem in honour of Earl Waltheof, Siward's son, composed by an Icelandic poet called Þorkell Skallason. This poem, *Valþjófsflokkr* (*Poem about Waltheof*), of which only two stanzas now survive, was composed after Waltheof's death in 1076, but the skald had evidently been part of the earl's retinue while he was alive.[202] So here we have an Old Norse poem being composed for an earl of Northumbria as late as the decade after the Norman Conquest – strong evidence that the Norse language continued to have an audience, at least in elite circles, well into the eleventh century. Siward, Waltheof's father, seems to have been one of the new wave of Scandinavian magnates who entered England with Cnut's conquest, rather than coming from a family established in England since the ninth century, but Þorkell's *Valþjófsflokkr* still dates from over half a century after Cnut's accession; this is no transitory production from the brief years of Cnut's conquest, but rather a second-generation poem that has roots in the north of England of at least five decades' standing. What is more, we know that Waltheof had an English mother, Ælfflæd of Bernicia: this suggests that, even in the eleventh century, it was not inevitable that the child of an English mother and a Scandinavian father would automatically follow his mother's tongue (though we should, no doubt, assume that Waltheof possessed competence in both). So it is certainly possible that Norse speech was still to be heard in some parts, or some circles, in eleventh-century Yorkshire.

By the time of Þorkell's poetry, though, 200 years had passed since the fall of York to the Viking Great Army. The world of Earl Waltheof, say, or of Orm Gamalson, or of York's urban elite, was in no way the same as that of the early settlers of the 870s, those who had benefited from Halfdan's sharing out of the land. Orm's church at Kirkdale was built in the early 1060s – at exactly the same time, in other words, when the county of Yorkshire seems to have been constituted as a formal administrative entity. The establishment of the county of Yorkshire can be taken as the point at which the polity and society created by the Vikings in southern Northumbria – the Viking kingdom of York, founded on the earlier Anglo-Saxon kingdom of Deira – becomes definitively incorporated into a southern-centred English state (though as we shall see in the next chapter, for a few years this incorporation was disputed through a great deal of bloodshed). Moreover, when Orm's church at Kirkdale was built or re-built at this time, a number of Scandinavian crosses, from 150 years earlier, were re-used as building material, and built into its walls, either for symbolic reasons or simply because they were suitable materials and close at hand: their re-use thus provides a poignant demonstration of the passing of time, and a reminder that the world of the Middleton warriors, with which we began this book, was becoming increasingly distant history (and some of the Middleton stones themselves were built into an eleventh-century church tower).[203] Nonetheless, and as we have seen, it is not difficult also to perceive a strong element of continuity between the age of Halfdan and the age of Orm: in descent, in language, in culture, and perhaps also in some aspects of political allegiance. By the mid eleventh century, we can conclude, some of the earlier markers of Scandinavian culture and identity were in decline, or had disappeared; but by no means all. Yorkshire, on the eve of the Norman Conquest, still bore the profound impress of its Scandinavian history, and possessed a continuing Scandinavian heritage.

EPILOGUE

1066 AND BEYOND

Rebellion and Conquest

Within a Europe-wide perspective, the Viking Age is conventionally viewed as extending from approximately 800 to 1050. By the mid eleventh century, the society and polities of Scandinavia had experienced a number of changes which served to bring them much more into line with the rest of Europe: above all, conversion to Christianity and the establishment of strong, centralized kingships. But the history of the Vikings in England is usually narrated according to a more precise bracket of dates, namely 793 (the date of the attack on Lindisfarne) and 1066 (the date of the Battle of Stamford Bridge, prologue to the Battle of Hastings). There are good grounds, however, for extending the narrative of Viking Age Yorkshire, at least in outline, by ten or fifteen years beyond 1066. The great change in life in Northumbria came in the decade after 1066, not in that year itself, in terms of northern England's experience of Norman rule, and the consequences of this for the Northumbrian — that is, the native Anglo-Scandinavian — aristocracy and gentry. The 1060s and 1070s saw the greatest tumult and changes in the north since the 860s and 870s, and it is these events and changes that this last chapter will sketch out, before finally glancing at some of the echoes and memories of Yorkshire's Scandinavian heritage up to the present day.

Edward the Confessor died on 5 January 1066, leaving no offspring. Cnut, the Danish conqueror, had reigned from 1016 to 1035, before being succeeded by his sons Harthacnut (1035-40) and Harold Harefoot (1040-42). With the deaths of Harthacnut and Harold (and also of Cnut's other son, Swein, who did not rule in England), the line of Cnut and Swein Forkbeard came to an end, and the house of Alfred re-occupied the throne of Anglo-Saxon England, in the person of Æthelred's son, Edward. Edward had spent the years of Danish rule in Normandy, and his return to England marked the beginnings of the French or Norman impact on English politics and culture, a full twenty-five years before the Battle of Hastings.[1]

In Northumbria, the events of 1066 really began a year earlier, in 1065. And the story of 1065 begins a decade earlier, in 1055. In that year, as we saw in the previous chapter, Earl Siward died, and was buried in the church which he had had dedicated to St Olaf, in York. As his replacement as earl of Northumbria, King Edward appointed Tostig, son of Earl Godwine (and brother-in-law of the king himself), a member of the most powerful aristocratic family in England.[2] Tostig was the first earl of Northumbria to be appointed with no prior connection to either the northern or eastern Danelaw, or to the region of Bernicia; the power-base of the Godwinesons lay firmly in the south.[3] But he was half-Danish: Godwine's wife was Gytha, the sister of Cnut's brother-in-law, and both Tostig and a number of his brothers bore Norse names – including his brother Harold (Old Norse *Haraldr*). His own wife, Judith, was sister of the count of Flanders, and both Tostig and Judith were remembered as generous patrons of the church, not least in Durham.[4]

Tostig spent much of his time in the south of England, and at the royal court, and his deputy on the ground in Yorkshire seems to have been a local thegn named Copsig (Old Norse *Kofsi*).[5] Some of our sources do, however, show Tostig acting in close connection with Ealdred, as, respectively, earl of Northumbria and archbishop of York. So, for example, Tostig accompanied Ealdred to Rome in 1061, only for them both to be set upon by brigands on their way home.[6] While Tostig was away, the Scots raided Lindisfarne and annexed Cumbria, so undoing much of the hard work that Siward had put into defending Northumbria's northern borders.[7] But it was the events of autumn 1065 that proved decisively that Tostig's decade as earl was a disaster. As the *Anglo-Saxon Chronicle* records (here quoted from version D):

> All the thegns in Yorkshire and in Northumberland came together and outlawed their Earl Tostig and killed his bodyguard, and all they could get at, both English and Danish, and took all his weapons in York, and gold and silver and all his treasure they could hear about anywhere.[8]

The near-contemporary (and pro-Tostig) *Life of King Edward* states that 'many were slaughtered in the cities of York and Lincoln', and that 'whosoever could be identified as having been at some time a member of Tostig's household was dragged to the torments of death without trial'.[9] But the fullest account of these events is given in a later source, John of Worcester's early twelfth-century *Chronicle*, and this enables us to identify some of the leaders of the revolt, and also some of the causes:

After the feast of St Michael the Archangel, on Monday, 3 October, the Northumbrian thegns, Gamalbarn, Dunstan, son of Æthelnoth, and Glonieorn, son of Heardwulf, came with 200 soldiers to York, and, on account of the disgraceful death of the noble Northumbrian thegns Gospatric (whom Queen Edith, on account of her brother Tostig, had ordered to be killed in the king's court on the fourth night of Christmas by treachery), Gamal, son of Orm, and Ulf, son of Dolfin (whose murders Earl Tostig had treacherously ordered the preceding year at York in his own chamber, under cover of a peace-treaty), and also of the huge tribute which Tostig had unjustly levied on the whole of Northumbria, they, on that same day, slew first his Danish house-carls, Amund and Ravenswart, hauled back from flight, beyond the city walls, and on the following day more than 200 men from his court, on the north side of the River Humber. They also broke open his treasury, and, having taken away all his goods, they withdrew.[10]

The three rebel leaders seem to have been prominent thegns from the West Riding, and we should note the cultural diversity of their names: one Norse, one English, and one Irish.[11]

Tostig himself was not in York or Northumbria, but down south in the king's company. The rebels soon voiced their demands, and marched southwards to try to enforce them:

And they sent for Morcar, son of Earl Ælfgar, and chose him as their earl, and he went south with all the people of the shire, and of Nottinghamshire, Derbyshire, and Lincolnshire until he came to Northampton. And his brother Edwin came to meet him with the men that were in his earldom, and also many Welsh came with him. Thereupon Earl Harold [Tostig's brother] came to meet them, and they entrusted him with a message to King Edward, and also sent messengers with him, and asked that they might be allowed to have Morcar as their earl. And the king granted this and sent Harold back to them at Northampton.[12]

In other words, Edward gave in to the rebels' demands, seemingly against his will (the *Life of King Edward* claims that the king wished to crush the rebellion, but 'horror was felt at [the prospect of] what seemed civil war').[13] Tostig and his family and retinue departed into exile, going first to the court of Judith's brother in Flanders. The *Anglo-Saxon Chronicle* records two other elements in the dénouement of the rebellion. First, that while the rebels were waiting for the king's response, they 'did much damage round Northampton', killing the locals, burning their houses and corn, and capturing both cattle and even (the *Chronicle* claims) people, to be taken back north with them: it seems significant that, like Swein Forkbeard before them, the northern rebels waited until they had come to Watling Street, the old Danelaw boundary, before they began to waste the surrounding countryside.[14] And second, the *Chronicle* records that Edward conciliated the rebel forces at Northampton by 'renew[ing] there the law of King Cnut'.

207

This last piece of information leads us on to the question of the grounds for the rebellion. Why did the revolt take place? What had Tostig done, or not done? These issues have been much discussed.[15] 'Whatever his particular oppressions,' as one modern historian has written, 'there is good reason to think that his general offence was insufficient regard for traditional modes of northern government'.[16] For whatever reason, it was clearly felt by the rebels that the laws of Cnut – drafted by Archbishop Wulfstan II of York – were more acceptable to northern sensibilities than the policies and practices of the current regime; perhaps they were viewed as a safeguard against unfair or over-intrusive government.[17] The sympathetic *Life of King Edward* claims that the rebellion was an ungrateful response to the admirable firmness with which Tostig had brought law and order to the unruly north: 'this distinguished earl, a son and lover of divine peace, had in his time so reduced the number of robbers and cleared the country of them by mutilating or killing them and by sparing no one, however noble, who was caught in this crime, that any man, even with any of his goods, could travel at will even alone without fear of attack'.[18]

Two further explanations for the revolt, as we have seen, are given by John of Worcester. The first, an alternative perspective on the *Life of King Edward's* interpretation, is that Tostig had unjustly killed a number of important Northumbrian thegns: those named are a certain Gospatric, Gamal, son of Orm, and Ulf, son of Dolfin. Although definitive identifications are impossible, the first of these was probably a member of the family of the earls of Bamburgh; the second was probably the father of Orm Gamalson of Kirkdale (though possibly his son); and the third was probably the son of a Northumbrian thegn who had been killed fighting alongside Earl Siward in Scotland. All three, in other words, were members of prominent Northumbrian families, and all three seem to have had some connection, either through descent or marriage, with the earls of Bamburgh.[19] So it looks as if Tostig may have been trying to eliminate political rivals in the north, perhaps even weighing in on the famed 'Northumbrian bloodfeud'.

John of Worcester's second explanation is that Tostig had 'unjustly levied' a 'huge tribute' on Northumbria. We should therefore remind ourselves that the earliest references to Yorkshire as a shire date from the early 1060s, immediately before the rebellion, and that one of the main reasons why Anglo-Saxon kings imposed the shire system was for purposes of tax-collecting, and maximizing revenue. Is it a coincidence that the first appearance of Yorkshire as a shire comes just before the Northumbrian revolt? It may be so, but it seems more likely that it was these new burdens of the southern yoke, legal as well as financial, that provided the kindling to be sparked into flame by Tostig's killing of prominent thegns.

All our sources, then, whatever their stance, indicate that it was Tostig's authoritarian ways that provoked the rebellion, as he endeavoured to impose, either justly or unjustly, a degree of central control not hitherto experienced in the north; and this rebellion erupted shortly, it seems, after the formal institution of the county of Yorkshire. So it may be an irony, at least for later generations of Yorkshire patriots, that the creation of the county of Yorkshire was a profoundly unwelcome act in the locality: the name and institution of Yorkshire may have represented to contemporaries not proud northern independence, but oppressive southern rule. But we should note the limit of the rebels' demands. What they wished for was to change their earl, not to get rid of earls altogether; this was a movement demanding reform and devolution, but not separation from the kingdom of England.[20]

The appointment as Tostig's successor of Morcar, of the Leofwineson family of the earls of Mercia, re-asserted a late tenth-century pattern in which Mercia and Northumbria belonged together as a sort of political 'greater north' of Anglo-Saxon England beyond the Thames. Morcar himself returned control of Bernician Northumbria to Oswulf of Bamburgh, grandson of the Earl Uhtred who had been killed in 1016.[21] Tostig's estates in the north were carved up and re-distributed: Morcar received the majority of the estates, but a number passed into the possession of his brother, Earl Edwin, and also of Tostig's elder brother, Harold Godwineson.[22] King Edward died just a few weeks after the Northumbrian revolt, his decline accelerated by the stress of events. And the day after Edward's death, Harold Godwineson was proclaimed king, even though he was not of royal descent. William of Malmesbury records that, on Harold's accession, 'the only people to put off taking allegiance were the Northumbrians, 'with all the pride of their race' [a quotation from the Latin poet Statius]; as they frequently put it, they did not care to see their northern granite subject to those softies in the south [*australi mollitie*]'.[23] This explains why, according to the *Anglo-Saxon Chronicle*, Harold made a visit to York immediately after his proclamation as king, to secure his recognition in the north.[24]

But of course Harold was not the only person in 1066 who believed that they had a claim on Edward's throne.[25] The belief in Normandy was that, at an earlier date, Edward had indicated Duke William to be his chosen heir; moreover, Harold Godwineson had supposedly recognized William as his lord when he himself was in Normandy. Yet a third claimant to the throne was King Harald Hardrada of Norway, who demands introduction at this point.

Harald was the half-brother of the St Olaf whom Earl Siward had venerated, and in the years after Olaf's death in 1030 he had enjoyed service and adventures out in Byzantium, as a member of the Varangian Guard of Scandinavian mercenaries.[26] Following the demise of Cnut's dynasty, in 1046 he had returned to Norway and claimed a share of the throne from his nephew Magnus, Olaf's son. Magnus died the following year, after which Harald assumed sole rule of the kingdom. His nickname, seemingly a contemporary one, comes from the Old Norse *harðráði* 'hard-rule', and later saga accounts depict him as a stern and old-fashioned warrior-king.[27] He was also distinguished as an energetic patron of poets, and seems to have composed poetry himself: a later Icelandic text known as *Skáldatal* or the 'List of Poets' records that no fewer than thirteen poets composed in his honour – the highest number known for any Scandinavian king.[28] Harald believed himself to have a claim on the English kingdom via his nephew Magnus, who had supposedly reached an agreement with Cnut's son Harthacnut, then king of England and Denmark, that whichever of them outlived the other would inherit the other's domains; and for much of his reign Harald had been at war with Harthacnut's successor in Denmark, Swein Estrithson.[29] The final impetus that sent Harald towards England in 1066 may have been supplied by the exiled Tostig, who established an understanding that he would support the Norwegian king in any attack on England. But we should realize that this was not Harald's first move in that direction: back in 1058, the *Chronicle* records, 'a naval force came from Norway', and Irish sources indicate that this was a serious fleet, with purposes of conquest, led by Harald's son (also called Magnus).[30]

Very little is known about this Norwegian assault of 1058, whereas that of 1066 is well recorded in contemporary or near-contemporary sources from both the English and Scandinavian sides.[31] The *Anglo-Saxon Chronicle* offers a relatively full account, while Harald's patronage of poets meant that his English expedition was celebrated and commemorated in a sizeable body of skaldic verse.[32] Such verse, and perhaps other oral traditions, were later to be blended with continental Latin sources to provide the basis for very extensive narratives about Harald's last campaigns in thirteenth-century kings' sagas; but while such sources undoubtedly have some value, they also contain a fair dash of imaginative fiction, and it is the skaldic poetry which should be prioritized as more authoritative.[33]

Among the versions of the *Anglo-Saxon Chronicle*, it is the C-text that gives the fullest account of Harald's campaign, though the D-text is also important.[34] Version C records that Harald and Tostig had a rendezvous at the River Tyne (the D-text says Scotland), and then sailed up the Humber and Ouse towards York, with Harald's fleet of 300 ships. John of Worcester claims that Harald's fleet was in fact 500-strong, and Gaimar, in his *History of the English*, specifies 470. These two twelfth-century sources also disagree as to where Harald came ashore: John of Worcester says Riccall [ER], some ten miles south of York, while Gaimar states cryptically 'at St Wilfrid's', which (it has been suggested) may be a reference to Brayton [WR] near Selby, five miles further south than Riccall, where the church is dedicated to St Wilfrid.[35] As soon as Harold Godwineson learned of Harald's landing, he marched north 'day and night as quickly as he could to assemble his force'.[36] But he did not arrive in time for the first battle:

Then before Harold could get there Earl Edwin and Earl Morcar assembled from their earldom as large a force as they could muster, and fought against the invaders and caused them heavy casualties, and many of the English host were killed and drowned and put to flight, and the Norwegians remained masters of the field.[37]

This battle took place at Fulford, just south of York, on 20 September 1066; the place is named by both the *History of the Kings* and Gaimar.[38] Modern investigations have suggested that the precise site of the battle was in the low ground around the stream now known as Germany Beck.[39] Further details of the battle, of a heroic, panegyric sort, are supplied by some of the commemorative verses composed by Harald's skalds. Arnórr Þórðarson, for example, declares that 'The leader reddened weighty iron blades ruthlessly on the English hard by the Ouse, and never will greater slaughter come upon a bold host', while other verses state that many English perished around the stream: Steinn Herdísarson records that 'many people died in the river; submerged men drowned; not a few warriors soon lay [dead] around young Morcar', while the anonymous *Haraldsstikki* claims that the English forces 'lay fallen down in the marsh, hacked by weapons, so that the battle-bold Norwegians could walk across on corpses alone'.[40] Some of the dead may have been buried at St Andrew's Church, Fishergate: a group of a dozen mid to late eleventh-century male skeletons have been uncovered there showing weapon injuries.[41]

Neither Morcar nor Edwin were killed at Fulford, but the battle did leave the city of York in Harald's power. He and Tostig entered the city, and exchanged hostages to secure their position. Moreover, Harald was supplied with provisions from the city and 'settled a complete peace, arranging that they [the hostages? a Northumbrian force?] should all go with him southwards and subdue this country'.[42] It is, of course, notable that Harald should have chosen to begin his attempted conquest in the north, as if there was expectation of less resistance there, or perhaps even a positive reception.

Five days after the Battle of Fulford, Harald and most of his army were seven miles east of York at Stamford Bridge [ER], 'because they had been promised for certain that hostages would be brought to them there out of all the shire'.[43] Stamford Bridge, on the River Derwent, was well placed for such a purpose in terms of its nodal position in the local road system. But this meant that it was also easily accessible from the south, and on 25 September Harold Godwineson and his army, having passed through York, fell upon Harald's Norwegian force, who seem to have been wholly unaware of the nearness of the English king:

Then Harold, king of the English, came against them by surprise beyond the bridge, and there they joined battle, and went on fighting strenuously till late in the day. And there Harald, king of Norway, was killed and Earl Tostig, and numberless men with them both Norwegians and English, and the Norwegians fled from the English.

This is the version of the near-contemporary C-text, to which a later hand has added an anecdote of the battle of a sort found elsewhere in heroic poetry:

> There was one of the Norwegians there who withstood the English host so that they could not cross the bridge nor win victory. Then an Englishman shot an arrow, but it was no use, and then another came under the bridge and stabbed him under the corselet. Then Harold, king of the English, came over the bridge and his host with him [...][44]

A more expansive version of this anecdote is found in William of Malmesbury ('Called upon to surrender [...] he spurned the invitation and kept taunting the enemy, saying they were a poor lot if they could not deal with a single man').[45] Heroic postures are also prominent in the skaldic accounts of the battle, mostly associated with Harald himself: according to Stúfr Þórðarson, for instance, 'the warden of spears' rain [i.e. Harald], who not at all heeded his life, went there, exultant, through battle like the wind', while Arnórr Þórðarson (no relation) states that 'the prince, shunning mediocrity, had no small courage in himself, and the battle-swift heart of the king did not tremble in the helmet-din [i.e. battle]'.[46] But there is also a touch of criticism of the king, for having led himself and his warriors into defeat, with Harald's old-style heroic virtues themselves proving his downfall, and perhaps also proving no longer appropriate in the changed world of the eleventh century: so, Arnórr attributes Harald's death in 'the blizzard of steel' to 'excess of heroism [*ofrausn*]', but Þjóðólfr Arnórsson remarks less equivocally that 'people have paid a dire penalty [...] Harald commanded troops onto this expedition westwards needlessly [*þarflaust*]'.[47] Nonetheless, Arnórr re-assures his listeners that 'the death of the fearsome king was not unadorned [...] All the liegemen of the gracious prince chose much rather to fall beside the battle-swift commander than wishing quarter'.[48]

The D-text of the *Chronicle* tells that, after the battle, the English army pursued the fleeing Norwegians right back to their ships (presumably still at Riccall): 'some were drowned, and some burned, and some destroyed in various ways so that few survived'.[49] One who did survive was Harald's son Olaf (later known as Olaf 'the Quiet', and king of Norway 1067-93); another was the earl of Orkney. After they had sworn pledges of peace to Harold, Olaf and the remnants of the Norwegian fleet were allowed to creep home, only 20 or 24 ships out of the several hundreds who had made landfall only a few days earlier.[50]

The graves of those who died at Stamford Bridge have so far not been discovered; a cemetery at Riccall has been found and excavated, but the bodies uncovered were those of the local population (between the seventh and twelfth centuries), not the Norwegian dead.[51] Tostig himself, according to William of Malmesbury, was buried in York ('recognized by the evidence of a wart between the shoulder-blades', which suggests that his body may have been mutilated or even decapitated).[52] William also states that Harold Godwineson entrusted to Edwin and Morcar the booty acquired through his victory, whereas Gaimar gives that role to Archbishop Ealdred of York, and also adds that Harold left the magnate Merleswein in command on the ground.[53] But Harold had no time to linger in the north: news reached him that William of Normandy had landed at Pevensey in Sussex on 28 September, a mere three days after the Battle of Stamford Bridge. And so Harold's men fought a second time, sixteen days after the first, and on 14 October 1066 the last Anglo-Saxon king of England was defeated and killed at the Battle of Hastings. Two months later, on Christmas Day at Westminster, William was crowned king of England by Archbishop Ealdred of York.[54] The word 'Norman' comes, of course, from 'Northman': the duchy of Normandy was established in the early tenth century as a Scandinavian polity, though it had changed and evolved over the following century and a half of French influence.[55]

William did not begin his reign in England by stripping the native aristocracy and gentry of their lands and giving them to his own followers, at least not in the north. But such a course of action was soon expedited by a series of revolts against his rule: in other words, it was not the events of 1066 that led to the fall of the Northumbrian elite, but those of the few years that followed.[56] These revolts were motivated variously by grievance, resistance, and disenfranchisement, and in response to heavy burdens of taxation. In William Kapelle's view, these early northern revolts against Norman rule also marked the continuation of a strain of Northumbrian separatism which was of long standing and had previously expressed itself most forcefully in the 1065 rebellion against Tostig; indeed, Tostig, in this view, may be blamed for feeding and provoking this rebelliousness, which was eventually to lead to disaster rather than reconciliation in the years after 1066.[57] Even in the twelfth century, Hugh the Chanter, in his *History of the Church of York*, attributes to Lanfranc, the Norman archbishop of Canterbury, the opinion that 'it was expedient for the union and solidarity of the kingdom that all Britain should be subject to one man as primate; it might otherwise happen [...] that some one of the Danes, Norwegians, or Scots, who used to sail up to York in their attacks on the realm, might be made king by the archbishop of York and the fickle and treacherous Yorkshiremen, and the kingdom disturbed and divided'.[58]

To begin with, in January 1067, William received the submission of a number of magnates, including Edwin and Morcar, and Tostig's old deputy, Copsig.[59] But then the rebellions began, not helped by William's appointment of the abhorred Copsig as earl of Bernician Northumbria. (His earldom was short-lived, as he was murdered within a month of taking up the office.[60]) Edwin and Morcar rebelled briefly against William in 1068, but were soon brought back into submission when William came north to York and built a castle there, probably the one at the site later known as Clifford's Tower.[61] A more substantial revolt was put together in the months following, centred around the person of Edgar 'the Atheling', a grandson of Edmund Ironside who had spent most of his life in exile in Hungary.[62] Edwin and Morcar were not among Edgar's supporters, but the group did include some who had been part of the short-lived rebellion of 1068: Earl Gospatric of Bamburgh; Merleswein, the Sheriff of Lincoln whom Harold Godwineson had left in charge of York in 1066; the sons of Carl, inheritors of the 'Northumbrian bloodfeud'; and a powerful Yorkshire thegn named Arnkell or Arnketill, whose urban estates in York may be commemorated by the later place-name Arkilltofts.[63] Our fullest source on these Northumbrian rebellions is the twelfth-century writer Orderic Vitalis, in his *Ecclesiastical History* (*Historia Ecclesiastica*), who gives an eloquent account of the nobles of the north being driven by 'anger at the loss of their patrimonies and the deaths of their kinsmen and fellow countrymen'.[64]

Early in 1069, William's garrisons at both Durham and then York were attacked by the rebels, but again the king was quickly able to re-assert control. As the *Anglo-Saxon Chronicle* (D-text) records:

> The atheling Edgar came to York with all the Northumbrians, and the citizens made peace with him. And King William came on them by surprise from the south with an overwhelming army and routed them, and killed those who could not escape, which was many hundreds of men, and ravaged the city [...] And the atheling went back to Scotland.[65]

William then built a second castle at York, at Old Baile, in a further attempt to secure the city. For the rebels were still at large: they had been routed and weakened, but not definitively beaten.

However, internal revolts formed only half of William's problems in the north after 1066, as indicated by the speech put into Lanfranc's mouth by Hugh the Chanter. The other half was the continuation of attacks from mainland Scandinavia, as Harald Hardrada's defeat at Stamford Bridge had not extinguished the desires of Scandinavian kings to re-conquer England; and it is possible that such subsequent attacks preferred to come up the Humber because they expected a supportive reception from the people of the north.[66] In late summer 1069 King Swein Estrithson of Denmark sent a fleet of 240 or 300 ships, led by his sons and their uncle, to attack England. Swein himself told Adam of Bremen that he had a claim on the throne of England: supposedly (and incredibly), Edward the

Confessor had designated Swein 'to be, on his death, the next heir to the English throne, even if Edward had sons'.[67] Swein's fleet sailed up the Humber and met the leaders of the English rebels – Edgar atheling and his supporters, now joined, significantly, by Waltheof, son of Earl Siward – together with (in the words of the *Anglo-Saxon Chronicle* D-text) 'the Northumbrians and all the people, riding and marching with an immense army rejoicing exceedingly'. It was just a few days later, at this profoundly ominous moment, that the venerable Archbishop Ealdred died, and was buried in York. Ealdred had had a difficult time since he had crowned William as king: according to Orderic, in 1068, for example, 'the city of York [had been] seething with discontent, and showed no respect for the holy office of its archbishop when he tried to appease it', while John of Worcester records that Ealdred was 'much affected with distress' at the arrival of Swein's fleet.[68]

The *Anglo-Saxon Chronicle* continues:

> So they all went resolutely to York, and stormed and razed the castle and captured an incalculable treasure in it, and killed many hundreds of Frenchmen and took many with them to the ships. And before the shipmen got there the Frenchmen had burned the city, and had also thoroughly ravaged and burnt the holy minster of St Peter.[69]

This loss of York in September 1069 has been described as 'the heaviest defeat which the Normans ever suffered in England'.[70] William of Malmesbury preserves a vignette of Waltheof slaughtering 'many of the Normans single-handed, beheading them one by one as they issued from the gate', while Orderic states that, when the Danes reached York, 'a general rising of the inhabitants swelled their ranks'.[71] The Conqueror's response was ferocious. He marched north again to suppress the rebellion, this time for good, and forced the Danish fleet to over-winter at the Isle of Axholme, on the south side of the Humber. William himself spent Christmas 1069 in York, ceremonially wearing his crown to demonstrate forcefully that it was he who was the king of England.[72] In the spring, though, a further Danish fleet appeared in the Humber, led by King Swein in person. The *Anglo-Saxon Chronicle* states that 'the local people came to meet him and made a truce with him – they expected that he was going to conquer the country'.[73] But by now the Danish assault was petering out in rather pointless fashion, and its final activities before withdrawal in 1070 played out south rather than north of the Humber, in the revolt associated with Hereward 'the Wake'.

The *Chronicle* also states that, as an aftermath to his re-capture of York in 1069, William exacted a terrible punishment on the territory of Yorkshire itself: he 'utterly ravaged and laid waste that shire'.[74] This is the so-called 'Harrying of the North', and several twelfth-century writers elaborated on the appalling destruction and displacement that William caused.[75] But the extent and significance of the Harrying have been much discussed by modern historians, especially in the light of Domesday Book's designation of many estates as 'waste [*vasta*]' in 1086.[76] Many interpreters would now take the view that, while William's army undoubtedly caused a very great deal of suffering – more than enough to create an unparalleled impression on twelfth-century commentators – there is also a limit to what they could have achieved within a finite, three-month period of winter. So, Domesday's 'waste' might indicate not only land that had been rendered unfarmable on account of the Harrying, but also land that happened not to be tenanted or cultivated at the time of inquiry, or even, possibly, land whose position under the plough was simply not known by the Domesday commissioners. It is certainly true that many Yorkshire estates declined in value and yield between 1066 and 1086, but the Harrying of the North may not have been the only reason for this; as we have just seen, the years immediately after the Conquest were a time of enormous turmoil and uncertainty – not unlike, of course, the 860s and 870s – and, as an index of this, several coin hoards have been found in Yorkshire from this period.[77]

The English rebellion and Danish attack of 1069-70 were not quite the last of their kind, though they were by far the most serious for William, and by early 1070, with the Danes departed, the Harrying accomplished, and the English rebels either in submission or permanently removed to Scotland, William's military subjugation of Yorkshire was effectively complete. In 1071, though, Edwin and Morcar rebelled again, for the last time: Edwin was killed and Morcar subsequently imprisoned.[78] Siward's son, Waltheof, had been forgiven by the King for his part in the 1069 rebellion, even so far as to be married to the king's niece, and in 1072 he was appointed as earl of Bernician Northumbria (at which point, as we saw in the previous chapter, he played the final move in the 'Northumbrian bloodfeud').[79] But in 1075 Waltheof was involved in plans for yet another rebellion. William seemed at first to offer him forgiveness once more; but in 1076 he was beheaded for treason – William's only political execution in England – and soon he was being culted as a saint.[80] As we have seen, Waltheof had a Norse poet in his retinue, named Þorkell Skallason, and Þorkell's words form a fitting epitaph for this last major casualty of northern rebellion:

> William, who reddened weapons, the one who cut the rime-flecked sea from the south, has indeed betrayed the bold Waltheof under safe conduct. It is true that killings will be slow to cease in England, but my lord was brave; a more splendid munificent prince will not die.[81]

Waltheof's death further marked the end of the rule in Northumbria of the long line of Bamburgh earls.

1075 also saw the last assault launched by Swein Estrithson, again led by one of his sons, Cnut. 'Two hundred ships came from Denmark', says the *Anglo-Saxon Chronicle*, 'and they dared not fight with King William but went to York and broke into St Peter's Minster and captured a large amount of property there and so departed'.[82] And then after that, there were no more Danish attacks, though a threatened one in 1085 (again by Cnut, by now king of Denmark) caused great anxiety, and may have been one of the motivations for the Domesday survey.[83]

In the midst of this political and military turmoil, changes were also afoot in the ecclesiastical sphere. After the death of Ealdred, the next archbishop of York was the Norman Thomas of Bayeux, appointed in 1070, who promptly re-built the minster from the ground up, on a different alignment, in a clear break from the pre-Conquest past.[84] New monasteries also began to be founded, patronized by Norman nobles, the first of which was Selby Abbey in 1069.[85] A significant twist here, though, is that at least some of the early founders of these post-Conquest monasteries were inspired by Bede's *Ecclesiastical History*, and by the vision of ancient Northumbrian piety which that text propagated: so we should be careful to think of continuities, or at least re-commencements, as well as abrupt breaks with the past.

But it is the secular sphere that especially concerns us here, rather than the ecclesiastical. It was the sequence of revolts in the north that led to the loss of land and wealth by the Northumbrian elite: after every revolt that William stamped out, further nobles were deprived of their property. As early as 1069 at the latest (and possibly a year or two earlier), one of William's writs begins 'King William greets in a friendly fashion all my thegns in Yorkshire, both French and English', so indicating that at least some Norman lords were settled in the county by this point.[86] But as he did with Waltheof, William's tendency, at least at first, was sometimes to show leniency, and the most prominent rebels were not automatically deprived of their lands after they had (re-)submitted to the king: so, for example, the sons of Carl were still in possession of their estate at Settrington in 1073 or 1074, when Waltheof's forces set upon them and killed them.[87] Nonetheless, as Domesday Book attests, a gradual re-distribution of lands took place in Yorkshire during and after the years of rebellion, by the end of which, 'nearly all of the families belonging to [the Anglo-Scandinavian] aristocracy were either deprived of their lands or reduced to the level of subtenants'.[88] William's main practice was to re-distribute land according to lordship rather than territory: that is to say, his Norman followers received the whole package of properties previously held by one or more Anglo-Scandinavian lords, rather than a particular parcel of land that cut across pre-Conquest lordships, and in Domesday Book these 1066 lords are known as the *antecessores* or antecedents of the 1086 lords. But by the mid 1070s, it may be that all the major Anglo-Scandinavian lords had been dispossessed, and so it is possible that William complemented the 'antecessorial' approach with a 'hundredal' or territorial one, giving to a particular Norman lord most or all of the remaining properties within a particular hundred or wapentake.[89] It will have been at this stage, probably, that the minor land-holders and sokemen, Stenton's 'free peasantry', lost their lands or were reduced to the status of subtenants or villeins, with burdens owed to their new Norman lords.[90] If we revisit the minor lordlings whom we met in the previous chapter, those small local figures who held only one piece of land in one place, we can observe their demise in the pages of Domesday Book: the land of Reiði in Little Hatfield [ER] passed to Drogo de la Beuvrière, that of Búi in Anley [WR] to Roger the Poitevin, and that of Mylnu-Grímr in Croome [ER] to the king himself.[91]

Some 1066 land-holders did still remain in place in 1086, but not many as a proportion of the whole; and Ann Williams has shown that the chances of survival were greatest for those who fulfilled a role in regional administration, for example as a reeve or other local official.[92] And no doubt there were many people in Yorkshire for whom the Norman Conquest brought less momentous changes, such as lesser craftsmen and non-free peasants at the bottom of the social scale – though even here, the burdens placed upon them after 1066 may have been greater than before, as part of the more oppressive tenurial revolution which the Conquest effected.[93] So the fundamental story of the late 1060s and early 1070s is of the dispossession and subjugation of numerous individuals, many of them far from grand, whose families may have held for up to two centuries the lands or rights which they lost after 1066. As the Norman motte-and-bailey castles were being built across the county, this loss of land and status was, by at least one important means of measurement, the end of Anglo-Scandinavian Yorkshire.

After the Viking Age: Yorkshire's Scandinavian heritage

Not everything changed immediately, of course, and no doubt the majority of those who lost land and independence nonetheless stayed put. Signs of Scandinavian culture did not suddenly vanish in the 1080s, even though a new Norman elite was now in place; indeed, some features only come properly into view after the Conquest. So, for example, the 1106 letter concerning the customs of York Minster reveals that a number of local 'lawmen' (*lagamen*) played a prominent role in York's governance, as they did in other Anglo-Scandinavian cities such as Lincoln, and one of the 1106 figures is described as lawman 'by hereditary right'.[94] Names of York moneyers become even more dominantly Norse in the first 75 years of Norman rule.[95] It has been suggested that earlier Scandinavian art-styles, Jellinge and Borre – or at least echoes of those styles – may have persisted later in York than in Scandinavia itself, even into the twelfth century, and twelfth-century sculpture from Kirkburn [ER] has been seen as bearing traces of the Urnes style.[96] A celebrated piece of ironwork on the twelfth-century door of Stillingfleet church [ER] shows a ship of seeming Scandinavian design.[97]

Nor did contacts and connections between England and Scandinavia cease with the waning of the Viking Age, though they did change in nature and frequency.[98] Military conflict was replaced by mercantile and ecclesiastical exchange, though the Norwegian king Eysteinn Haraldsson raided down the east coast of England in 1151, including at Whitby.[99] Trade between England and Scandinavia became increasingly lucrative, focused especially on fish, with ships sailing out of Hull, Scarborough, and other Yorkshire ports. The hundred years from 1400 onwards, for example, are dubbed 'the English century' in Icelandic historiography, and at that time Icelandic merchants and sailors were certainly to be found in the cities of Hull and York.[100]

But as the post-Conquest centuries proceeded, Northumbria's Viking past began to seem more remote. One sign of this is the manner in which Latin historians' accounts of England's Viking Age grow more and more colourful, with stereotyped tropes of fire and the sword, and gruesome embellishments such as babies spitted on spears.[101] It was also at this point that the Scandinavian settlements started to perform one of their most important functions, offering an aetiological or originary explanation as to why certain features of culture or conduct were different in the north of England from the south (and this question is, of course, one that endures to the present day in scholarly debate: how far does the Danelaw's Scandinavian history provide an explanation for regional difference?). Many of the origins claimed were far-fetched, though, such as Gerald of Wales' late twelfth-century assertion that the distinctive Yorkshire practice of part-singing was derived from 'the Danes and Norwegians, who so often invaded those parts of the island and held them longer under their dominion'.[102]

Tales of the Viking Age also began to feature in vernacular poetry and story-telling, in Anglo-Norman and Middle English, though there is nothing from medieval Yorkshire to compare with the great Lincolnshire legend of Havelok the Dane, centred on the port of Grimsby (though it is often said that the historical prototype of the hero was Olaf *cuaran*, king of York in the 940s).[103] The legends of Earl Siward might seem the most likely counterpart from north of the Humber, but Eleanor Parker has argued recently that our extant tales about Siward (in Latin) are more plausibly to be associated with the region around Crowland in Lincolnshire, where Siward's son Waltheof was culted as a saint.[104] The story of the fall of York in 866 did, however, receive considerable elaboration, as recorded above all in Geffrei Gaimar's verse-history (also composed in Lincolnshire): Gaimar has a long story which explains the Danish conquest of York on the grounds that Osberht, one of the two kings in Northumbria in 866, had raped the wife of a local nobleman called Buern Bucecarle, who then 'organized and brought the Danes over here from Denmark' (in a thirteenth-century Latin version of the story, it is the other king, Ælle, who is the villain).[105] Gaimar also claims that the Great Army that subsequently arrived was made up three elements: an 'elite corps' on horseback, a sizeable contingent in ships, and 'more than 20,000 foot soldiers as well'.

Re-tellings and re-interpretations were taking place in Scandinavia, too, culminating in the Icelandic sagas of the thirteenth and fourteenth centuries. In the sagas, the north of England's Viking past is certainly not forgotten, but it is re-imagined and re-packaged for a new set of contexts, with a liberal helping of fantasy and forgetfulness.[106] Stories about the fall of York are among the most important to be elaborated in Scandinavian tradition as well (as noted in Chapter 2), as also the Stamford Bridge campaign of two centuries later. There is also an awareness of the history of Scandinavian settlement in Yorkshire, as for example in Snorri Sturluson's *Heimskringla*:

> Northumbria is reckoned to be a fifth part of England. [Eric Bloodaxe] had his residence in York, where it is said that earlier the sons of Loðbrók had resided. Northumbria had been mostly inhabited by Norwegians after the sons of Loðbrók conquered the land. Danes and Norwegians had often made raids on it after rule of the land had passed from them. Many place-names there are derived from the Norse tongue, Grímsbœr [Grimsby] and Hauksfljót [?] and many others.[107]

One particular site for which a Scandinavian origin was proposed was Scarborough [NR]: according to *Kormak's Saga*, the settlement there was founded by the poet Kormak and his brother, Thorgils *skarði* (hence Old Norse *Skarðaborg* 'Skarði's fortification'). Modern place-name study, however, gives little support for this romantic tradition, and suggests instead an Old English, pre-Viking origin for the name (probably *scearde burh* 'the notched fortification', perhaps a reference to the old Roman signal station on the headland).[108]

Language was the most enduring feature of Scandinavian culture in England, as it was elsewhere in the British Isles. William of Malmesbury, in the twelfth century, wrote that 'the whole speech of the Northumbrians, especially that of the men of York, grates so harshly upon the ear that it is completely unintelligible to us southerners'.[109] William's observations enjoyed a long shelf-life: in the late fourteenth century, they were still being used in John Trevisa's translation of Ranulph Higden's *Polychronicon*: 'Al the longage of the Northumbres, and specialych at York, ys so scharp, slyttyng and frotyng and unschape [piercing and grating and ugly] that we southeron men may that longage unnethe [scarcely] undurstonde'.[110] William himself attributed this to the Northumbrians' 'proximity to barbaric tribes and their distance from the kings of the land', but other southern commentators had a different explanation for the harshness of northern speech: according to Gerald of Wales, southern English was 'purer than elsewhere' because 'it retains more features of the original language and the old ways of speaking English, whereas the northern regions have been greatly corrupted by the Danish and Norwegian invasions'.[111]

In some respects, of course, Gerald was absolutely right (though 'corrupted' is a value term that no modern linguist would use). What distinguished northern English of the twelfth century from more southerly varieties was the presence of a large number of loanwords from Old Norse (as well as some possible influences in syntax and grammar). Although significant numbers of Norse loanwords are recorded in Old English texts, they are vastly outnumbered by the quantity that are first recorded in Middle English, in the thirteenth and fourteenth centuries.[112] Partly this may be a trick of the evidence, as we have relatively few vernacular texts from the north of England from the eleventh and twelfth centuries, but that is unlikely to be the whole story. Rather, we should imagine that the greatest influence of Norse upon the English language occurred when Norse speakers finally gave up their own language (at different times in different places), as they – or more likely, the next generation – switched to speaking English. At this point, Norse words, constructions, and (perhaps above all) pronunciations were imported into English, so that a heavily Scandinavianized variety of English came to be spoken in the north.[113] Take, for example, the minor river-name Backstone Beck [NR], first recorded as *Bacstainbek* ('bake-stone beck') only in 1314.[114] The form of its middle element ('stone') shows derivation, or influence, from Old Norse *steinn* rather than Old English *stān*. Whether the place-name was an early coinage or a late one, examples such as this indicate the remarkably long-lived effect that Norse speech habits had on Yorkshire phonology for centuries after the demise of Old Norse as an independent language.

Classic Norse loans include words such as *egg, ill, leg, skill, skirt, sky, take, want,* and *window*.[115] But in addition to these, we find examples of English and Norse variants existing side-by-side, often with subsequent differentiation of meaning (for example, *whole* and *hail*, and *leap* and *lope*) – a monument to the Danelaw's dual linguistic history. Among the most important loans in English are the pronouns *they, them,* and *their*; and *she* may possibly show Norse influence as well. Many of the Norse loans were subsequently generalized through other varieties of English – in other words, they spread geographically beyond the areas of Scandinavian settlement, as other English speakers adopted them, and this process was greatly assisted by heavy migration to London from the central and southern Danelaw.[116] But not all loanwords spread, and many remained geographically restricted in their distribution, never entering into standard written English, and awaiting, as it were, discovery and cataloguing in nineteenth- and early twentieth-century interest in regional dialect. A few Yorkshire examples – from among many – include *femmer* 'weak, frail', *gizzen* 'to sneer', *gleg* 'clear-sighted', and *hawbaw* 'a clumsy fellow' (seemingly from Old Norse *haugbúi* 'mound-dweller, ghost').[117]

Norse personal names lasted longer in the north than the Norse language itself did; indeed, the continued use of Norse personal names in Yorkshire can be regarded as the most tenacious feature of Scandinavian culture in the high medieval period. The common practice among the peasantry of Yorkshire (including the upper peasantry) of giving Norse names lasted into the early thirteenth century.[118] Norman and Biblical or saints' names were already entering the northern name-stock in the twelfth century, but the generational shift becomes more apparent in the early thirteenth century, when legal records present us with a series of Yorkshire examples in which a father bears a Norse name but his son bears a Norman or Biblical/saint's one: Walter son of Gamal, Geoffrey son of Grimkell, Thomas son of Siward, and so on.[119] David Postles therefore concludes that, at least before the thirteenth century, not only were non-Norman names free from any sort of 'social dishonour' among the peasantry of the north, but even that the giving of such names might possess an 'oppositional or resistant nature to a dominant discourse of culture, that of the new overlords'.[120] Such an oppositional practice has not, it should be said, been observed among scholars studying naming patterns further south, so it may be that here we have yet another symptom of that Northumbrian instinct towards separatism which the Scandinavian settlements in the north re-inforced.[121]

When it did come, though, the change in naming practices was profound, and the repertoire of names shrank greatly, not only in Yorkshire but across the country, so that a very small number of names were used over and over again; in the 1379 poll tax for the East Riding, for example, 33% of adult males were called John, and 21% William.[122] It is this reduction in range which signals that the triumph of Norman and Biblical/saints' names in England, and the abandonment of native names, was a very different process from that in which Norse names were introduced into northern and eastern England four centuries earlier. The Norse names, it may be recalled from Chapter 4, represented a diverse and ever-changing repertoire, and indicate that what was transplanted to England was a living, evolving tradition of naming, rather than just a closed list of a very small number of names.[123] But even in the shift to the new set of names, we should not assume that a global 'fashion' or 'prestige' is the best explanation: rather, it seems that an important factor in name-choice may have been the name of the local lord of the manor, who increasingly elected to stand as sponsor or god-parent to children being baptized; so the naming indicates spiritual kinship.[124]

The demise of native personal names, and their replacement by a much more limited set of Norman/Biblical names, is related to another development in naming practices at approximately this time or a little later, the rise of hereditary surnames.[125] The most common categories of surnames are those which derive from place-names, from personal names, from occupational names, and from nicknames. It is in the first two of these categories, and above all the first, that the surnames of Yorkshire show a strong Scandinavian character. Surnames derived from place-names are usually subdivided into locative names (that is, names from a particular place, such as Askwith or Quarmby) and topographical names (names from a natural or man-made feature, such as Fell or Sykes); and clearly a very large number of surnames of the locative type have arisen from Norse settlement-names in Yorkshire (Beckwith, Danby, Gowthorpe, Holtby, Huby, Lazenby, Scargill, Skelton, Slingsby, Snaith, Stainton, and hundreds of others). Surnames derived from Norse personal names are much fewer in number, for the obvious reason that Norse names had largely been ousted by Norman names by the time that hereditary surnames took shape.[126] Nonetheless, plausible Yorkshire examples include Gamble, Kettle, and Oddy (from Old Norse *Gamall*, *Ketill*, and *Oddr*).[127] Finally, we should note that surnames ending in –*son* are especially common in the north of England (Robinson, Smithson, and so on). It is quite possible that the Scandinavian practice of patronymics and metronymics (Orm Gamalson, for example) was a contributory factor in the evolution and frequency of this type of surname, but it was probably not the only one, and some scholars have cautioned against seeing a Scandinavian genesis for such names.[128]

As the Middle Ages gave way to the early modern period, then, the Scandinavian heritage in Yorkshire was carried forward most pervasively in terms of the county's place-names and locative surnames; but of course the fact that such names had a Scandinavian origin was more or less forgotten. By the sixteenth and seventeenth centuries, most of the historical figures and events of Viking Age Northumbria had slipped out of memory, though a few were remembered: the fame of Earl Siward, for example, was perpetuated by his appearance in Shakespeare's *Macbeth*. But at a popular level, the beginnings of learned antiquarianism – which involved, as it did, the local collecting of traditions – revealed that 'the Danes' had come to play a very full role in England's folklore, and not only within the old counties of the Danelaw.[129] Indeed, it has been said that 'more references to the Danes occur in popular lore of the [early modern] period than to any other invading host, from the Romans to the Normans'.[130] In particular, folk traditions were eager to interpret prehistoric earthworks and tumuli as the monuments and burial mounds of the Danes, a considerable number of which remain so labelled on modern Ordnance Survey maps. Examples from Yorkshire include Danes' Dyke near Flamborough, and Danes' Graves at Nafferton and Skipwith [all ER]. A variant on this is the biographical tradition that the hill of Siward's Howe in York was in fact the earl's burial mound.[131]

In their colourful, larger-than-life villainy, the characterization of the Danes in much early modern folklore is also similar – and, presumably, related – to that found in Latin histories of the later Middle Ages. An illustrative example from Yorkshire may be the story of St Alkelda or Alhhild. Only two churches in the country are dedicated to this obscure saint, at Giggleswick [WR] and Middleham

[NR]. No medieval texts mention Alkelda, and her very existence has been doubted, but local traditions recorded in post-medieval sources claim that 'Alkelda was a Saxon princess, strangled for her faith by two Danish women at the time of the Viking invasions'.[132] The remembrance of Vikings as persecutors of the church was also kept alive through the ghastly tradition of 'Danes' skins': until quite recently, a number of churches sported (supposedly) the flayed skins of Danes nailed to their doors, including Stillingfleet [ER] in Yorkshire.[133]

From the mid eighteenth century onwards, antiquarianism and literary culture began to be influenced by a new, and better informed, interest in ancient Scandinavia, as Old Norse texts began to be read again by British scholars, and to be translated by poets such as Thomas Gray as part of an interest in Gothic primitivism.[134] But the real take-off for Viking studies came in the nineteenth century, when a wider range of Norse texts and resources was made available for Anglophone readers, and the study of the past was revolutionized by new movements in philology and history.[135] An especially important landmark was the publication in 1852 of J.J.A. Worsaae's *An Account of the Danes and Norwegians in England, Scotland, and Ireland*. Written by a brilliant Danish archaeologist, this was the book that, more than any other work, encouraged the British people to regard their Viking past with enthusiasm rather than distaste, and to celebrate the Scandinavian contribution to Britain's making and greatness.

Worsaae's book also coincided with a wider shift in British (and especially English) self-perceptions. From the middle of the nineteenth century, it has been argued, the English started to view themselves as an essentially 'mongrel' people, beneficially shaped by successive waves of immigration and cultural contact into a whole that was greater than any of its constituent parts.[136] For just one reflection of this view, we might turn to the verse-drama *Harold* (1877) by the Poet Laureate Alfred Tennyson – in which two of the characters, incidentally, are 'Aldred, Archbishop of York' and 'Gamel (son of Orm), a Northumbrian Thane'. Tennyson's drama is concerned not only with the Battle of Hastings in 1066, but also with the 1065 Northumbrian rebellion against Tostig, and its aftermath. Act IV Scene I is set 'in Northumbria', in the brief period between the battles of Fulford and Stamford Bridge. Harold, newly arrived from the south, is met by a crowd of surly Northumbrians, and an anonymous local tells him that 'Thou art but a West Saxon: we are Danes', to which Harold pointedly responds:

> My mother is a Dane, and I am English;
> There is a pleasant fable in old books,
> Ye take a stick, and break it; bind a score
> All in one faggot, snap it over knee,
> Ye cannot.[137]

224

In other words, the people of Northumbria need to realize not only that they are indeed part of England, but also that the English are made up of both Danes and West Saxons combined, and are the better and stronger for it. One could not find a better illustration of the new attitude to the Scandinavian past, and to English identity, which took hold in the second half of the nineteenth century.

But Worsaae's demonstration of Britain's Viking history was worked out in particular at a local or regional level, rather than a national one, with the Victorian proliferation of antiquarian study and antiquarian societies.[138] Yorkshire produced its fair share of eminent antiquaries in the nineteenth century, many of them clergymen, of whom just two may be cited here to exemplify the quickening of interest in the county's Scandinavian past in the decades after 1850. The first is Isaac Taylor (1829-1901), who distinguished himself in various fields, including the history of alphabets, and from 1875 until his death was vicar of Settrington [ER] – the scene of the last killings in the 'Northumbrian bloodfeud', where Waltheof's soldiers massacred the sons of Carl. Taylor was a pioneering scholar of place-names, with his two works *Words and Places* (1864) and *Names and their Histories* (1896) highly influential and much reprinted; he was also an important early student of the Yorkshire Domesday.[139]

The second example is John Christopher Atkinson (1814-1900), often known as Canon Atkinson, as – like Taylor – he was appointed a canon of York Minster.[140] For over half a century (from 1847), Atkinson was the vicar of the remote rural parish of Danby [NR], and his most famous work is *Forty Years in a Moorland Parish* (1891), an undisputed classic of folkloric antiquarianism. But among his many other works, Atkinson also produced an impressive *Glossary of the Cleveland Dialect* (1868), in which he traced Norse etymologies for many local words, and was the first scholar to note the importance of the lost *Thingwala* place-name in the vicinity of Whitby.[141] He also reported the Kildale weapon burials to the Society of Antiquaries, thereby stimulating a correspondence with Worsaae in Denmark.[142] In *Forty Years in a Moorland Parish*, amid a host of other topics and inquiries, Atkinson probed deeply into the Scandinavian origins of the Danby region: his essential view was that 'the people of his own district continued for ages to be a Danish-speaking people', on the grounds that it was 'impossible to suppose that of the scores of subordinate local names [...] the preponderating amount could have been given by any other than a folk continuing to speak Danish for generation after generation'; in other words, Atkinson perceived the important point that it is likely to be minor place-names rather than major ones which give the best guide to the intensity of Scandinavian settlement.[143]

As Atkinson's example indicates, and as noted earlier, the second half of the nineteenth century was also the boom period for the collection and celebration of local dialect vocabulary – especially as such vocabulary was felt to be under threat from increased mobility and standard education. The climax on a national scale was the compilation of the six-volume *English Dialect Dictionary* (1898-1905) by the Yorkshireman Joseph Wright (1855-1930) – an extraordinary figure, who began by working in the mills at Saltaire as a boy, but ended up as Professor of Comparative Philology at the University of Oxford.[144] As a result of work done for Wright's *Dictionary*, the Yorkshire Dialect Society was founded in 1897, the *Transactions* of which regularly cast light on the Norse provenance of much local dialect.[145] From 1904, one energetic member of the Society was Frederic W. Moorman, Professor of English Language at the University of Leeds, where he established a tradition of dialect study and attempted to close the gap between academic philology and working-class self-expression; he also published a study of the place-names of the West Riding.[146] Moorman died in 1919, in a drowning accident; his successor at Leeds was none other than J.R.R. Tolkien, trained under Wright at Oxford, who in 1928, as another member of the Yorkshire Dialect Society, was to write an approving foreword to a glossary of Huddersfield dialect, pointing out to its readers that 'this dialect is full of Scandinavian words, some rare, some found in many other places'.[147]

In York, the city's Viking remains were also beginning to attract attention. Here a crucial figure was the architect George Benson (1856-1935), who in the early years of the twentieth century was the first person properly to identify and record Viking Age structures.[148] An important contemporary was George Augustus Auden (1872-1957), a doctor in York, who reported on local finds to the Viking Club of London – and, for good measure, passed on his Scandinavian enthusiasms to his son, the poet W.H. Auden.[149] In 1908, the Cumbrian antiquary W.G. Collingwood published his survey of Anglian and Viking Age sculpture from the city, as part of his ground-breaking survey of the whole of Yorkshire.[150]

With figures such as Moorman and Collingwood, in the early decades of the twentieth century, we find ourselves truly at the beginnings of modern study, with no fundamental interruptions or revolutions in understanding; we are back where we began in Chapter 1. So we can now conclude by reflecting briefly on the role played by the Viking past in Yorkshire's contemporary culture and identity.

Yorkshire's Scandinavian heritage is now regarded as a given thing – in some respects, the central fact in the county's pre-industrial history – and this can be observed in many ways. Fictional Yorkshire place-names, for example, are often given a Scandinavian flavour by ending in *–by*, from James Herriot's *Darrowby* to J.L. Carr's *Oxgodby* in *A Month in the Country* (1980). More swaggeringly, in 2013 Yorkshire County Cricket Club decided to re-name its one-day team as the Yorkshire Vikings. 'We wanted a new name that has relevance to the region', the Club's Commercial Director explained; 'the Vikings have been ingrained in Yorkshire for over 1000 years and are woven into the fabric of the County's history'.[151] One contemporary view of the Vikings, then, invests them with a set of values and associations that are, for Yorkshire audiences at least, fundamentally positive: Yorkshire's Viking legacy can be deployed to express a form of regional pride, an inherent, independent northernism that can be made sharply contradistinctive to ideas of the south, and of government from the south.

It is therefore no surprise that the Vikings play an important role in heritage tourism, in business and advertising, and in the articulation of local identities – a role greatly facilitated by the fact that (like the Romans, but unlike, say, the Anglo-Saxons) the Vikings possess 'brand identity', a well-established set of traits and visual hooks, from longships and interlace to beards and (unhistorical) horned helmets. The launch event for the name-change of the Yorkshire Vikings took place at the Jorvik Viking Centre in York – far and away, of course, the most important Viking tourist site in the British Isles, which has attracted over 17 million visitors since it opened in 1984. The Centre also runs an extremely popular 'Jorvik Viking Festival' in the February half-term holidays, which swells the city's tourist population on an annual basis. On account of its 'theme park' qualities, and the power of its tourist pull, it is not always appreciated what a serious exercise in archaeological reconstruction the Jorvik Viking Centre represents. Not only is the Centre on the site of the Coppergate dig itself, but the buildings and interpretation are very closely modelled on the Coppergate finds; so one is touring the excavation site as the same time as one is marvelling at the reconstructed sights and sounds. A less famous, but in many ways complementary, attraction, just outside York at Murton Park, is the Yorkshire Museum of Farming's Danelaw Centre for Living History, a hands-on Viking village that is popular for school visits and re-enactment events.

In terms of business and advertising, an extraordinary array of firms and services, especially in the vicinity of York, play on Yorkshire's Viking past, presumably on the assumption that 'Vikings connote qualities such as dynamism, success, and go-getting'.[152] The York phone book for 2013/14 lists, among others: The Viking Loom (a craft shop), Viking Management Systems, and Viking Vehicle Services; Jorvik Physiotherapy, Jorvik Podiatry Centre, and Jorvik Supreme Flooring; and Yorvik Electrical Contractors and Yorvik Homes. It is not possible to walk around the city of York without seeing the image of a Viking on an advertizing hoarding or the side of a bus.

Local village and civic identities are also bound up with the Viking past. The modern street names of Stamford Bridge commemorate the events of 1066 – Viking Road, Hardrada Way, Tostig Close – as do monuments, pub-signs, and even a floral planter in the shape of a Viking ship [Figure 28]. Controversy has arisen over plans to build a new housing development on the likely site of the Battle of Fulford.[153] The village of Burnsall [WR], home of an important array of Viking Age sculpture, has recently instituted its own 'Viking Festival'. And in the millennium celebrations of 2000, many local communities looked back 1000 years to identify and commemorate Scandinavian origins. In all this popular and communal engagement with Yorkshire's Viking past, it goes without saying that – as has been the case ever since the time of Gerald of Wales – some of the meanings and identifications that are claimed are unimpeachably well-founded, whereas others are romantic over-interpretations, and at least a few are pure fantasy.

It is, perhaps, a reductive question to ask what, in the final analysis, modern Yorkshire owes to its Viking past in terms of historical inheritance – and our engagement with history is not to be justified or quantified simply in terms of its demonstrable contribution to present existence. But it is not superficial to point out that, as this book has explored, the 200 years of Viking Age Yorkshire (866-1066) represent a period in which permanently important changes took part in the region – many, though not all, to be attributed to the arrival of the Vikings themselves. The Vikings cannot be said to have created Yorkshire itself: the county, as a county, was formally a West Saxon institution, and the extent of the Viking kingdom (which became the county) had earlier been the Anglo-Saxon kingdom of Deira. But still, the Scandinavian centuries were a defining period, not only on account of the events and developments of the period itself, but also for the regional sense of self, and sense of difference, which the period consolidated and bequeathed. These centuries saw both the 'urban moment' for the city of York, and the 'village moment' for many smaller settlements, when prior patterns of land-holding were shaken up, and homes and streets were laid out in their enduring form. Churchyards were founded, parish churches were built and re-built, and a geography of habitation took shape which was familiar for generations afterwards – and still is, in the county's non-urbanized areas. And although the county of Yorkshire cannot strictly be said to have been a Scandinavian creation, it may be that the ridings were.

It was also in Yorkshire's Viking period, very importantly, that many places in the county received the names that they still possess. To repeat the statistics given in Chapter 1: according to one calculation, approximately 49% of place-names in the East Riding in Domesday Book are either Old Norse in origin or Scandinavianized in form, 46% in the North Riding, and 31% in the West Riding.[154] These figures, of course, apply only to major names: many thousands of minor names, most of them first recorded after Domesday Book, are also Norse in some way, and speak of the defining role that the Scandinavians played in the naming of Yorkshire. So if we want to appreciate the importance of Yorkshire's Viking past, probably the best thing we can do is just to look at a map, or at the signposts and name-plates of the county – which point eloquently to a rich history as well as to the places of the present.

REFERENCES

CHAPTER 1

1. Crosland and Hayes 1955; Lang 1991, 182.
2. Binns 1956, 16-18; Binns 1963, 43-44.
3. Lang 1973.
4. Thompson 2004, 148-52.
5. Wilson and Klindt-Jensen 1980, 103.
6. Lang 1973; Lang 1991, 33-36, 39-42.
7. Thompson 2004, 150.
8. Lang 1991, 181-87.
9. Dumville 1997, 8-14; Price 2002.
10. Taylor and Taylor 1965, I, 418-24.
11. *PNNRY*, 80.
12. Bailey 1980, 209-14.
13. Lang 1991, 187; Morris 2011, 188-89.
14. Faull and Stinson 1986, 299b, 380d.
15. *ASC*, xi-xxiii; Jorgensen 2010, 4-17; Keynes 2012.
16. Bately 1986; Taylor 1983; O'Brien O'Keeffe 2001; Cubbin 1996; Irvine 2004; Baker 2000.
17. Brooks 2010.
18. Stafford 2008.
19. Baxter 2007b.
20. Whitelock 1954, 28-30; Stafford 2007, 42-49.
21. Wormald 1993; Cubbin 1996, lxxviii-lxxxi.
22. Stafford 2011, 153-56.
23. Keynes 1978, 229-32.
24. Mac Airt and Mac Niocaill 1983.
25. Stevenson 1904; Keynes and Lapidge 1983.
26. Campbell 1962; Ashley 2007; Baxter 2007, 79-85.
27. Townend 2002, 110-28.
28. Dumville and Lapidge 1985.
29. Darlington and McGurk 1995; Mynors, Thomson, and Winterbottom 1998-99.
30. Short 2009.
31. Arnold 1882-85; *EHD*, 239-54 (no. 3); Rollason 1998b.
32. Rollason 2000.
33. *EHD*, 118-19; Blair 1963, 104-06; Downham 2003, 36-38.
34. Angus 1940.
35. Blair 1939, 98.
36. Coxe 1841-42; *EHD*, 119, 254-58 (no. 4).
37. Binns 1963, 46-52; Binns 1965.
38. Stafford 2008, 108-09.
39. Johnson South 2002; Aird 1998.
40. Binns 1963, 49-50; Frank 1981, 126-29; Johnson South 2002, 48-51.
41. Simpson 1989; Johnson South 2002, 25-36.
42. Hart 1975; Woodman 2012.

43. Faull and Stinson 1986;
    Williams and Martin 1992;
    Darby and Maxwell 1962;
    Faull 1984.
44. Sawyer 1985; Holt 1987a;
    Roffe 2000a; Roffe 2007;
    Erskine and Williams 2003;
    Baxter 2007.
45. Roffe 1990a; Palliser 1993,
    14-20.
46. Roffe 1990a, 324.
47. Fellows-Jensen 1972, 169.
48. *PNNRY*; *PNERY*; *PNWRY*.
49. Fellows-Jensen 1973, 2-3, 5-
    6.
50. Fellows-Jensen 1968;
    Fellows-Jensen 1972;
    Fellows-Jensen 1978a;
    Fellows-Jensen 1985a.
51. Gelling 1988; Cameron
    1996a; Carroll and Parsons
    2013.
52. Ong 1982; Brink 2005.
53. Jesch 2001a, 15-33; Jesch
    2005.
54. Binns 1966.
55. Sawyer 2000; Spurkland
    2005; Barnes 2012.
56. Holman 1996; Barnes and
    Page 2006.
57. Okasha 1971.
58. Carver 2001, 2.
59. Samson 1991b, 128-33;
    Blackburn 2003, 22-23;
    Graham-Campbell 2011, 151.
60. Halsall 2000, 267-68; Price
    2008, 270.
61. Blackburn 2004.
62. Williams 2009.
63. Collingwood 1907; Collingwood
    1908; Collingwood 1911;
    Collingwood 1912; Colingwood
    1914; Collingwood 1915;
    Townend 2009.

64. Lang 1991; Lang 2001;
    Coatsworth 2008; Cramp
    1984; Bailey and Cramp
    1988; Bailey 2010.
65. Blair 1994; Sawyer 1998.
66. Higham 1993; Rollason 2003.
67. Binns 1963.
68. Keynes 1999a, 420.
69. Roffe 2010, 41-44;
    Molyneaux 2011, 83-85.
70. Keynes 1999a, 421.
71. Blair 1949, 49; Higham 2006,
    395-96.
72. Blair 1949.
73. Blair 1948; *ASC*, 67, 71;
    Higham 2006, 404-12.
74. Aird 1998, 65-66; Rollason
    2003, 213.
75. Watts 1995.
76. Cameron 1996a, 54-55.
77. Palliser 1992, 4-5.
78. Toop 2011; Clark 2011.
79. Rollason 2003, 20-53.
80. Binns 1963, 10-11.
81. Williams 2009, 80; Williams
    2011a, 67; Williams 2013a,
    478-80.
82. Blackburn 2004, 347-49;
    Gooch 2011, 117.
83. Phythian-Adams 1996;
    Dumville 1997, 31-32;
    Downham 2007, 160-61;
    Phythian-Adams 2011.
84. Higham 2006, 412-17.
85. Harmer 1989, 137; Woodman
    2012, 220-23 (no. 13).
86. *ASC*, 137-38; Cubbin 1996,
    77.
87. *ASC*, 137; O'Brien O'Keeffe
    2001, 117; Irvine 2004, 86.
88. *ASC*, 144; O'Brien O'Keeffe
    2001, 122.
89. *ASC*, 95; Cubbin 1996, 60-61.

90. *PNERY*, 275-80; Fellows-Jensen 1987a; Rollason 1998a, 226-37.
91. Stewart and Lyon 1992, 63; Townend 1998, 44-46.
92. Rollason 2003, 215; Williams 2013b, 23-25.
93. Blair 1948, 98-104; Higham 2006, 393-404.
94. *ASC*, 67-68; Bately 1986, 69.
95. *ASC*, 68-69; Cubbin 1996, 41.
96. *ASC*, 73; Cubbin 1996, 45.
97. Whitelock 1959; Higham 1993, 211-12, 223-27.
98. *ASC*, 54, 59, 61; Bately 1986, 55, 62, 63.
99. Campbell 1962, 51.
100. Townend 1998, 57-59.
101. Arnold 1882-85, II, 94; *EHD*, 253 (no. 3).

102. *ASC*, 67; O'Brien O'Keeffe 2001, 76.
103. *ASC*, 72; Cubbin 1996, 44.
104. Whitelock 1959, 81; Higham 1999.
105. Binns 1963, 24-25.
106. Abrams 2001a, 128-33; Holman 2001; Holman 2007, 157-64.
107. Pons-Sanz 2007, 70-72.
108. Fell 1987; Wawn 2000, 3-4; Brink 2008b.
109. Jesch 2002.
110. Fellows-Jensen 1968, 338-39.
111. Fell 1986.
112. Mawer 1913, 1-2.
113. Hall 2000, 311-14.

CHAPTER 2

1. *ASC*, 45.
2. Keynes and Lapidge 1983, 76.
3. Stevenson 1904, 22-23.
4. Johnson South 2002, 51.
5. Rollason 2000, 97.
6. Rollason 2000, 97-99.
7. Rollason 1998a, 71.
8. Smyth 1999, 21; Hall 2001, 50.
9. Hadley 2009a, 203-04; McLeod 2014, 184-85.
10. Arnold 1882-85, I, 225; Wood 1987; Rollason 1998a, 26.
11. Whaley 2012, II, 651.
12. Townend 1997; Kries 2003.
13. Smyth 1977; McTurk 1991; Rowe 2012.
14. Frank 1984; Einarsson 1986; Smyth 1999, 16-20.

15. Johnson South 2002, 50-53.
16. Wormald 1982a, 142-43; Rowe 2012.
17. Downham 2007, 1-9; Rowe 2012, 122-23, 127-28.
18. Binns 1963; Smyth 1978, 9.
19. Keynes and Lapidge 1983, 125.
20. Norton 1998.
21. Hawkes 1996.
22. Wormald 1983; Wormald 1992; Brooks 1999.
23. Stenton 1971; Campbell 1982.
24. Garrison, Nelson, and Tweddle 2001.
25. Godman 1982, 7.
26. Godman 1982, 123-25.
27. Garrison 2012.
28. Godman 1982, 119.

29. Campbell 1967; Lapidge 1990.
30. Campbell 1967, 50.
31. Tweddle 1992.
32. Lang 1991, 83-84.
33. Lund 1995; Myhre 2003; Hedeager 2008.
34. Myhre 1998; Sawyer 2003; Barrett 2008.
35. Tschan 2002, 211.
36. Clover 1988; Wicker 1998.
37. Sawyer 2013.
38. Barrett 2008; Sindbæk 2011.
39. Wamers 1983; Wamers 1998; Sheehan 2013.
40. Lindkvist et al 2003.
41. Wormald 1982a, 144-48.
42. Whaley 2012, I, cxcvi-cxcviii.
43. Fell 1975, 5.
44. Roesdahl 1991, 78-93; Bill 2008.
45. Allott 1974, 18; *EHD*, 776 (no. 193).
46. *ASC*, 36.
47. Allott 1974, 19.
48. Cramp 1984, I, 206-07.
49. Bullough 1993, 95-98.
50. Allott 1974, 36.
51. Coupland 1991.
52. Godman 1985, 126-39.
53. Allott 1974, 19.
54. Hines 1984, 291-301; Myhre 1993.
55. *ASC*, 35, Bately 1986, 39.
56. Bourne 2012; Parsons 2013, 54-56.
57. Campbell 1962, 27; Dumville and Lapidge 1985, 39.
58. Allott 1974, 40.
59. Downham 2008, 342; *EHD*, 255 (no. 4).
60. Dumville 2008, 353.
61. *ASC*, 41.
62. *ASC*, 41; Bately 1986, 42.

63. *EHD*, 256 (no. 4).
64. Pagan 1969; Grierson and Blackburn 1986, 301-03.
65. *ASC*, 42.
66. *ASC*, 45; Bately 1986, 47.
67. Dumville 2004, 91.
68. Smyth 1975-79; Smyth 1977.
69. Page 1982; Wormald 1982a, 141-44.
70. Downham 2007; Woolf 2007.
71. *ASC*, 45.
72. Keynes 1997, 54; Rowe 2012, 134-35; McLeod 2014.
73. McLeod 2014, 149-51.
74. McLeod 2014, 132-33.
75. Halsall 2003; Lavelle 2010.
76. Sawyer 1962, 117-44.
77. Brooks 1979; Smyth 1999, 5-6.
78. Williams 2014.
79. Higham 1993, 178; Heather 2009, 483-84.
80. Downham 2012, 4-5.
81. Brooks 1979, 8-9.
82. *ASC*, 46.
83. *ASC*, 46; Bately 1986, 47.
84. Blackburn 2011, 221-64.
85. Biddle and Kjølbye-Biddle 2001.
86. *ASC*, 48; Bately 1986, 49; McLeod 2014, 173-203.
87. *ASC*, 48; Bately 1986, 49.
88. *ASC*, 48.
89. Hall 2011, 78.
90. Hall 2011, 78.
91. Ager and Williams 2007.
92. Blackburn 2009, 49, n. 37; Richards and Naylor 2010, 341; Williams 2013b, 17-19; Williams 2014; www.britishmuseum.org.
93. Rollason 1998a, 63; Rollason 2000, 99; *EHD*, 251 (no. 3).
94. Rollason 2000, 99.
95. *EHD*, 251 (no. 3).

96. *ASC*, 48.
97. Keynes and Lapidge 1983, 83.
98. Rollason 1998a, 63; Rollason 2003, 215, 228; McLeod 2014, 177-80.
99. Woolf 2007, 71-79; Sawyer 1994, 8-10.
100. Grierson and Blackburn 1986, 295-303.
101. Williams 2011c, 354.
102. Rogers 1993, 1443; Kemp 1996, 83.
103. Booth 1997.
104. Grierson and Blackburn 1986, 301; Blackburn 2003, 23-24, 30-31; Hall 2004b, 490.
105. Pagan 1969, 11.
106. Campbell 1962, 35, 43.
107. Mac Airt and Mac Niocaill 1983, 329; Downham 2007, 23.
108. Smyth 1974-77; Dumville 2004, 83-84; Valante 2008, 66-69; Etchingham 2010; Downham 2011.
109. Mac Airt and Mac Niocaill 1983, 333; Smyth 1977, 255-66; Downham 2007, 24.
110. Johnson South 2002, 53.
111. *ASC*, 49; Rowe 2012, 147-48.
112. Johnson South 2002, 53.
113. Campbell 1962, 51.
114. Keynes and Lapidge 1983, 96, 262-63.
115. Aird 1998, 29-32.
116. Fellows-Jensen 2003, 48.
117. Binns 1963, 11; Rollason 2000, lxxiv; Johnson South 2002, 87-88, 119-20.
118. Dumville 2004, 87-88.
119. *ASC*, 54.
120. Campbell 1962, 50, 51; McLeod 2014, 119-20.
121. Stenton 1927a, 205-07.
122. Johnson South 2002, 69-71.
123. Johnson South 2002 116-17; Downham 2007, 144.
124. Dolley 1965; Dolley 1978; Blunt, Stewart, and Lyon 1989; Blackburn 2004.
125. Blackburn 2004, 325.
126. Blackburn 2004, 329-32; Williams 2011a, 43-47.
127. Blackburn 1989, 18-20.
128. Mac Airt and Mac Niocaill 1983, 347; Downham 2007, 79, 268.
129. Smyth 1975-79, I, 47-52.
130. Williams 2012.
131. Blackburn 2004, 329-31.
132. Blackburn 2004, 338-39, 342; McLeod 2014, 145-49.
133. Blackburn 2007.
134. Blackburn 2007, 197.
135. Graham-Campbell 2001; Williams 2009.
136. Higham 1992.
137. Mac Airt and Mac Niocaill 1983, 353.
138. Wainwright 1975, 131-61; Cavill, Harding, and Jesch 2000.
139. Graham-Campbell 1992b, 114; Graham-Campbell 2011.
140. *ASC*, 58-59; O'Brien O'Keeffe 2001, 71.
141. Dumville 1979; Lavelle 2009.
142. Blunt 1985; Williams 2011a, 45.
143. *ASC*, 59; O'Brien O'Keeffe 2001, 72.
144. Campbell 1962, 52.
145. Taylor 1983, 49; Hart 1992, 511-15.
146. *ASC*, 60.
147. *ASC*, 60 n. 4; Campbell 2001a, 21-22.
148. Brooks and Kelly 2013, II, 958-63 (no. 124)

149. *ASC*, 60.
150. *ASC*, 61; O'Brien O'Keeffe 2001, 73.
151. Horovitz 2010.
152. *EHD*, 252 (no. 3); *ASC*, 61-62; Campbell 1962, 52-53.
153. Campbell 1962, 53.

154. Lehiste 1958.
155. Blunt, Stewart, and Lyon 1989, 103-06; Stewart and Lyon 1992; Blackburn 2004, 332-35.
156. Blackburn and Pagan 2002.

CHAPTER 3

1. *ASC*, 62-67; Hill 1981, 54-59.
2. John 1996, 83-98.
3. Dumville 1997, 1-2; Downham 2007, 31-33.
4. Griffiths 2010, 129; Hadley and ten Harkel 2013.
5. Downham 2009.
6. *ASC*, 67-68; Bately 1986, 69; Cubbin 1996, 41.
7. Davidson 2001.
8. *EHD*, 252 (no. 3); Arnold 1882-85, II, 93; Mac Airt and Mac Niocaill 1983, 373.
9. Campbell 1962, 53; Mac Airt and Mac Niocaill 1983, 361.
10. Mac Airt and Mac Niocaill 1983, 369.
11. Johnson South 2002, 61.
12. Campbell 1942, 85-91; Wainwright 1975, 163-79.
13. Johnson South 2002, 105-07; Woolf 2007, 142-44; Downham 2007, 91-94.
14. Abrams 1997; Abrams 2010.
15. Woolf 2007, 145.
16. Johnson South 2002, 60-63.
17. McTurk, 1991, 98-114; Rowe 2012, 175-76.
18. Blunt and Stewart 1983; Blunt, Stewart, and Lyon 1989, 105; Blackburn 2004, 333-35.
19. Dolley 1965, 21.

20. Stewart 1991, 181; Stewart and Lyon 1992, 59-60.
21. Woolf 2007, 139.
22. Campbell 1962, 52.
23. Downham 2007, 88.
24. *ASC*, 67; O'Brien O'Keeffe 2001, 76.
25. *ASC*, 67.
26. Rollason 2003, 214-30; Rollason 2004, 307-14; McLeod 2014, 239-41.
27. Rollason 2003, 228.
28. Rollason 2003, 229, 230.
29. Higham 1993, 208-10.
30. Rollason 1998a, 70.
31. Raine 1879-94, II, 339.
32. Foot 2011, 129.
33. Cramp 1967, 13; Blackburn 2003, 34-35.
34. Blunt, Stewart, and Lyon 1989, 102; Rollason 2003, 225; Sawyer 2013, 2.
35. Blackburn 2004, 333.
36. Stewart and Lyon 1992, 59; Blackburn 2004, 338.
37. *ASC*, 68; Foot 2011, 38-40.
38. Breeze 1998.
39. Mac Airt and Mac Niocaill 1983, 367-71; Downham 2007, 33.
40. Smyth 1975-79, I, 70.
41. Poole 1991, 122-25; Townend 2003, 55-57.

42. Mac Airt and Mac Niocaill 1983, 371-73.
43. Graham-Campbell 1993, 83.
44. Williams 2011b; Williams 2013a, 461-66.
45. Blunt, Stewart, and Lyon 1989, 107; Blackburn 2004, 335.
46. *ASC*, 68; Cubbin 1996, 41.
47. Foot 2011, 44-52.
48. *ASC*, 68; Mac Airt and Mac Niocaill 1983, 379.
49. *EHD*, 257 (no. 4).
50. Thacker 2001, 257-58.
51. *ASC*, 69.
52. Mac Airt and Mac Niocaill 1983, 369.
53. Mynors, Thomson, and Winterbottom 1998-99, I, 215.
54. Mac Airt and Mac Niocaill 1983, 379.
55. Foot 2011, 160-62.
56. Mynors, Thomson, and Winterbottom 1998-99, I, 215.
57. Smyth 1977, 182-84; Rollason 1998, 166.
58. Graham-Campbell 1993; Graham-Campbell 2001, 212-17.
59. Williams 2008; Williams and Ager 2010; Ager and Williams 2011.
60. Ager 2011, 122-27; Wamers 2011, 133-35.
61. Williams and Ager 2010, 43.
62. www.finds.org.uk (ID: YORYM-BC3AB2).
63. *ASC*, 68-69.
64. Mynors, Thomson, and Winterbottom 1998-99, I, 215.
65. Lapidge 1981, 83-93, 98; Zacher 2011, 91-96.
66. Lapidge 1981, 89.
67. Foot 2011, 154-55, 212-16.
68. Blackburn 2004, 335-36.
69. Blackburn 2004, 341-42.
70. Foot 2011, 90, 168-69.
71. *ASC*, 69; Woolf 2007, 158-68; Foot 2011, 164-69.
72. Wilson 2003; Foot 2011, 243-45.
73. Johnson South 2002, 65.
74. Rollason 1989; Foot 2011, 119-24, 208-10.
75. *EHD*, 505-08 (no. 104); Woodman 2012, 86-97 (no. 1).
76. Higham 1992; Watson 2011.
77. Raine 1879-94, II, 339.
78. Townend 2002, 5.
79. *PNER Y*, 14-15; Fellows-Jensen 1989.
80. *ASC*, 61-62; Cubbin 1996, 38.
81. Downham 2007, 35-42.
82. Campbell 1962, 54.
83. Smyth 1975-79, II, 41-61; Wood 1980; Hart 1992, 515-25; Halloran 2005; Wood 2013.
84. Cavill 2008; Cavill 2011.
85. Darlington and McGurk 1995, 393; Binns 1963, 17-18; Wood 2013, 147-50.
86. Campbell 1938; Livingston 2011a.
87. Townend 2000a; Bredehoft 2011.
88. Walker 1992.
89. *ASC*, 69-70; O'Brien O'Keeffe 2001, 77-79.
90. Carroll 2007, 230-32.
91. Mynors, Thomson, and Winterbottom 1998-99, I, 210-11, 220-23.

92. Lapidge 1981, 62-71; Mynors, Thomson, and Winterbottom 1998-99, II, 116-18; Wood 1999, 149-68; Foot 2011, 251-58; Wood 2013, 152-54.

93. Kries 2003; Poole 2013, 582-84.

94. Fell 1975, 187; Einarsson 2003, 82-83.

95. Livingston 2011a.

96. Downham 2007, 105.

97. Livingston 2011b, 25.

98. *EHD*, 253 (no. 3); Arnold 1882-85, II, 94.

99. Smyth 1975-79, II, 89, 94-95.

100. *EHD*, 380-81 (no. 34).

101. *ASC*, 71; Whitelock 1959, 72-73.

102. Keynes 1999b; Downham 2007, 114-15; Woodman 2012, 53-55.

103. *EHD*, 257 (no. 4).

104. Smyth 1975-79, II, 96.

105. Blunt, Stewart, and Lyon 1989, 219-21; Blackburn 2004, 336, 343.

106. Townend 2002, 189-96.

107. Blackburn 2004, 336.

108. Smyth 1975-79, II, 96.

109. *EHD*, 253 (no. 3); Arnold 1882-85, II, 94.

110. Smyth 1975-79, II, 97-98; Woolf 2007, 235-36.

111. Breeze 1997.

112. Downham 2003; Downham 2007, 107-12; Halloran 2013.

113. Beaven 1918; Blunt, Stewart, and Lyon 1989, 216-23, 226-28.

114. Stenton 1971, 358.

115. Mynors, Thomson, and Winterbottom 1998-99, I, 215.

116. *ASC*, 71; O'Brien O'Keeffe 2001, 79.

117. Mawer 1923; Downham 2009.

118. *ASC*, 71.

119. *ASC*, 71.

120. Campbell 1962, 54.

121. Blunt, Stewart, and Lyon 1989, 221-23; Blackburn 2004, 336-37; Downham 2003, 42-43.

122. *ASC*, 72; Cubbin 1996, 44; Faull 1981, 190.

123. *EHD*, 257 (no. 4).

124. *ASC*, 72.

125. Woolf 2001; Hudson 2005.

126. Whaley 2012, I, 213-16.

127. *ASC*, 72-73; Cubbin 1996, 44-45; Irvine 2004, 55-56.

128. Sawyer 1995.

129. Woolf 1998.

130. Rollason 1998a, 170; Faull 1981, 190-91.

131. Finlay and Faulkes 2011, 89-90; Woolf 1998; Williams 2010, 86-90.

132. Blunt, Stewart, and Lyon 1989, 223-25, 228-29; Blackburn 2004, 337-38; Williams 2010, 98-102.

133. McDougall and McDougall 1998, 5, 58-59.

134. Finlay 2004, 56-58; Finlay and Faulkes 2011, 80-90.

135. Woolf 2001, 39; Downham 2004.

136. Irvine 2004, 55.

137. Downham 2004, 76.

138. Fell 1975, 198-200; Einarsson 2003, 155-62.

139. Fell 1975, 192; Einarsson 2003, 110.

140. Gade 2009, I, 16.

141. Finlay 2004, 52-54; Finlay and Faulkes 2011, 84-85.

142. Mynors, Thomson, and Winterbottom 1998-99, I, 217; Page 1981, 113-16.
143. Foot 2011, 54-55.
144. Finlay and Faulkes 2011, 88; Abrams 1995, 216-20; Williams 2001.
145. Cubbin 1996, 80.
146. John 1996, 96.
147. Campbell 1942, 91-97.
148. Townend 2003.
149. Hines 1995.
150. Townend 2003, 51-52.
151. Fell 1975, 190-92; Einarsson 2003, 106-12.
152. Jones 1952; Einarsson 1955.
153. Hines 1995.

154. Coxe 1841-42, I, 402-03; *EHD*, 257 (no. 4).
155. Thornton 1997; Williams 2010, 111-12.
156. Finlay and Faulkes 2011, 69; Williams 2010, 41-53.
157. Finlay 2004, 58.
158. Einarsson 1985, 77-79; Whaley 2012, II, 1003-13.
159. Finlay and Faulkes 2011, 90.
160. Williams 2010, 107-09.
161. *EHD*, 511 (no. 107).
162. *ASC*, 74.
163. *ASC*, 73.
164. *EHD*, 254 (no. 3); Arnold 1882-85, II, 94.

CHAPTER 4

1. *ASC*, 48; Bately 1986, 50.
2. *ASC*, 57.
3. *ASC*, 49, 50; Bately 1986, 50, 51.
4. Woodman 2012, 98, 110; Pons-Sanz 2013, 98-100, 134.
5. Stenton 1971, 514.
6. Keynes and Lapidge 1983, 83; Stevenson 1904, 38.
7. *EHD*, 256 (no. 4).
8. Johnson South 2002, 53.
9. Johnson South 2002, 58-59.
10. Johnson South 2002, 60.
11. Morris 1977; Morris 1981, 223-27.
12. Dalton 1994, 78.
13. Foot 2011, 150.
14. Bailey 1996, 84-85; Hadley 2008, 275-78; Kopár 2012, 111-13.
15. Redmonds, King, and Hey 2011.
16. Evison 2000.

17. Helgason et al 2000a; Helgason et al 2000b; Helgason et al 2001.
18. Bowden et al 2008.
19. Capelli et al 2003.
20. Capelli et al 2003, 981.
21. Hadley 2009b, 217.
22. Halsall 2000; Richards 2002; Hadley 2006, 237-71; Redmond 2007.
23. Svanberg 2003; Price 2008.
24. Richards 2002, 162.
25. Wilson 1967; Hadley 2000c.
26. Redmond 2007, 3.
27. Richards 2004; Griffiths 2010, 72-99.
28. Redmond 2007, 92-116.
29. Hadley 2000c; Hadley 2002a; Redmond 2007, 116-20; Hadley 2013, 110-11.
30. Hall 2011, 78.
31. Redmond 2007, 97.
32. Pedersen 2008.

33. Wilson 1965, 41-42; Halsall 2000, 269; Redmond 2007, 100, 112.
34. Morris 1981, 233-35.
35. Redmond 2007, 108-10, lv-lxviii.
36. Lang 1984; Page and Barnes 2006.
37. Scott Burns 1986, 115.
38. Hadley 2008, 271-75.
39. Speed and Walton Rogers 2004.
40. Redmond 2007, 95, 99.
41. Kershaw 2013, 96-97.
42. Speed and Walton Rogers 2004, 73.
43. Kershaw 2013, 98-99.
44. Budd et al 2004.
45. McLeod 2011; McLeod 2014, 90-101.
46. Blackburn 2011, 246-47.
47. Hough 2002, 65-68, 85-89; Jesch 2008.
48. *ASC*, 55, 57; Jesch 1991, 96-98.
49. Johnson South 2002, 53.
50. Woolf 2007, 78-79.
51. Richards and Naylor 2010; Richards and Naylor 2011.
52. Kirk 1927; Hall 1976, 12.
53. Watkin and Mann 1981; Thomas 2000.
54. Kershaw 2013; Kershaw 2009; Leahy and Paterson 2001.
55. Kershaw 2013, 21.
56. Kershaw 2013, 96-100; www.finds.org.uk (ID: NCL-A16CB5).
57. Wilson and Klindt-Jensen 1980; Graham-Campbell 2013.
58. Kershaw 2013, 182.
59. Kershaw 2013 (and database: http://dx.doi.org/10.5284/1012709).
60. Gelling 1988.
61. Fellows-Jensen 1975a; Abrams and Parsons 2004; Townend 2013.
62. Sawyer 1962; Hadley 1997.
63. Townend 2002.
64. Redmonds 2004; Townend 2007.
65. Sawyer 1994, 18-20.
66. Trafford 2000; Heather 2009, 1-35.
67. Woolf 2007, 289-93.
68. Jespersen 1956, 55-77; Miller 2012, 91-147; Durkin 2014, 173-221.
69. Durkin 2014, 223-97.
70. Stenton 1927a, 230-31; Fellows-Jensen 1968; Insley 1994.
71. Tomasson 1980, 58; Karlsson 2000, 15; Byock 2001, 9.
72. Barnwell and Roberts 2011.
73. Gregson 1985; Hadley 1996a.
74. Sawyer 1982, 105-07; Higham 1993, 195-97; Sawyer 1994, 15-18; Richards 2000a, 41-42; Rollason 2003, 231-33; Kelly 2009, 31-33.
75. Faith 1997, 153-77; Fleming 2003, 107-14; Jones 2013, 191-98.
76. Jones 1965, 77.
77. Wormald 1982b, 147; Smyth 1999, 13-14.
78. Hadley 1996a, 7; Townend 2002, 5.
79. *ASC*, 57; Bately 1986, 59.
80. Blunt and Dolley 1959, 221; Pagan 1966; Brooks and Graham-Campbell 1986, 106; Blackburn 2004, 347.
81. Morris 1977; Morris 1984.

238

82. Fox 1989, 90-94; Gelling 2004; Gelling 2006.
83. Gelling 2004, 351.
84. Morris and McDonnell 1990-91; Fellows-Jensen 1978b, 41-42; Fellows-Jensen 1995a, 183-84; Fellows-Jensen 2013, 90-92.
85. Dyer 2003, 17-26; Baxter 2011, 101-02.
86. Smith 1956, II, 188-98; Fellows-Jensen 1978b, 31-37; Cameron 1996a, 143-49.
87. Parsons 2001, 308; Townend 2013, 117-21.
88. Townend 2013, 113-15; McLeod 2014, 43-108.
89. Fellows-Jensen 1972, 195-251.
90. Fellows-Jensen 1972, 241-42; Abrams and Parsons 2004, 400.
91. Cameron 1996a, 143-44; Fellows-Jensen 2012, 352-53.
92. *PNWRY*, VI, 55; Fellows-Jensen 1995a, 174.
93. Watts 2004, 567, 570-71.
94. *ASC*, 65; *PNWRY*, IV, 80; Fellows-Jensen 1995b, 25-26; Fellows-Jensen 2012, 355.
95. *PNNRY*, 238; Fellows-Jensen 2008, 128, 132.
96. Fellows-Jensen 2012, 353-56.
97. Pálsson and Edwards 1972.
98. Fellows-Jensen 1972, 109-30.
99. *PNNRY*, 37; Fellows-Jensen 1972, 56, 255.
100. Watts 2004, 263.
101. Fellows-Jensen 1972, 220; Fellows-Jensen 1975b, 6.
102. Bailey 1980, 213-14.
103. *PNNRY*, 54-55.
104. Townend 2002, 51-52, 187-89.
105. Smith 1956, I, 66-72; Parsons and Styles 2000, 104-08; Fellows-Jensen 2013, 83-88.
106. Fellows-Jensen 1972, 5-41; Fellows-Jensen 1995a, 175.
107. Fellows-Jensen 1972, 176.
108. Fellows-Jensen 1972, 9-17; Abrams and Parsons 2004, 395-98.
109. Abrams and Parsons 2004, 398.
110. Abrams and Parsons 2004, 401.
111. Fellows-Jensen 1995a, 175-80.
112. *PNERY*, 47; Fellows-Jensen 1972, 8, 24.
113. Fox 1989, 90-94.
114. Fellows-Jensen 1972, 42-71; Cullen, Jones, and Parsons 2011, 25 n. 12, 185-97.
115. Cullen, Jones, and Parsons 2011.
116. Cameron 1965; Cameron 1970; Cameron 1971.
117. Binns 1963, 24-25; Fellows-Jensen 1972, 175-79.
118. Ekwall 1937-45, 33-34.
119. Unwin 1988, 97.
120. Banham 2009.
121. Fellows-Jensen 1972, 72-108.
122. Gelling 1984.
123. Townend 2000, 99-100; Townend 2002, 43-87.
124. *PNNRY*, 146.
125. *PNNRY*, 15, 87; *PNWRY*, II, 22-23, V, 86; Fellows-Jensen 2011, 79-80.
126. Fellows-Jensen 1972, 131-68.
127. *PNERY*, 49-50; *PNWRY*, I, 312-13, IV, 24-25.
128. *PNNRY*, 253, 255; *PNWRY*, IV, 184, VI, 31.
129. *PNWRY*, VI, 71-72.

130. Fellows-Jensen 1974; Cameron 1996b; Parsons 2006.
131. Abrams and Parsons 2004, 402-03.
132. *PNNRY*, 324-33; *PNERY*, 318-29.
133. *PNNRY*, 65, 68, 69, 80, 86, 147, 257; *PNERY*, 133, 169; *PNWRY*, VI, 261.
134. *PNNRY*, 148.
135. Ekwall 1928.
136. Ekwall 1928; Fellows-Jensen 1986.

CHAPTER 5

1. Rollason 2003; Higham 2007.
2. *EHD*, 433 (no. 52).
3. Roesdahl and Sørensen 2003; Abrams 2012a.
4. Fellows-Jensen 1972, 13, 50, 189-90.
5. Worsaae 1852.
6. Kershaw 2013, 128.
7. Smith 1928-29; Fellows-Jensen 1985b; Fellows-Jensen 1987a; Downham 2009, 157-63.
8. Smith 1956, I, 66-72; Parsons and Styles 2000, 105.
9. *PNWRY*, VII, 294-95; Fellows-Jensen 1968, xxvi-xxviii; Fellows-Jensen 1972, 9-12.
10. *PNNRY*, xxiv-xxix; *PNERY*, xxiii-xxv; *PNWRY*, VII, 52-62; Fellows-Jensen 1972, 189-94.
11. Fellows-Jensen 1972, 13, 189-90.
12. Smith 1956, I, 187-88; *PNWRY*, II, 65-66, IV, 41.
13. Faull 1981, 197; Johnson South 2002, 50-51; Besteman 2005; Woolf 2007, 71-73; McLeod 2014, 133-41.
14. Fellows-Jensen 1972, 13, 49-50.
15. Smart 1986, 178-79; Blunt, Stewart, and Lyon 1989, 229-34; Blackburn 2004, 342.
16. Smith 1927.
17. Grant 2002; Parsons 2011.
18. Janzén 1960.
19. Grant 2002, 71-73; Edmonds 2009, 8-12.
20. Smith 1927; *PNNRY*, 324; *PNERY*, 317; *PNWRY*, VII, 296.
21. Janzén 1960, 78-80.
22. Lang 2001, 36-38.
23. Fanning 1994; Thomas 2000, 246-49; Hall 2000, 320; McLeod 2014, 122-27.
24. Sheehan 2009; Sheehan 2011; Graham-Campbell 2011, 87-104.
25. www.finds.org.uk (ID: YORYM-CEE620).
26. Dumville 2004, 87; McLeod 2014, 112-32.
27. Bailey 1978, 178; Lang 1995, 439.
28. Parsons 2011, 135.
29. Edmonds 2009, 11-12.
30. Townend 2000a.
31. Townend 2002.
32. Fellows-Jensen 1972, 131-68; Townend 2002, 45-87.
33. *PNNRY*, 54-55; Fellows-Jensen 1972, 166.

34. Stafford 2008, 108-09.
35. Townend 2002, 195-96;
    Blackburn 2004, 336.
36. Holman 1996; Barnes and
    Page 2006.
37. Holman 1996, 79-81; Lang
    2001, 195-97; Barnes and
    Page 2006, 301-07.
38. Okasha 1971, 114; Barnes
    and Page 2006, 303-05.
39. Page 1971, 168-70; Holman
    1996, Appendix I, i-v; Barnes
    and Page 2006, 24-25,
    340-41; Redmond 2007, 108,
    lv.
40. Hines 1991; Barnes 1993;
    Townend 2002; Pons-Sanz
    2013.
41. Pons-Sanz 2000.
42. Okasha 1971, 47; Fellows-
    Jensen 1991, 110-11;
    Townend 2012, 97-99.
43. Mitchell 1994; Townend
    2002, 196-201.
44. Abrams 2000, 136; Foote
    1993.
45. Turville-Petre 1964; Abram
    2011.
46. McKinnell 1994; Brink 2007.
47. Fletcher 1997, 369-416;
    Carver 2004; Winroth 2012.
48. Price 2002, 391.
49. Smyth 1999, 26-28.
50. Coupland 1991; Townend
    2002, 174-76.
51. Brooks 1979, 13-14;
    Townend 2002, 173-74.
52. Foot 1991; Kelly 2009,
    29-32.
53. Wamers 1983; Wamers 1998.
54. Johnson South 2002, 51-53;
    Rollason 2000, 97.
55. Blair 2005, 121-34.
56. Wormald 1982a, 138; Barrow
    2000, 156-61.

57. Abrams 2001b, 33.
58. Binns 1965, 185.
59. Brooks 1984, 151.
60. Smyth 1999, 4.
61. Garrison 2012.
62. Wormald 1982a, 139; Abrams
    2001b, 33-34.
63. Carver 2011, 191; Dumville
    1992, 37; Kelly 2009, 31-33.
64. Sawyer 1994, 8.
65. Hadley 1996b; Hadley 2000a,
    216-97; Barrow 2000; Blair
    2005, 291-323; Hadley 2006,
    192-236; Pickles 2012.
66. Hadley 2000a, 220-57;
    Barrow 2000, 166.
67. Barrow 2000, 166, 169.
68. Abrams 2000, 142.
69. PNNRY, 164; Jesch 2011,
    15-16.
70. Pope 1967-68, II, 684.
71. Smith 1956, I, 235-36;
    Gelling 1988, 137-38; Gelling
    and Cole 2000, 174
72. *PNNRY*, 66, 249, 251-52.
73. Fellows-Jensen 1992, 267.
74. *PNWRY*, I, 210-11, IV, 239,
    VII, 57, 66.
75. Price 2008, 261.
76. Dent 1984.
77. Graham-Campbell 2011,
    125-26, 160; Jesch 2011,
    17-19; McLeod 2014, 249-51.
78. Jesch 2011, 17;
    www.finds.org.uk
    (ID: SWYOR-489283).
79. Wilson 1957.
80. Johnson South 2002, 61-63.
81. Wormald 1982a, 139-40.
82. Meaney 2004.
83. Abrams 2000, 139.
84. Abrams 2001, 39.
85. *EHD*, 820 (no. 227); Abrams
    2000, 142.

86. Keynes and Lapidge 1983, 107.
87. Lapidge 2009, 17.
88. Lapidge 2009, 19.
89. Turner and Muir 2006, 13-15, 219-21.
90. *EHD*, 253 (no. 3).
91. Keynes and Lapidge 1983, 103; Abrams 2001, 37.
92. Brooks 1984, 222-37.
93. Wareham 1996.
94. Blackburn 2007.
95. Fletcher 1997.
96. Abrams 1997; Abrams 2010.
97. *EHD*, 257 (no. 4).
98. *ASC*, 71.
99. *PNWRY*, VIII, 104; Fellows-Jensen 1987c.
100. Pickles 2012, 31-33.
101. Bailey 1981, 87.
102. Collingwood 1927; Bailey 1996.
103. Sawyer 2000; Spurkland 2005.
104. Lang 1991; Lang 2001; Coatsworth 2008.
105. Stocker 2000, 193, 198.
106. Lang 1984.
107. Morris 1989, 140-67; Blair 2005, 385-96.
108. Stocker 2000, 182, 200; Everson and Stocker 2012, 215-20.
109. Bailey 1978; Bailey 1980, 45-75.
110. Wilson and Klindt-Jensen 1980; Graham-Campbell 2013.
111. Lang 1978c, 20; Bailey 1996, 81-82.
112. Wilson and Klindt-Jensen 1980, 103; Bailey 1996, 14; Graham-Campbell 2013, 94.
113. Collingwood 1926; Bailey 1980, 70-71.
114. Kopár 2012, xxxvi n. 13.
115. Bailey 1980, 101-42; McKinnell 2001; Buckland 2010; Kopár 2012.
116. McKinnell 1987; Kopár 2012, 106-23.
117. Lang 1976a; Kopár 2012, 3-56.
118. McKinnell 1990; McKinnell 2001, 331-33.
119. Pálsson and Edwards 1972, 97.
120. Stocker 2000, 191-200.
121. McKinnell 1987, 335-36.
122. Bailey 1980, 116-25.
123. Thompson 2004, 165-66.
124. Kopár 2012, 167-79.
125. Wilcox 1994, 116-19.
126. Gunnell and Lassen 2013.
127. Bailey 1985, 60-61.
128. Cramp 1982, 18.
129. Jesch 2004.
130. Bailey 1980, 143-75.
131. Mynors, Thomson, and Winterbottom 1998, I, 196-97.
132. Darlington and McGurk 1995, 443.
133. Fletcher 1997.
134. Lang 1991, 220-21; Kershaw 2013, 22.
135. Lang 1991, 158-59.
136. Pattison 1973; Lang 1976b; Lang 1991, 189-93; Foys 2007, 159-88.
137. Lang 1984.
138. Schoenfelder and Richards 2011.
139. Kershaw 2013, 152-55.
140. Kershaw 2013, 2.
141. Kershaw 2013, 229-36.
142. Kershaw 2013, 233.
143. Kershaw 2013, 56-65.

144. Kershaw 2013 (and database: http://dx.doi.org/10.5284/1012709).
145. Kershaw 2013, 247, 248.
146. Curta 2011, 542.
147. Ashby 2011; Ashby 2013; Ashby 2014.
148. Ashby 2014, 62-64, 133-34.
149. Pope 1967-68, II, 667-724; Townend 2000b, 93-95.
150. Townend 2002, 185-86.
151. Kemble 1839-48, IV, 84 (no. 772); Harmer 1989, 576; Fellows-Jensen 1995b, 8-9.
152. Barlow 1992, 34-35.
153. Stenton 1927a, 230-31; Fellows-Jensen 1968, lxiv-lxvi.
154. Leonard 2012, 121-23.
155. Keynes and Lapidge 1983, 126.
156. Foot 1996.
157. Bartlett 1994; Ashby 2014, 67-97.
158. Allott 1974, 19.
159. *EHD*, 825 (no. 232); Clayton 2002.
160. Brooks 1986, 2-4.
161. Vaughan 1958, 60.
162. *ASC*, 86; Cubbin 1996, 51.
163. Keynes 2007.
164. Innes 2000; Hadley 2000b; Hadley 2002b.

CHAPTER 6

1. Ottaway 2013, 130.
2. Hall 1994, 21-30; Hall 2004a.
3. Abrams 2012a, 24.
4. Lapidge 2009, 150-51.
5. Fletcher 2002, 48.
6. Hall 1994, 42; Hall 2004c, 287.
7. Ottaway 2013.
8. Rollason 1999; Spall and Toop 2008; Palliser 2014, 23-50.
9. Tweddle, Moulden, and Logan 1999; Hall 2001, 43-50; Hall 2011, 75-77.
10. Hall 2011, 79-81.
11. Phillips and Heywood 1995; Graham-Campbell 1996, 73-74.
12. Hall 1994, 100-01.
13. Lindkvist 1926; *PNERY*, 280-300; Palliser 1978; Fellows-Jensen 2004.
14. Hall 1994, 31-41; Hall 2004b.
15. Norton 1998.
16. *PNERY*, 291-92; Fellows-Jensen 2004, 370.
17. Fell 1975, 199; Einarsson 2003, 157, 158.
18. Hall 1991, 92; Hall 1994, 53-54.
19. Abrams 2008, 186; Woodman 2012, 7-8.
20. Hall 1991, 88-91.
21. Brooks 1979.
22. Keynes and Lapidge 1983, 76.
23. Johnson South 2002, 52-53.
24. Richards 2000a, 63.
25. Mynors, Thomson, and Winterbottom 1998-99, I, 215.
26. Smyth 1977, 182-84; Rollason 1998a, 166.
27. Hall 2004c, 292.

28. Hall 1994, 34; Wilson and Mee 2002, 26-28; Hall 2014, 604.
29. Brooks 1971.
30. Blackburn 2004.
31. Sawyer 2013, 89.
32. Graham-Campbell 2008; Graham-Campbell 2011, 87-104.
33. Graham-Campbell 2011, 104-09, 160, 379.
34. Ager 2007.
35. Williams and Ager 2010, 22-23.
36. Mynors, Thomson, and Winterbottom 1998-99, I, 215.
37. Graham-Campbell 2002; Graham-Campbell and Williams 2007; Graham-Campbell, Sindbæk, and Williams 2011.
38. Edwards 1985; Graham-Campbell 2011, 10.
39. Blackburn 2004, 344-46; Williams 2009, 80-82.
40. Blackburn 2004, 347; Williams 2009, 78, 80.
41. Blackburn 2004, 348.
42. Hadley and ten Harkel 2013.
43. Fell 1975, 190.
44. Mainman and Rogers 2000, 2559-64.
45. *EHD*, 257 (no. 4).
46. *ASC*, 76.
47. Molyneaux 2011, 86-87; Sawyer 2013, 105.
48. Palliser 2014, 4-5.
49. Hall 1984.
50. Hall and Kenward 2004, 372-77, 394-95.
51. Hall et al 2004.
52. Mainman and Rogers 2004.
53. Pirie 1986, 33-43; Graham-Campbell 1996, 77-78; Richards 2000a, 128-30; Blackburn 2004, 340-41.
54. Mainman 1990; Richards 2000a, 103-07; Mainman and Rogers 2004, 459-63; McLeod 2014, 153-56.
55. Hall 1994, 55-69; Hall 2014.
56. Mainman and Rogers 2004, 480.
57. Mainman and Rogers 2004, 476-82.
58. Hall and Kenward 2004, 385.
59. Morris 2000.
60. Hall 1994, 83-88; Hall 2000, 315-17.
61. Walton 1989; Fleming 2007.
62. Morris 1982, 86-88.
63. Hall 1994, 106.
64. Hall and Kenward 2004, 378, 412-14.
65. Hall and Kenward 2004.
66. O'Connor 1989; O'Connor 2004; Barrett, Locker, and Roberts 2004.
67. Hall and Kenward 2004, 397-98.
68. Tweddle 2004.
69. Mainman and Rogers 2000, 2500-17.
70. Hall 2000, 316.
71. Hall 2000, 316.
72. Kershaw 2013, 134-36, 206, 235.
73. Cameron and Mould 2004.
74. Tweddle 2004.
75. Stenton 1927b, 10.
76. Phillips and Heywood 1995.
77. Lang 1991; Lang 1995; Richards 2002, 163-64.
78. Lang 1978b; Lang 1978c.
79. Lang 1991, 39-40.
80. Lang 1993, 266.

81. Palliser 1984; Morris 1986; Rees Jones 2013, 43-44.
82. Stocker 2000, 203-05; Hall 2001, 63.
83. Wenham et al 1987, 80; Hall 1994, 44-45.
84. Janzén 1960, 48, 80-81.
85. Richards 2000c, 50.
86. *PNNRY*, 48; *PNERY*, 47; *PNWRY*, I, 125-26, V, 14, VI, 45-46, 85-86.
87. Ross 1968.
88. Stenton 1927c, 147; Stenton 1971, 504 n. 1; Higham 1993, 180; Sawyer 1998, 133-39.
89. *PNNRY*, xiv-xv.
90. Byock 2002, 6-9.
91. Richards and Naylor 2010, 345, 349; www.finds.org.uk.
92. Kruse 1988; Blackburn and Bonser 1990; www.finds.org.uk.
93. Wilson and Klindt Jensen 1980, 103-04; Bailey 1996, 95.
94. Lang 1973; Lang 1991, 33-36, 39-42.
95. Lang 1978c, 11; Lang 1978b.
96. Cramp 1984, I, 86-87; Lang 1991, 28.
97. Lang 1984; Lang 2001, 47-49.
98. Pattison 1973; Lang 1976b; Lang 1978b; Lang 1978c; Lang 1991, 105-07; Foys 2007, 175-76.
99. Lang 1991, 30.
100. Lang 2001, 9, 44-47.
101. Lang 1991, 38-42; Lang 2001, 44-50; Coatsworth 2008, 74-77.
102. Bailey 1981, 84.
103. Firby and Lang 1981; Lang 1991, 215-16.
104. Morris 2009, 229-33.
105. Lang 2001, 44-47.
106. Coatsworth 2008, 75.
107. Wilson 2008, 116-18; Griffiths 2010, 109-15.
108. Stocker 2000.
109. Atkinson 1879, 1; Lang 2001, 250; Graham-Campbell 1980, 8 (no. 2).
110. Hall 1994, 98; Wilson 2008, 49; Lang 2001, 17, 19.
111. Faull and Stinson 1986, 305a; Pickles 2009.
112. Lang 2001, 153-67, 231-66.
113. Cambridge 1995, 140-43.
114. Stocker 2000, 200.
115. Kroebel 2011.
116. Addyman 1984, 20; Hall 2003, 176-79.
117. Richards 2000b, Richards 2000c; Hadley 2006, 104-18.
118. Richards 2000b, 295-96; Richards 2001, 270, 276.
119. Richards 2000b, 300-02; Hall 2003, 176-77.
120. Richards 2000b, 298.
121. King 1978; Coggins, Fairless, and Batey 1983; Dickinson 1985; Coggins 2004; King 2004.
122. Morris 1981, 236-41.
123. Richards 1999; Richards 2000b, 303-06; Richards 2003; Richards 2013.
124. Richards 2008, 371.
125. Wrathmell 2012.
126. Fox 1989, 90-94; Richards 2000d; Richards 2001, 274-75; Wrathmell 2012, 203-08.
127. Fellows-Jensen 1995a, 180-81; Gelling 2004; Gelling 2006.
128. Wrathmell 2012, 82-96.
129. Wrathmell 2012, 98.

130. Richards 2013, 265.
131. Banham 2009; Cullen, Jones, and Parsons 2011.
132. Higham 1977-78.
133. Fellows-Jensen 1977-78; Fellows-Jensen 1980; Parsons and Styles 1997, 31.
134. *PNNRY*, 47, 72, 134, 147, 164; *PNERY*, 198; *PNWRY*, III, 246; Smith 1956, I, 210; Janzén 1960, 63-76.
135. *PNNRY*, 8-9, 198; *PNERY*, 108-09; *PNWRY*, IV, 242-43, V, 27, VI, 38, 63; Smith 1955; Atkin 1977-78.
136. *PNNRY*, 146, 212, 215, 218-19, 327; *PNERY*, 233; *PNWRY*, VI, 95, 153.
137. *PNWRY*, VI, 80.
138. *PNERY*, 128-29; Fellows-Jensen 1972, 108.
139. *PNWRY*, I, 106-07, VII, 65; Parsons and Styles 2000, 112.
140. *PNNRY*, 59, 146, 157, 205; *PNERY*, 107, 172; Smith 1956, II, 245.
141. Fellows-Jensen 1993.
142. Atkinson 1879, 3; *PNNRY*, 128.
143. *PNNRY*, 213; *PNWRY*, I, 168-69, V, 207; Jones 1965, 79-81.
144. Stenton 1971, 504-05.
145. Loyn 1992, 111-34.
146. Thorn 1992; Hart 1992, 281-88; Campbell 1994, 45-46; Roffe 2000b, 11-13; Wrathmell 2012, 195-96.
147. Stenton 1927a, 238-41; Stenton 1971, 647-48; Hart 1992, 288-335; Sawyer 1998, 137-38.
148. Palliser 1992, 16.
149. *PNNRY*, 42; *PNERY*, 120; Anderson 1934.
150. *PNWRY*, VII, 62.
151. *PNNRY*, 42-43; *PNERY*, 14-15; Fellows-Jensen 1989.
152. *PNNRY*, 326; *PNERY*, 33; *PNWRY*, VII, 66.
153. Jesch 2001a, 216-32; Goetting 2006.
154. Kapelle 1979, 71-72; Roffe 2000b, 10; Everson and Stocker 2012, 212-13.
155. *PNERY*, 81, 323; *PNWRY*, IV, 226, 229.
156. *PNERY*, 170-71, 324; *PNWRY*, III, 223; Smith 1956, I, 191-92; Barlow 1963, 196-98; Jesch 2001a, 239-41.
157. Karras 1988; Pelteret 1991.
158. Pelteret 1991, 183; Pons-Sanz 2013, 69-70, 207-08.
159. *PNERY*, 326.
160. *PNNRY*, 160, 210; *PNWRY*, IV, 107; Fellows-Jensen 1968, 186-87.
161. Stenton 1927a, 219; Pelteret 1991, 184-85.
162. Stenton 1910; Stenton 1927a; Stenton 1969.
163. *PNERY*, 205; Everson and Stocker 2012, 210.
164. Davis 1955; Sawyer 1957.
165. Margeson 1997.
166. Kapelle 1979, 50-85; Hall 1993; Hadley 1996a; Hadley 2000a; Baxter 2007a, 257-61.
167. Loyn 1994, 95.
168. Stenton 1927a, 215.

CHAPTER 7

1. Campbell 1995; Fletcher 2002, 31-57; Aird 2009.
2. Whitelock 1959, 71.
3. Simpson 1989.
4. Whitelock 1954, 28-30; Stafford 2007, 42-49.
5. Woodman 2012, 11.
6. Stafford 2007, 48; Rollason 2003, 257-74.
7. Roffe 2010, 41-44; Molyneaux 2011, 80-85.
8. Sawyer 1998, 133-39; Marten 2008.
9. Whitelock 1959, 83-85.
10. Farrer 1914, 86-87 (no. 88); Bates 1998, 193 (no. 32); Green 1990, 89; Rollason 2003, 270; Baxter 2007a, 121-23.
11. Williams and Martin 2002, 884; Sawyer 1998, 18; Palliser 2014, 5-6.
12. Attenborough 1922, 121, 205; Liebermann 1903-16, I, 458-61; *EHD*, 432-33 (no. 52(B)); Wormald 1999a, 391-94.
13. *ASC*, 96; Cubbin 1996, 62.
14. *ASC*, 119; Cubbin 1996, 70.
15. Sawyer 1998, 149-54.
16. *ASC*, 114; Irvine 2004, 80.
17. *EHD*, 254 (no. 3).
18. Downham 2007, 121-22; Edmonds 2009, 8.
19. Whitelock 1930, 46-51, 151-60; *EHD*, 541-43 (no. 125); Molyneaux 2011, 82-83.
20. Palliser 1978, 6; Parsons and Styles 1997, 120.
21. Lapidge and Winterbottom 1991, 22-25.
22. Treharne 2004, 152-53.
23. Baxter 2007a, 138-51.
24. Whitelock 1959, 86-87; Baxter 2007a, 51-52, 144-45.
25. Whitelock 1959, 73; Woodman 2012, 96-97.
26. Lapidge 2009, 151.
27. *ASC*, 102; Smyth 1999, 43.
28. Blackburn 2004, 325, 344.
29. Fleming 1993; Campbell 2001b; Rees Jones 2013, 61-66.
30. Faull and Stinson 1986, 298a-d; Palliser 1990.
31. Rollason 1998a, 179-225.
32. Rees Jones 2013, 23-59.
33. Chadwick 1905, 161-97; Baxter 2007a.
34. Whitelock 1959.
35. Hall 1994, 54-55; Rollason 2004, 314-15; Baxter 2007a, 62; Rees Jones 2014, 50-54.
36. Whitelock 1959; Rollason 1998, 74-76; Rollason 2004, 314-16.
37. *ASC*, 76; Whitelock 1959, 77-79.
38. *EHD*, 397-401 (no. 41); Wormald 1999a, 317-20.
39. Hadley 2002b, 48-49; Abrams 2008, 177-79.
40. Woodman 2012, 118-27 (no. 4).
41. Whitelock 1959, 78; Kelly 2009, 240-47 (no. 14); Woodman 2012, 127-33 (no. 5).
42. Woodman 2012, 132; Le Patourel, Long, and Pickles 1993.
43. Vaughan 1958, 54; Keynes 1986, 87; Abrams 2008, 186 n. 78.

44. John 1996, 99-123; Cubitt 1997.
45. Kelly 2009, 240-47.
46. Ker 1957, 352; Faull 1981, 191-95; Tamoto 2013.
47. *ASC*, 78.
48. Whitelock 1959, 78-80.
49. *EHD*, 521-22 (no. 114); Woodman 2012, 133-39 (no. 6); Baxter 2004.
50. Woodman 2012, 352-55 (no. 18).
51. *ASC*, 82.
52. *EHD*, 50; Freeland 2005, 105, 132.
53. Johnson South 2002, 67.
54. *EHD*, 402-05 (no. 43); Neff 1989; Wormald 1999a, 328-29.
55. Whitelock 1959, 72, 80-81.
56. *ASC*, 202; Bolton 2007a.
57. Sawyer 1979.
58. Whitelock 1930, 47.
59. *ASC*, 87; Darlington and McGurk 1995, 456-59; Keynes 1980, 209-14.
60. Whitelock 1959, 82.
61. Whitelock 1959, 73-76.
62. Barrow 2000, 161-63; Barrow 2004.
63. Woodman 2012, 97-118 (nos 2 and 3).
64. Baxter 2007a, 65.
65. Woodman 2012, 134 (no. 6).
66. Woodman 2012, 134-35 (no. 6).
67. Arnold 1882-85, I, 226; Whitelock 1959, 75 n. 6.
68. Brooks and Cubitt 1996; Brooks 2004.
69. Lapidge 2009.
70. *EHD*, 521-22 (no. 114); Robertson 1956, 110-13, 357-60 (no. 54); Woodman 2012, 133-39 (no. 6).

71. Wormald 2004a; Hill 2004, 311-12.
72. *ASC*, 84.
73. Wilcox 2000.
74. Barker 1986; Norton 2004; Heslop 2004.
75. Stevenson 1912; Keynes 1986; Wood 1987; Baxter 2004; Woodman 2012, 139-48 (no. 7).
76. Wormald 2004a; Townend 2004; Lionarons 2010.
77. Ker 1971.
78. Wormald 1999b.
79. Holman 2001; Pons-Sanz 2007; Pons-Sanz 2013.
80. Keynes 1991.
81. *ASC*, 90.
82. *EHD*, 857-58 (no. 240).
83. *ASC*, 92; Cubbin 1996, 58.
84. *ASC*, 92.
85. *ASC*, 93.
86. Short 2009, 227.
87. *ASC*, 93.
88. *ASC*, 95.
89. *ASC*, 96; Cubbin 1996, 62.
90. Whaley 2012, II, 772.
91. Whitelock 1959, 87.
92. *ASC*, 95; Cubbin 1996, 61.
93. Darlington and McGurk 1995, 483.
94. *ASC*, 96; Cubbin 1996, 62.
95. Barlow 1963; Fleming 2001; Smith, Fleming, and Halpin 2001; O'Donnell, Townend, and Tyler 2013.
96. Wormald 2004b.
97. *ASC*, 98.
98. *EHD*, 414-16 (no. 48); Keynes 1986, 95-96; Treharne 2012, 18-27.
99. Jost 1959; Swanton 1975, 125-38.
100. Whitelock 1965; Norton 2004; Baxter 2004.

101. Crook 2004.
102. Cooper 1970, 14-18.
103. Woodman 2012, 148-57 (no. 8).
104. Cooper 1970, 18-23.
105. Liebermann 1903-16, I, 380-85; *EHD*, 434-39 (no. 53); Wormald 1999a, 396-97.
106. Chadwick 1905, 24-25, 44-47; Pons-Sanz 2013, 199-201.
107. Barlow 1963, 86-90; Cooper 1970, 23-29; King 1996; Lawson 2004.
108. Winterbottom and Thomson 2002, 35.
109. *ASC*, 114, 120.
110. *ASC*, 116, 129, 135.
111. *ASC*, 134; Cubbin 1996, 76.
112. Lawson 2004, 553.
113. Wormald 1993; Cubbin 1996, lxxviii-lxxxi; Stafford 2011; Raine 1879-94, II, 344-54.
114. Lapidge 1983.
115. Liebermann 1903-16, I, 473-74; Wormald 1999a, 395; Woodman 2012, 244-45.
116. Woodman 2012, 173-265.
117. Armstrong, Tomlinson, and Evans 1991; Hall and Whyman 1996.
118. Morris and Cambridge 1989; Lapidge 2009, 170-73; Woodman 2012, 183-85.
119. Wilson 2003; *ASC*, 72.
120. Barlow 1963, 176; Brooks 1984, 227-31.
121. Coatsworth 2008, 235-36; Kopár 2012, 39-40; Woodman 2012, 242-43.
122. *PNERY*, 194-97; Armstrong, Tomlinson, and Evans 1991, 155-56; Kershaw 2013, 78.
123. Gem 1988; Morris 1989, 140-67; Blair 2005, 407-17.
124. Barrow 2000, 165-69.
125. Rees Jones 2013, 66-71.
126. Okasha 1971, 131; Wenham et al 1987; Lang 1991, 99-101.
127. Wrathmell 2012, 207-08.
128. Taylor and Taylor 1965; Wenham et al 1987; McClain 2011; Morris 2011.
129. Hall, Kendall, and Briden 2008.
130. Lang 1991, 146-48; Jones 1992, 81-83; Hawkes 1993; Pickles 2012.
131. Lang 1991, 144-45.
132. Taylor and Taylor 1965, I, 326-28.
133. Adams 1990; Adams 1996; Hadley 2000c; Hadley 2002a.
134. Mytum 1993.
135. Woodman 2012, 379; Stevenson 1912, 9.
136. Gittos 2005, 66.
137. Keen 1993; Norton 2004, 230-32.
138. Norton 2004, 211-13; Rees Jones 2013, 51-52; Palliser 2014, 83.
139. *EHD*, 434-39 (no. 53).
140. Okasha 1971, 87-88; Lang 1991, 163-66.
141. Taylor and Taylor 1965, I, 357-61.
142. Lang 1991, 123-24, 133-35, 195; Wall 1997.
143. *PNNRY*, 66; Lang 1991, 161-63; Rahtz and Watts 2004.
144. Morris 1990; Blair 2010.
145. Wrathmell 2012, 182-88; Pickles 2012, 36-38.
146. Keynes 1994; Fellows-Jensen 1994; Bolton 2009, 109-26.

147. Whitelock 1959, 82-83; Keynes 1994, 57-58; Whaley 2012, I, cxc-cxci.
148. Whaley 2012, I, 510.
149. Barlow 1992, 35.
150. Bolton 2007b.
151. Wright 1939, 127-35, 267-70; Parker 2014.
152. Stenton 1971, 417.
153. Morris 1992, 5; Keynes 1994, 65-66.
154. *ASC*, 128-29; Kapelle 1979, 27-49.
155. Baxter 2007a, 103; Rees Jones 2013, 52-53.
156. *ASC*, 130.
157. Phelpstead 2001.
158. Dickins 1937-45; Townend 2005.
159. Hart 1975, 143-50; Morris 1992; Fletcher 2002.
160. Morris 1992, 2.
161. Johnson South 2002, 67, 111-12.
162. Morris 1992, 3.
163. Morris 1992, 3.
164. Morris 1992, 3-4.
165. Miller 1990.
166. Kapelle 1979, 17-26; Aird 1998, 47-49, 92-93; Fletcher 2002.
167. Rollason 1998a, 211; Wrathmell 2012, 186; Rees Jones 2013, 65.
168. Kapelle 1979, 19-20.
169. Liebermann 1903-16, I, 458-61; *EHD*, 432-33 (no. 52(B)); Wormald 1999, 392-93.
170. Wrathmell 2012, 180-96; Bolton 2009, 114-22.
171. Roffe 1990a; Palliser 1992.
172. Clarke 1994, 132-35, 322-24.

173. Faull and Stinson 1986, 301b; Roffe 2000b; Everson and Stocker 2012.
174. Faull and Stinson 1986, 300a, 300c, 301a.
175. Faull and Stinson 1986, 301a, 301b, 330d.
176. Faull and Stinson 1986, 301b, 324d, 332a.
177. Parsons 2002; von Feilitzen 1937.
178. Townend 2007.
179. Stenton 1927b, 4-5; Smart 1986, 178-82.
180. Stevenson 1912, 12-13; Woodman 2012, 380-81.
181. Lindkvist 1922; Cooper 1969; Keynes 1986, 98-99; Woodman 2012, 381-82.
182. Sawyer 1994, 18-20; Sawyer 1998, 106.
183. Sawyer 1998, 106.
184. Smith 1927, 40-46; Edmonds 2009, 11-12.
185. Kershaw 2013, 151.
186. Williams 1997.
187. www.finds.org.uk.
188. Graham-Campbell 1991; Richards and Naylor 2010, 346-47, 349-50.
189. Fellows-Jensen 1994; Bolton 2009.
190. Wilson and Klindt-Jensen 1980; Graham-Campbell 2013.
191. Owen 2001; Richards and Naylor 2010, 347.
192. Hall 1994, 117; Tweddle 2004, 453, 455-56.
193. Bailey 1980, 57; Lang 1991, 177-78; Coatsworth 2008, 76.
194. Bailey 1980, 58; Coatsworth 2008, 226-27.
195. Lang 1991, 80; Tweddle 2004, 456.
196. Thompson 2004, 161-63.

197. Kershaw 2008.
198. *ASC*, 109-11.
199. Page 1971; Parsons 2001.
200. Townend 2002, 189-96.
201. Stenton 1927b, 10-11;
    PNERY, 287; Rollason 1998a,

199-201; Rees Jones 2013,
162-64.
202. Scott 1953-57; Jesch 2001b,
321-23; Gade 2009, I, 382-84.
203. Lang 1991, 158-60, 163;
    O'Sullivan 2011.

CHAPTER 8

1. Lewis 1994.
2. Barlow 2003; Mason 2004;
   Aird 2004a.
3. Whitelock 1959, 83-84.
4. Rollason 2000, 174-77.
5. Rollason 2000, 181; Fletcher
   2002, 157; Aird 2004b.
6. *ASC*, 135; Barlow 1992,
   55-57; Winterbottom and
   Thomson 2002, 43.
7. Kapelle 1979, 90-94; Fletcher
   2002, 151-54.
8. *ASC*, 137-38.
9. Barlow 1992, 77.
10. Darlington and McGurk 1995,
    597-99.
11. Fletcher 2002, 160.
12. *ASC*, 138.
13. Barlow 1992, 81.
14. *ASC*, 138; Innes 2000, 69-71.
15. Wilkinson 1939; Kapelle
    1979, 86-101; Higham 1993,
    236-37; Aird 1998, 54-61;
    Innes 2000, 68-71; Fletcher
    2002, 149-62.
16. Wormald 1994, 2.
17. Wormald 1999a, 133;
    Wormald 2004b, 25.
18. Barlow 1992, 79.
19. Kapelle 1979, 94-95; Fletcher
    2002, 157-58.
20. Wormald 1994, 6.

21. Stevenson 1987, 143; Aird
    1998, 61-62; Baxter 2007a,
    50-51.
22. Baxter 2007a, 51-52.
23. Winterbottom and Thomson
    2002, 56-57.
24. *ASC*, 140.
25. Körner 1964; Stenton 1970,
    545-621.
26. Gade 2009, I, lxxxiii-lxxxiv.
27. Magnusson and Pálsson 1966;
    Andersson and Gade 2000;
    Finlay 2004.
28. Jónsson 1954, 344; Turville-
    Petre 1968; Fidjestøl 1997,
    117-32.
29. Körner 1964, 145-54.
30. *ASC*, 134; Anderson 1922, II,
    1; Darlington and McGurk
    1995, 585.
31. Brooks 1956; DeVries 1999;
    Jones 2006.
32. Gade 2009, I, lxxxiv.
33. Rowe 1994; White 2005.
34. *ASC*, 140-45; O'Brien
    O'Keeffe 2001, 119-23;
    Cubbin 1996, 79-81.
35. Darlington and McGurk 1995,
    603; Short 2009, 283, 428.
36. *ASC*, 143.
37. *ASC*, 143.
38. Stevenson 1987, 131; Short
    2009, 283.
39. Jones 2006; Jones 2011.

40. Gade 2009, I, 268, 368, II, 807.
41. Daniell 2001.
42. *ASC*, 143-44; Darlington and McGurk 1995, 603.
43. *ASC*, 144.
44. *ASC*, 144-45.
45. Mynors, Thomson, and Winterbottom 1998-99, I, 421.
46. Gade 2009, I, 272, 357.
47. Gade 2009, I, 175, 273.
48. Gade 2009, I, 274.
49. *ASC*, 142.
50. *ASC*, 142; Darlington and McGurk 1995, 605; Short 2009, 285.
51. Hall et al 2008.
52. Mynors, Thomson, and Winterbottom 1998-99, I, 469.
53. Short 2009, 285.
54. *ASC*, 144-45.
55. Abrams 2012b.
56. Higham 1993, 242-48.
57. Kapelle 1979.
58. Johnson 1990, 5.
59. Chibnall 1969, 195; Williams 1995, 7-8.
60. Aird 1998, 64-68; Fletcher 2002, 169-70.
61. Williams 1995, 24-27; Rollason 1998a, 181; Fletcher 2002, 172-73; Baxter 2007a, 273-74; Rees Jones 2013, 87-88.
62. Hooper 1985; Baxter 2007a, 274-76.
63. Williams 1995, 27-33; Fletcher 2002, 175-77; Rees Jones 2013, 65.
64. Chibnall 1969, 223.
65. *ASC*, 149.
66. Holman 2006, 183-89.
67. Tschan 2002, 108; Williams 1995, 35-38.
68. Chibnall 1969, 217; McGurk 1998, 9.
69. *ASC*, 150; Fletcher 2002, 177-79.
70. Stenton 1971, 603.
71. Mynors, Thomson, and Winterbottom 1998-99, I, 469; Chibnall 1969, 227.
72. Chibnall 1969, 233; Williams 1995, 32-33, 38.
73. *ASC*, 151.
74. *ASC*, 150.
75. Palliser 1993, 3-5; Williams 1995, 40-43; Fletcher 2002, 180-84.
76. Darby and Maxwell 1962, 444-54; Kapelle 1979, 117-19, 173-74; Palliser 1992, 33-38; Palliser 1993; Dalton 1994, 23-27; Roffe 2007, 250-56.
77. Blackburn and Pagan 1986, 299; Palliser 1993, 7-8.
78. Baxter 2007a, 278-80.
79. Scott 1952; Lewis 2004.
80. Williams 1995, 58-65; Aird 1998, 91-94.
81. Gade 2009, I, 383.
82. *ASC*, 157-58.
83. Holt 1987b, 62.
84. Norton 2001.
85. Burton 1999.
86. Bates 1998, 191-92 (no. 31); Fletcher 2002, 174.
87. Morris 1992, 3-4; Williams 1995, 59; Fletcher 2002, 182-83.
88. Dalton 1994, 19.
89. Roffe 1990b; Fleming 1991, 107-82; Palliser 1992, 29-33; Dalton 1994, 70-77; Garnett 2005, 24-33.

90. Farrer 1912, 146-48; Kapelle 1979, 176-78; Palliser 1992, 26-27.
91. Faull and Stinson 1986, 301b, 324d, 332a.
92. Michelmore 1981, 251-53; Williams 1995, 71-125.
93. Baxter 2011.
94. Rollason 1998a, 221; Stenton 1927b, 11-14; Palliser 2014, 80.
95. Stenton 1927b, 6.
96. Tweddle 2004, 456; Owen 2001, 219.
97. Addyman and Goodall 1979.
98. Leach 1921; Holman 2007, 181-204.
99. Taylor 1965; Gade 2009, II, 556.
100. Þorsteinsson 1969; Karlsson 2000, 118-22; Barrett, Locker, and Roberts 2004.
101. Page 1987; Keynes 2007.
102. Thorpe 1978, 243.
103. Dunn 1965; Smithers 1987; Weiss 1992, 141-58; Phythian-Adams 1999; Turville-Petre 2001.
104. Parker 2014.
105. Short 2009, 141-55; Wright 1939, 107-16; McTurk 1991, 215-25; Rowe 2012, 84-88.
106. Binns 1966; Townend 2003; Fjalldal 2005; Rowe 2009; Rowe 2012.
107. Finlay and Faulkes 2011, 89.
108. *PNNRY*, 105-06; Whaley 2002, 65; Whaley 2010.
109. Preest 2002, 139.
110. Pearsall 1999, 231.
111. Thorpe 1978, 231.
112. Björkman 1900-02; Dance 2003; Pons-Sanz 2013.
113. Samuels 1985; Thomason and Kaufman 1988, 275-304; Townend 2002, 201-10; Townend 2012.
114. *PNNRY*, 231.
115. Miller 2012, 91-147; Durkin 2014, 173-221.
116. Rynell 1948; Samuels 1963.
117. Wright 1898-1905; Thorson 1936.
118. Fellows-Jensen 1968.
119. Postles 2007, 123-27.
120. Postles 2007, 127, 135.
121. Clark 1987, 17.
122. Redmonds 2004, 30.
123. Stenton 1927a, 230-31; Townend 2007, 15-17.
124. Clark 1987; Redmonds 2004.
125. Reaney 1967; McKinley 1990; Hey 2000.
126. Fellows-Jensen 2003, 46-47.
127. Redmonds 1973; Fellows-Jensen 2003.
128. Reaney 1967, 75-90; Sørensen 1983; Postles 2007, 34-71.
129. Woolf 1991, 193-97; Westwood and Simpson 2005, 530-31.
130. Woolf 1991, 193.
131. Westwood and Simpson 2005, 838-39.
132. Edwards 2004, 135.
133. Swanton 1976; Addyman and Goodall 1979, 82-83.
134. Omberg 1976; Clunies Ross 1998; Sweet 2004, 219-29.
135. Wawn 2000; Townend 2009.
136. Young 2008.
137. Tennyson 1877, 101.
138. Levine 1986.
139. Cheesman 2004.
140. Scott Burns 1986; Sheils 2004.

141. Atkinson 1868, xii-xiii; Atkinson 1879, xx-xxii.
142. Atkinson 1891, 432; Scott Burns 1986, 113-15.
143. Atkinson 1891, xxxviii-xxxix.
144. Wright 1932.
145. Kellett and Dewhirst 1997.
146. Marshall 2011.
147. Tolkien 1928, xv.
148. Hall 2004a, 294-97.
149. Haraldsson 1994.
150. Collingwood 1908; Townend 2009
151. www.yorkshireccc.com/news (7 March 2013).
152. Tyas 2010, 19.
153. Jones 2011.
154. Fellows-Jensen 1972, 169.

BIBLIOGRAPHY

Abram, Christopher. 2011. *Myths of the Pagan North: The Gods of the Norsemen* (London).

Abrams, Lesley. 1995. 'The Anglo-Saxons and the Christianization of Scandinavia', *Anglo-Saxon England* 24, 213-49.

—— 1997. 'The Conversion of the Scandinavians of Dublin', *Anglo-Norman Studies* 20, 1-29.

—— 2000. 'Conversion and Assimilation', in Hadley and Richards 2000, 135-53.

—— 2001a. 'Edward the Elder's Danelaw', in Higham and Hill 2001, 128-43.

—— 2001b. 'The Conversion of the Danelaw', in Graham-Campbell et al 2001, 31-44.

—— 2008. 'King Edgar and the Men of the Danelaw', in Donald Scragg (ed.), *Edgar, King of the English 959-75: New Interpretations* (Woodbridge), 171-91.

—— 2010. 'Conversion and the Church in Viking-Age Ireland', in Sheehan and Ó Corráin 2010, 1-10.

—— 2012a. 'Diaspora and Identity in the Viking Age', *Early Medieval Europe* 20, 17-38.

—— 2012b. 'Early Normandy', *Anglo-Norman Studies* 35, 45-64.

Abrams, Lesley, and David N. Parsons. 2004. 'Place-Names and the History of Scandinavian Settlement in England', in Hines, Lane, and Redknap 2004, 379-431.

Abramson, Tony, ed. 2011. *Studies in Early Medieval Coinage: Volume 2 New Perspectives* (Woodbridge).

Adams, Kenneth A. 1990. 'Monastery and Village at Crayke, North Yorkshire', *Yorkshire Archaeological Journal* 62, 29-50.

Adams, Max. 1996. 'Excavation of a Pre-Conquest Cemetery at Addingham, West Yorkshire', *Medieval Archaeology* 40, 151-91.

Addyman, P.V. 1984. 'York in its Archaeological Setting', in Addyman and Black 1984, 7-21.

Addyman, P.V., and V.E. Black, eds. 1984. *Archaeological Papers from York Presented to M.W. Barley* (York).

Addyman, P.V., and Ian H. Goodall. 1979. 'The Norman Church and Door at Stillingfleet, North Yorkshire', *Archaeologia* 106, 75-105.

Ager, Barry. 2007. 'York area: Viking gold armring', *Treasure Annual Report 2004* (London), 63-64 (no. 76).

—— 2011. 'A Preliminary Note on the Artefacts from the Vale of York Viking Hoard', in Abramson 2011, 121-34.

Ager, Barry, and Gareth Williams. 2007. 'North Yorkshire area: Closely associated group of Viking-period and Late Saxon objects and coins', *Treasure Annual Report 2004* (London), 91-93 (no. 137).

—— 2011. 'The Vale of York Viking Hoard: Preliminary Catalogue', in Abramson 2011, 135-45.

Aird, William M. 1998. *St Cuthbert and the Normans: The Church of Durham, 1071-1153*, Studies in the History of Medieval Religion 14 (Woodbridge).

255

— 2004a. 'Tostig, Earl of Northumbria (c.1029-1066)', in Matthew and Harrison 2004, 55, 67-70.

— 2004b. 'Copsi [Coxo], Earl of Northumbria (d. 1067)', in Matthew and Harrison 2004, 13, 377.

— 2009. 'Northumbria', in Stafford 2009, 302-21.

Allott, Stephen, trans. 1974. *Alcuin of York: His Life and Letters* (York).

Anderson, Alan Orr, trans. 1922. *Early Sources of Scottish History AD 500 to 1286*, 2 vols (Edinburgh).

Anderson, Olof S. 1934. *The English Hundred-Names* (Lund).

Andersson, Theodore M., and Kari Ellen Gade, trans. 2000. *Morkinskinna: The Earliest Icelandic Chronicle of the Norwegian Kings (1030-1157)*, Islandica 51 (Ithaca).

Angus, W.S. 1940. 'The Annals for the Tenth Century in Symeon of Durham's Historia Regum', *Durham University Journal* 32, 213-29.

Armstrong, Peter, David Tomlinson, and D.H. Evans. 1991. *Excavations at Lurk Lane, Beverley, 1979-82*, Sheffield Excavation Reports 1 (Sheffield).

Arnold, Thomas, ed. 1882-85. *Symeonis Monachi Opera Omnia*, 2 vols, Rolls Series 75 (London).

ASC = Whitelock 1961

Ashby, Steven P. 2011. 'A Study in Regionality: Hair Combs and Bone/Antler Craft in North-east England c. AD 800-1100', in Petts and Turner 2011, 303-19.

— 2013. 'Making a Good Comb: Mercantile Identity in 9th- to 11th-Century England', in Hadley and ten Harkel 2013, 193-208.

— 2014. *A Viking Way of Life: Combs and Communities in Early Medieval Britain* (Stroud).

Ashley, Scott. 2007. 'The Lay Intellectual in Anglo-Saxon England: Ealdorman Æthelweard and the Politics of History', in Patrick Wormald and Janet L. Nelson (eds), *Lay Intellectuals in the Carolingian World* (Cambridge), 218-45.

Atkin, Mary. 1977-78. 'Viking Race-Courses? The distribution of *skeið* place-name elements in northern England', *Journal of the English Place-Name Society* 10, 26-39.

Atkinson, J.C. 1868. *A Glossary of the Cleveland Dialect: Explanatory, Derivative, and Critical* (London).

— ed. 1879. *Cartularium Abbathiæ de Whiteby Ordinis S. Benedicti Fundatæ Anno MLXXVIII*, Surtees Society 72 (Durham).

— 1891. *Forty Years in a Moorland Parish: Reminiscences and Researches in Danby in Cleveland*, 2nd ed. (London).

Attenborough, F.L., ed. 1922. *The Laws of the Earliest English Kings* (Cambridge).

Bailey, Richard N. 1978. 'The Chronology of Viking Age Sculpture in Northumbria', in Lang 1978a, 173-88.

— 1980. *Viking Age Sculpture in Northern England* (London).

— 1981. 'The Hammer and the Cross', in Roesdahl et al 1981, 83-94.

— 1985. 'Aspects of Viking-Age Sculpture in Cumbria', in Baldwin and Whyte 1985, 53-63.

— 1996. *England's Earliest Sculptors*, Publications of the Dictionary of Old English 5 (Toronto).

— 2010. *Cheshire and Lancashire,* Corpus of Anglo-Saxon Stone Sculpture 9 (Oxford).

Bailey, Richard N., and Rosemary Cramp. 1988. *Cumberland, Westmorland and Lancashire North-of-the-Sands,* Corpus of Anglo-Saxon Stone Sculpture 2 (Oxford).

Baker, Peter S., ed. 2000. *MS F,* The Anglo-Saxon Chronicle: A Collaborative Edition 8 (Cambridge).

Baldwin, John R., and Ian D. Whyte, eds. 1985. *The Scandinavians in Cumbria* (Edinburgh).

Banham, Debby. 2009. 'Race and Tillage: Scandinavian Influence on Anglo-Saxon Agriculture?', in Matti Kilpiö et al (eds), *Anglo-Saxons and the North: Essays Reflecting the Theme of the 10th Meeting of the International Society of Anglo-Saxonists in Helsinki, August 2001,* Medieval and Renaissance Texts and Studies 364 (Tempe), 165-91.

Barker, Nicolas, ed. 1986. *The York Gospels: A Facsimile with Introductory Essays* (London).

Barlow, Frank. 1963. *The English Church 1000-1066: A Constitutional History* (London).

— ed. 1992. *The Life of King Edward who Rests at Westminster,* 2nd ed. (Oxford).

— 2003. *The Godwins: The Rise and Fall of a Noble Dynasty* (London).

Barnes, Michael P. 1993. 'Norse in the British Isles', in Faulkes and Perkins 1993, 65-84.

— 2012. *Runes: A Handbook* (Woodbridge).

Barnes, Michael. P., and R.I. Page. 2006. *The Scandinavian Runic Inscriptions of Britain,* Runrön 19 (Uppsala).

Barnwell, P.S., and Brian K. Roberts, eds. 2011. *Britons, Saxons, and Scandinavians: The Historical Geography of Glanville R.J. Jones,* Medieval Countryside 7 (Turnhout).

Barrett, James H. 2008. 'What caused the Viking Age?', *Antiquity* 82, 671-85.

Barrett, James H., Alison M. Locker, and Callum M. Roberts. 2004. '"Dark Age Economics" Revisited: the English fish bone evidence AD 600-1600', *Antiquity* 78, 618-36.

Barrow, Julia. 2000. 'Survival and Mutation: Ecclesiastical Institutions in the Danelaw in the Ninth and Tenth Centuries', in Hadley and Richards 2000, 155-76.

— 2004. 'Oscytel [Oskytel] (*d.* 971)', in Matthew and Harrison 2004, 42, 41-42.

Bartlett, Robert. 1994. 'Symbolic Meanings of Hair in the Middle Ages', *Transactions of the Royal Historical Society* 6th Series 4, 43-60.

Bately, Janet M., ed. 1986. *MS A,* The Anglo-Saxon Chronicle: A Collaborative Edition 3 (Cambridge).

Bates, David, ed. 1998. *Regesta Regum Anglo-Normannorum: The Acta of William I (1066-1087)* (Oxford).

Baxter, Stephen. 2004. 'Archbishop Wulfstan and the Administration of God's Property', in Townend 2004, 161-205.

— 2007a. *The Earls of Mercia: Lordship and Power in Late Anglo-Saxon England* (Oxford).

— 2007b. 'MS C of the Anglo-Saxon Chronicle and the Politics of Mid-Eleventh-Century England', *English Historical Review* 122, 1189-1227.

— 2011. 'Lordship and Labour', in Julia Crick and Elisabeth van Houts (eds), *A Social History of England 900-1200* (Cambridge), 98-114.

Beaven, Murray L.R. 1918. 'King Edmund I and the Danes of York', *English Historical Review* 33, 1-9.

Bessinger, Jess B., Jr, and Robert P. Creed, eds. 1965. *Franciplegius: Medieval and Linguistic Studies in Honor of Francis Peabody Magoun, Jr* (New York).

Besteman, Jan. 2005. 'Vikings and Frisia from an Archaeological Perspective', in Jørgen Højgaard Jørgensen and Hans Frede Nielsen (eds), *Beretning fra Fireogtyvende Tværfaglige Vikingesymposium* (Aarhus), 17-36.

Biddle, Martin, and Birthe Kjølbye-Biddle. 2001. 'Repton and the 'Great Heathen Army', 873-4', in Graham-Campbell et al 2001, 45-96.

Bill, Jan. 2008. 'Viking Ships and the Sea', in Brink 2008a, 170-80.

Binns, A.L. 1956. *Tenth Century Carvings from Yorkshire and the Jellinge Style*, Universitetet i Bergen Årbok 1956, Historisk-antikvarisk rekke 2 (Bergen).

— 1963. *The Viking Century in East Yorkshire*, East Yorkshire Local History Series 15 (York).

— 1965. 'The York Viking Kingdom: Relations between Old English and Old Norse Culture', in Small 1965, 179-89.

— 1966. *East Yorkshire in the Sagas*, East Yorkshire Local History Series 22 (York).

Björkman, Erik. 1900-02. *Scandinavian Loan-Words in Middle English*, Studien zur englischen Philologie 7 (Halle).

Blackburn, M.A.S., ed. 1986. *Anglo-Saxon Monetary History: Essays in Memory of Michael Dolley* (Leicester).

— 1989. 'The Ashdon (Essex) Hoard and the Currency of the Southern Danelaw in the Late Ninth Century', *British Numismatic Journal* 59, 13-38 (reprinted in Blackburn 2011, no. VIII).

— 2003. ''Productive' Sites and the Pattern of Coin Loss in England, 600-1180', in Pestell and Ulmschneider 2003, 20-36.

— 2004. 'The Coinage of Scandinavian York', in Hall et al 2004, 325-49 (reprinted in Blackburn 2011, no. XII).

— 2007. 'Crosses and Conversion: The Iconography of the Coinage of Viking York ca. 900', in Karen Louise Jolly, Catherine E. Karkov, and Sarah Larratt Keefer (eds), *Cross and Culture in Anglo-Saxon England: Studies in Honor of George Hardin Brown*, Medieval European Studies 9 (Morgantown), 172-200 (reprinted in Blackburn 2011, no. XIII).

— 2009. 'Currency under the Vikings. Part 5: The Scandinavian Achievement and Legacy', *British Numismatic Journal* 79, 43-71 (reprinted in Blackburn 2011, no. V).

— 2011. *Viking Coinage and Currency in the British Isles*, British Numismatic Society Special Publication 7 (London).

Blackburn, M.A.S., and M.J. Bonser. 1990. 'A Viking-Age Silver Ingot from Near Easingwold, Yorks', *Medieval Archaeology* 34, 149-50.

Blackburn, M.A.S., and H.E. Pagan. 1986. 'A Revised Check-List of Coin Hoards from the British Isles c. 500-1100', in Blackburn 1986, 291-313,

— 2002. 'The St Edmund Coinage in the Light of a Parcel from a Hoard of St Edmund Pennies', *British Numismatic Journal* 72, 1-14 (reprinted in Blackburn 2011, No. XI).

Blair, John. 1994. *Anglo-Saxon Oxfordshire* (Stroud).

— 2005. *The Church in Anglo-Saxon Society* (Oxford).

— 2010. 'The Kirkdale Dedication Inscription and its Latin Models: *Romanitas* in Late Anglo-Saxon Yorkshire', in Alaric Hall et al (eds), *Interfaces Between Language and Culture in Medieval England: A Festschrift for Matti Kilpiö* (Leiden), 139-45.

Blair, Peter Hunter. 1939. 'Symeon's History of the Kings', *Archaeologia Æliana* 4th Series 16 (1939), 87-100 (reprinted in Blair 1984, no. II).

— 1948. 'The Northumbrians and their Southern Frontier', *Archaeologia Æliana* 4th Series 26, 98-126 (reprinted in Blair 1984, no. IV).

—1949. 'The Boundary Between Bernicia and Deira', *Archaeologia Æliana* 4th Series 27, 46-59 (reprinted in Blair 1984, no. V),

— 1963. 'Some Observations on the 'Historia Regum' Attributed to Symeon of Durham', in N.K. Chadwick (ed.), *Celt and Saxon: Studies in the Early British Border* (Cambridge), 63-118 (reprinted in Blair 1984, no. IX).

— 1984. *Anglo-Saxon Northumbria*, ed. Michael Lapidge and Peter Hunter Blair (London).

Blunt, C.E. 1985. 'Northumbrian Coins in the Name of Alwaldus', *British Numismatic Journal* 55, 192-94.

Blunt, C.E., and R.H.M. Dolley. 1959. 'The Hoard Evidence for the Coins of Alfred', *British Numismatic Journal* 29, 220-47.

Blunt, C.E., and B.H.I.H. Stewart. 1983. 'The Coinage of Regnald I of York and the Bossall Hoard', *Numismatic Chronicle* 143, 146-63.

Blunt, C.E., B.H.I.H. Stewart, and C.S.S. Lyon. 1989. *Coinage in Tenth-Century England: From Edward the Elder to Edgar's Reform* (Oxford).

Bolton, Timothy. 2007a. 'Ælfgifu of Northampton: Cnut the Great's 'Other Woman'', *Nottingham Medieval Studies* 51, 247-68.

— 2007b. 'Was the Family of Earl Siward and Earl Waltheof a Lost Line of the Ancestors of the Danish Royal Family?', *Nottingham Medieval Studies* 51, 41-71.

— 2009. *The Empire of Cnut the Great: Conquest and the Consolidation of Power in Northern Europe in the Early Eleventh Century*, Northern World 40 (Leiden).

Bonner, Gerald, David Rollason, and Clare Stancliffe, eds. 1989. *St Cuthbert, His Cult and His Community to AD 1200* (Woodbridge).

Booth, James. 1997. 'Northumbrian Coinage and the Productive Site at South Newbald', *Yorkshire Numismatist* 3, 15-38.

Bourne, Jill. 2012. 'Kingston – the place-name and its contexts', in Jones and Semple 2012, 260-83.

Bowden, Georgina R., et al. 2008. 'Excavating Past Population Structures by Surname-Based Sampling: the Genetic Legacy of the Vikings in Northwest England', *Molecular Biology and Evolution* 25, 301-09.

Bredehoft, Thomas A. 2011. '*The Battle of Brunanburh* in Old English Studies', in Livingston 2011a, 285-94.

Breeze, Andrew. 1997. 'The *Anglo-Saxon Chronicle* for 949 and Olaf Cuaran', *Notes and Queries* New Series 44, 160-61.

— 1998. 'The Irish Nickname of Sitric Caoch (d. 927) of York', *Saga-Book of the Viking Society* 25, 86-87.

Brink, Stefan. 2005. '*Verba Volant, Scripta Manent?* Aspects of Early Scandinavian Oral Society', in Hermann 2005, 77-135.

— 2007. 'How Uniform Was the Old Norse Religion?', in Judy Quinn, Kate Heslop, and Tarrin Wills (eds), *Learning and Understanding in the Old Norse World: Essays in Honour of Margaret Clunies Ross*, Medieval Texts and Cultures of Northern Europe 18 (Turnhout), 105-36.

— ed. 2008a. *The Viking World* (London).

— 2008b. 'Who were the Vikings?', in Brink 2008a, 4-7.

Brooks, F.W. 1956. *The Battle of Stamford Bridge*, East Yorkshire Local History Series 6 (York).

Brooks, Nicholas. 1971. 'The Development of Military Obligations in Eighth- and Ninth-Century England', in Clemoes and Hughes 1971, 69-84.

— 1979. 'England in the Ninth Century: The Crucible of Defeat', *Transactions of the Royal Historical Society* 5th Series 29, 1-20.

— 1984. *The Early History of the Church of Canterbury: Christ Church from 597 to 1066* (London).

— 1986. *History and Myth, Forgery and Truth*, Inaugural Lecture (Birmingham).

— 1999. *Bede and the English*, Jarrow Lecture (Jarrow).

— 2004. 'Oswald [St Oswald] (*d.* 992)', in Matthew and Harrison 2004, 42, 79-84.

— 2010. 'Why is the Anglo-Saxon Chronicle About Kings?', *Anglo-Saxon England* 39, 43-70.

Brooks, Nicholas, and Catherine Cubitt, eds. 1996. *St Oswald of Worcester: Life and Influence* (London).

Brooks, Nicholas, and James Graham-Campbell. 1986. 'Reflections on the Viking-Age Silver Hoard from Croydon, Surrey', in Blackburn 1986, 91-110.

Brooks, Nicholas, and S.E. Kelly, eds. 2013. *Charters of Christ Church Canterbury*, 2 vols, Anglo-Saxon Charters 17-18 (Oxford).

Buckland, Paul C. 2010. 'Ragnarök and the Stones of York', in Sheehan and Ó Corráin 2010, 47-59.

Budd, Paul, et al. 2004. 'Investigating Population Movement by Stable Isotope Analysis: a report from Britain', *Antiquity* 78, 127-41.

Bullough, D.A. 1993. 'What has Ingeld to do with Lindisfarne?', *Anglo-Saxon England* 22, 95-125.

Burton, Janet. 1999. *The Monastic Order in Yorkshire, 1069-1215*, Cambridge Studies in Medieval Life and Thought 4th Series 40 (Cambridge).

Byock, Jesse. 2001. *Viking Age Iceland* (Harmondsworth).

— 2002. 'The Icelandic Althing: Dawn of Parliamentary Democracy', in J.M. Fladmark (ed.), *Heritage and Identity: Shaping the Nations of the North* (Shaftesbury), 1-18.

Cambridge, Eric. 1995. 'Archaeology and the Cult of St Oswald in Pre-Conquest Northumbria', in Clare Stancliffe and Eric Cambridge (eds), *Oswald: Northumbrian King to European Saint* (Stamford), 128-63.

Cameron, Esther, and Quita Mould. 2004. 'Saxon Shoes, Viking Sheaths? Cultural Identity in Anglo-Scandinavian York', in Hines, Lane, and Redknap 2004, 457-66.

260

Cameron, Kenneth. 1965. *Scandinavian Settlement in the Territory of the Five Boroughs: The Place-Name Evidence*, Inaugural Lecture (Nottingham) (reprinted in Cameron 1975).

— 1970. 'Scandinavian Settlement in the Territory of the Five Boroughs: the place-name evidence, part II, place-names in thorp', *Mediaeval Scandinavia* 3, 35-49 (reprinted in Cameron 1975).

— 1971. Scandinavian Settlement in the Territory of the Five Boroughs: the place-name evidence, part III, the Grimston-hybrids', in Clemoes and Hughes 1971, 147-63 (reprinted in Cameron 1975).

— ed. 1975. *Place-Name Evidence for the Anglo-Saxon Invasion and Scandinavian Settlements* (Nottingham).

— 1996a. *English Place Names*, new ed. (London).

— 1996b. 'The Scandinavian Element in Minor Names and Field-Names in North-East Lincolnshire', *Nomina* 19, 5-27.

Campbell, Alistair, ed. 1938. *The Battle of Brunanburh* (London).

— 1942. 'Two Notes on the Norse Kingdoms in Northumbria', *English Historical Review* 57, 85-97.

— ed. 1962. *The Chronicle of Æthelweard* (London).

— ed. 1967. *Æthelwulf: De Abbatibus* (Oxford).

Campbell, James, ed. 1982. *The Anglo-Saxons* (London).

— 1994. 'The Late Anglo-Saxon State: A Maximum View', *Proceedings of the British Academy* 87, 39-65 (reprinted in Campbell 2000, no. 1).

— 1995. 'The United Kingdom of England: The Anglo-Saxon Achievement', in Alexander Grant and K.J. Stringer (eds), *The Making of English History* (London), 31-47 (reprinted in Campbell 2000, no. 2).

— 2000. *The Anglo-Saxon State* (Hambledon).

— 2001a. 'What is Not Known about the Reign of Edward the Elder', in Higham and Hill 2001, 12-24.

— 2001b. 'Power and Authority 600-1300', in D.M. Palliser (ed.), *The Cambridge Urban History of Britain: Volume I 600-1540* (Cambridge), 51-78.

Capelli, Cristian, et al. 2003. 'A Y Chromosome Census of the British Isles', *Current Biology* 13, 979-84.

Carroll, Jayne. 2007. 'Concepts of Power in Anglo-Scandinavian Verse', in Brenda Bolton and Christine Meek (eds), *Aspects of Power and Authority in the Middle Ages*, International Medieval Research 14 (Turnhout), 217-33.

Carroll, Jayne, and David N. Parsons, eds. 2013. *Perceptions of Place: Twenty-First-Century Interpretations of English Place-Name Studies* (Nottingham).

Carver, Martin. 2001. 'Why That? Why There? Why Then? The Politics of Early Medieval Monumentality', in Helena Hamerow and Arthur MacGregor (eds), *Image and Power in the Archaeology of Early Medieval Britain: Essays in honour of Rosemary Cramp* (Oxford), 1-22.

— ed. 2004. *The Cross Goes North: Processes of Conversion in Northern Europe, AD 300-1300* (York).

— 2011. 'Intellectual Communities in Early Northumbria', in Petts and Turner 2011, 185-206.

Cavill, Paul. 2008. 'The Site of the Battle of *Brunanburh*: manuscripts and maps, grammar and geography', in Padel and Parsons 2008, 303-19.

— 2011. 'The Place-Name Debate', in Livingston 2011a, 327-49.

Cavill, Paul, Stephen E. Harding, and Judith Jesch. 2000. *Wirral and its Viking Heritage*, English Place-Name Society Popular Series 2 (Nottingham).

Chadwick, H. Munro. 1905. *Studies on Anglo-Saxon Institutions* (Cambridge).

Chase, Colin, ed. 1981. *The Dating of Beowulf* (Toronto).

Cheeseman, C.E.A. 2004. 'Taylor, Isaac (1829-1901)', in Matthew and Harrison 2004, 53, 913-14.

Chibnall, Marjorie, ed. 1969. *The Ecclesiastical History of Orderic Vitalis: Volume II* (Oxford).

Clark, Cecily. 1987. ' *Willelmus Rex?* vel alius *Willelmus?*', *Nomina* 11, 7-33.

Clark, Felicity H. 2011. 'Thinking about Western Northumbria', in Petts and Turner 2011, 113-28.

Clarke, Howard B., Máire Ní Mhaonaigh, and Raghnall Ó Floinn, eds. 1998. *Ireland and Scandinavia in the Early Viking Age* (Dublin).

Clarke, Peter A. 1994. *The English Nobility under Edward the Confessor* (Oxford).

Clayton, Mary. 2002. 'An Edition of Ælfric's *Letter to Brother Edward* ', in Elaine Treharne and Susan Rosser (eds), *Early Medieval English Texts and Interpretations: Studies Presented to Donald G. Scragg*, Medieval and Renaissance Texts and Studies 252 (Tempe), 263-83.

Clemoes, Peter, and Kathleen Hughes, eds. 1971. *England Before the Conquest: Studies in Primary Sources Presented to Dorothy Whitelock* (Cambridge).

Clover, Carol J. 1988. 'The Politics of Scarcity: Notes on the Sex Ratio in Early Scandinavia', *Scandinavian Studies* 60, 147-88.

Clunies Ross, Margaret. 1998. *The Norse Muse in Britain 1750-1820* (Trieste).

Coatsworth, Elizabeth. 2008. *Western Yorkshire*, Corpus of Anglo-Saxon Stone Sculpture 8 (Oxford).

Coggins, Denis. 2004. 'Simy Folds: Twenty Years On', in Hines, Lane and Redknap 2004, 325-34.

Coggins, Dennis, K.J. Fairless, and C.E. Batey. 1983. 'Simy Folds: An Early Medieval Settlement Site in Upper Teesdale, Co. Durham', *Medieval Archaeology* 27, 1-26.

Collingwood, W.G. 1907. 'Anglian and Anglo-Danish Sculpture in the North Riding of Yorkshire', *Yorkshire Archaeological Journal* 19, 267-413.

— 1908. 'Anglian and Anglo-Danish Sculpture in York', *Yorkshire Archaeological Journal* 20, 149-213.

— 1911. 'Anglian and Anglo-Danish Sculpture in the East Riding', *Yorkshire Archaeological Journal* 21, 254-302.

— 1912. 'Anglo-Saxon Sculptured Stones', in Page 1912, 109-31.

— 1914. 'The Early Crosses of Leeds', in *Misclllanea*, Publications of the Thoresby Society 22 (Leeds), 269-338.

— 1915. 'Anglian and Anglo-Danish Sculpture in the West Riding', *Yorkshire Archaeological Journal* 23, 129-299.

— 1926. 'The Dispersion of the Wheel-Cross', *Yorkshire Archaeological Journal* 28, 322-31.

— 1927. *Northumbrian Crosses of the Pre-Norman Age* (London).

Cooper, Janet M. 1969. 'The List of Ælfric's Festermen in the York Gospels', *Yorkshire Archaeological Journal* 42, 328-32.

— 1970. *The Last Four Anglo-Saxon Archbishops of York*, Borthwick Paper 38 (York).

Coupland, Simon. 1991. 'The Rod of God's Wrath or the People of God's Wrath? The Carolingian Theology of the Viking Invasions', *Journal of Ecclesiastical History* 42, 535-54.

Coxe, Henry O., ed. 1841-42. *Rogeri de Wendover Chronica, sive Flores Historiarum*, 4 vols (London).

Cramp, Rosemary. 1967. *Anglian and Viking York*, Borthwick Paper 33 (York).

— 1982. 'The Viking Image', in Farrell 1982, 8-19.

— 1984. *County Durham and Northumberland*, 2 vols, Corpus of Anglo-Saxon Stone Sculpture 1 (Oxford).

Crawford, Barbara E., ed. 1995. *Scandinavian Settlement in Northern Britain: Thirteen Studies of Place-Names in their Historical Context* (London).

Crook, John. 2004. '"Vir optimus Wlstanus': The Post-Conquest Commemoration of Archbishop Wulfstan of York at Ely Cathedral', in Townend 2004, 501-24.

Crosland, R.W., and R.H. Hayes. 1955. 'Bound Dragon Crosses at Middleton, Pickering', *Yorkshire Archaeological Journal* 38, 453-55.

Cubbin, G.P., ed. 1996. *MS D*, The Anglo-Saxon Chronicle: A Collaborative Edition 6 (Cambridge).

Cubitt, Catherine. 1997. 'The Tenth-Century Benedictine Reform in England', *Early Medieval Europe* 6, 77-94.

Cullen, Paul, Richard Jones, and David N. Parsons. 2011. *Thorps in a Changing Landscape*, Explorations in Local and Regional History 4 (Hatfield).

Curta, Florin. 2011. 'Medieval Archaeology and Ethnicity: Where are We?', *History Compass* 9, 537-48.

Dalton, Paul. 1994. *Conquest, Anarchy and Lordship: Yorkshire, 1066-1154*, Cambridge Studies in Medieval Life and Thought 4th Series 27 (Cambridge).

Dance, Richard. 2003. *Words Derived from Old Norse in Early Middle English: Studies in the Vocabulary of the South-West Midland Texts*, Medieval and Renaissance Texts and Studies 246 (Tempe).

Daniell, Chris. 2001. 'Battle and Trial: weapon injury burials of St Andrew's Church, Fishergate, York', *Medieval Archaeology* 45, 220-26.

Darby, H.C., and I.S. Maxwell. 1962. *The Domesday Geography of Northern England* (Cambridge).

Darlington, R.R., and P. McGurk, eds. 1995. *The Chronicle of John of Worcester: Volume II The Annals from 450 to 1066* (Oxford).

Davidson, Michael R. 2001. 'The (Non) Submission of the Northern Kings in 920', in Higham and Hill 2001, 200-11.

Davis, R.H.C. 1955. 'East Anglia and the Danelaw', *Transactions of the Royal Historical Society* 5th Series 5, 23-39.

Dent, John. 1984. 'Skerne', *Current Archaeology* 91, 251-53.

DeVries, Kelly. 1999. *The Norwegian Invasion of England in 1066* (Woodbridge).

Dickins, Bruce. 1937-45. 'The Cult of S. Olave in the British Isles', *Saga-Book of the Viking Society* 12, 53-80.

Dickinson, Steve. 1985. 'Bryant's Gill, Kentmere: another 'Viking-period' Ribblehead?', in Baldwin and Whyte 1985, 83-88.

Dolley, Michael. 1965. *Viking Coins of the Danelaw and of Dublin* (London).

— 1978. 'The Anglo-Danish and Anglo-Norse coinages of York', in Hall 1978, 26-31.

Downham, Clare. 2003. 'The Chronology of the Last Scandinavian Kings of York, AD 937-954', *Northern History* 40, 25-51.

— 2004. 'Eric Bloodaxe – Axed? The Mystery of the Last Scandinavian King of York', *Mediaeval Scandinavia* 14, 51-77.

— 2007. *Viking Kings of Britain and Ireland: The Dynasty of Ívarr to AD 1014* (Edinburgh).

— 2008. 'Vikings in England', in Brink 2008a, 341-49.

— 2009. '"Hiberno-Norwegians" and "Anglo-Danes": Anachronistic Identities and Viking Age England', *Mediaeval Scandinavia* 19, 139-69.

— 2011. 'Viking Identities in Ireland: it's not all black and white', *Medieval Dublin* 11, 185-201.

— 2012. 'Viking Ethnicities: A Historiographic Overview', *History Compass* 10/1, 1-12.

Dumville, David N. 1979. 'The Ætheling: a study in Anglo-Saxon constitutional history' *Anglo-Saxon England* 8, 1-33.

— 1992. *Wessex and England from Alfred to Edgar: Six Essays on Political, Cultural, and Ecclesiastical Revival* (Woodbridge).

— 1997. *The Churches of North Britain in the First Viking-Age*, Whithorn Lecture 1996 (Whithorn).

— 2004. 'Old Dubliners and New Dubliners in Ireland and Britain: a Viking-Age Story', *Medieval Dublin* 6, 78-93.

— 2008. 'Vikings in Insular Chronicling', in Brink 2008a, 350-67.

Dumville, David N., and Michael Lapidge, eds. 1985. *The Annals of St Neots with Vita Prima Sancti Neoti*, The Anglo-Saxon Chronicle: a Collaborative Edition 17 (Cambridge).

Dunn, Charles W. 1965. 'Havelok and Anlaf Cuaran', in Bessinger and Creed 1965, 244-49.

Durkin, Philip. 2014. *Borrowed Words: A History of Loanwords in English* (Oxford).

Dyer, Christopher. 2003. *Making a Living in the Middle Ages: The People of Britain 850-1520* (London).

Edmonds, Fiona. 2009. 'History and Names', in Graham-Campbell and Philpott 2009, 3-12.

Edwards, B.J.N. 1985. 'Viking Silver Ingots from Bowes Moor, Yorkshire', *Antiquaries Journal* 65, 457-59.

Edwards, Heather. 2004. 'The Saint of Middleham and Giggleswick', *Yorkshire Archaeological Journal* 76, 135-44.

EHD = Whitelock 1955

Einarsson, Bjarni, ed. 1985. *Ágrip af Nóregskonunga Sögum. Fagrskinna – Nóregs Konunga Tal*, Íslenzk Fornrit 29 (Reykjavík).

— 1986. 'De Normannorum Atrocitate, or on the Execution of Royalty by the Aquiline Method', *Saga-Book of the Viking Society* 22, 79-82.

— ed. 2003. *Egils Saga* (London).

Einarsson, Stefán. 1955. 'The Origin of Egill Skallagrímsson's Runhenda', in *Scandinavica et Finno-Ugrica: Studier tillägnade Björn Collinder den 22 juli 1954* (Stockholm), 54-60.

Ekwall, Eilert. 1928. *English River Names* (Oxford).

— 1937-45. 'The Proportion of Scandinavian Settlers in the Danelaw', *Saga-Book of the Viking Society* 12, 19-34.

Erskine, R.W.H., and Ann Williams, eds. 2003. *The Story of Domesday Book*, new ed. (Chichester).

Etchingham, Colmán. 2010. '*Laithlinn*, 'Fair Foreigners' and 'Dark Foreigners': the identity and provenance of Vikings in ninth-century Ireland', in Sheehan and Ó Corráin 2010, 80-88.

Everson, Paul, and David Stocker. 2012. 'Why at Wharram? The foundation of the nucleated settlement', in Wrathmell 2012, 208-20.

Evison, Martin Paul. 2000. 'All in the Genes? Evaluating the Biological Evidence of Contact and Migration', in Hadley and Richards 2000, 277-94.

Faith, Rosamond. 1997. *The English Peasantry and the Growth of Lordship* (London).

Fanning, Thomas. 1994. *Viking Age Ringed Pins from Dublin*, Medieval Dublin Excavations 1962-81, Series B Volume 4 (Dublin).

Farrell, R.T., ed. 1982. *The Vikings* (London).

Farrer, William. 1912. 'Introduction to the Yorkshire Domesday', in Page 1912, 133-89.

— ed. 1914. *Early Yorkshire Charters: Volume I* (Edinburgh).

Faulkes, Anthony, and Richard Perkins, eds. 1993. *Viking Revaluations: Viking Society Centenary Symposium 14-15 May 1992* (London).

Faull, Margaret L. 1981. 'The Late Anglo-Saxon Period (AD 867-1066)', in Faull and Moorhouse 1981, I, 187-202.

— 1984. 'Late Anglo-Saxon Settlement Patterns in Yorkshire', in Margaret L. Faull (ed.), *Studies in Late Anglo-Saxon Settlement* (Oxford), 129-42.

Faull, Margaret L., and Stephen A. Moorhouse, eds. 1981. *West Yorkshire: An Archaeological Survey to AD 1500*, 3 vols (Wakefield).

Faull, Margaret L., and Marie Stinson, eds. 1986. *Domesday Book: Yorkshire*, 2 vols, Domesday Book 30 (Chichester).

Fell, Christine, trans. 1975. *Egils Saga* (London).

— 1986. 'Old English *wicing*: A Question of Semantics', *Proceedings of the British Academy* 72, 295-316.

— 1987. 'Modern English *Viking*', *Leeds Studies in English* New Series 18, 111-23.

Fellows-Jensen, Gillian. 1968. *Scandinavian Personal Names in Lincolnshire and Yorkshire*, Navnestudier udgivet af Institut for Navneforskning 7 (Copenhagen).

— 1972. *Scandinavian Settlement Names in Yorkshire*, Navnestudier udgivet af Institut for Navneforskning 11 (Copenhagen).

— 1973. 'Place-Name Research and Northern History: A Survey', *Northern History* 8, 1-23.

— 1974. 'English Field-Names and the Danish Settlement', in Poul Andersen et al (eds), *Festskrift til Kristian Hald* (Copenhagen), 45-55.

— 1975a. 'The Vikings in England: a review', *Anglo-Saxon England* 4, 181-206.

— 1975b. 'Vikingens forhold til stednavne i Yorkshire [The attitude of the Vikings to English place-names in Yorkshire]', *Selskab for Nordisk Filologi: Årsberetning for 1971-1973* (Copenhagen), 5-12.

— 1977-78. 'A Gaelic-Scandinavian Loan-Word in English Place-Names', *Journal of the English Place-Name Society* 10, 18-25.

— 1980. 'Common Gaelic *áirge*, Old Scandinavian *ærgi* or *erg*?', *Nomina* 4, 67-74.

— 1978a. *Scandinavian Settlement Names in the East Midlands*, Navnestudier udgivet af Institut for Navneforskning 16 (Copenhagen).

— 1978b. 'Place-Names and Settlement in the North Riding of Yorkshire', *Northern History* 14, 19-46.

— 1985a. *Scandinavian Settlement Names in the North-West*, Navnestudier udgivet af Institut for Navneforskning 25 (Copenhagen).

— 1985b. 'Scandinavian Settlement in Cumbria and Dumfriesshire: The Place-Name Evidence', in Baldwin and Whyte 1985, 65-82.

— 1986. 'Danish Lake- and River-Names in England', in Vibeke Dalberg and Gillian Fellows-Jensen (eds), *Mange Bække Små: Til John Kousgård Sørensen på tresårsdagen 6.12.1985* (Copenhagen).

— 1987a. 'York', *Leeds Studies in English* New Series 18, 141-55 (reprinted, in edited form, as 'The Origin and Development of the Name York', in Rollason 1998a, 226-37).

— 1987b. 'To Divide the Danes from the Norwegians: on Scandinavian Settlement in the British Isles', *Nomina* 11, 35-60.

— 1987c. 'The Vikings' Relationship with Christianity in the British Isles: the evidence of place-names containing the element *kirkja*', in James E. Knirk (ed.), *Proceedings of the Tenth Viking Congress, Larkollen, Norway, 1985* (Oslo), 295-307.

— 1989. '*Amounderness* and *Holderness*', in Lena Peterson and Svante Strandberg (eds), *Studia Onomastica: festskrift till Thorsten Andersson 23 den februari 1989* (Stockholm), 87-94.

— 1991. 'Of Danes – and Thanes – and Domesday Book', in Wood and Lund 1991, 107-21.

— 1992. 'Cultic Place-Names: a view from the Danelaw', *NORNA-Rapporter* 48, 265-72.

— 1993. 'Tingwall, Dingwall and Thingwall', *North-Western European Language Evolution* 21/22, 53-67.

— 1994. 'Danish Place-Names and Personal Names in England: the influence of Cnut?', in Rumble 1994, 125-40.

— 1995a. 'Scandinavian Settlement in Yorkshire – through the rear-view mirror', in Crawford 1995, 170-86.

— 1995b. *The Vikings and their Victims: the Verdict of the Names*, Dorothea Coke Memorial Lecture (London).

— 2003. 'In Quest of Lost Danes: the Scandinavian element in English surnames', in Della Hooke and David Postles (eds), *Names, Time and Place: Essays in Memory of Richard McKinley* (Oxford), 41-57.

— 2004. 'The Anglo-Scandinavian Street-Names of York', in Hall et al 2004, 357-71.

— 2008. 'Grimston revisited', in Padel and Parsons 2008, 125-35.

— 2011. 'Light Thrown by Scandinavian Place-Names on the Anglo-Saxon Landscape', in Higham and Ryan 2011, 69-83.

— 2012. 'Grimston and Grimsby: the Danes as re-namers', in Jones and Semple 2012, 352-63.

— 2013. 'The Scandinavian Background to English Place-Names', in Carroll and Parsons 2013, 75-101.

Fidjestøl, Bjarne. 1997. *Selected Papers*, ed. Odd Einar Haugen and Else Mundal, Viking Collection 9 (Odense).

Finlay, Alison, trans. 2004. *Fagrskinna: A Catalogue of the Kings of Norway*, Northern World 7 (Leiden).

Finlay, Alison, and Anthony Faulkes, trans. 2011. *Snorri Sturluson: Heimskringla. Volume I The Beginnings to Óláfr Tryggvason* (London).

Firby, Margaret, and James T. Lang. 1981. 'The Pre-Conquest Sculpture at Stonegrave', *Yorkshire Archaeological Journal* 53, 17-29.

Fjalldal, Magnús. 2005. *Anglo-Saxon England in Icelandic Medieval Texts* (Toronto).

Fleming, Robin. 1991. *Kings and Lords in Conquest England*, Cambridge Studies in Medieval Life and Thought 4th Series 15 (Cambridge).

— 1993. 'Rural Elites and Urban Communities in Late-Saxon England', *Past and Present* 141, 3-37.

— 2001. 'The New Wealth, the New Rich and the New Political Style in Late Anglo-Saxon England', *Anglo-Norman Studies* 23, 1-22.

— 2003. 'Lords and Labour', in Wendy Davies (ed.), *From the Vikings to the Normans* (Oxford), 107-37.

— 2007. 'Acquiring, Flaunting and Destroying Silk in Late Anglo-Saxon England', *Early Medieval Europe* 15, 127-58.

Fletcher, Richard. 1997. *The Conversion of Europe: From Paganism to Christianity 371-1386 AD* (London).

— 2002. *Bloodfeud: Murder and Revenge in Anglo-Saxon England* (London).

Foot, Sarah. 1991. 'Violence Against Christians: The Vikings and the Church in Ninth-Century England', *Medieval History* 1.3, 3-16.

— 1996. 'The Making of *Angelcynn*: English Identity before the Norman Conquest', *Transactions of the Royal Historical Society* 6th Series 6, 25-49.

— 2011. *Æthelstan: The First King of England* (New Haven).

Foote, Peter. 1993. 'Historical Studies: conversion moment and conversion period', in Faulkes and Perkins 1993, 137-44.

Fox, H.S.A. 1989. 'The People of the Wolds in English Settlement History', in Michael Aston, David Austin, and Christopher Dyer (eds), *The Rural Settlements of Medieval England: Studies Dedicated to Maurice Beresford and John Hurst* (Oxford), 77-101.

Foys, Martin K. 2007. *Virtually Anglo-Saxon: Old Media, New Media, and Early Medieval Studies in the Late Age of Print* (Gainesville).

Frank, Roberta. 1981. 'Skaldic Verse and the Date of *Beowulf*', in Chase 1981, 123-39.

— 1984. 'Viking Atrocity and Skaldic Verse: The Rite of the Blood-Eagle', *English Historical Review* 99, 332-43.

Gade, Kari Ellen, ed. 2009. *Poetry from the Kings' Saga 2: From c.1035 to c.1300*, 2 vols, Skaldic Poetry of the Scandinavian Middle Ages 2 (Turnhout).

Gameson, Richard, ed. 2012. *The Cambridge History of the Book in Britain: Volume I c.400-1100* (Cambridge).

Gammeltoft, Peder, and Bent Jørgensen (eds), *Names through the Looking-Glass: Festschrift in Honour of Gillian Fellows-Jensen, July 5th 2006*, Navnestudier udgivet af Afdeling for Navneforskning 39 (Copenhagen, 2006).

Garnett, George. 2005. *Conquered England: Kingship, Succession, and Tenure, 1066-1166* (Oxford).

Garrison, Mary. 2012. 'The Library of Alcuin's York', in Gameson 2012, 633-64.

Garrison, Mary, Janet L. Nelson, and Dominic Tweddle. 2001. *Alcuin and Charlemagne: The Golden Age of York* (York).

Gelling, Margaret. 1984. *Place-Names in the Landscape* (London).

— 1988. *Signposts to the Past: Place-Names and the History of England*, 2nd ed. (Chichester).

— 2004. 'A Regional Review of Place-Names', in Philip Rahtz and Lorna Watts (eds), *The North Manor Area and North-West Enclosure*, Wharram: A Study of Settlement on the Yorkshire Wolds 9 (York), 347-51.

— 2006. 'Anglo-Norse Place-Names on the Yorkshire Wolds', in Gammeltoft and Jørgensen 2006, 85-93.

Gelling, Margaret, and Ann Cole. 2000. *The Landscape of Place-Names* (Stamford).

Gem, Richard. 1988. 'The English Parish Church in the 11th and Early 12th Centuries: A Great Rebuilding?', in John Blair (ed.), *Minsters and Parish Churches: The Local Church in Transition 950-1200* (Oxford), 21-30.

Gittos, Helen. 2005. 'Is There Any Evidence for the Liturgy of Parish Churches in Late Anglo-Saxon England? The Red Book of Darley and the Status of Old English', in Francesca Tinti (ed.), *Pastoral Care in Late Anglo-Saxon England* (Woodbridge), 63-82.

Godman, Peter, ed. 1982. *Alcuin: The Bishops, Kings, and Saints of York* (Oxford).

— ed. 1985. *Poetry of the Carolingian Renaissance* (London).

Goetting, Lauren. 2006. '*Þegn* and *drengr* in the Viking Age', *Scandinavian Studies* 78, 375-403.

Gooch, Megan. 2011. 'Viking Kings, Political Power and Monetisation', in Abramson 2011, 111-20.

Graham-Campbell, James. 1980. *Viking Artefacts: A Select Catalogue* (London).

— 1991. 'Anglo-Scandinavian Equestrian Equipment in Eleventh-Century England', *Anglo-Norman Studies* 14, 77-89.

— ed. 1992a. *Viking Treasure from the North West: The Cuerdale Hoard in its Context*, National Museums and Galleries on Merseyside Occasional Papers 5 (Liverpool).

— 1992b. 'The Cuerdale Hoard: Comparisons and Context', in Graham-Campbell 1992a, 107-15.

— 1993. 'A 'Vital' Yorkshire Viking Hoard Revisited', in Martin Carver (ed.), *In Search of Cult: Archaeological investigations in honour of Philip Rahtz* (Woodbridge), 79-84.

— 1996. 'The Archaeology of Anglian and Anglo-Scandinavian York: progress to publication', *Early Medieval Europe* 5, 71-82.

— 2001. 'The Northern Hoards: from Cuerdale to Bossall/Flaxton', in Higham and Hill 2001, 212-29.

— 2002. 'The Dual Economy of the Danelaw', *British Numismatic Journal* 71, 49-59.

— 2008. 'Two Viking-Age Silver Arm-Rings from Near Selby, North Yorkshire', *Medieval Archaeology* 52, 307-10.

— 2011. *The Cuerdale Hoard and Related Viking-Age Silver and Gold from Britain and Ireland in the British Museum*, British Museum Research Publication 185 (London).

— 2013. *Viking Art* (London).

Graham-Campbell, James, and Robert Philpott, eds. 2009. *The Huxley Viking Hoard: Scandinavian Settlement in the North West* (Liverpool).

Graham-Campbell, James, and Gareth Williams, eds. 2007. *Silver Economy in the Viking Age* (Walnut Creek).

Graham-Campbell, James, Søren M. Sindbæk, and Gareth Williams, eds. 2011. *Silver Economies, Monetisation and Society in Scandinavia, AD 800-1100* (Aarhus).

Graham-Campbell, James, et al, eds. 2001. *Vikings and the Danelaw: Select Papers from the Proceedings of the Thirteenth Viking Congress, Nottingham and York, 21-30 August 1997* (Oxford).

Grant, Alison. 2002. 'A New Approach to the Inversion Compounds of North-West England', *Nomina* 25, 65-90.

Green, Judith A. 1990. *English Sheriffs to 1154*, Public Record Office Handbooks 24 (London).

Gregson, Nicky. 1985. 'The Multiple Estate Model: some critical questions', *Journal of Historical Geography* 11, 339-51.

Grierson, Philip, and Mark Blackburn. 1986. *Medieval European Coinage: Volume I The Early Middle Ages (5th-10th Centuries)* (Cambridge).

Griffiths, David. 2010. *Vikings of the Irish Sea: Conflict and Assimilation AD 790-1050* (Stroud).

Gunnell, Terry, and Annette Lassen, eds. 2013. *The Nordic Apocalypse: Approaches to Völuspá and Nordic Days of Judgement*, Acta Scandinavica 2 (Turnhout).

Hadley, Dawn M. 1996a. 'Multiple Estates and the Origins of the Manorial Structure of the Northern Danelaw', *Journal of Historical Geography* 22, 3-15.

— 1996b. 'Conquest, Colonization and the Church: Ecclesiastical Organization in the Danelaw', *Historical Research* 69, 109-28.

— 1997. '"And they proceeded to plough and to support themselves": the Scandinavian Settlement of England', *Anglo-Norman Studies* 19, 69-96.

— 2000a. *The Northern Danelaw: Its Social Structure, c.800-1100* (London).

— 2000b. '"Cockle amongst the Wheat': The Scandinavian Settlement of England', in William O. Frazer and Andrew Tyrrell (eds), *Social Identity in Early Medieval Britain* (London), 111-35.

— 2000c. 'Burial Practices in the Northern Danelaw, c.650-1100', *Northern History* 36, 199-216.

— 2002a. 'Burial Practices in Northern England in the Later Anglo-Saxon Period', in Lucy and Reynolds 2002, 209-28.

— 2002b. 'Viking and Native: re-thinking identity in the Danelaw', *Early Medieval Europe* 11, 45-70.

— 2006. *The Vikings in England: Settlement, Society and Culture* (Manchester).

— 2008. 'Warriors, Heroes and Companions: Negotiating Masculinity in Viking-Age England', *Anglo-Saxon Studies in Archaeology and History* 15, 270-84.

— 2009a. 'Viking Raids and Conquest', in Stafford 2009, 195-211.

— 2009b. 'Scandinavian Settlement', in Stafford 2009, 212-30.

— 2013. 'Whither the Warrior in Viking-Age Towns?', in Hadley and ten Harkel 2013, 103-18.

Hadley, Dawn M., and Julian D. Richards, eds. 2000. *Cultures in Contact: Scandinavian Settlement in England in the Ninth and Tenth Centuries*, Studies in the Early Middle Ages 2 (Turnhout).

Hadley, Dawn M., and Letty ten Harkel, eds. 2013. *Everyday Life in Viking-Age Towns: Social Approaches to Towns in England and Ireland, c.800-1100* (Oxford).

Hall, Allan, and Harry Kenward. 2004. 'Setting People in their Environment: Plant and Animal Remains from Anglo-Scandinavian York', in Hall et al 2004, 372-426.

Hall, K. Mary. 1993. 'Pre-Conquest Estates in Yorkshire', in Le Patourel, Long, and Pickles 1993, 25-38.

Hall, Richard. 1976. *The Viking Kingdom of York* (York).

— ed. 1978. *Viking Age York and the North*, Council for British Archaeology Research Report 27 (London).

— 1984. *The Viking Dig: The Excavations at York* (London).

— 1991. 'Sources for Pre-Conquest York', in Wood and Lund 1991, 83-94.

— 1994. *Viking Age York* (London).

— 2000. 'Anglo-Scandinavian Attitudes: Archaeological Ambiguities in Late Ninth- to Mid-Eleventh-Century York', in Hadley and Richards 2000, 311-24.

— 2001. 'Anglo-Saxon and Viking-Age York', in Patrick Nuttgens (ed.), *The History of York, Yorkshire: From Earliest Times to the Year 2000* (Pickering), 39-67.

— 2003. 'Yorkshire AD 700-1066', in T.G. Manby, Stephen A. Moorhouse, and Patrick Ottaway (eds), *The Archaeology of Yorkshire: an assessment at the beginning of the 21st century*, Yorkshire Archaeological Society Occasional Paper 3 (Leeds), 171-80.

— 2004a. 'A Historiographical Introduction to Anglo-Scandinavian York', in Hall et al 2004, 293-304.

— 2004b. 'The Topography of Anglo-Scandinavian York', in Hall et al 2004, 488-97.

— 2004c. '*Jórvík*: A Viking-Age City', in Hines, Lane, and Redknap 2004, 283-95

— 2011. 'Recent Research into Early Medieval York and its Hinterland', in Petts and Turner 2011, 71-84.

— 2014. *Anglo-Scandinavian Occupation at 16-22 Coppergate: Defining a Townscape*, Archaeology of York 8/5 (York).

Hall, Richard, and Mark Whyman. 1996. 'Settlement and Monasticism at Ripon, North Yorkshire, from the 7th to 11th Centuries AD', *Medieval Archaeology* 40, 62-150.

Hall, Richard, Toby Kendall, and Colin Briden. 2008. 'St Helen's Church, Skipwith, North Yorkshire', *Archaeological Journal* 165, 399-470.

Hall, Richard, et al. 2004. *Aspects of Anglo-Scandinavian York*, Archaeology of York 8/4 (York).

— 2008. 'The Medieval Cemetery at Riccall Landing: A Reappraisal', *Yorkshire Archaeological Journal* 80, 55-92.

Halloran, Kevin. 2005. 'The Brunanburh Campaign: A Reappraisal', *Scottish Historical Review* 84, 133-48.

— 2013. 'Anlaf Guthfrithson at York: A Non-Existent Kingship?', *Northern History* 50, 180-85.

Halsall, Guy. 2000. 'The Viking Presence in England? The Burial Evidence Reconsidered', in Hadley and Richards 2000, 259-76.

— 2003. *Warfare and Society in the Barbarian West, 450-900* (London).

Haraldsson, Sveinn. 1994. '"The North Begins Inside': Auden, Ancestry and Iceland', in Andrew Wawn (ed.), *Northern Antiquity: The Post-Medieval Reception of Edda and Saga* (Enfield Lock), 255-84.

Harmer, Florence E., ed. 1989. *Anglo-Saxon Writs*, 2nd ed. (Stamford).

Hart, Cyril. 1975. *The Early Charters of Northern England and the North Midlands* (Leicester).

— 1992. *The Danelaw* (London).

Hawkes, Jane. 1993. 'Mary and the Cycle of Resurrection: the Iconography of the Hovingham Panel', in Spearman and Higgitt 1993, 254-60.

— 1996. *The Golden Age of Northumbria* (Morpeth).

Heather, Peter. 2009. *Empires and Barbarians* (London).

Hedeager, Lotte. 2008. 'Scandinavia before the Viking Age', in Brink 2008a, 11-22.

Helgason, Agnar, et al. 2000a. 'mtDNA and the Origin of the Icelanders: Deciphering Signals of Recent Population History', *American Journal of Human Genetics* 66, 999-1016.

— 2000b. 'Estimating Scandinavian and Gaelic Ancestry in the Male Settlers of Iceland', *American Journal of Human Genetics* 67, 697-717.

— 2001. 'mtDNA and the Islands of the North Atlantic: Estimating the Proportions of Norse and Celtic Ancestry', *American Journal of Human Genetics* 68, 723-37.

Helle, Knut, ed. 2003. *The Cambridge History of Scandinavia: Volume I Prehistory to 1520* (Cambridge).

Hermann, Pernille, ed. 2005. *Literacy in Medieval and Early Modern Scandinavian Culture*, Viking Collection 16 (Odense).

Heslop, T.A. 2004. 'Art and the Man: Archbishop Wulfstan and the York Gospelbook', in Townend 2004, 279-308.

Hey, David. 2000. *Family Names and Family History* (London).

Higham, Mary. 1977-78. 'The "erg" Place-Names of Northern England', *Journal of the English Place-Name Society* 10, 7-17.

Higham, Nicholas J. 1992. 'Northumbria, Mercia and the Irish Sea Norse, 893-926', in Graham-Campbell 1992a, 21-30.

— 1993. *The Kingdom of Northumbria, AD 350-1100* (Stroud).

— 1999. 'Five Boroughs', in Lapidge et al 1999, 186.

— 2006. 'Northumbria's Southern Frontier: a review', *Early Medieval Europe* 14, 391-417.

— ed. 2007. *Britons in Anglo-Saxon England* (Woodbridge).

271

Higham, Nicholas J., and David Hill, eds. 2001. *Edward the Elder 899-924* (London).

Higham, Nicholas J., and Martin J. Ryan, eds. 2011. *Place-Names, Language and the Anglo-Saxon Landscape* (Woodbridge).

Hill, David. 1981. *An Atlas of Anglo-Saxon England* (Toronto).

Hill, Joyce. 2004. 'Archbishop Wulfstan: Reformer?', in Townend 2004, 309-24.

Hines, John. 1984. *The Scandinavian Character of Anglian England in the Pre-Viking Period*, British Archaeological Reports British Series 124 (Oxford).

— 1991. 'Scandinavian English: A Creole in Context', in P. Sture Ureland and George Broderick (eds), *Language Contact in the British Isles* (Tübingen), 403-27.

— 1995. 'Egill's *Höfuðlausn* in Time and Place', *Saga-Book of the Viking Society* 24, 83-104.

Hines, John, Alan Lane, and Mark Redknap, eds. 2004. *Land, Sea and Home: Proceedings of a Conference on Viking-period Settlement, at Cardiff, July 2001*, Society for Medieval Archaeology Monograph 20 (Leeds).

Holman, Katherine. 1996. *Scandinavian Runic Inscriptions in the British Isles: Their Historical Context*, Senter for Middelalderstudier Skrifter 4 (Trondheim).

— 2001. 'Defining the Danelaw', in Graham-Campbell et al 2001, 1-11.

— 2007. *The Northern Conquest: Vikings in Britain and Ireland* (Oxford).

Holt, J.C., ed. 1987a. *Domesday Studies* (Woodbridge).

— 1987b. '1086', in Holt 1987a, 41-64.

Hooper, Nicholas. 1985. 'Edgar the Ætheling: Anglo-Saxon prince, rebel and crusader', *Anglo-Saxon England* 14, 197-214.

Horovitz, David. 2010. *Notes and Materials on the Battle of Tettenhall 910 A.D., and Other Researches* (Stafford).

Hough, Carole. 2002. 'Women in English Place-Names', in Hough and Lowe 2002, 41-106.

Hough, Carole, and Kathryn A. Lowe, eds. 2002. *'Lastworda Betst': Essays in Memory of Christine E. Fell* (Donington).

Hudson, Benjamin. 2005. *Viking Pirates and Christian Princes: Dynasty, Religion, and Empire in the North Atlantic* (New York).

Innes, Matthew. 2000. 'Danelaw Identities: Ethnicity, Regionalism, and Political Allegiance', in Hadley and Richards 2000, 65-88.

Insley, John. 1994. *Scandinavian Personal Names in Norfolk: A Survey Based on Medieval Records and Place-Names*, Acta Academiae Regiae Gustavi Adolphi 62 (Uppsala).

Irvine, Susan, ed. 2004. *MS E*, The Anglo-Saxon Chronicle: A Collaborative Edition 7 (Cambridge).

Janzén, Assar. 1960. 'Are there so-called Inversion Compounds in Yorkshire Place-Names?', *Namn och Bygd* 48, 43-81.

Jesch, Judith. 1991. *Women in the Viking Age* (Woodbridge).

— 2001a. *Ships and Men in the Late Viking Age: The Vocabulary of Runic Inscriptions and Skaldic Verse* (Woodbridge).

— 2001b. 'Skaldic Verse in Scandinavian England', in Graham-Campbell et al 2001, 313-25.

— 2002. 'Old Norse *víkingr*: A Question of Contexts', in Hough and Lowe 2002, 107-21.

— 2004. 'Scandinavians and 'Cultural Paganism' in Late Anglo-Saxon England', in Paul Cavill (ed.), *The Christian Tradition in Anglo-Saxon England: Approaches to Current Scholarship and Teaching* (Woodbridge), 55-68.

— 2005. 'Skaldic Verse, a Case of Literacy *Avant la Lettre?*', in Hermann 2005, 187-210.

— 2008. 'Scandinavian Women's Names in English Place-Names', in Padel and Parsons 2008, 154-62.

— 2011. 'The Norse Gods in England and the Isle of Man', in Daniel Anlezark (ed.), *Myths, Legends, and Heroes: Essays on Old Norse and Old English Literature in Honour of John McKinnell* (Toronto), 11-24.

Jespersen, Otto. 1956. *Growth and Structure of the English Language*, 9th ed. (Oxford).

John, Eric. 1996. *Reassessing Anglo-Saxon England* (Manchester).

Johnson, Charles, ed. 1990. *Hugh the Chanter: The History of the Church of York 1066-1127*, rev. ed., rev. Martin Brett, C.N.L. Brooke, and Michael Winterbottom (Oxford).

Johnson South, Ted, ed. 2002. *Historia de Sancto Cuthberto: A History of Saint Cuthbert and a Record of His Patrimony*, Anglo-Saxon Texts 3 (Cambridge).

Jones, Charles. 2006. *The Forgotten Battle of 1066: Fulford* (Stroud).

— 2011. *Finding Fulford: The Search for the First Battle of 1066* (London).

Jones, Glanville R.J. 1965. 'Early Territorial Organization in Northern England and its Bearing on the Scandinavian Settlement', in Small 1965, 67-84.

— 1992. 'The Multiple Estates of (Holy) Islandshire, Hovingham and Kirkby Moorside', in *Rural Settlement: Pre-printed Papers Volume 8* (York), 79-84.

Jones, Gwyn. 1952. 'Egill Skallagrímsson in England', *Proceedings of the British Academy* 38, 127-44.

Jones, Richard. 2013. 'Settlement Archaeology and Place-Names', in Carroll and Parsons 2013, 181-207.

Jones, Richard, and Sarah Semple, eds. 2012. *Sense of Place in Anglo-Saxon England* (Donington).

Jónsson, Guðni, ed. 1954. *Edda Snorra Sturlusonar* (Reykjavík).

Jorgensen, Alice. 2010. 'Introduction: Reading the Anglo-Saxon Chronicle', in Alice Jorgensen (ed.), *Reading the Anglo-Saxon Chronicle: Language, Literature, History*, Studies in the Early Middle Ages 23 (Turnhout), 1-28.

Jost, Karl, ed. 1959. *Die 'Institutes of Polity, Civil and Ecclesiastical': ein Werk Erzbischof Wulfstans von York*, Schweizer anglistische Arbeiten 47 (Bern).

Kapelle, William E. 1979. *The Norman Conquest of the North: The Region and Its Transformation, 1000-1135* (London).

Karlsson, Gunnar. 2000. *Iceland's 1100 Years: The History of a Marginal Society* (London).

Karras, Ruth Mazo. 1988. *Slavery and Society in Medieval Scandinavia* (New Haven).

Keen, Laurence. 1993. 'Pre-Conquest Glazed Relief Tiles from All Saints Church, Pavement, York', *Journal of the British Archaeological Association* 146, 67-86.

Kellett, Arnold, and Ian Dewhirst, eds. 1997. *A Century of Yorkshire Dialect: Selections from the Transactions of the Yorkshire Dialect Society* (Otley).

Kelly, S.E., ed. 2009. *Charters of Peterborough Abbey*, Anglo-Saxon Charters 14 (Oxford).

Kemble, J.M., ed. 1839-48. *Codex Diplomaticus Ævi Saxonici*, 6 vols (London).

Kemp, Richard L. 1996. *Anglian Settlement at 46-54 Fishergate*, Archaeology of York 7/1 (York).

Ker, N.R. 1957. *Catalogue of Manuscripts Containing Anglo-Saxon* (Oxford).

— 1971. 'The Handwriting of Archbishop Wulfstan', in Clemoes and Hughes 1971, 315-31.

Kershaw, Jane F. 2008. 'The Distribution of the "Winchester" Style in Late Saxon England: Metalwork Finds from the Danelaw', *Anglo-Saxon Studies in Archaeology and History* 15, 254-69.

— 2009. 'Culture and Gender in the Danelaw: Scandinavian and Anglo-Scandinavian Brooches', *Viking and Medieval Scandinavia* 5, 295-325.

— 2013. *Viking Identities: Scandinavian Jewellery in England* (Oxford) (and database: http://dx.doi.org/10.5284/1012709).

Keynes, Simon. 1978. 'The Declining Reputation of King Æthelred the Unready', in David Hill (ed.), *Ethelred the Unready: Papers from the Millenary Conference*, British Archaeological Reports British Series 59 (Oxford), 227-53.

— 1980. *The Diplomas of King Æthelred 'the Unready': A Study in their Use as Historical Evidence*, Cambridge Studies in Medieval Life and Thought 3rd Series 13 (Cambridge).

— 1986. 'The Additions in Old English', in Barker 1986, 81-99.

— 1991. 'The Historical Context of the Battle of Maldon', in Donald Scragg (ed.), *The Battle of Maldon AD 991* (Oxford), 81-113.

— 1994. 'Cnut's Earls', in Rumble 1994, 43-88.

— 1997. 'The Vikings in England, c.790-1016', in Peter Sawyer (ed.), *The Oxford Illustrated History of the Vikings* (Oxford), 48-82.

— 1999a. 'Shire', in Lapidge et al 1999, 420-22.

— 1999b. 'Wulfstan I', in Lapidge et al 1999, 492-93.

— 2007. 'The Massacre of St Brice's Day (13 November 1002)', in Niels Lund (ed.), *Beretning fra Seksogtyvende Tværfaglige Vikingesymposium* (Aarhus), 32-67.

— 2012. 'Manuscripts of the *Anglo-Saxon Chronicle*', in Gameson 2012, 537-52.

Keynes, Simon, and Michael Lapidge, trans. 1983. *Alfred the Great: Asser's Life of King Alfred and other contemporary sources*, Penguin Classics (London).

King, Alan. 1978. 'Gauber High Pasture, Ribblehead – an interim report', in Hall 1978, 21-25.

— 2004. 'Post-Roman Upland Architecture in the Craven Dales and the Dating Evidence', in Hines, Lane, and Redknap 2004, 335-44.

King, Vanessa. 1996. 'Ealdred, Archbishop of York: The Worcester Years', *Anglo-Norman Studies* 18, 123-37.

Kirk, John. 1927. 'Trefoil Brooch from Yorkshire', *Antiquaries Journal* 7, 526-28.

Kopár, Lilla. 2012. *Gods and Settlers: The Iconography of Norse Mythology in Anglo-Scandinavian Sculpture*, Studies in the Early Middle Ages 25 (Turnhout).

Körner, Sten. 1964. *The Battle of Hastings, England, and Europe 1035-1066*, Bibliotheca Historica Lundensis 14 (Lund).

Kries, Susanne. 2003. '"Westward I Came Across the Sea": Anglo-Scandinavian History through Scandinavian Eyes', *Leeds Studies in English* New Series 34, 47-76.

Kroebel, Christiane. 2011. *Anglo-Saxon and Scandinavian Mulgrave: the Communities from Aislaby to Staithes near Whitby, North Yorkshire* (Staithes).

Kruse, Susan E. 1988. 'Ingots and Weight Units in Viking Age Silver Hoards', *World Archaeology* 20, 285-301.

Lang, James T. 1973. 'Some Late Pre-Conquest Crosses in Ryedale, Yorkshire: A Reappraisal', *Journal of the British Archaeological Association* 3rd Series 36, 16-25.

— 1976a. 'Sigurd and Weland in Pre-Conquest Carving from Northern England', *Yorkshire Archaeological Journal* 48, 83-94.

— 1976b. 'The Sculptors of the Nunburnholme Cross', *Archaeological Journal* 133, 75-94.

— ed. 1978a. *Anglo-Saxon and Viking Age Sculpture and its Context: Papers from the Collingwood Symposium on Insular Sculpture from 800 to 1066*, British Archaeological Reports British Series 49 (Oxford).

— 1978b. 'Continuity and Innovation in Anglo-Scandinavian Sculpture: A Study of the Metropolitan School at York', in Lang 1978a, 145-55.

— 1978c. 'Anglo-Scandinavian Sculpture in Yorkshire', in Hall 1978, 11-20.

— 1984. 'The Hogback: A Viking Colonial Monument', *Anglo-Saxon Studies in Archaeology and History* 3, 86-176.

— 1991. *York and Eastern Yorkshire*, Corpus of Anglo-Saxon Stone Sculpture 3 (Oxford).

— 1993. 'Survival and Revival in Insular Art: Northumbrian Sculpture of the 8th to 10th Centuries', in Spearman and Higgitt 1993, 261-67.

— 1995. 'Pre-Conquest Sculpture', in Phillips and Heywood 1995, II, 433-67.

— 2001. *Northern Yorkshire*, Corpus of Anglo-Saxon Stone Sculpture 6 (Oxford).

Lapidge, Michael. 1981. 'Some Latin Poems as Evidence for the Reign of Athelstan', *Anglo-Saxon England* 9, 61-98 (reprinted in Lapidge 1993, no. 2).

— 1983. 'Ealdred of York and MS. Cotton Vitellius E. XII', *Yorkshire Archaeological Journal* 55, 11-25 (reprinted in Lapidge 1993, no. 16).

— 1990. 'Aediluulf and the School of York', in Albert Lehner and Walter Berschin (eds), *Lateinische Kultur im VIII. Jahrhundert: Traube-Gedenkschrift* (St Ottilien), 161-78 (reprinted in Michael Lapidge, *Anglo-Latin Literature 600-899* (London, 1996), no. 14).

— 1993. *Anglo-Latin Literature 900-1066* (London).

— ed. 2009. *Byrhtferth of Ramsey: The Lives of St Oswald and St Ecgwine* (Oxford).

Lapidge, Michael, and Michael Winterbottom, eds. 1991. *Wulfstan of Winchester: The Life of St Æthelwold* (Oxford).

Lapidge, Michael, et al, eds. 1999. *The Blackwell Encyclopaedia of Anglo-Saxon England* (Oxford).

Lavelle, Ryan. 2009. 'The Politics of Rebellion: The *Ætheling* Æthelwold and West Saxon Royal Succession, 899-902', in Patricia Skinner (ed.), *Challenging the Boundaries of Medieval History: The Legacy of Timothy Reuter*, Studies in the Early Middle Ages 22 (Turnhout), 51-80.

— 2010. *Alfred's Wars: Sources and Interpretations of Anglo-Saxon Warfare in the Viking Age* (Woodbridge).

Lawson, M.K. 2004. 'Ealdred [Aldred] (*d.* 1069)', rev. Vanessa King, in Matthew and Harrison 2004, 17, 552-54.

Leach, Henry Goddard. 1921. *Angevin Britain and Scandinavia* (Cambridge, MA).

Leahy, Kevin, and Caroline Paterson. 2001. 'New Light on the Viking Presence in Lincolnshire: the artefactual evidence', in Graham-Campbell et al 2001, 181-202.

Lees, Clare A., ed. 2013. *The Cambridge History of Early Medieval English Literature* (Cambridge).

Lehiste, Ilse. 1958. 'Names of Scandinavians in *The Anglo-Saxon Chronicle*', *Publications of the Modern Language Association* 73, 6-22.

Leonard, Stephen Pax. 2012. *Language, Society and Identity in Early Iceland*, Publications of the Philological Society 45 (Oxford).

Le Patourel, H.E. Jean, Moira H. Long, and May F. Pickles, eds. 1993. *Yorkshire Boundaries* (Leeds).

Levine, Philippa. 1986. *The Amateur and the Professional: Antiquarians, Historians and Archaeologists in Victorian England, 1838-1886* (Cambridge).

Lewis, C.P. 1994. 'The French in England Before the Norman Conquest', *Anglo-Norman Studies* 17, 123-44.

— 2004. 'Waltheof, Earl of Northumbria (*c*.1050-1076)', in Matthew and Harrison 2004, 57, 187-89.

Liebermann, Felix, ed. 1903-16. *Die Gesetze der Angelsachsen*, 3 vols (Halle).

Lindkvist, Harald. 1922. 'Some Notes on Elfric's Festermen', *Beiblatt zur Anglia* 33, 130-44.

— 1926. 'A Study on Early Medieval York', *Anglia* 50, 345-94.

Lindkvist, Thomas, et al. 2003. 'Early Political Organisation', in Helle 2003, 160-234.

Lionarons, Joyce Tally. 2010. *The Homiletic Writings of Archbishop Wulfstan* (Woodbridge).

Livingston, Michael, ed. 2011a. *The Battle of Brunanburh: A Casebook* (Exeter).

— 2011b. 'The Roads to Brunanburh', in Livingston 2011a, 1-26.

Loyn, Henry. 1992. *Society and Peoples: Studies in the History of England and Wales, c.600–1200*, Westfield Publications in Medieval Studies 6 (London).

— 1994. *The Vikings in Britain*, rev. ed. (Oxford).

Lucy, Sam, and Andrew Reynolds, eds. 2002. *Burial in Early Medieval England and Wales*, Society for Medieval Archaeology Monograph Series 17 (London).

Lund, Niels. 1995. 'Scandinavia, *c*.700-1066', in Rosamond McKitterick (ed.), *The New Cambridge Medieval History: Volume II c.700-c.900* (Cambridge), 202-27.

Mac Airt, Séan, and Gearóid Mac Niocaill, eds. 1983. *The Annals of Ulster (to AD 1131)* (Dublin).

Magnusson, Magnus, and Hermann Pálsson, trans. 1966. *Snorri Sturluson: King Harald's Saga*, Penguin Classics (Harmondsworth).

Mainman, A.J. 1990. *Anglo-Scandinavian Pottery from Coppergate*, Archaeology of York 16/5 (York).

Mainman, A.J., and N.S.H. Rogers. 2000. *Craft, Industry and Everyday Life: Finds from Anglo-Scandinavian York*, Archaeology of York 17/14 (York).

— 2004. 'Craft and Economy in Anglo-Scandinavian York', in Hall et al 2004, 459-83.

Margeson, Sue. 1997. *The Vikings in Norfolk* (Norwich).

Marshall, William. 2011. 'An Eisteddfod for Yorkshire? Professor Moorman and the Uses of Dialect', *Yorkshire Archaeological Society* 83, 199-217.

Marten, Lucy. 2008. 'The Shiring of East Anglia: an alternative hypothesis', *Historical Research* 81, 1-27.

Mason, Emma. 2004. *The House of Godwine: The History of a Dynasty* (London).

Matthew, H.C.G., and Brian Harrison, eds. 2004. *The Oxford Dictionary of National Biography*, 60 vols (Oxford) (online edition: www.oxforddnb.com).

Mawer, Allen. 1913. *The Vikings* (Cambridge).

— 1923. 'The Redemption of the Five Boroughs', *English Historical Review* 38, 551-57.

McClain, Aleksandra. 2011. 'Local Churches and the Conquest of the North: Elite Patronage and Identity in Saxo-Norman Northumbria', in Petts and Turner 2011, 151-78.

McDougall, David, and Ian McDougall, trans. 1998. *Theodoricus Monachus: Historia de Antiquitate Regum Norwagiensium. An Account of the Ancient History of the Norwegian Kings*, Viking Society for Northern Research Text Series 11 (London).

McGurk, P., ed. 1998. *The Chronicle of John of Worcester: Volume III The Annals from 1067 to 1140 with the Gloucester Interpolations and the Continuation to 1141* (Oxford).

McKinley, R.A. 1990. *A History of British Surnames* (London).

McKinnell, John. 1987. 'Norse Mythology and Northumbria: A Response', *Scandinavian Studies* 59, 325-37.

— 1990. 'The Context of *Völundarkviða*', *Saga-Book of the Viking Society* 23, 1-27.

— 1994. *Both One and Many: Essays on Change and Variety in Late Norse Heathenism* (Rome).

— 2001. 'Eddic Poetry in Anglo-Scandinavian Northern England', in Graham-Campbell et al 2001, 327-44.

McLeod, Shane. 2011. 'Warriors and Women: the sex ratio of Norse migrants to eastern England up to 900 AD', *Early Medieval Europe* 19, 332-53.

— 2014. *The Beginning of Scandinavian Settlement in England: The Viking 'Great Army' and Early Settlers, c.865-900*, Studies in the Early Middle Ages 29 (Turnhout).

McTurk, Rory. 1991. *Studies in Ragnars saga loðbrókar and its Major Scandinavian Analogues*, Medium Ævum Monographs New Series 15 (Oxford).

Meaney, Audrey L. 2004. "'And we forbeodað eornostlice ælcne hæðenscipe': Wulfstan and Late Anglo-Saxon and Norse 'Heathenism'", in Townend 2004, 461-500.

Michelmore, D.J.H. 1981. 'Township and Tenure', in Faull and Moorhouse 1981, II, 231-64.

Miller, D. Gary. *External Influences on English: From its Beginnings to the Renaissance* (Oxford).

Miller, William Ian. 1990. *Bloodtaking and Peacemaking: Feud, Law, and Society in Saga Iceland* (Chicago).

Mitchell, Bruce. 1994. 'The Englishness of Old English', in Malcolm Godden, Douglas Gray, and Terry Hoad (eds), *From Anglo-Saxon to Early Middle English: Studies Presented to E.G. Stanley* (Oxford), 163-81.

Molyneaux, George. 2011. 'Why were some Tenth-Century English Kings presented as Rulers of Britain?', *Transactions of the Royal Historical Society* 6th Series 21, 59-91.

Morris, Carole A. 2000. *Wood and Woodworking in Anglo-Scandinavian and Medieval York*, Archaeology of York 17/13 (York).

Morris, Christopher D. 1977. 'Northumbria and the Viking Settlement: The Evidence of Land-Holding', *Archaeologia Æliana* 5th Series 5, 81-103.

—— 1981. 'Viking and Native in Northern England: A Case-Study', in Hans Bekker-Nielsen, Peter Foote, and Olaf Olsen (eds), *Proceedings of the Eighth Viking Congress, Mediaeval Scandinavia* Supplements 2 (Odense), 223-44.

—— 1982. 'The Vikings in the British Isles: some aspects of their settlement and economy', in Farrell 1982, 70-94.

—— 1984. 'Aspects of Scandinavian Settlement in Northern England: A Review', *Northern History* 20, 1-22.

—— 2009. 'Revisiting Anglo-Scandinavian Settlement and Sculpture', in Catherine E. Karkov (ed.), *Poetry, Place, and Gender: Studies in Medieval Culture in Honor of Helen Damico* (Kalamazoo), 211-33.

Morris, Christopher J. 1992. *Marriage and Murder in Eleventh-Century Northumbria: A Study of the 'De Obsessione Dunelmi'*, Borthwick Paper 82 (York).

Morris, G.E., and J. McDonnell. 1990-91. "Thwaite' Place-Names on the North York Moors', *Ryedale Historian* 15, 24-29.

Morris, Richard. 1986. 'Alcuin, York, and the *alma sophia*', in L.A.S. Butler and Richard Morris (eds), *The Anglo-Saxon Church: Papers on History, Architecture, and Archaeology in Honour of Dr H.M. Taylor*, Council for British Archaeology Research Report 60 (London), 80-89.

—— 1989. *Churches in the Landscape* (London).

—— 1990. 'A Note on St Gregory's Minster, Kirkdale, North Yorkshire', *Bulletin of the C.B.A. Churches Committee* 27, 4-6.

—— 2011. 'Local Churches in the Anglo-Saxon Countryside', in David A. Hinton, Sally Crawford, and Helena Hamerow (eds), *The Oxford Handbook of Anglo-Saxon Archaeology* (Oxford), 172-97.

Morris, Richard, and Eric Cambridge. 1989. 'Beverley Minster Before the Early Thirteenth Century', in Christopher Wilson (ed.), *Medieval Art and Architecture in the East Riding of Yorkshire*, British Archaeological Association Conference Transactions 9 (Leeds), 9-32.

Myhre, Bjørn. 1993. 'The Beginning of the Viking Age – some current archaeological problems', in Faulkes and Perkins 1993, 182-204.

—— 1998. 'The Archaeology of the Early Viking Age in Norway', in Clarke, Ní Mhaonaigh, and Ó Floinn 1998, 3-36.

—— 2003. 'The Iron Age', in Helle 2003, 60-93.

Mynors, R.A.B., R.M. Thomson, and Michael Winterbottom, eds. 1998-99. *William of Malmesbury: Gesta Regum Anglorum. The History of the English Kings*, 2 vols (Oxford).

Mytum, Harold. 1993. 'Kellington Church', *Current Archaeology* 133, 15-17.

Neff, Charlotte. 1989. 'Scandinavian Elements in the Wantage Code of Æthelred II', *Journal of Legal History* 10, 285-316.

Norton, Christopher. 1998. 'The Anglo-Saxon Cathedral at York and the Topography of the Anglian City', *Journal of the British Archaeological Association* 151, 1-42.

— 2001. *Archbishop Thomas of Bayeux and the Norman Cathedral at York*, Borthwick Paper 100 (York).

— 2004. 'York Minster in the Time of Wulfstan', in Townend 2004, 207-234.

O'Brien O'Keeffe, Katherine, ed. 2001. *MS C, The Anglo-Saxon Chronicle: A Collaborative Edition 5* (Cambridge).

O'Connor, T.P. 1989. *Bones from Anglo-Scandinavian Levels at 16-22 Coppergate*, Archaeology of York 15/3 (York).

— 2004. 'Animal Bones from Anglo-Scandinavian York', in Hall et al 2004, 427-45.

O'Donnell, Thomas, Matthew Townend, and Elizabeth M. Tyler. 2013. 'European Literature and Eleventh-Century England', in Lees 2013, 607-36.

Okasha, Elisabeth. 1971. *Handlist of Anglo-Saxon Non-Runic Inscriptions* (Cambridge).

Omberg, Margaret. 1976. *Scandinavian Themes in English Poetry, 1760-1800* (Uppsala).

Ong, Walter J. 1982. *Orality and Literacy* (London).

O'Sullivan, Deirdre. 2011. 'Normanising the North: The Evidence of Anglo-Saxon and Anglo-Scandinavian Sculpture', *Medieval Archaeology* 55, 163-91.

Ottaway, Patrick. 2013. *Roman Yorkshire: People, Culture and Landscape* (Pickering).

Owen, Olwyn. 2001. 'The Strange Beast that is the English Urnes Style', in Graham-Campbell et al 2001, 203-22.

Padel, O.J., and David N. Parsons, eds. 2008. *A Commodity of Good Names: Essays in Honour of Margaret Gelling* (Donington).

Pagan, H.E. 1966. 'The Gainford Hoard', *British Numismatic Journal* 35, 190-91.

— 1969. 'Northumbrian Numismatic Chronology in the Ninth Century', *British Numismatic Journal* 38, 1-15.

Page, R.I. 1971. 'How Long did the Scandinavian Language Survive in England? The epigraphical evidence', in Clemoes and Hughes 1971, 165-81.

— 1981. 'The Audience of *Beowulf* and the Vikings', in Chase 1981, 113-22.

— 1982. 'A Tale of Two Cities', *Peritia* 1, 335-51.

— 1987. *'A Most Vile People': Early English Historians on the Vikings*, Dorothea Coke Memorial Lecture (London).

Page, William, ed. 1912. *The Victoria History of the County of York: Volume II* (London).

Palliser, D.M. 1978. 'The Medieval Street-Names of York', *York Historian* 2, 2-16.

— 1984. 'York's West Bank: Medieval Suburb or Urban Nucleus?', in Addyman and Black 1984, 101-08.

— 1990. *Domesday York*, Borthwick Paper 78 (York).

— 1992. 'An Introduction to the Yorkshire Domesday', in Williams and Martin 1992, I, 1-38.

— 1993. 'Domesday Book and the 'Harrying of the North'', *Northern History* 29, 1-23.

— 2014. *Medieval York 600-1540* (Oxford)

Pálsson, Hermann, and Paul Edwards, trans. 1972. *The Book of Settlements: Landnámabók*, University of Manitoba Icelandic Studies 1 (Winnipeg).

Parker, Eleanor. 2014. 'Siward the Dragon-Slayer: Mythmaking in Anglo-Scandinavian England', *Neophilologus*, 98, 481-93.

Parsons, David N. 2001. 'How Long did the Scandinavian Language Survive in England? Again', in Graham-Campbell et al 2001, 299-312.

— 2002. '*Anna, Dot, Thorir* … Counting Domesday Personal Names', *Nomina* 25, 29-52.

— 2006. 'Field-Name Statistics, Norfolk and the Danelaw', in Gammeltoft and Jørgensen 2006, 165-88.

— 2011. 'On the Origin of 'Hiberno-Norse Inversion-compounds'', *Journal of Scottish Name Studies* 5, 115-52.

— 2013. 'Churls and Athelings, Kings and Reeves: some reflections on place-names and early English society', in Carroll and Parsons 2013, 43-72.

Parsons, David N., and Tania Styles. 1997. *The Vocabulary of English Place-Names (Á-Box)* (Nottingham).

— 2000. *The Vocabulary of English Place-Names (Brace-Cæster)* (Nottingham).

Pattison, I.R. 1973. 'The Nunburnholme Cross and Anglo-Danish Sculpture in York', *Archaeologia* 104, 209-34.

Pearsall, Derek, ed. 1999. *Chaucer to Spenser: An Anthology of Writings in English 1375-1575* (Oxford).

Pedersen, Anne. 2008. 'Viking Weaponry', in Brink 2008, 204-11.

Pelteret, David. 1991. 'Slavery in the Danelaw', in Samson 1991, 179-88.

Pestell, Tim, and Katharina Ulmschneider, eds. 2003. *Markets in Early Medieval Europe: Trading and 'Productive' Sites, 650-850* (Macclesfield).

Petts, David, and Sam Turner, eds. 2011. *Early Medieval Northumbria: Kingdoms and Communities, AD 450-1100*, Studies in the Early Middle Ages 24 (Turnhout).

Phelpstead, Carl, ed. 2001. *A History of Norway and The Passion and Miracles of the Blessed Óláfr*, trans. Devra Kunin, Viking Society for Northern Research Text Series 13 (London).

Phillips, Derek, and Brenda Heywood, *Excavations at York Minster: Volume I From Roman Fortress to Norman Cathedral*, ed. Martin Carver, 2 vols (London).

Phythian-Adams, Charles. 1996. *Land of the Cumbrians: A Study in British Provincial Origins AD 400-1120* (Aldershot).

— 1999. 'Environments and Identities: Landscape as Cultural Projection in the English Provincial Past', in Paul Slack (ed.), *Environments and Historical Change: The Linacre Lectures 1998* (Oxford), 118-46.

— 2011. 'From Peoples to Regional Societies: The Problem of Early Medieval Cumbrian Identities', *Transactions of the Cumberland and Westmorland Antiquarian and Archaeological Society* 3rd Series 11, 51-64.

Pickles, Thomas. 2009. '*Biscopes-tūn, muneca-tūn* and *prēosta-tūn*: dating, significance and distribution', in Eleanor Quinton (ed.), *The Church in English Place-Names*, English Place-Name Society Extra Series 4 (Nottingham), 39-107.

— 2012. *Power, Religious Patronage and Pastoral Care: Religious Communities, Mother Parishes and Local Churches in Ryedale, c.650 – c.1250*, Kirkdale Lecture 2009 (Kirkdale).

Pirie, E.J.E. 1986. *Post-Roman Coins from York Excavations 1971-81*, Archaeology of York 18/1 (York).

PNERY = Smith 1937

PNNRY = Smith 1928

PNWRY = Smith 1961-63

Pons-Sanz, Sara M. 2000. *Analysis of the Scandinavian Loanwords in the Aldredian Glosses to the Lindisfarne Gospels*, Studies in English Language and Linguistics 9 (Valencia).

— 2007. *Norse-Derived Vocabulary in Late Old English Texts: Wulfstan's Works, a Case Study*, North-Western European Language Evolution Supplement 22 (Odense).

— 2013. *The Lexical Effects of Anglo-Scandinavian Linguistic Contact on Old English*, Studies in the Early Middle Ages 1 (Turnhout).

Poole, Russell. 1991. *Viking Poems on War and Peace: A Study in Skaldic Narrative*, Toronto Medieval Texts and Translations 8 (Toronto).

— 2013. 'Crossing the Language Divide: Anglo-Scandinavian language and literature', in Lees 2013, 579-606.

Pope, John C. ed. 1967-68. *Homilies of Ælfric: A Supplementary Collection*, Early English Text Society Original Series 259-60 (Oxford).

Postles, David. 2007. *The North through its Names: A Phenomenology of Medieval and Early-Modern Northern England*, English Surnames Survey 8 (Oxford).

Preest, David, trans. 2002. *William of Malmesbury: The Deeds of the Bishops of England (Gesta Pontificum Anglorum)* (Woodbridge).

Price, Neil S. 2002. *The Viking Way: Religion and War in Late Iron Age Scandinavia*, Aun 31 (Uppsala).

— 2008. 'Dying and the Dead: Viking Age mortuary behaviour', in Brink 2008a, 257-73.

Rahtz, Philip, and Lorna Watts. 2004. 'Three Ages of Conversion at Kirkdale, North Yorkshire', in Carver 2004, 289-309.

Raine, James, ed. 1879-94. *The Historians of the Church of York and Its Archbishops*, 3 vols, Rolls Series 71 (London).

Reaney, P.H. 1967. *The Origin of English Surnames* (London).

Redmond, Angela Z. 2007. *Viking Burial in the North of England: A Study of Contact, Interaction and Reaction between Scandinavian Migrants with Resident Groups, and the Effect of Immigration on Aspects of Cultural Continuity*, British Archaeological Reports British Series 429 (Oxford).

Redmonds, George. 1973. *Yorkshire: West Riding*, English Surnames Series 1 (Chichester).

— 2004. *Christian Names in Local and Family History* (London).

Redmonds, George, Turi King, and David Hey. 2011. *Surnames, DNA, and Family History* (Oxford).

Rees Jones, Sarah. 2013. *York: The Making of a City 1068-1350* (Oxford).

Reynolds, Andrew, and Leslie Webster, eds. 2013. *Early Medieval Art and Archaeology in the Northern World: Studies in Honour of James Graham-Campbell*, Northern World 58 (Leiden).

Richards, Julian D. 1999. 'Cottam: An Anglian and Anglo-Scandinavian Settlement in the Yorkshire Wolds', *Archaeological Journal* 156, 1-110.

— 2000a. *Viking Age England*, rev. ed. (Stroud).

— 2000b. 'Identifying Anglo-Scandinavian Settlements', in Hadley and Richards 2000, 295-309.

— 2000c. 'Defining Settlements: York and its Hinterland AD 700-1000', in Sarah Rees Jones, Richard Marks, and A.J. Minnis (eds), *Courts and Regions in Medieval Europe* (Woodbridge), 45-74.

— 2000d. 'The Anglo-Saxon and Anglo-Scandinavian Evidence', in Stamper and Croft 2000, 195-200.

— 2001. 'Finding the Vikings: the search for Anglo-Scandinavian rural settlement in the northern Danelaw', in Graham-Campbell et al 2001, 269-77.

— 2002. 'The Case of the Missing Vikings: Scandinavian Burial in the Danelaw', in Lucy and Reynolds 2002, 156-70.

— 2003. 'The Anglian and Anglo-Scandinavian Sites at Cottam, East Yorkshire', in Pestell and Ulmschneider 2003, 155-66.

— 2004. 'Excavations at the Viking Barrow Cemetery at Heath Wood, Ingleby, Derbyshire', *Antiquaries Journal* 84, 23-116.

— 2008. 'Viking Settlement in England', in Brink 2008, 368-74.

— 2013. 'Cottam, Cowlam and Environs: An Anglo-Saxon Estate on the Yorkshire Wolds', *Archaeological Journal*, 70, 201-71.

Richards, Julian D., and John Naylor. 2010. 'The Metal Detector and the Viking Age in England', in Sheehan and Ó Corráin 2010, 338-52.

— 2011. 'Settlement, Landscape, and Economy in Early Medieval Northumbria: The Contribution of Portable Antiquities', in Petts and Turner 2011, 129-49.

Robertson, A.J., ed. 1956. *Anglo-Saxon Charters*, 2nd ed. (Cambridge).

Roesdahl, Else. 1991. *The Vikings* (London).

Roesdahl, Else, and Preben Meulengracht Sørensen. 2003. 'Viking Culture', in Helle 2003, 121-46.

Roesdahl, Else, et al, eds. 1981. *The Vikings in England* (London).

Roffe, David. 1990a. 'Domesday Book and Northern Society: a reassessment', *English Historical Review* 105, 311-36.

— 1990b. 'From Thegnage to Barony: Sake and Soke, Title, and Tenants-in-Chief', *Anglo-Norman Studies* 12, 157-76.

— 2000a. *Domesday: The Inquest and the Book* (Oxford).

— 2000b. 'The Early History of Wharram Percy', in Stamper and Croft 2000, 1-16.

— 2007. *Decoding Domesday* (Woodbridge).

— 2010. 'The Danes and the Making of the Kingdom of the English', in Hirokazu Tsurushima (ed.), *Nations in Medieval Britain* (Donington), 32-44.

Rogers, N.S.H. 1993. *Anglian and Other Finds from 46-54 Fishergate*, Archaeology of York 17/9 (York).

Rollason, David. 1989. 'St Cuthbert and Wessex: The Evidence of Cambridge, Corpus Christi College MS 183', in Bonner, Rollason, and Stancliffe 1989, 413-24.

— 1998a. *Sources for York History to AD 1100*, Archaeology of York 1 (York).

— ed. 1998b. *Symeon of Durham: Historian of Durham and the North*, Studies in North-Eastern History 1 (Stamford).

— 1999. 'Historical Evidence for Anglian York', in Tweddle, Moulden, and Logan 1999, 117-40.

— ed. 2000. *Symeon of Durham: Libellus de Exordio atque Procursu istius hoc est Dunhelmensis Ecclesie. Tract on the Origins and Progress of this the Church of Durham* (Oxford).

— 2003. *Northumbria, 500-1100: Creation and Destruction of a Kingdom* (Cambridge).

— 2004. 'Anglo-Scandinavian York: The Evidence of Historical Sources', in Hall et al 2004, 305-24.

Ross, Alan S.C. 1968. 'The Earliest Occurrence of "Riding"?', *Notes and Queries* 15, 444.

Rowe, Elizabeth Ashman. 1994. 'Historical Invasions / Historiographical Interventions: Snorri Sturluson and the Battle of Stamford Bridge', *Mediaevalia* 17, 149-76.

— 2009. 'Helpful Danes and Pagan Irishmen: Saga Fantasies of the Viking Age in the British Isles', *Viking and Medieval Scandinavia* 5, 1-21.

— 2012. *Vikings in the West: The Legend of Ragnarr Loðbrók and His Sons*, Studia Medievalia Septentrionalia 18 (Vienna).

Rumble, Alexander R., ed. 1994. *The Reign of Cnut: King of England, Denmark and Norway* (London).

Rynell, Alarik. 1948. *The Rivalry of Scandinavian and Native Synonyms in Middle English, especially taken and nimen*, Lund Studies in English 13 (Lund).

Samson, Ross, ed. 1991a. *Social Approaches to Viking Studies* (Glasgow).

— 1991b. 'Fighting with Silver: Rethinking Trading, Raiding, and Hoarding', in Samson 1991a, 123-33.

Samuels, M.L. 1963. 'Some Applications of Middle English Dialectology', *English Studies* 44, 81-94.

— 1985. 'The Great Scandinavian Belt', in Roger Eaton et al (eds), *Papers from the 4th International Conference on English Historical Linguistics*, Current Issues in Linguistic Theory 41 (Amsterdam), 269-81.

Sawyer, Birgit. 2000. *The Viking-Age Rune-Stones: Custom and Commemoration in Early Medieval Scandinavia* (Oxford).

Sawyer, Peter. 1957. 'The Density of the Danish Settlement in England', *University of Birmingham Historical Journal* 6, 1-17.

— 1962. *The Age of the Vikings* (London).

— ed. 1979. *Charters of Burton Abbey*, Anglo-Saxon Charters 2 (Oxford).

— 1982. *Kings and Vikings: Scandinavia and Europe AD 700-1100* (London).

— ed. 1985. *Domesday Book: A Reassessment* (London).

— 1994. *Scandinavians and the English in the Viking Age*, H.M. Chadwick Memorial Lecture 5 (Cambridge).

— 1995. 'The Last Scandinavian Kings of York', *Northern History* 31, 39-44.

— 1998. *Anglo-Saxon Lincolnshire*, History of Lincolnshire 3 (Lincoln).

— 2003. 'The Viking Expansion', in Helle 2003, 105-20.

— 2013. *The Wealth of Anglo-Saxon England* (Oxford).

Schoenfelder, Meagan, and Julian D. Richards. 2011. 'Norse Bells – a Scandinavian Colonial Artefact', *Anglo-Saxon Studies in Archaeology and History* 17, 151-68.

Scott, Forrest S. 1952. 'Earl Waltheof of Northumbria', *Archaeologia Æliana* 4th Series 30, 149-215.

— 1953-57. 'Valþjófr jarl: An English Earl in Icelandic Sources', *Saga-Book of the Viking Society* 14, 78-94.

Scott Burns, Tom. 1986. *Canon Atkinson and his Country* (Middlesbrough).

Sheehan, John. 2009. 'The Huxley Hoard and Hiberno-Scandinavian Arm-Rings', in Graham-Campbell and Philpott 2009, 58-69.

— 2011. '"Bullion-Rings' in Viking Age Britain and Ireland', in Svavar Sigmundsson (ed.), *Viking Settlements and Viking Society: Papers from the Proceedings of the Sixteenth Viking Congress, Reykjavík and Reykholt, 16-23 August 2009* (Reykjavík), 393-406.

— 2013. 'Viking Raiding, Gift-Exchange and Insular Metalwork in Norway', in Reynolds and Webster 2013, 809-23.

Sheehan, John, and Donnchadh Ó Corráin, eds. 2010. *The Viking Age: Ireland and the West. Papers from the Proceedings of the Fifteenth Viking Congress, Cork, 18-27 August 2005* (Dublin).

Sheils, William Joseph. 2004. 'Atkinson, John Christopher (1814-1900)', in Matthew and Harrison 2004, 2, 836-37.

Short, Ian, ed. 2009. *Geffrei Gaimar: Estoire des Engleis / History of the English* (Oxford).

Simpson, Luisella. 1989. 'The King Alfred/St Cuthbert Episode in the *Historia de Sancto Cuthberto*: Its Significance for mid-tenth-century English History', in Bonner, Rollason, and Stancliffe 1989, 397-411.

Sindbæk, Søren M. 2011. 'Silver Economies and Social Ties: Long-Distance Interaction, Long-term Investments – and why the Viking Age happened', in Graham-Campbell, Sindbæk, and Williams 2011, 41-65.

Small, Alan, ed. 1965. *The Fourth Viking Congress: York, August 1961* (Edinburgh).

Smart, Veronica. 1986. 'Scandinavians, Celts, and Germans in Anglo-Saxon England: the evidence of moneyers' names', in Blackburn 1986, 169-84.

Smith, A.H. 1927. 'Some Aspects of Irish Influence on Yorkshire', *Révue Celtique* 44, 34-58.

— 1928. *The Place-Names of the North Riding of Yorkshire*, English Place-Name Society 5 (Cambridge).

— 1928-29. 'Danes and Norwegians in Yorkshire', *Saga-Book of the Viking Society* 10, 188-215.

— 1937. *The Place-Names of the East Riding of Yorkshire and York*, English Place-Name Society 14 (Cambridge).

— 1956. 'Horse Fighting in Viking England', *Arv* 2, 104-08.

— 1956. *English Place-Name Elements*, 2 vols, English Place-Name Society 25-26 (Cambridge).

— 1961-63. *The Place-Names of the West Riding of Yorkshire*, 8 vols, English Place-Name Society 30-37 (Cambridge).

Smith, Mary Frances, Robin Fleming, and Patricia Halpin. 2001. 'Court and Piety in Late Anglo-Saxon England', *Catholic Historical Review* 87, 569-602.

Smithers, G.V., ed. 1987. *Havelok* (Oxford).

Smyth, Alfred P. 1974-77. 'The Black Foreigners of York and the White Foreigners of Dublin', *Saga-Book of the Viking Society* 19, 101-17.

— 1975-79. *Scandinavian York and Dublin: The History and Archaeology of Two Related Viking Kingdoms*, 2 vols (Dublin).

— 1977. *Scandinavian Kings in the British Isles, 850-880* (Oxford).

— 1978. 'The Chronology of Northumbrian History in the Ninth and Tenth Centuries', in Hall 1978, 8-10.

— 1999. 'The Effect of Scandinavian Raiders on the English and Irish Churches: a preliminary reassessment', in Brendan Smith (ed.), *Britain and Ireland 900-1300: Insular Responses to Medieval European Change* (Cambridge), 1-38.

Sørensen, John Kousgård. 1983. *Patronymics in Denmark and England*, Dorothea Coke Memorial Lecture (London).

Spall, Cecily A., and Nicola J. Toop. 2008. 'Before *Eoforwic*: New Light on York in the 6th-7th Centuries', *Medieval Archaeology* 52, 1-25.

Spearman, R. Michael, and John Higgitt, eds. 1993. *The Age of Migrating Ideas: Early Medieval Art in Northern Britain and Ireland* (Edinburgh).

Speed, Greg, and Penelope Walton Rogers. 2004. 'A Burial of a Viking Woman at Adwick-le-Street, South Yorkshire', *Medieval Archaeology* 48, 51-90.

Spurkland, Terje. 2005. *Norwegian Runes and Runic Inscriptions* (Woodbridge).

Stafford, Pauline. 2007. 'The Anglo-Saxon Chronicles, Identity and the Making of England', *Haskins Society Journal* 19, 28-50.

— 2008. '"The Annals of Æthelflæd': Annals, History and Politics in Early Tenth-Century England', in Julia Barrow and Andrew Wareham (eds), *Myth, Rulership, Church and Charters: Essays in Honour of Nicholas Brooks* (Aldershot), 101-16.

— ed. 2009. *A Companion to the Early Middle Ages: Britain and Ireland c.500-c.1100* (Oxford).

— 2011. 'Archbishop Ealdred and the D Chronicle', in David Crouch and Kathleen Thompson (eds), *Normandy and its Neighbours, 900-1250: Essays for David Bates*, Medieval Texts and Cultures of Northern Europe 14 (Turnhout), 135-56.

Stamper, P.A., and R.A. Croft, eds. 2000. *The South Manor Area*, Wharram: A Study of Settlement on the Yorkshire Wolds 8 (York).

Stenton, F.M. 1910. *Types of Manorial Structure in the Northern Danelaw*, Oxford Studies in Social and Legal History 2 (Oxford).

— 1927a. 'The Danes in England', *Proceedings of the British Academy* 13, 203-46.

— 1927b. *York in the Eleventh Century*, York Minster Historical Tracts 8 (York).

— 1927c. 'Lindsey and its Kings', in H.W.C. Davis (ed.), *Essays in History Presented to Reginald Lane Poole* (Oxford), 136-50.

— 1969. *The Free Peasantry of the Northern Danelaw* (Oxford).

— 1971. *Anglo-Saxon England*, Oxford History of England 2, 3rd ed. (Oxford).

Stevenson, J., trans. 1987. *Simeon of Durham: A History of the Kings of England*, reprint of 1858 translation (Llanerch).

Stevenson, W.H., ed. 1904. *Asser's Life of King Alfred* (Oxford).

— 1912. 'Yorkshire Surveys and Other Eleventh-Century Documents in the York Gospels', *English Historical Review* 27, 1-25.

Stewart, Ian. 1991. 'On the Date of the Bossall Hoard', *Numismatic Chronicle* 151, 175-82.

Stewart, Ian, and Stewart Lyon. 1992. 'Chronology of the St Peter Coinage', *Yorkshire Numismatist* 2, 45-73.

Stocker, David. 2000. 'Monuments and Merchants: Irregularities in the Distribution of Stone Sculpture in Lincolnshire and Yorkshire in the Tenth Century', in Hadley and Richards 2000, 179-212.

Svanberg, Fredrik. 2003. *Death Rituals in South-East Scandinavia AD 800-1000: Decolonizing the Viking Age 2* (Stockholm).

Swanton, Michael, trans. 1975. *Anglo-Saxon Prose* (London).

— 1976. "Dane-Skins': Excoriation in Early England', *Folklore* 87, 21-28.

Sweet, Rosemary. 2004. *Antiquaries: The Discovery of the Past in Eighteenth-Century Britain* (London).

Tamoto, Kenichi, ed. 2013. *The Macregol Gospels or the Rushworth Gospels* (Amsterdam).

Taylor, A.B. 1965. 'Eysteinn Haraldsson in the West, *c*.1151: Oral Traditions and Written Record', in Small 1965, 119-34.

Taylor, H.M., and Joan Taylor. 1965. *Anglo-Saxon Architecture*, 2 vols (Cambridge).

Taylor, Simon, ed. 1983. *MS B*, The Anglo-Saxon Chronicle: A Collaborative Edition 4 (Cambridge).

Tennyson, Alfred. 1877. *Harold: A Drama* (London).

Thacker, Alan. 2001. 'Dynastic Monasteries and Family Cults: Edward the Elder's sainted kindred', in Higham and Hill 2001, 248-63.

Thomas, Gabor. 2000. 'Anglo-Scandinavian Metalwork from the Danelaw: Exploring Social and Cultural Interaction', in Hadley and Richards 2000, 237-55.

Thomason, Sarah Grey, and Terrence Kaufman. 1988. *Language Contact, Creolization, and Genetic Linguistics* (Berkeley).

Thompson, Victoria. 2004. *Dying and Death in Later Anglo-Saxon England* (Woodbridge).

Thorn, F.R. 1992. 'Hundreds and Wapentakes', in Williams and Martin 1992, I, 39-70.

Thornton, David E. 1997. 'Hey, Mac! The Name *Maccus*, Tenth to Fifteenth Centuries', *Nomina* 20, 67-98.

Thorpe, Lewis, trans. 1978. *Gerald of Wales: The Journey through Wales and The Description of Wales*, Penguin Classics (Harmondsworth).

Thorson, Per. 1936. *Anglo-Norse Studies: An Inquiry into the Scandinavian Elements in the Modern English Dialects* (Amsterdam).

Tolkien, J.R.R. 1928. 'Foreword', in Walter E. Haigh, *A New Glossary of the Dialect of the Huddersfield District* (London), xiii-xviii.

Tomasson, Richard F. 1980. *Iceland: The First New Society* (Minneapolis).

Toop, Nicola J. 2011. 'Northumbria in the West: Considering Interaction through Monumentality', in Petts and Turner 2011, 85-111.

Townend, Matthew. 1997. '*Ella*: An Old English Name in Old Norse Poetry', *Nomina* 20, 23-35.

— 1998. *English Place-Names in Skaldic Verse*, English Place-Name Society Extra Series 1 (Nottingham).

— 2000a. 'Pre-Cnut Praise-Poetry in Viking Age England', *Review of English Studies* New Series 51, 349-70.

— 2000b. 'Viking Age England as a Bilingual Society', in Hadley and Richards 2000, 89-105.

— 2002. *Language and History in Viking Age England: Linguistic Relations between Speakers of Old Norse and Old English*, Studies in the Early Middle Ages 6 (Turnhout).

— 2003. 'Whatever Happened to York Viking Poetry? Memory, tradition and the transmission of skaldic verse', *Saga-Book of the Viking Society* 27, 48-90.

— ed. 2004. *Wulfstan, Archbishop of York: The Proceedings of the Second Alcuin Conference*, Studies in the Early Middle Ages 10 (Turnhout).

— 2005. 'Knútr and the Cult of St Óláfr: Poetry and Patronage in Eleventh-Century Norway and England', *Viking and Medieval Scandinavia* 1, 251-79.

— 2007. *Scandinavian Culture in Eleventh-Century Yorkshire*, Kirkdale Lecture 2007 (Kirkdale).

— 2009. *The Vikings and Victorian Lakeland: the Norse medievalism of W.G. Collingwood and his contemporaries*, Cumberland and Westmorland Antiquarian and Archaeological Society Extra Series 34 (Kendal).

— 2012. 'Contacts and Conflicts: Latin, Norse, and French', in Lynda Mugglestone (ed.), *The Oxford History of English*, rev. ed. (Oxford), 75-105.

— 2013. 'Scandinavian Place-Names in England', in Carroll and Parsons 2013, 103-26.

Trafford, Simon. 2000. 'Ethnicity, Migration Theory, and the Historiography of the Scandinavian Settlement of England', in Hadley and Richards 2000, 17-39.

Treharne, Elaine, ed. 2004. *Old and Middle English c.890–c.1400: An Anthology*, 2nd ed. (Oxford).

— 2012. *Living Through Conquest: The Politics of Early English, 1020-1220* (Oxford).

Tschan, Francis J., trans. 2002. *Adam of Bremen: History of the Archbishops of Hamburg-Bremen*, new ed. (New York).

Turner, Andrew J., and Bernard J. Muir, eds. 2006. *Eadmer of Canterbury: Lives and Miracles of Saints Oda, Dunstan, and Oswald* (Oxford).

Turville-Petre, Gabriel. 1964. *Myth and Religion of the North: The Religion of Ancient Scandinavia* (London).

— 1968. *Haraldr the Hard-ruler and his Poets*, Dorothea Coke Memorial Lecture (London).

Turville-Petre, Thorlac. 2001. 'Representations of the Danelaw in Middle English Literature', in Graham-Campbell et al 2001, 345-55.

Tweddle, Dominic. 1992. *The Anglian Helmet from 16-22 Coppergate*, Archaeology of York 17/8 (London).

— 2004. 'Art in Pre-Conquest York', in Hall et al 2004, 446-58.

Tweddle, Dominic, Joan Moulden, and Elizabeth Logan, *Anglian York: A Survey of the Evidence*, Archaeology of York 7/2 (York).

Tyas, Shaun. 2010. 'Medievalism in British and Irish Business Names', *Nomina* 33, 5-25.

Unwin, Tim. 1988. 'Towards a Model of Anglo-Scandinavian Rural Settlement in England', in Della Hooke (ed.), *Anglo-Saxon Settlements* (Oxford), 77-98.

Valante, Mary A. 2008. *The Vikings in Ireland: Settlement, Trade and Urbanization* (Dublin).

Vaughan, Richard. 1958. 'The Chronicle Attributed to John of Wallingford', in *Camden Miscellany XXI* (London).

von Feilitzen, Olof. 1937. *The Pre-Conquest Personal Names of Domesday Book*, Nomina Germanica 3 (Uppsala).

Wainwright, F.T. 1975. *Scandinavian England: Collected Papers*, ed. H.P.R. Finberg (Chichester).

Walker, Simon. 1992. 'A Context for *Brunanburh*', in Timothy Reuter (ed.), *Warriors and Churchmen in the High Middle Ages: Essays Presented to Karl Leyser* (London), 21-39.

Wall, John. 1997. 'Anglo-Saxon Sundials in Ryedale', *Yorkshire Archaeological Journal* 69, 93-117.

Walton, Penelope. 1989. *Textiles, Cordage and Raw Fibre from 16-22 Coppergate*, Archaeology of York 17/5 (York).

Wamers, Egon. 1983. 'Some Ecclesiastical and Secular Insular Metalwork Found in Norwegian Viking Graves', *Peritia* 2, 277-306.

— 1998. 'Insular Finds in Viking Age Scandinavia and the State Formation of Norway', in Clarke, Ní Mhaonaigh, and Ó Floinn 1998, 37-72.

— 2011. 'The Halton Moor Cup and the Carolingian Metalwork in the Cuerdale Hoard', in Graham-Campbell 2011, 133-39.

Wareham, Andrew. 1996. 'Saint Oswald's Family and Kin', in Brooks and Cubitt 1996, 46-63.

Watkin, Jeffrey, and Faith Mann. 1981. 'Some Late Saxon Finds from Lilla Howe, N. Yorks. and their Context', *Medieval Archaeology* 25, 153-57.

Watson, Richard. 2011. 'Viking-Age Amounderness: A Reconsideration', in Higham and Ryan 2011, 125-41.

Watts, Victor. 1995. 'Northumberland and Durham: the place-name evidence', in Crawford 1995, 206-13.

— 2004. *The Cambridge Dictionary of English Place-Names* (Cambridge).

Wawn, Andrew. 2000. *The Vikings and the Victorians: Inventing the Old North in Nineteenth-Century Britain* (Cambridge).

Weiss, Judith, trans. 1992. *The Birth of Romance: An Anthology* (London).

Wenham, L.P., et al. 1987. *St Mary Bishophill Junior and St Mary Castlegate*, Archaeology of York 8/2 (York).

Westwood, Jennifer, and Jacqueline Simpson. 2005. *The Lore of the Land: A Guide to England's Legends, from Spring-Heeled Jack to the Witches of Warboys* (London).

Whaley, Diana, ed. 2002. *Sagas of Warrior-Poets*, Penguin Classics (London).

— 2010. 'Scarborough Revisited', *Nomina* 33, 87-100.

— ed. 2012. *Poetry from the Kings' Saga 1: From the Beginnings to 1035*, 2 vols, Skaldic Poetry of the Scandinavian Middle Ages 1 (Turnhout).

White, Paul A. 2005. *Non-Native Sources for the Scandinavian Kings' Sagas* (London).

Whitelock, Dorothy, ed. 1930. *Anglo-Saxon Wills* (Cambridge).

— ed. 1954. *The Peterborough Chronicle (The Bodleian Manuscript Laud Misc. 636)*, Early English Manuscripts in Facsimile 4 (Copenhagen).

— ed. 1955. *English Historical Documents: Volume I c.500-1042* (London).

— 1959. 'The Dealings of the Kings of England with Northumbria in the Tenth and Eleventh Centuries', in Peter Clemoes (ed.), *The Anglo-Saxons: Studies in Some Aspects of their History and Culture Presented to Bruce Dickins* (London), 70-88.

— trans. 1961. *The Anglo-Saxon Chronicle: A Revised Translation* (London).

— 1965. 'Wulfstan at York', in Bessinger and Creed 1965, 214-31.

Wicker, Nancy L. 1998. 'Selective Female Infanticide as Partial Explanation for the Dearth of Women in Viking Age Scandinavia', in Guy Halsall (ed.), *Violence and Society in the Early Medieval West* (Woodbridge), 205-21.

Wilcox, Jonathan, ed. 1994. *Ælfric's Prefaces*, Durham Medieval Texts 9 (Durham).

— 2000. 'The St Brice's Day Massacre and Archbishop Wulfstan', in Diane Wolfthal (ed.), *Peace and Negotiation: Strategies for Co-Existence in the Middle Ages and Renaissance* (Turnhout), 79-91.

Wilkinson, Bertie. 1939. 'Northumbrian Separatism in 1065 and 1066', *Bulletin of the John Rylands Library* 23, 504-26.

Williams, Ann. 1995. *The English and the Norman Conquest* (Woodbridge).

Williams, Ann, and G.H. Martin, eds. 1992. *The Yorkshire Domesday*, 3 vols (London).

— eds. 2002. *Domesday Book: A Complete Translation* (London).

Williams, David. 1997. *Late Saxon Stirrup-Strap Mounts: A Classification and Catalogue*, Council for British Archaeology Research Report 111 (York).

Williams, Gareth. 2001. 'Hákon *Aðalsteins fóstri*: Aspects of Anglo-Saxon Kingship in Tenth-Century Norway', in Thomas R. Liszka and Lorna E.M. Walker (eds), *The North Sea World in the Middle Ages: Studies in the Cultural History of North-Western Europe* (Dublin), 108-26.

— 2008. 'The Coins from the Vale of York Viking Hoard: Preliminary Report', *British Numismatic Journal* 78, 227-34.

— 2009. 'Viking Hoards of the Northern Danelaw from Cuerdale to the Vale of York', in Graham-Campbell and Philpott 2009, 73-83.

— 2010. *Eirik Bloodaxe* (Hafrsfjord).

— 2011a. 'The Cuerdale Coins', in Graham-Campbell 2011, 39-71.

— 2011b. 'The Coins from Goldsborough', in Graham Campbell 2011, 236-37.

— 2011c. 'Silver Economies, Monetisation and Society: An Overview', in Graham-Campbell, Sindbæk, and Williams 2011, 337-72.

— 2012. 'A New Coin Type (And a New King?) From Viking Northumbria', *Yorkshire Numismatist* 4, 261-75.

— 2013a. 'The 'Northern Hoards' Revisited: Hoards and Silver Economy in the Northern Danelaw in the Early Tenth Century', in Reynolds and Webster 2013, 459-86.

— 2013b. 'Towns and Identities in Viking England', in Hadley and ten Harkel 2013, 14-34.

— 2014. 'Viking Camps in England and Ireland', in Gareth Williams, Peter Pentz, and Matthias Wemhoff (eds), *Vikings: Life and Legend* (London), 120-21.

Williams, Gareth, and Barry Ager. 2010. *The Vale of York Hoard* (London).

Wilson, Barbara, and Frances Mee. 2002. *'The Fairest Arch in England'. Old Ouse Bridge, York, and its Buildings: The Pictorial Evidence*, Archaeology of York Supplementary Series 1/2 (York).

Wilson, David M. 1957. 'An Unpublished Fragment from the Goldsborough Hoard', *Antiquaries Journal* 37, 72-73.

— 1965. 'Some Neglected Late Anglo-Saxon Swords', *Medieval Archaeology* 9, 32-54.

— 1967. 'The Vikings' Relationship with Christianity in Northern England', *Journal of the British Archaeological Association* 3rd Series 30, 37-46.

— 2008. *The Vikings in the Isle of Man* (Aarhus).

Wilson, David M., and Ole Klindt-Jensen. 1980. *Viking Art*, 2nd ed. (London).

Wilson, Susan E. 2003. 'King Athelstan and St John of Beverley', *Northern History* 40, 5-23.

Winroth, Anders. 2012. *The Conversion of Scandinavia: Vikings, Merchants, and Missionaries in the Remaking of Northern Europe* (New Haven).

Winterbottom, Michael, and R.M. Thomson, eds. 2002. *William of Malmesbury: Saints' Lives* (Oxford).

Wood, Ian. 1987. 'Anglo-Saxon Otley: An Archiepiscopal Estate and its Crosses in a Northumbrian Context', *Northern History* 23, 20-38.

Wood, Ian, and Niels Lund, eds. 1991. *People and Places in Northern Europe 500-1600: Essays in Honour of Peter Hayes Sawyer* (Woodbridge).

Wood, Michael. 1980. 'Brunanburh Revisited', *Saga-Book of the Viking Society* 20, 200-17.

— 1999. *In Search of England: Journeys into the English Past* (London).

— 2013. 'Searching for Brunanburh: The Yorkshire Context of the 'Great War' of 937', *Yorkshire Archaeological Journal* 85, 138-59.

Woodman, D.A., ed. 2012. *Charters of Northern Houses*, Anglo-Saxon Charters 16 (Oxford).

Woolf, Alex. 1998. 'Erik Bloodaxe Revisited', *Northern History* 34, 189-93.

— 2001. 'Amlaíb Cuarán and the Gael, 941-81', *Medieval Dublin* 3, 34-43.

— 2007. *From Pictland to Alba 789-1070*, New Edinburgh History of Scotland 2 (Edinburgh).

Woolf, Daniel. 1991. 'Of Danes and Giants: Popular Beliefs about the Past in Early Modern England', *Dalhousie Review* 71, 166-209.

Wormald, Patrick. 1982a. 'Viking Studies: Whence and Whither?', in Farrell 1982, 128-53.

— 1982b. 'The Ninth Century', in Campbell 1982, 132-59.

— 1983. 'Bede, the *Bretwaldas*, and the Origin of the *Gens Anglorum*', in Patrick Wormald (ed.), *Ideal and Reality in Frankish and Anglo-Saxon Society: Studies Presented to J.M. Wallace-Hadrill* (Oxford), 99-129.

— 1992. 'The Venerable Bede and the "Church of the English"', in Geoffrey Rowell (ed.), *The English Religious Tradition and the Genius of Anglicanism* (Wantage), 13-32.

— 1993. *How do we know so much about Anglo-Saxon Deerhurst?* Deerhurst Lecture 1991 (Deerhurst).

— 1994. '*Engla Lond*: the Making of an Allegiance', *Journal of Historical Sociology* 7, 1-24.

— 1999a. *The Making of English Law: King Alfred to the Twelfth Century. Volume I Legislation and its Limits* (Oxford).

— 1999b. 'Archbishop Wulfstan and the Holiness of Society', in David Pelteret (ed.), *Anglo-Saxon History: Basic Readings* (New York), 191-224.

— 2004a. 'Wulfstan [Lupus] (*d*. 1023)', in Matthew and Harrison 2004, 60, 558-62.

— 2004b. 'Archbishop Wulfstan: Eleventh-Century State-Builder', in Townend 2004, 9-27.

Worsaae, J.J.A. 1852. *An Account of the Danes and Norwegians in England, Scotland, and Ireland* (London).

Wrathmell, Stuart, ed. 2012. *A History of Wharram Percy and Its Neighbours*, Wharram: A Study of Settlement on the Yorkshire Wolds 13 (York).

Wright, C.E. 1939. *The Cultivation of Saga in Anglo-Saxon England* (Edinburgh).

Wright, Elizabeth Mary. 1932. *The Life of Joseph Wright*, 2 vols (Oxford).

Wright, Joseph. 1898-1905. *The English Dialect Dictionary* (Oxford).

www.finds.org.uk (Portable Antiquities Scheme).

Young, Robert J.C. 2008. *The Idea of English Ethnicity* (Oxford).

Zacher, Samantha. 2011. 'Multilingualism at the Court of King Æthelstan: Latin Praise Poetry and *The Battle of Brunanburh*', in Elizabeth M. Tyler (ed.), *Conceptualizing Multilingualism in Medieval England, c.800-c.1250*, Studies in the Early Middle Ages 27 (Brepols), 77-103.

Þorsteinsson, Björn. 1969. *Enskar Heimildir um Sögu Íslendinga á 15. og 16. Öld* (Reykjavík).

INDEX

306